LONDON SCHOOL OF ECONOMICS
MONOGRAPHS ON SOCIAL ANTHROPOLOGY

Managing Editor: Anthony Forge

POLITICAL SYSTEMS OF HIGHLAND BURMA
A STUDY OF KACHIN SOCIAL STRUCTURE

LONDON SCHOOL OF ECONOMICS
MONOGRAPHS ON SOCIAL ANTHROPOLOGY
No. 44

POLITICAL SYSTEMS OF HIGHLAND BURMA

A Study of Kachin Social Structure

BY

E. R. LEACH

UNIVERSITY OF LONDON
THE ATHLONE PRESS

Published by
THE ATHLONE PRESS
UNIVERSITY OF LONDON
at 2 Gower Street, London, WC1
Distributed by Tiptree Book Services Ltd
Tiptree, Essex

Australia and New Zealand
Melbourne University Press

First edition (G. Bell & Son Ltd) 1954
Reprinted 1964
Reprinted (Athlone Press) 1970

© *E. R. Leach,* 1964

ISBN 0 485 19644 1

Reprinted by photolitho by
FLETCHER AND SON LTD, NORWICH

FOREWORD

To have been asked by Dr. Leach to write a foreword to this book is a tribute to an old friendship and academic association.

It is generally expected of a foreword that it will introduce the book either to a wider public than knows its author, or that it will make manifest some hidden virtue which the book contains. Neither of these objectives is sought here. The author is already known not only to his British colleagues, but also internationally, as a leading social anthropologist. He is also by the force and clarity of his thought fully capable of presenting the merits of his own work. What then can this foreword do? By our ordinary conventions the writer of a foreword is presumably restrained from reviewing the book when it appears. He cannot compensate by reviewing it in his introduction. But what he may do is to give some notice in advance of some of the themes which he sees as being of major significance in any discussion of its merits.

'Dynamic' is an overworked word. But if one says that the primary feature in Dr. Leach's analysis is its attempt to provide the elements of a dynamic theory for social anthropology, the point will be generally understood. What is meant is an analysis of forces in movement or principles in action. Much of social anthropology nowadays is concerned with institutions in change. But the treatment is usually mainly descriptive, or where it becomes abstract the concepts are apt to become over-elaborate, highly artificial, and out of relation to the real world of observed human actions in specific societies. What Dr. Leach is attempting to do is to handle dynamic theory at a higher level of abstraction than has been done heretofore in social anthropology while still using the materials from empirical social observation among named groups.

He works forcibly and elegantly. To do this he makes certain assumptions. These involve the notion of descriptions of social systems as models of a social reality. There is a growing tendency in social anthropology, and rather a slipshod one, to call any set of assumptions or abstractions used as a

v

basis for discussion, a model. At times the notion serves as an excuse for an evasion of reality, by emphasising the personal character of the construct. But with the author a model is clearly a representation of a structure with the parts articulated or related in such manner that manipulation of them is possible for the illustration of further relations. Dr. Leach has already demonstrated his skill in such manipulation in his article on Jinghpaw Kinship Terminology,[1] which he described as 'an experiment in ethnographic algebra'. The essential feature of this analysis was the demonstration that by taking a limited set of assumptions about kinship structure, and by relating them in operation in the simplest possible manner, a behaviour scheme was found adequate to provide an explanation in terms of ideal rules for the noted events in a real society.

A consequence of Dr. Leach's analysis was to stress again the distinction drawn by Malinowski and others between 'ideal' and 'real' (or 'normal') patterns of behaviour. But in Dr. Leach's hands this distinction assumes a new importance. To him it is the ideal patterns—the social relations which are regarded as 'correct'—which are expressed in the model which gives the structural description of a social system. The necessary equilibrium of the model as a construct means that essentially it is debarred from providing in itself a dynamic analysis. The difficulty lies not so much in introducing time abstractly as a factor into the model as in getting into it a true expression of what is really relevant in actual conditions. Application must therefore be made to the observation of what people actually do in their normal everyday life to give a basis for a dynamic consideration, a consideration of structural change. The situation here is analogous to that in economic theory. But the social anthropologist has an advantage over the economist in that from the beginnings of the science, it has been the 'real world' that he has studied at first hand. The anthropologist is already familiar with the raw stuff of social change.

In actual life individuals are continually faced by choices between alternatives for action. When they make these choices Dr. Leach believes their decisions are made commonly to gain power—that is, access to office or to esteem which will lead to

[1] *Journal of the Royal Anthropological Institute*, vol. LXXV, 1945, pp. 59–72.

office. The development of this argument is pursued with a
wealth of detail and subtlety of interpretation that must command the admiration of every careful reader. His challenges
to accepted views may not please everyone, but the reader
will gain much by the way from the author's direct presentation, his complete intellectual honesty, and the freshness of
his approach. Some of us, for example, have not hesitated
to tell our students in private that ethnographic facts may
be irrelevant—that it does not matter so much if they get
the facts wrong so long as they can argue the theories logically.
But few of us would be prepared to say in print, as Dr.
Leach has done, that he is usually bored by the facts which
his anthropological colleagues present. And who of us also
usually feels inclined to state so bluntly at a point in his argument that his interpretation is completely at variance with
almost everything that has previously been published on the
subject? This is refreshing candour; it awakes the reader's
expectations and he will not be disappointed.

As yet Dr. Leach's dynamic theory is still largely a special,
not a general, one. This is so for two reasons. The first is
that it is intended as yet primarily to refer to, and to explain,
the behaviour of people in North Burma. It is true that
examples from remote fields are cited. Yet while in boundary
terms many 'tribes' must be ethnographic fictions, this is not
so everywhere. The notions of 'becoming something else' in
this situation, as Kachins become Shans, or *gumsa* people
become *gumlao*, are specific ethnographic phenomena that may
have only a restricted analogy. They are indeed almost an
'ideal type' of the phenomenon of becoming another social
being.

Secondly, some of Dr. Leach's concepts are of a special order.
I do not refer here to his redefinitions of myth and of ritual,
which in their novelty offer a stimulating way of considering
social relationships. Nor do I refer to his use of the terms 'social
structure' and 'social organisation', for which each of us has
his personal idiom. But I refer to his thesis that seeking for
power is the basis of social choice. The Italian Renaissance
and our own recent history have good examples to support
him. And his contention is in line with many trends of modern
thought. Yet the concentration of power and status on the

quest for esteem as leading to office, suggests either an undue restriction of the field of motivation or a re-interpretation of the power notion in terms so wide as to include almost any social action. I would, from my own Tikopia material, give support to Dr. Leach's views both as regards the role of myth and the cardinal importance of power notions for group action. I would think that the study of other Polynesian people, such as the Samoans or the Maori, would corroborate this too. And yet one feels that there is some speciousness in such a monolithic explanation. For the operation of social affairs in Polynesian communities to seem explicable, allowance must be made empirically for notions of loyalty and obligation which cut across the narrow confines of group power interests. And in other ethnographic fields it would seem that valuations of a moral and religious order enter and jostle the power and status-seeking elements.

All this is to indicate that the stimulation of Dr. Leach's theories is wider than the ethnographic province with which he has primarily dealt. The book will appeal to those who are interested in problems of government in undeveloped territories as well as to those who wish to have a really good first-hand study of one of the more primitive types of South-East Asian society. But to me its prime importance is as a major contribution to the theory of social systems. The book is a superb piece of craftsmanship done to an exciting design ; the best tribute one can pay to it is to hope that before too long the author will have the opportunity to repeat the design, with modifications to suit another material of as interesting quality.

RAYMOND FIRTH

INTRODUCTORY NOTE TO THE 1964 REPRINT

Professor Firth's generously worded foreword provided such excellent sales talk that the first edition of this book rather rapidly went out of print. This new edition is a photographically reproduced copy of the original.

Early professional comment was distinctly tepid but, in retrospect, the book's appearance seems to have marked the beginning of a trend. My own feeling at the time was that British Social Anthropology had rested too long on a crudely oversimplified set of equilibrium assumptions derived from the use of organic analogies for the structure of social systems. Even so I recognised the great power of this type of equilibrium analysis and the difficulty of evading it within the general framework of current sociological theory. My book was an attempt to find a way out of this dilemma. In brief, my argument is that although historical facts are never, in any sense, in equilibrium, we can gain genuine insights if, for the purpose of analysis, we force these facts within the constraining mould of an *as if* system of ideas, composed of concepts which are treated *as if* they were part of an equilibrium system. Furthermore I claim to demonstrate that this fictional procedure is not merely an analytical device of the social anthropologist, it also corresponds to the way the Kachins themselves apprehend their own system through the medium of the verbal categories of their own language. It is not an entirely satisfactory argument—there are many threads in the story which might have been much better expressed—but in 1964 it no longer represents a solitary point of view. Professor Gluckman, who has always been my most vigorous opponent in matters theoretical and who has consistently sustained the type of organic equilibrium theory to which I have referred, has recently admitted that for many years 'I [Gluckman] thought too much in terms of organic analysis, whereby I saw the cycle of rebellions as maintaining the system, with some implication that it strengthened the state'[1] and two pages later he even refers with guarded approval to the argument of this book while still maintaining that I have

[1] Max Gluckman, *Order and Rebellion in Tribal Africa*, (London, 1963), p. 35.

misunderstood my colleagues and misused the English language. Gluckman asserts that the Kachin system which I describe is properly described as one of 'stable equilibrium', which seems to me true at the level of ideas but quite untrue at the level of facts, and that 'British anthropologists have always thought in terms of this kind of equilibrium',[2] which seems to me untrue altogether. In this last connection the reader should bear in mind that comments in this book on the work of my fellow anthropologists refer to work already published in 1952. Others besides Professor Gluckman have modified their position since then.

When I wrote this book the general climate of anthropological thinking in England was that established by Radcliffe-Brown. Social systems were spoken of as if they were naturally existing real entities and the equilibrium inherent in such systems was intrinsic, a fact of Nature. In 1940 Fortes wrote:

> At every level of Tale social organisation ... the tendency towards an equilibrium is apparent. ... This does not mean that Tale society was ever stagnant. Tension is implicit in the equilibrium. ... But conflict could never develop to the point of bringing about complete disintegration. The homogeneity of Tale culture, the undifferentiated economic system, the territorial stability of the population, the network of kinship ties, the ramifications of clanship, and especially the mystical doctrines and ritual practices determining the native conception of the common good—all these are factors, restricting conflict and promoting restoration of equilibrium.[3]

If Professor Gluckman supposes that the Kachins have a system which is in equilibrium in any sense which is even approximately equivalent to the equilibrium here described by Fortes, he has completely misunderstood the argument of my book. I fully appreciate that a great deal of sociological analysis of the very highest quality makes it appear that social systems are naturally endowed with an equilibrium which is a demonstrable fact. It is the thesis of this book that this appearance is an illusion, and my over-all purpose in writing the book at all was to examine the nature of this particular illusion in a particular case.

[2] op. cit., p. 37.
[3] M. Fortes, 'The Political System of the Tallensi of the Northern Territories of the Gold Coast' in *African Political Systems*, eds. M. Fortes and E. E. Evans-Pritchard, (London, 1940), p. 271.

The data of social anthropology are in the first instance historical incidents, intrinsically non-repetitive, but when the anthropologist insists that his concern is with 'sociology' rather than with 'history', he at once imposes upon the evidence an assumption that systemic order may be discerned among the confusions of empirical fact. Such systemic order cannot be described without introducing notions of equilibrium and to that extent the argument of this book is itself an equilibrium analysis. But it differs from most monographic studies by social anthropologists in two particular respects. Firstly, I have attempted to expand the time-span within which the equilibrium is assumed to operate to a period of about 150 years, and secondly, I have attempted to make explicit the fictional (idealist) nature of the equilibrium assumptions. The argument itself is not novel, only its application. It is an accident of presentation that the text of the book contains no direct reference to the work of Pareto so that *Traité de Sociologie Générale*[4] does not appear in the bibliography; thus readers have failed to appreciate that a model for my *gumsa/gumlao* oscillation is to be found in Pareto's discussion of the alternating dominance of the 'lions' and the 'foxes' (§2178) and in his conception of a 'moving equilibrium' (§2067). This latter model presupposes that the total phenomenon which is in equilibrium is a social system which has extension in time as well as in space. It is true that a comparable model underlies much of Professor Fortes' work,[5] but Fortes' argument and my own are very different. Fortes' case is that if we are to understand the set of data observable simultaneously at any one point of time we must take account of the fact that each of the individuals whom we observe is separately progressing through a developmental cycle from infancy through adulthood to death, and that the groupings directly observable by the anthropologist (e.g. domestic groups) are themselves passing through a derivative sequence of phases. Thus the 'moving equilibrium' with which Fortes is concerned is anchored to biology; there is nothing in

[4] A new edition, *The Mind and Society*, ed. Arthur Livingston, was published in 1963 by Dover Publications, New York.

[5] e.g. M. Fortes, 'Time and Social Structure: An Ashanti Case Study', in *Social Structure: Studies presented to A. R. Radcliffe-Brown*, (Oxford, 1949); Fortes' Introduction to *The Development Cycle in Domestic Groups*, ed. J. R. Goody, Cambridge Papers in Social Anthropology No. 1, 1958.

the least 'illusory' about the systemic order which he discerns in his data. But Fortes' developmental cycles take no account of history; they are conceived of as sequences within a total system that is static and 'integrated' in Malinowski's sense of the term. All the facts under observation at *one* time cohere together to form *one* system; in theory there should be no loose ends (see quotation from *African Political Systems* above).

My own postulate of a *gumsa/gumlao* developmental cycle is of a different scale and quality. In the first place, since the total moving equilibrium system is presumed to incorporate all the events occurring within a time-span of a century or more, the model implies that the facts under observation at any one time will appear to belong to several quite different 'systems'. No amount of re-sorting of the synchronous data can produce a pattern which is 'integrated' in Malinowski's sense. But further-more, whereas Fortes' analysis is based on an empirical fact, the biological ageing process, my own attempt to find sys-temic ordering in historical events depends upon the changing evaluation of verbal categories and is, in the final analysis, illusory.

Nearly one-third of this book consists of Chapter V entitled 'The Structural Categories of Kachin *Gumsa* Society'. It is concerned with the interpretation of a series of verbal concepts and their interconnections. This long chapter is placed between a relatively short account of a particular Kachin community directly observed (Chapter IV) and a series of chapters (VI, VII, VIII) containing secondhand ethnographic and historical evidence. My critics, with their different assumptions about the nature of social reality, seem to have been puzzled by this arrangement. It arises logically from the circumstance that I do not consider that social systems are a natural reality. In my view, the facts of ethnography and of history can only *appear* to be ordered in a systematic way if we impose upon these facts a figment of thought. We first devise for ourselves a set of verbal categories which are nicely arranged to form an ordered system, and we then fit the facts to the verbal categories, and hey presto the facts are 'seen' to be systemically ordered! But in that case the *system* is a matter of the relations between concepts and not of relations 'actually existing' within the raw factual data, as Radcliffe-Brown and some of his followers have persistently maintained. The organic analogy is sometimes helpful, but society is *not* an organism, nor even a machine.

I do not believe in historical determinism in any shape or form, and those who have imagined that I here claim to discern an everlasting cyclical process in the slender facts of recorded Kachin history have quite misunderstood what I intended to say. The argument is rather that the set of verbal categories described in Chapter V form a persistent structured set and that it is always in terms of such categories as these that Kachins seek to interpret (to themselves and to others) the empirical social phenomena which they observe around them. The special interest of the Kachin material is that Kachin verbal usage allows the speaker to structure his categories in more than one way. *Gumsa* and *gumlao* use the same words to describe the categories of their own political system and that of their opponents but they make different assumptions about the relations between the categories in the two cases.

Considered as category structures the *gumsa* political order and the *gumlao* political order are alike ideal types which necessarily, at all times and in all places, correspond rather badly with the empirical facts on the ground. If this be so, it seems reasonable to enquire whether there is any analysable social process which can be attributed to the persistent discrepancy between the facts on the ground and the two polarised structures of ideal categories. The thesis of Chapters VII and VIII is that the outcome, for any one part of the Kachin region, is a long-phase political oscillation, though, since the facts at the end of the cycle are quite different from the facts at the beginning of the cycle, the 'system on the ground' is not in equilibrium in the same way as the 'system of ideas'. There are many details in this part of the book which now seem to me very unsatisfactory. It is not that the evidence is irrelevant but that I have often put the stress in the wrong place.

Over the past ten years I have come to a much clearer understanding of the distinction (often blurred in this book) between the structure which can exist within a set of verbal categories and the lack of structure which ordinarily exists within any directly observed set of empirical facts. Certainly I noted this discrepancy—a particularly clear example of what I mean is cited at pp. 279–81—but I tended to treat it as an abnormality, whereas it is really our common experience. Events only come to be structured in so far as they are endowed with order by the imposition of verbal categories.

My unorthodox treatment of 'ritual' (summarised at pp. 10–14) is related to this proposition. 'Ritual' is a term which anthropologists employ in diverse senses.[6] My own view is that while we only run into paradox if we try to apply this term to some distinct class of behaviours, we can very usefully think of 'ritual' as an aspect of all behaviour, namely the communicative aspect. This view, which attributes to certain features of culturally defined behaviour the qualities of a language, is really the same as that presented above where I say that events (i.e. items of behaviour) are only seen as structured when they are ordered by means of verbal categories. Had I developed this thesis more lucidly in the first place, the interdependence of the idealism of Chapter V and the factual evidence recorded elsewhere might have been easier to understand. Incidentally, in a friendly comment, Professor Gellner has flatly written off my whole argument as one of 'idealist error'.[7] Truth and error are complicated matters but it seems to me that in suggesting indirectly that the Kachins have a rather simple-minded philosophy which presumes a relationship between 'idea' and 'reality' not very different from that postulated by Plato, I am not arguing that Plato was correct. The errors of Platonism are very common errors which are shared not only by anthropologists but also by the people whom anthropologists study.

The main body of the book is concerned with the theme that empirical political behaviour among the Kàchin is a compromise response to the polarised political doctrines of *gumsa* and *gumlao*. In Chapter IX, I attempted to show how these polar doctrines are actually presented to the actor through the medium of conflicting mythologies, any of which might conveniently serve as a charter for social action. Re-reading this chapter now it seems to me 'useful but inadequate'. Professor Lévi-Strauss' numerous writings on the study of myth have all appeared since this book first went to press, and they certainly have much relevance for the understanding of Kachin tradition.

[6] See *Essays on the Ritual of Social Relations*, ed. Max Gluckman (Manchester University Press, 1962), pp. 20-3.

[7] E. Gellner, 'Time and Theory in Social Anthropology', *Mind*, Vol. 67 N.S., No. 266, April 1958.

The book ends with the suggestion that this unconventional style of analysis might have relevance outside the Kachin Hills, more particularly for areas to the west where the ethnographic record is particularly lavish. This suggestion has been justified. F. K. Lehman has combined personal research with a survey of a wide range of Chin materials.[8] The result greatly enhances our understanding of the Chins, but also, less directly, it provides a useful confirmation of the value of my Kachin interpretation, for in Lehman's hands the discrepancies of Chin ethnography fall into a pattern. Viewed over-all, Chins turn out to be even more like Kachins than most of us would have expected.

It now seems clear that, in this whole region, the concept 'tribe' is of quite negative utility from the viewpoint of social analysis. The significance of particular features of particular tribal organisations cannot be discovered by functional investigations of the more usual kind. It is rather that we come to understand the qualities of 'Tribe A' only when we measure these qualities against their antithesis in 'Tribe B' (as in the *gumsa-gumlao* case). I reaffirm my opinion that, even at this late date, the extensive ethnographic literature of the Nagas would repay study from such a dialectical 'cross-tribal' point of view.

E.R.L.

Cambridge
January 1964

[8] F. K. Lehman, *The Structure of Chin Society*, (University of Illinois Press, 1963).

ACKNOWLEDGEMENTS

I wish to thank the following individuals for assistance in connection with the preparation of this book:—Mr. G. E. Harvey, Mr. R. S. Wilkie and Mr. J. L. Leyden for making available documents which would not otherwise have been accessible; Col. J. H. Green and the Librarian of the Haddon Library, Cambridge, for permission to print the material given in Appendix III; the Editor of the Journal of the Royal Anthropological Institute for permission to reprint part of the material given in Appendix IV; Professor I. Schapera for invaluable assistance in proof reading and many helpful comments; Professor Raymond Firth for writing the Foreword and for teaching me most of what I know about anthropology.

E. R. L.

CONTENTS

page

MAPS

DIAGRAMS

PART I

THE PROBLEM AND ITS SETTING

CHAPTER I

INTRODUCTION

This book is concerned with the Kachin and Shan population of North-East Burma, but it is also intended to provide a contribution to anthropological theory. It is not intended as an ethnographic description. Most of the ethnographic facts to which I refer have been previously recorded in print. Any originality is not therefore to be found in the facts with which I deal, but in the interpretation of the facts.

The population with which we are concerned is that which occupies the area marked KACHIN on Map 1 and shown in large scale on Map 2. This population speaks a number of different languages and dialects and there are wide differences of culture between one part of the area and another. Nevertheless, it is usual to refer to the whole of this population under the two heads Shan and Kachin. In this book I shall refer to the whole region as the *Kachin Hills Area*.

At a crude level of generalisation Shans occupy the river valleys where they cultivate rice in irrigated fields; they are a relatively sophisticated people with a culture somewhat resembling that of the Burmese. The Kachins on the other hand occupy the hills where they cultivate rice mainly by the slash and burn techniques of shifting cultivation. The literature throughout the past century has almost always treated these Kachins as if they were primitive and warlike savages, so far removed from the Shans in appearance, language and general culture that they must be regarded as of quite different racial origin.[1]

That being so, it is quite within the normal conventions of anthropology that monographs about Kachins should ignore

[1] e.g. Malcom (1837); Eickstedt (1944).

the Shans and monographs about Shans should ignore the Kachins. Nevertheless Kachins and Shans are almost every-where close neighbours and in the ordinary affairs of life they are much mixed up together.

Consider, for example, the following piece of documenta-tion. It is part of the verbatim record of the evidence of a witness at a confidential Court of Enquiry held in the Northern Shan States in 1930.[2]

'Name of witness: Hpaka Lung Hseng
Race: Lahtawng Kachin (Pawyam, Pseudo-Shan)
Age: 79
Religion: Zawti Buddhist
Lives at: Man Hkawng, Mong Hko
Born at: Pao Mo, Mong Hko
Occupation: Retired headman
Father: Ma La, sometime Duwa of Pao Mo

When I was a boy some 70 years ago, the (Shan) Regent Sao Hkam Hseng who then reigned in Mong Mao sent a relative of his, Nga Hkam by name, to negotiate an alliance with the Kachins of Mong Hko. After a while Nga Hkam settled down in Pao Mo and later he exchanged names with my ancestor Hko Tso Li and my grandfather Ma Naw, then Duwas of Pao Mo ; after that we became Shans and Buddhists and prospered greatly and, as members of the Hkam clan, whenever we went to Mong Mao we stayed with the Regent, conversely in Mong Hko our house was theirs. . . .'

It appears that this witness considered that for the past 70 years or so all his family have been simultaneously Kachins and Shans. As a Kachin the witness was a member of the Pawyam lineage of the Lahtaw(ng) clan. As a Shan he was a Buddhist, and a member of the Hkam clan, the royal house of Möng Mao State.

Furthermore Möng Mao—the well-known Shan state of that name in Chinese territory—is treated here as being a political entity of the same kind and much the same status as Möng Hko, which in the eyes of British administrators of 1930 was no more than a Kachin administrative 'circle' in North Hsenwi State.

Data of this kind cannot readily be fitted into any ethno-

[2] Harvey and Barton (1930), p. 81.

graphic scheme which, on linguistic grounds, places Kachins and Shans in different 'racial' categories.

The problem, however, is not simply one of sorting out Kachins from Shans; there is also the difficulty of sorting out Kachins from one another. The literature discriminates between several varieties of Kachin. Some of these sub-categories are primarily linguistic, as when Jinghpaw-speaking Kachins are distinguished from Atsi, Maru, Lisu, Nung, etc.; others are mainly territorial, as when the Assam Singpho are distinguished from the Burma Jinghpaw, or the Hkahku of the Upper Mali Hka area (Triangle) from the Gauri, East of Bhamo. But the general tendency has been to minimise the significance of these distinctions and to argue that the essentials of Kachin culture are uniform throughout the Kachin Hills Area.[3] Books with such titles as *The Kachin Tribes of Burma*; *The Kachins, their Religion and Mythology*; *The Kachins, their Customs and Traditions*; *Beitrag zur Ethnologie der Chingpaw (Kachin) von Ober-Burma*[4] refer by implication to all Kachins wherever they may be found, that is to a population of some 300,000 persons thinly scattered over an area of some 50,000 square miles.[5]

It is not part of my immediate problem to consider how far such generalisations about the uniformity of Kachin culture are in fact justifiable ; my interest lies rather in the problem of how far it can be maintained that a single type of social structure prevails throughout the Kachin area. Is it legitimate to think of Kachin society as being organised throughout according to one particular set of principles or does this rather vague category Kachin include a number of different forms of social organisation?

Before we can attempt to investigate this question we must first be quite clear as to what is meant by continuity and change with regard to social systems. Under what circumstances can we say of two neighbouring societies A and B that 'these two societies have fundamentally different social structures' while as between two other societies C and D we may argue that 'in these two societies the social structure is essentially the same'?

---

[3] e.g. Hanson (1913), p. 13.
[4] Carrapiett (1929); Gilhodes (1922); Hanson (1913); Wehrli (1904).
[5] See Appendix V.

Throughout the remainder of this opening chapter my concern is to explain the theoretical standpoint from which I approach this fundamental issue.

The argument in brief is as follows. Social anthropologists who, following Radcliffe-Brown, use the concept of social structure as a category in terms of which to compare one society with another, in fact presuppose that the societies with which they deal exist throughout time in stable equilibrium. Is it then possible to describe at all, by means of ordinary sociological categories, societies which are *not* assumed to be in stable equilibrium?

My conclusion is that while conceptual models of society are necessarily models of equilibrium systems, real societies can never be in equilibrium. The discrepancy is related to the fact that when social structures are expressed in cultural form, the representation is imprecise compared with that given by the exact categories which the sociologist, *qua* scientist, would like to employ. I hold that these inconsistencies in the logic of ritual expression are always necessary for the proper functioning of any social system.

Most of my book is a development of this theme. I hold that social structure in practical situations (as contrasted with the sociologist's abstract model) consists of a set of ideas about the distribution of power between persons and groups of persons. Individuals can and do hold contradictory and inconsistent ideas about this system. They are able to do this without embarrassment because of the form in which their ideas are expressed. The form is cultural form; the expression is ritual expression. The latter part of this introductory chapter is an elaboration of this portentous remark.

But first to get back to social structure and unit societies.

Social Structure

At one level of abstraction we may discuss social structure simply in terms of the principles of organisation that unite the component parts of the system. At this level the form of the structure can be considered quite independently of the cultural content.[6] A knowledge of the form of society among the Gilyak hunters of Eastern Siberia[7] and among the Nuer

---

[6] cf. Fortes (1949), pp. 54–60.   [7] Lévi-Strauss (1949), Chapter XVIII.

pastoralists of the Sudan[8] helps me to understand the form of Kachin society despite the fact that the latter for the most part are shifting cultivators inhabiting dense monsoon rain forest.

At this level of abstraction it is not difficult to distinguish one formal pattern from another. The structures which the anthropologist describes are models which exist only as logical constructions in his own mind. What is much more difficult is to relate such abstraction to the data of empirical field work. How can we really be sure that one particular formal model fits the facts better than any other possible model?

Real societies exist in time and space. The demographic, ecological, economic and external political situation does not build up into a fixed environment, but into a constantly changing environment. Every real society is a process in time. The changes that result from this process may usefully be thought of under two heads.[9] Firstly, there are those which are consistent with a continuity of the existing formal order. For example, when a chief dies and is replaced by his son, or when a lineage segments and we have two lineages where formerly there was only one, the changes are part of the process of continuity. There is no change in the formal structure. Secondly, there are changes which do reflect alterations in the formal structure. If, for example, it can be shown that in a particular locality, over a period of time, a political system composed of equalitarian lineage segments is replaced by a ranked hierarchy of feudal type, we can speak of a change in the formal social structure.

When, in this book, I refer to changes of social structure, I always mean changes of this latter kind.

Unit Societies

In the context of the Kachin Hills Area the concept of 'a society' presents many difficulties which will become increasingly apparent in the course of the next few chapters. For the time being I will follow Radcliffe-Brown's unsatisfactory advice and interpret 'a society' as meaning 'any convenient locality'.[10]

Alternatively, I accept Nadel's arguments. By 'a society' I really mean any self-contained political unit.[11]

[8] Evans-Pritchard (1940).   [9] cf. Fortes, op. cit., pp. 54–5.
[10] Radcliffe-Brown (1940).   [11] cf. Nadel (1951), p. 187.

Political units in the Kachin Hills Area vary greatly in size and appear to be intrinsically unstable. At one end of the scale one may encounter a village of four households firmly asserting its right to be considered as a fully independent unit. At the other extreme we have the Shan state of Hsenwi which, prior to 1885, contained 49 sub-states (*möng*), some of which in turn contained over a hundred separate villages. Between these two extremes one may distinguish numerous other varieties of 'society'. These various types of political system differ from one another not only in scale but also in the formal principles in terms of which they are organised. It is here that the crux of our problem lies.

For certain parts of the Kachin Hills Area genuine historical records go back as far as the beginning of the 19th century. These show clearly that during the last 130 years the political organisation of the area has been very unstable. Small autonomous political units have often tended to aggregate into larger systems; large-scale feudal hierarchies have fragmented into smaller units. There have been violent and very rapid shifts in the overall distribution of political power. It is therefore methodologically unsound to treat the different varieties of political system which we now find in the area as independent types; they should clearly be thought of as part of a larger total system in flux. But the essence of my argument is that the process by which the small units grow into larger ones and the large units break down into smaller ones is not simply part of the process of structural continuity; it is not merely a process of segmentation and accretion, it is a process involving structural change. It is with the mechanism of this change process that we are mainly concerned.

There is no doubt that both the study and description of social change in ordinary anthropological contexts presents great difficulties. Field studies are of short duration, historical records seldom contain data of the right kind in adequate detail. Indeed, although anthropologists have frequently declared a special interest in the subject, their theoretical discussion of the problems of social change has so far merited little applause.[12]

Even so it seems to me that at least some of the difficulties

[12] e.g. Malinowski (1945); G. and M. Wilson (1945); Herskovits (1949).

arise only as a by-product of the anthropologist's own false assumptions about the nature of his data.

English social anthropologists have tended to borrow their primary concepts from Durkheim rather than from either Pareto or Max Weber. Consequently they are strongly prejudiced in favour of societies which show symptoms of 'functional integration', 'social solidarity', 'cultural uniformity', 'structural equilibrium'. Such societies, which might well be regarded as moribund by historians or political scientists, are commonly looked upon by social anthropologists as healthy and ideally fortunate. Societies which display symptoms of faction and internal conflict leading to rapid change are on the other hand suspected of 'anomie' and pathological decay.[13]

cf Barth

This prejudice in favour of 'equilibrium' interpretations arises from the nature of the anthropologist's materials and from the conditions under which he does his work. The social anthropologist normally studies the population of a particular place at a particular point in time and does not concern himself greatly with whether or not the same locality is likely to be studied again by other anthropologists at a later date. In the result we get studies of Trobriand society, Tikopia society, Nuer society, *not* 'Trobriand society in 1914', 'Tikopia society in 1929', 'Nuer society in 1935'. When anthropological societies are lifted out of time and space in this way the interpretation that is given to the material is necessarily an equilibrium analysis, for if it were not so, it would certainly appear to the reader that the analysis was incomplete. But more than that, since, in most cases, the research work has been carried out once and for all without any notion of repetition, the presentation is one of *stable* equilibrium; the authors write as if the Trobrianders, the Tikopia, the Nuer are as they are, now and for ever. Indeed the confusion between the concepts of equilibrium and of stability is so deep-rooted in anthropological literature that any use of either of these terms is liable to lead to ambiguity. They are not of course the same thing. My own position is as follows.

[13] Homans (1951), pp. 336 f.

Model Systems

When the anthropologist attempts to describe a social system he necessarily describes only a model of the social reality. This model represents in effect the anthropologist's hypothesis about 'how the social system works'. The different parts of the model system therefore necessarily form a coherent whole—it is a system in equilibrium. But this does not imply that the social reality forms a coherent whole; on the contrary the reality situation is in most cases full of inconsistencies; and it is precisely these inconsistencies which can provide us with an understanding of the processes of social change.

In situations such as we find in the Kachin Hills Area, any particular individual can be thought of as having a status position in several different social systems at one and the same time. To the individual himself such systems present themselves as alternatives or inconsistencies in the scheme of values by which he orders his life. The overall process of structural change comes about through the manipulation of these alternatives as a means of social advancement. Every individual of a society, each in his own interest, endeavours to exploit the situation as he perceives it and in so doing the collectivity of individuals alters the structure of the society itself.

This rather complicated idea will receive frequent illustration in the pages which follow but the argument may be illustrated by a simple example.

In matters political, Kachins have before them two quite contradictory ideal modes of life. One of these is the Shan system of government, which resembles a feudal hierarchy. The other is that which in this book is referred to as the *gumlao* type organisation; this is essentially anarchistic and equalitarian. It is not uncommon to meet an ambitious Kachin who assumes the names and titles of a Shan prince in order to justify his claim to aristocracy, but who simultaneously appeals to *gumlao* principles of equality in order to escape the liability of paying feudal dues to his own traditional chief.

And just as individual Kachins are frequently presented with a choice as to what is morally right, so also whole Kachin communities may be said to be offered a choice as to the type of political system which shall serve as their ideal. Briefly,

my argument is that in terms of political organisation Kachin communities oscillate between two polar types—*gumlao* 'democracy' on the one hand, Shan 'autocracy' on the other. The majority of actual Kachin communities are neither *gumlao* nor Shan in type, they are organised according to a system described in this book as *gumsa*,[14] which is, in effect, a kind of compromise between *gumlao* and Shan ideals. In a later chapter I describe the *gumsa* system as if it were a third static model intermediate between the *gumlao* and Shan models, but the reader needs clearly to understand that actual *gumsa* communities are not static. Some, under the influence of favourable economic circumstances, tend more and more towards the Shan model, until in the end the Kachin aristocrats feel that they 'have become Shan' (*sam tai sai*), as in the case of the Möng Hko elder whom we encountered on p. 2; other *gumsa* communities shift in the opposite direction and become *gumlao*. Kachin social organisation, as it is described in the existing ethnographic accounts, is always the *gumsa* system; but my thesis is that this system considered by itself does not really make sense, it is too full of inherent inconsistencies. Simply as a model scheme it can be represented as an equilibrium system,[15] yet as Lévi-Strauss has perceived the structure thus represented contains elements which are 'en contradiction avec le système, et doit donc entraîner sa ruine'.[16] In the field of social reality *gumsa* political structures are essentially unstable, and I maintain that they only become fully intelligible in terms of the contrast provided by the polar types of *gumlao* and Shan organisation.

Another way of regarding phenomena of structural change is to say that we are concerned with shifts in the focus of political power within a given system.

The structural description of a social system provides us with an idealised model which states the 'correct' status relations existing between groups within the total system and between the social persons who make up particular groups.[17] The position of any social person in any such model

---

[14] Except where otherwise stated, all native words used in this book are words of the Jinghpaw language spelt according to the system of romanisation devised by Hanson; cf. Hanson (1906).   [15] Leach (1952), pp. 40–5.   [16] Lévi-Strauss (1949), p. 325.
[17] For this use of the expression 'social person' see especially Radcliffe-Brown (1940), p. 5.

system is necessarily fixed, though individuals can be thought of as filling different positions in the performance of different kinds of occupation and at different stages in their career.

When we refer to structural change we have to consider not merely changes in the position of individuals with regard to an ideal system of status relationships, but changes in the ideal system itself: Changes, that is, in the power structure.

Power in any system is to be thought of as an attribute of 'office holders', that is of social persons who occupy positions to which power attaches. Individuals wield power only in their capacity as social persons. As a general rule I hold that the social anthropologist is never justified in interpreting action as unambiguously directed towards any one particular end. For this reason I am always dissatisfied with func- tionalist arguments concerning 'needs' and 'goals' such as those advanced by Malinowski and Talcott Parsons,[18] but I consider it necessary and justifiable to assume that a conscious or unconscious wish to gain power is a very general motive in human affairs. Accordingly I assume that individuals faced with a choice of action will commonly use such choice so as to gain power, that is to say they will seek recognition as social persons who have power; or, to use a different language, they will seek to gain access to office or the esteem of their fellows which may lead them to office.

Esteem is a cultural product. What is admired in one society may be deplored in another. The peculiarity of the Kachin Hills type of situation is that an individual may belong to more than one esteem system, and that these systems may not be consistent. Action which is meritorious according to Shan ideas may be rated as humiliating according to the *gumlao* code. The best way for an individual to gain esteem in any particular situation is therefore seldom clear. This sounds diffi- cult, but the reader need not imagine that such uncertainty is by any means unusual; in our own society the ethically correct action for a Christian business man is often equally ambiguous.

Ritual

In order to elaborate this argument I must first explain my use of the concept *ritual*. Ritual, I assert, 'serves to express

[18] Malinowski (1944); Parsons (1949); Parsons and Shils (1951), Pt. II.

the individual's status as a social person in the structural system in which he finds himself for the time being'. Clearly the significance of such an aphorism must depend upon the meaning that is to be attached to the word *ritual*.

English social anthropologists have mostly followed Durkheim in distinguishing social actions into major classes—namely, religious rites which are *sacred* and technical acts which are *profane*. Of the many difficulties that result from this position one of the most important concerns the definition and classification of magic. Is there a special class of actions which can be described as magical acts and, if so, do they belong to the category 'sacred' or to the category 'profane', have they more of the nature and function of religious acts or of technical acts?

Various answers have been given to this question. Malinowski, for example, places magic in the terrain of the sacred[19]; Mauss seems to regard it as profane.[20] But no matter whether the major dichotomy is seen to lie between the magico-religious (sacred) and the technical (profane), or between the religious (sacred) and the magico-technical (profane), the assumption remains that somehow sacred and profane situations are distinct as wholes. Ritual is then a word used to describe the social actions which occur in sacred situations. My own use of the word is different from this.

From the observer's point of view, actions appear as means to ends, and it is quite feasible to follow Malinowski's advice and classify social actions in terms of their ends—i.e. the 'basic needs' which they appear to satisfy. But the facts which are thereby revealed are technical facts; the analysis provides no criterion for distinguishing the peculiarities of any one culture or any one society. In fact, of course, very few social actions have this elementary functionally defined form. For example, if it is desired to grow rice, it is certainly essential and functionally necessary to clear a piece of ground and sow seed in it. And it will no doubt improve the prospects of a good yield if the plot is fenced and the growing crop weeded from time to time. Kachins do all these things and, in so far as they do this, they are performing simple technical acts of a functional kind. These actions serve to satisfy 'basic needs'. But there is much

[19] Malinowski (1948), p. 67.   [20] Mauss (1947), p. 207.

more to it than that. In Kachin 'customary procedure', the routines of clearing the ground, planting the seed, fencing the plot and weeding the growing crop are all patterned according to formal conventions and interspersed with all kinds of technically superfluous frills and decorations. It is these frills and decorations which make the performance a *Kachin* performance and not just a simple functional act. And so it is with every kind of technical action; there is always the element which is functionally essential, and another element which is simply the local custom, an æsthetic frill. Such æsthetic frills were referred to by Malinowski as 'neutral custom',[21] and in his scheme of functional analysis they are treated as minor irrelevancies. It seems to me, however, that it is precisely these customary frills which provide the social anthropologist with his primary data. Logically, æsthetics and ethics are identical.[22] If we are to understand the ethical rules of a society, it is æsthetics that we must study. In origin the details of custom may be an historical accident; but for the living individuals in a society such details can never be irrelevant, they are part of the total system of interpersonal communication within the group. They are symbolic actions, representations. It is the anthropologist's task to try to discover and to translate into his own technical jargon what it is that is symbolised or represented.

All this of course is very close to Durkheim. But Durkheim and his followers seem to have believed that collective representations were confined to the sphere of the sacred, and since they held that the dichotomy between the sacred and the profane was universal and absolute, it followed that it was only specifically sacred symbols that called for analysis by the anthropologist.

For my part I find Durkheim's emphasis on the absolute dichotomy between the sacred and the profane to be untenable.[23] Rather it is that actions fall into place on a continuous scale. At one extreme we have actions which are entirely profane, entirely functional, technique pure and simple; at the other we have actions which are entirely sacred, strictly æsthetic, technically non-functional. Between these two

---

[21] Malinowski in Hogbin (1934), p. xxvi.   [22] Wittgenstein (1922), 6.421.
[23] Durkheim (1925), p. 53.

extremes we have the great majority of social actions which partake partly of the one sphere and partly of the other.

From this point of view technique and ritual, profane and sacred, do not denote *types* of action but *aspects* of almost any kind of action. Technique has economic material consequences which are measurable and predictable; ritual on the other hand is a symbolic statement which 'says' something about the individuals involved in the action. Thus from certain points of view a Kachin religious sacrifice may be regarded as a purely technical and economic act. It is a procedure for killing livestock and distributing the meat, and I think there can be little doubt that for most Kachins this seems the most important aspect of the matter. A *nat galaw* ('nat making', a sacrifice) is almost a synonym for a good feast. But from the observer's point of view there is a great deal that goes on at a sacrifice that is quite irrelevant as far as butchery, cooking and meat distribution are concerned. It is these other aspects which have meaning as symbols of social status, and it is these other aspects which I describe as ritual whether or not they involve directly any conceptualisation of the supernatural or the metaphysical.[24]

Myth, in my terminology, is the counterpart of ritual; myth implies ritual, ritual implies myth, they are one and the same. This position is slightly different from the textbook theories of Jane Harrison, Durkheim and Malinowski. The classical doctrine in English social anthropology is that myth and ritual are conceptually separate entities which perpetuate one another through functional interdependence—the rite is a dramatisation of the myth, the myth is the sanction or charter for the rite. This approach to the material makes it possible to discuss myths in isolation as constituting a system of belief, and indeed a very large part of the anthropological literature on religion concerns itself almost wholly with a discussion of the content of belief and of the rationality or otherwise of that content. Most such arguments seem to me to be scholastic nonsense. As I see it, myth regarded as a statement in words 'says' the same thing as ritual regarded as a statement

[24] cf. the distinction made by Merton (1951) between *manifest* and *latent* function.

in action.   To ask questions about the content of belief which are not contained in the content of ritual is nonsense.

If I draw a rough diagram of a motor-car on the blackboard and underneath I write 'this is a car', both statements—the drawing and the writing—'say' the same thing—neither says more than the other and it would clearly be nonsense to ask: 'Is the car a Ford or a Cadillac?'   In the same way it seems to me that if I see a Kachin killing a pig and I ask him what he is doing and he says *nat jaw nngai*—'I am giving to the nats', this statement is simply a description of what he is doing.   It is nonsense to ask such questions as: 'Do nats have legs?   Do they eat flesh?   Do they live in the sky?'

In parts of this book I shall make frequent reference to Kachin mythology but I shall make no attempt to find any logical coherence in the myths to which I refer.   Myths for me are simply one way of describing certain types of human behaviour; the anthropologist's jargon and his use of structural models are other devices for describing the same types of human behaviour.   In sociological analysis we need to make frequent use of these alternative languages, but we must always remember that a descriptive device can never have an autonomy of its own.   However abstract my representations, my concern is always with the material world of observable human behaviour, never with metaphysics or systems of ideas as such.

Interpretation

In sum then, my view here is that ritual action and belief are alike to be understood as forms of symbolic statement about the social order.   Although I do not claim that anthropologists are always in a position to interpret such symbolism, I hold nevertheless that the main task of social anthropology is to attempt such interpretation.[25]

I must admit here to a basic psychological assumption. I assume that all human beings, whatever their culture and whatever their degree of mental sophistication, tend to construct symbols and make mental associations in the same general sort of way.   This is a very large assumption, though

[25] The concept of *eidos* as developed by Bateson (1936) has relevance for this part of my argument.

all anthropologists make it.   The situation amounts to this:
I assume that with patience I, an Englishman, can learn to
speak any other verbal language—e.g. Kachin.   Furthermore,
I assume that I will then be able to give an *approximate* translation in English of any ordinary verbal statement made by a
Kachin.   When it comes to statements which, though verbal,
are entirely symbolic—e.g. as in poetry—translation becomes
very difficult, since a word for word translation probably carries
no associations for the ordinary English reader; nevertheless I
assume that I can, with patience, come to understand *approximately* even the poetry of a foreign culture and that I can then
communicate that understanding to others.   In the same way
I assume that I can give an approximate interpretation of even
non-verbal symbolic actions such as items of ritual.   It is difficult
entirely to justify this kind of assumption, but without it all
the activities of anthropologists become meaningless.

From this point we can go back to the problem I raised near
the beginning of this chapter, namely the relation between a
social structure considered as an abstract model of an ideal
society, and the social structure of any actual empirical society.

I am maintaining that wherever I encounter 'ritual' (in the
sense in which I have defined it) I can, as an anthropologist,
interpret that ritual.

Ritual in its cultural context is a pattern of symbols; the
words into which I interpret it are another pattern of symbols
composed largely of technical terms devised by anthropologists
—words like lineage, rank, status, and so on.   The two symbol
systems have something in common, namely a common *structure*.   In the same way, a page of music and its musical performance have a common structure.[26]   This is what I mean
when I say that ritual makes explicit the social structure.

The structure which is symbolised in ritual is the system of
socially approved 'proper' relations between individuals and
groups.   These relations are not formally recognised at all
times.   When men are engaged in practical activities in satisfaction of what Malinowski called 'the basic needs', the
implications of structural relationships may be neglected
altogether; a Kachin chief works in his field side by side with
his meanest serf.   Indeed I am prepared to argue that this

[26] Russell (1948), p. 479.

neglect of formal structure is essential if ordinary informal social activities are to be pursued at all.

Nevertheless if anarchy is to be avoided, the individuals who make up a society must from time to time be reminded, at least in symbol, of the underlying order that is supposed to guide their social activities. Ritual performances have this function for the participating group as a whole;[27] they momentarily make explicit what is otherwise a fiction.

Social Structure and Culture

My view as to the kind of relationship that exists between social structure and culture[28] follows immediately from this. Culture provides the form, the 'dress' of the social situation. As far as I am concerned, the cultural situation is a given factor, it is a product and an accident of history. I do not know *why* Kachin women go hatless with bobbed hair before they are married, but assume a turban afterwards, any more than I know *why* English women put a ring on a particular finger to denote the same change in social status; all I am interested in is that in this Kachin context the assumption of a turban by a woman does have this symbolic significance. It is a statement about the status of the woman.

But the structure of the situation is largely independent of its cultural form. The same kind of structural relationship may exist in many different cultures and be symbolised in correspondingly different ways. In the example just given, marriage is a structural relationship which is common to both English and Kachin society; it is symbolised by a ring in the one and a turban in the other. This means that one and the

---

[27] For the individual, participation in a ritual may also have other functions —e.g. a cathartic psychological one—but this, in my view, is outside the purview of the social anthropologist.

[28] As this book may be read by American as well as by English anthropologists I need to emphasise that the term *culture*, as I use it, is not that all-embracing category which is the subject matter of American cultural anthropology. I am a social anthropologist and I am concerned with the social structure of Kachin *society*. For me the concepts of culture and society are quite distinct. 'If society is taken to be an aggregate of social relations, then culture is the content of those relations. Society emphasises the human component, the aggregate of people and the relations between them. Culture emphasises the component of accumulated resources, immaterial as well as material, which the people inherit, employ, transmute, add to, and transmit' (Firth (1951), p. 27). For the somewhat different use of the term *culture* current among American anthropologists see Kroeber (1952) and Kroeber and Kluckhohn (1952).

same element of social structure may appear in one cultural dress in locality A and another cultural dress in locality B. But A and B may be adjacent places on the map. In other words there is no intrinsic reason why the significant frontiers of social systems should always coincide with cultural frontiers.

Differences of culture are, I admit, structurally significant, but the mere fact that two groups of people are of different culture does not necessarily imply—as has nearly always been assumed—that they belong to two quite different social systems. In this book I assume the contrary.

In any geographical area which lacks fundamental natural frontiers, the human beings in adjacent areas of the map are likely to have relations with one another—at least to some extent—no matter what their cultural attributes may be. In so far as these relations are ordered and not wholly haphazard there is implicit in them a social structure. But, it may be asked, if social structures are expressed in cultural symbols, how can the structural relations between groups of different culture be expressed at all? My answer to this is that the maintenance and insistence upon cultural difference can itself become a ritual action expressive of social relations.

In the geographical area considered in this book the cultural variations between one group and another are very numerous and very marked. But persons who speak a different language, wear a different dress, worship different deities and so on are not regarded as foreigners entirely beyond the pale of social recognition. Kachins and Shans are mutually contemptuous of one another, but Kachins and Shans are deemed to have a common ancestor for all that. In this context cultural attributes such as language, dress and ritual procedure are merely symbolic labels denoting the different sectors of a single extensive structural system.

For my purposes it is the underlying structural pattern and not the overt cultural pattern that has real significance. I am concerned not so much with the structural interpretation of a particular culture, but with how particular structures can assume a variety of cultural interpretations, and with how different structures can be represented by the same set of cultural symbols. In pursuing this theme I seek to demonstrate a basic mechanism in social change.

CHAPTER II

THE ECOLOGICAL BACKGROUND OF KACHIN SOCIETY

Before proceeding further it is necessary to give some general indication of the kind of economic life that is led by Kachins and their Shan neighbours.

Map 1, which shows the general location of the Kachin Hills Area, shows also the geographical position of the other major categories among the Hill Tribes of Burma,[1] namely the Karens, the Chins, the Nagas, the Palaungs, the Wa. In essence Burma comprises the drainage area of the Irrawaddy and the Lower Salween. The immediate neighbourhood of these great rivers and of their principal tributaries is low lying, flat and fertile; away from the rivers the country is generally mountainous, often precipitous. In the areas of heavy rainfall the normal vegetation cover is a dense semi-tropical monsoon forest; in the drier zones we find scrub, grassland and pine forest.[2]

An important distinction here is that in the rainbelts a dense secondary growth of jungle quickly replaces any abandoned clearings. In the drier zones on the other hand virgin forest, once cleared, tends to revert to grass or coarse scrub. In the absence of stock animals or systematic manuring, the continuing fertility of the land is thus much higher in the rainbelts than in the dry zones.

Along the river valleys irrigated rice cultivation is easy and cart tracks are readily constructed, but in the mountains which separate the valleys the construction of either roads or rice terraces is a feat of major engineering. It is hardly surprising, therefore, that the technical and economic organisation of the hill-dwelling peoples is very different from that of the peoples of the valleys, nor is it very surprising that the hill peoples in different parts of Burma all resort to much the same kind of technical device to overcome the difficulties of their environment.

[1] cf. Stevenson (1944).   [2] Stamp (1924) (a) and (b).

18

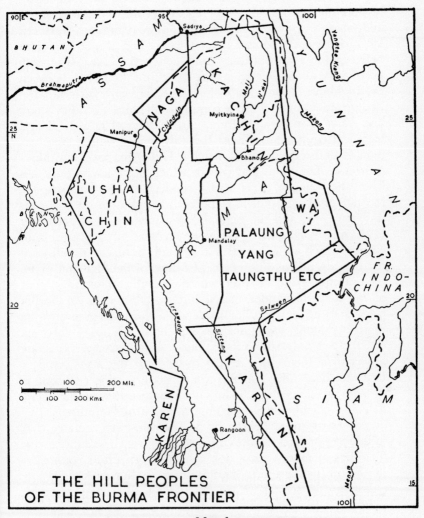

THE HILL PEOPLES
OF THE BURMA FRONTIER

MAP 1

The contrast between the highlanders and the lowlanders is thus in the first place ecological. Even if the two categories of population spoke the same language one might well expect to find marked cultural differences between the two groups and, on analogy with countries such as Scotland and Northern Italy, one might also anticipate a jealous and mutual contempt between the rival parties. And such is the case. The only peculiarity about Burma is that the cultural contrast between the highlanders and the lowlanders is so very marked. The two groups do not share a common language and they share few traits of material culture. In matters of household and technical equipment, almost the only objects which are common to both groups in the Kachin Hills Area are such things as iron cooking-pans and tripods which both parties purchase from the Chinese. Yet this is understandable enough, for technological equipment is necessarily adjusted to the conditions of life, and the highland and lowland mode of living is sharply contrasted. When one comes to the aspects of culture which are of 'ritual' rather than 'technical' significance matters are rather different. The dress of the highland males for example, is nearly everywhere a scruffy imitation of that of the local lowlander males, but women's dress is sharply contrasted as between highlanders and lowlanders and shows many regional variations among both groups. This sex difference is not without its sociological significance. It is one aspect of a theme that recurs throughout this book, namely that the highlander Kachins are constantly subject to contradictory pressures both to imitate and to oppose their valley dwelling neighbours. Incidentally much of the ethnography of Burma has been written by people who have assumed that differences of dress denotes differences of 'race'! On this basis members of more than a dozen 'races' turn up at Namhkam market in the Northern Shan States every five days.

But in this chapter we are concerned with ecology, not with politics or race. Briefly the technological situation can be summarised as follows:

The valley-dwelling peoples, that is the 'Burmese' and the 'Shans', mostly practise wet rice cultivation with moderate though adequate efficiency. This permits a system of continuous cultivation and continuous settlement even in areas where the annual rainfall is relatively slight.   Nearly all these valley peoples make use of animals for cultivation and transport.   Except in the central 'Dry Zone' of Burma, the mean density of population is nearly everywhere so low that land resources are ample.   Under normal conditions—that is in the absence of war and epidemics and similar disasters—the valley peoples can always easily raise more rice than is immediately required for the consumption of the actual cultivators. This secure economic basis permits the development of trade and small scale urbanisation and a moderate degree of general cultural sophistication.   As a broad generalisation it may be said that the valley peoples constitute a semi-literate peasantry. In an economic sense they live at a considerably 'higher' level of organisation than their neighbours in the surrounding mountains.

In contrast, the normal shifting cultivation techniques practised by the hill peoples can only be expected to yield a surplus under exceptional conditions of low population density and specially favourable terrain.   Wherever this technique proves inadequate, the hill peoples are forced into expedients of various kinds.   Some groups, such as the Central Chins, have developed quite elaborate schemes of crop rotation;[3] others, notably the Angami Nagas[4] and certain Kachin groups, have gone in for the construction of irrigated rice terraces cut out of the mountainside; others again have found a solution to their difficulties by achieving some form of political and economic alliance with their more prosperous neighbours of the plains.   This latter kind of symbiosis has assumed a variety of forms at different times in different places.   For example, the mountaineers are sometimes regarded as the political overlords of the valley, so that the valley people pay a feudal rent to the hill chieftains;[5] sometimes the hill peoples merely exploit the fact that they control the cross-country communications between the valleys and levy a toll on passing caravans;[6] sometimes the valley peoples have been willing to pay 'blackmail' provided the hillmen agreed not to raid the valley crops;[7]

---

[3] Stevenson (1943).   [4] Hutton (1921) (a).
[5] e.g. the Shan/Kachin relationship in the Hukawng Valley prior to 1926. See p. 242.
[6] e.g. the position of the Gauri chiefs throughout the 19th century.   See p. 224 f.
[7] e.g. the Assam posa system, see Butler (1846), pp. 213–17. Hamilton, A. (1912), pp. 36–9.

sometimes the valley chieftains have engaged the hillmen as mercenaries on a large scale.[8]

All such transactions are related to the fact that as a general rule the valley peoples are producers of rice surplus to their own requirements, while equally, as a general rule, the hill peoples suffer from a rice deficiency which must somehow be made good from outside. This crucial economic fact is of the utmost importance for the understanding of all long term social developments throughout the Burma area. It applies with particular force to the zone I am calling the Kachin Hills Area.

In this zone we have already seen that, at first approximation, the linguistic and territorial category Shan corresponds to 'valley dwellers and wet rice cultivators', while the vague category Kachin denotes the highlanders.

The mountain dwelling Kachins, however, do not all support themselves in the same way and we need to consider the different techniques employed and the different kinds of economy that result.

I propose to distinguish three types of hill agriculture which I shall call (a) monsoon *taungya*, (b) grassland *taungya*, (c) irrigated hill terraces. The merits and limitations of these different techniques are very relevant to our discussion.

The term *taungya* (hill field) is a Burmese term which describes a technique resembling that described as *jhum* in the literature of Assam and as *ladang* in the literature of Malaya. It has been the subject of much learned abuse but not much careful observation. A geographer has recently described the procedure as follows:

In *taungya* cultivation the larger trees are felled and the jungle burnt over. The resultant clearing is cultivated with such crops as dry hill rice, maize, millets, buckwheat and opium poppy. When the original fertility and that contributed by the wood ash are exhausted (say in one to four years) the clearing is abandoned and reverts to tangled scrub and bracken. As it is easier to clear fresh forest than the regrowth long abandoned *taungya* is rarely returned to and villages often shift bodily when the suitable land in their neighbourhood is exhausted. Naturally these practices are attended with serious deforestation and soil erosion.[9]

[8] e.g. at all known times the hill peoples have provided a major element in the Burma Army, and in armies of Shan chiefs. See pp. 186, 240.

[9] Spate (1945), p. 527.

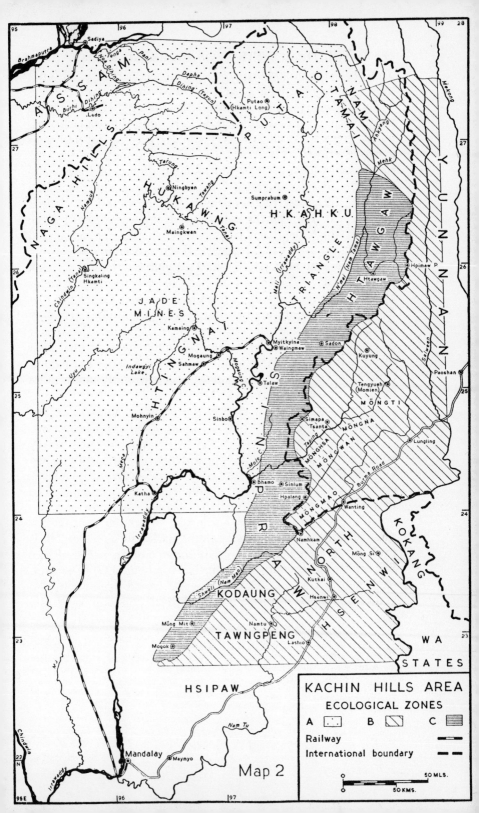

KACHIN HILLS AREA
ECOLOGICAL ZONES
A [·.·] B [///] C [▦]
Railway ————
International boundary — — —

Map 2

0 ___ 50 MLS.
0 ___ 50 KMS.

This decidedly prejudiced account distorts the reality.   Map 2 shows the Kachin Hills Area subdivided on a climatic basis.

Zone A is typical monsoon forest country.   Here the temperatures and rainfall are such that abandoned forest clearings, unless grossly abused, will very rapidly become covered with a strong growth of secondary jungle.   Throughout this area the Kachins have a clearly formulated theory of how *taung-ya* ought to be cultivated.   I call this procedure monsoon *taungya*.   The first requirement is that it should be cleared for one year only and then abandoned; the second that a piece of land which has been cleared once should not be cleared again for about 12 or 15 years.[10]   If this procedure is followed, then there is no deforestation and negligible soil loss.   In such conditions dry hill rice can be made to produce regular yields approaching those obtained from irrigated wet rice.[11]

Such a procedure implies that every piece of land as it goes out of cultivation is fallowed for at least 12 years.   Each unit of population therefore requires a formidably large total area of farmland, and anything in the way of a large permanent closely packed village community will find itself many miles from some of its outlying property.   To avoid this, Kachin communities very frequently consist of a cluster of small villages or hamlets widely scattered over the total community property.

There is a conflict here between the interests of military security, which call for large settlements enclosed within some kind of fortification, and the interests of economic convenience which call for small fragmented settlements situated close to the land used for cultivation.   British Administrators frequently complained at the Kachins' fondness for splitting up their settlements into smaller and smaller villages, and it is probably the case that the establishment of an enforced Pax Britannica did encourage the further fragmentation of Kachin settlement.   Groups, which formerly would have lived together for mutual protection within a common stockade,

[10] Kachins do not normally count the years of the fallow period; they merely judge when land is fit for re-use by the state of the secondary growth.   Competent agriculturalists have, however, shown that the necessary fallow period under North Burma monsoon conditions is about 12–15 years.   With a shorter period there are too many weeds; with a longer period the trunks and roots of the secondary trees are inconveniently large.

[11] This is the case, for example, in parts of the North Triangle area near Htingnan.   (Map 4, p. 33.)

preferred, under the British, to hive off and live on their own lands. However, the few records we have concerning the size of pre-British stockaded Kachin villages do not suggest that the settlement pattern then was very different from what it is now.[12]

However, this is the point. Although the average density of the population over the whole region is very low, and although there would be quite enough land to go round if this population were evenly distributed, the population is not in fact evenly distributed. There are local concentrations of population living at relatively high density. These concentrations are the result of past political events, such as local wars or external administrative interference; but, whatever their origin, they have the present-day consequence that there are a great many localities, even within the potentially fertile Zone A, where *taungya* is practised on a rotation cycle of substantially less than 12 years and in which crops are grown on the same land for more than one season at a time. In such circumstances, *taungya* methods do definitely lead in the long run to erosion and declining fertility. The Kachins themselves are well aware of this; they do not misuse their land by choice, they only reduce the fallow period of their cultivation cycle when local land scarcity makes it inevitable that they should do so.

In addition, the prosperity of certain parts of Zone A has been greatly affected in the past by the vicissitudes of the trade in special local products. Thus amber and salt and india-rubber were, even within recent times, of major importance for the Hukawng Valley, though they signify little at the present time. Similarly, the jade trade has been outstandingly erratic, while the iron and silver deposits of the Hkamti Long area, which were once of major local significance, are no longer considered worth exploiting at all. Such natural resources are elements in the ecological situation but their significance, at

[12] Wilcox (1832) and Bayfield (1873) between them mention the size of about a dozen Kachin villages: none of these contain more than 20 houses. The village of the Daipha Gam, who was virtually paramount chief of the Hukawng Valley, consisted in 1837 of two stockades (i.e. two separate hamlets) of 15 and 6 houses respectively. Bayfield assumes that each household averages 9–10 persons, whereas modern households average 4–5, but Bayfield may have been guessing. Michell (1883), pp. 132 f., gives a detailed inventory of 30 Singpho villages. The largest contained 40 houses; the average is estimated at 12 houses and 7 persons per house.

any particular time, is determined by economic and political factors which are external to the local environment.

Zone B is more or less outside the monsoon area. Temperatures and rainfall here are much lower. Pine and scrub and grass replace the wet forest. Here a clearing once made and abandoned recovers to jungle only very slowly if at all. *Taungya* in this kind of country is really a kind of crop rotation. The cultivation of dry hill rice is usually more or less impractical, either the rainfall is too unreliable or the altitudes are too high and the summer temperatures too low. Nevertheless, rice nearly always remains the preferred crop wherever local conditions permit its cultivation. In Zone B as a whole, the main cereal crops (apart from irrigated rice in the valleys) are maize, buckwheat, millet, wheat and barley. Beans are often grown as a first crop on newly opened grassland, but then several crops of one sort or another may be taken in succession before the land is finally allowed to revert to fallow grass again. It is unusual to find such crop rotations fully systematised as is apparently the case with the Central Chins in West Burma.[13] In Zone B, since cereal crops are normally poor and unrewarding, there is an incentive to resort to a cash crop economy. Crops such as tea, poppy and *hwang lien*[14] are often grown for trade purposes in preference to foodstuffs and sometimes with considerable success. The Palaung of Tawngpeng, for example, though a hill people, manage to maintain Shan standards of life by means of their long established trade in tea.[15] Tea, of course, is a plantation crop and does not involve *taungya* practice.

In general, grassland *taungya* of the ordinary Zone B type probably deserves much of the condemnation implied in my quotation from Spate. A village which relies exclusively on such *taungya* can seldom be self-sufficient in foodstuffs. There is consequently a much more marked tendency in Zone B than in Zone A for the hill villages and the valley villages to be interlocked in some sort of more or less permanent economic and political interdependence.

[13] Stevenson (1943). For details of grassland *taungya* see Scott and Hardiman (1901), Part I, Vol. II, pp. 355–6.

[14] *Hwang lien*—the plant *coptis teeta* used as a medicine by the Chinese; a major crop in the Nam Tamai, Ahkyang, Tarong area where it is called *numrin*.

[15] Milne (1924); cf. Scott and Hardiman, op. cit., p. 356 f.

In terms of climate and ecology, Zone C is intermediate between Zones A and B, as the following description of the Hpimaw district clearly shows:

North slopes are forested, south slopes are grass clad, so that looking north one sees all the south-facing slopes at once and the mountains appear somewhat bare, but looking south mainly north-facing slopes are exposed and they appear well timbered.[16]

The Kachins of this area practise both monsoon and grassland *taungya*, but, in addition, in a number of widely separated localities one finds elaborate systems of irrigated terracing used for the cultivation of wet-rice.

Such terrace systems are common enough in many parts of China, but when encountered among a so-called 'primitive' people, they invariably evoke the astonished admiration of ethnographers. The fact that the Angami Nagas and the Philippine Igorot both construct terraces of this type has been used by ethnologists to support the most fanciful theories concerning remote prehistoric migrations.[17]

British Administrators were equally impressed. It seemed only natural to suppose that people capable of such triumphs of engineering must be far more efficient farmers than those of their immediate neighbours who rely exclusively on *taungya* cultivation. In the belief that terracing was the only answer to the menace of the erosion which must result from the continued practice of *taungya*, the British constantly urged the Kachins to extend their areas of terraced cultivation. This propaganda was notably unsuccessful. Though government subsidy resulted in the construction of new terraces in one or two unlikely places, there is considerable evidence that fewer terraces were in use in 1940 than in 1870.

The fact is that official enthusiasm for terracing was not in accord with the economic facts. In general, terracing is not an economic procedure. It only becomes economic when local population densities are great enough to create a serious shortage of land. Under Pax Britannica the Kachin population as a whole tended to be spread more evenly over the total area, with the result that a good deal of terrace land previously

---

[16] Ward (1921), p. 106.   [17] e.g. Smith (1925), p. 159.

considered profitable became marginal and went out of use. Hill terraces are costly to construct and difficult to maintain; they often give a very poor return for the time and energy expended. When *taungyá* and hill terraces are both cultivated by the same community, as is often the case, the people concerned seem usually to regard *taungya* cultivation as the more rewarding.[18] On the other hand, since terraces can be cultivated year after year with little or no fallow period, relatively dense local aggregates of population are possible. Hill terraces are thus usually found associated with unusually large communities on permanent sites.

The real advantage of hill terrace systems seems to be military and political rather than economic. It is probably significant that the most notable terrace systems in this area lie athwart, or close to, the principal east-west trade routes from Yunnan into Burma—i.e. near Hpimaw, Sadon and Sinlum.[19] Military control of these trade routes was the original *raison d'être* for the relatively high concentrations of Kachin population found in these localities, and it was the profits of toll charges which originally made the construction of terrace systems worth while from the Kachin point of view.

Under the British, after the first few years, the Kachins were prohibited from levying toll charges on the trade caravans passing through their territory, and the original incentive for terracing largely disappeared. Once constructed, however, a terrace system represents a substantial investment of time and labour and is unlikely to be abandoned outright. The largest single village in the Kachin Hills (about 150 houses) is situated in the immediate vicinity of the Hpimaw Pass. Without terracing, the location would be almost uninhabitable, for most of the slopes are too steep for *taungya*. Simply as a place to live in, it is preposterous, but militarily speaking it is magnificent.

We must conclude, therefore, that while ecological factors have an important bearing upon the different modes of Kachin and Shan subsistence, political history has also had an important influence. The ecological situation is a limiting factor not a determinant of the social order.

I shall return to this theme in Chapter VIII.

[18] This observation is confirmed by Hutton ((1921) (*a*), p. 72); cf. also Leach (1949).   [19] See Map 2, p. 23.

CHAPTER III

THE CATEGORIES SHAN AND KACHIN AND THEIR SUBDIVISIONS

It must be apparent from what has already been said that a primary requirement for an understanding of the argument of this book is that the reader should be able to conceptualise for himself just what is meant by the categories Kachin and Shan and their various subdivisions, and also by the contrasted sub-categories *gumsa* Kachin and *gumlao* Kachin. The present chapter is an attempt to make these distinctions clear at the level of very superficial descriptive ethnography; the degree to which the categories can be distinguished at the level of social structure will only become apparent later on.

Shan

First let us consider the category Shan. The word in this form is derived from the Burmese. The English geographical expressions Assam and Siam are related terms. The Kachin (Jinghpaw) equivalent for Burmese *shan* is *sam*. The Burmese apply the term Shan fairly consistently to all the inhabitants of political Burma and of the Yunnan-Burma frontier area who call themselves Tai. In the west and south-west of Burma this involves some ambiguity since the Burmese distinguish Shans from Siamese, although both groups call themselves Tai. But for north-east Burma the definition is clear enough.

The Shans, so defined, are territorially scattered, but fairly uniform in culture. Dialect variations between different localities are considerable, but even so, apart from a few special exceptions, it can be said that all the Shans of North Burma and Western Yunnan speak one language, namely Tai. The exceptions are the Shans of Möng Hsa (the Maingtha or A'chang), who speak what seems to be a dialect of Maru, the Shans of the Kubaw Valley, who now speak a corrupted form of Burmese, and miscellaneous small pockets of Shans in the Upper Chindwin and Hukawng Valley areas, whose speech today would appear to be mainly Jinghpaw with a heavy

29

admixture of Tai and Assamese. Most of the population known as Kadu seem to fall into this category.[1] There is also a small group of people living on the Irrawaddy near Sinbo who live like Shans but speak a language called Hpon, more or less intermediate between Maru and Burmese. Most of the surviving Hpon speakers—there are only a few hundred in all—seem now to consider themselves Tai.

A most important criterion of group identity is that all Shans are Buddhists.[2] The majority, it is true, are not very devout, and Shan Buddhism includes a number of decidedly heretical sects, but being a Buddhist is symbolically important as an index of Shan sophistication. When, as not infrequently happens, a Kachin 'becomes a Shan' (*sam tai*), the adoption of Buddhism is a crucial part of the procedure. The individual who in present-day Burma (1951) holds the official title of 'Head of the Kachin State' is a Buddhist-Kachin-cum-Shan of this type.

A second general criterion is that 'all Shan settlements are associated with wet rice cultivation'. Here we can tie in the concept Shan with the data cited in Chapter II. North Burma is an area of hills and mountains. The Shans are scattered about in this area but not at random. Shan settlements only occur along the river valleys, or in pockets of level country in the hills. Such settlements are always found associated with irrigated wet paddy land. There is therefore a rough equation between culture and sophistication. In this region, the prosperity that comes from plains of wet paddy cultivation implies Buddhism, which implies membership of a Shan feudal state. The only exceptions to this generalisation fall more or less outside the area we are considering. The Palaung derive their economic prosperity from tea cultivation instead of wet paddy; they are Buddhists and have a Shan type social system, but they live in the mountains.[3] There are also certain sophisticated inhabitants of the Wa States who have grown rich on the proceeds of opium poppy cultivation. They still live in the mountains, but have adopted Buddhism and are known as Tai Loi (i.e. Hill Shans).

[1] See also p. 45.
[2] In Indo-China there is a group known as the 'Black Tai' who are not Buddhist, but I am concerned here only with the Shans of the Kachin Hills Area.
[3] Milne (1924); Cameron (1911); Lowis (1906).

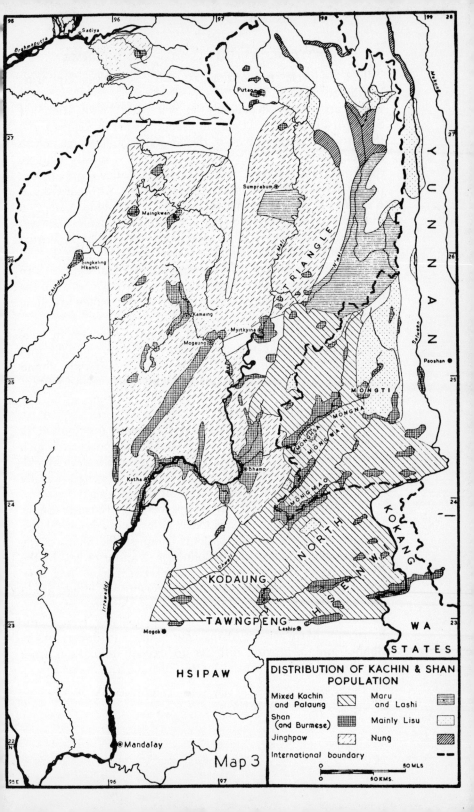

DISTRIBUTION OF KACHIN & SHAN POPULATION

Mixed Kachin and Palaung

Shan (and Burmese)

Jinghpaw

International boundary

Maru and Lashi

Mainly Lisu

Nung

Map 3

0   50 MLS
0   60 KMS.

The converse proposition is only approximately true. Within the Kachin Hills Area most (but not all) communities which are wholly dependent on wet paddy cultivation are Shan (or Burmese). The main exceptions are as follows. To the east in the upper part of the Shweli drainage area, north of Tengyueh, the rice-growing population is mostly Chinese speaking. Further west in the Hukawng Valley there are wet paddy areas where the inhabitants today regard themselves as Kachins (Jinghpaw) rather than Shans. Finally in Assam, on the western frontier of the area, the ordinary Assamese peasant is a cultivator of wet rice. I should also add that in the Burma administrative districts of Bhamo and Myitkyina the former Shan states no longer exist as separate political entities. In these areas no very clear distinction can be drawn between the Shan and the Burmese components of the valley dwelling population.

Shan rice cultivation is almost always carried on in level areas which permit the use of buffalo-drawn ploughs and harrows. Shan communities are very occasionally found associated with systems of hill terracing such as were mentioned in Chapter II, but most hill terrace systems within the area are worked by Kachins.

I have tried to indicate the approximate distribution of Shan settlements on Maps 3 and 4, but the pockets of such settlements are often so small that only a large-scale map can give a true indication of the extent to which, geographically speaking, Shans and Kachins are 'all mixed up'.

The Burmese make a distinction between Burmese Shans (*Shan B'mah*),[4] Chinese Shans (*Shan Tayok*) and Hkamti Shans. Roughly speaking, Burmese Shans comprise the Shans of the Burmese Shan states, where Buddhism is more or less of the Burmese type and where the princes (*saohpa*) have long been nominally subordinate to the Burmese King. Chinese Shans are the Shans of the Shan states in Yunnan, the most important of which lie in the area south of Tengyueh and west of the Salween. Many of the Shans now resident in Burma in the Bhamo and Myitkyina districts are recent immigrants from the Yunnan and are classed by the Burmese as Chinese Shans.

[4] This expression is apparently only current in the Bhamo and Myitkyina districts; see Bennison (1933), p. 189.

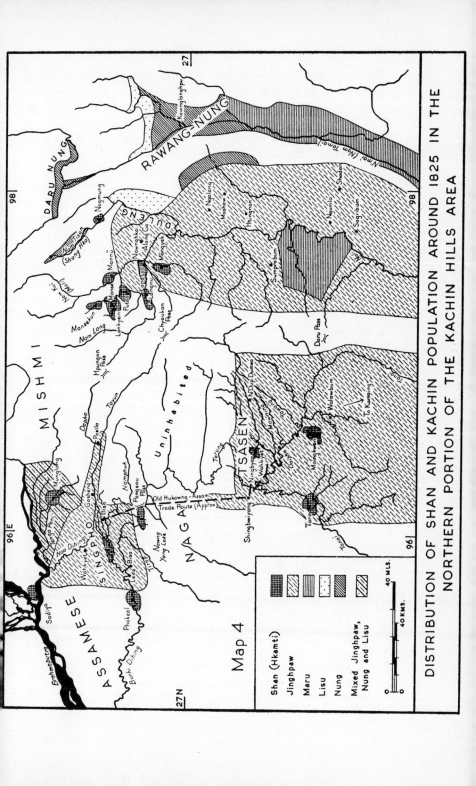

Map 4

DISTRIBUTION OF SHAN AND KACHIN POPULATION AROUND 1825 IN THE
NORTHERN PORTION OF THE KACHIN HILLS AREA

Shan (Hkamti)

Jinghpaw

Maru

Lisu

Nung

Mixed Jinghpaw,
Nung and Lisu

40 MLS.

40 KMS.

Hkamti Shans are looked upon as a sub-type of Burmese Shan. They may be defined as Shans who, on historical grounds, might be regarded as having had some political allegiance to the former Shan state of Mogaung (Möng Kawng).

Until the middle of the 18th century the Shan states of North Burma retained a considerable degree of independence and tended to owe fealty to China rather than Burma. In the latter part of the 18th century, in the course of a series of somewhat indecisive wars between Burma and China, the various Shan principalities of the Upper Irrawaddy area (Mogaung, Mohnyin, Waingmaw, Bhamo) appear to have sided with the Chinese and, as a consequence, suffered destruction at the hands of the Burmese armies.[5] From the end of the 18th century there were no regular Shan princes (*saohpa*) in these states. They were treated as direct feudal dependencies of the Burmese crown. The perquisites of the office of *myosa* were in the gift of the King and the state governor (*myowun*) was appointed direct from Ava.

Hkamti[6] appears to have been originally a title associated with the royal family of Mogaung. After the elimination of Mogaung as an independent political unit, it continued to serve as a description of those Shan principalities which had formerly been political dependencies of Mogaung in a feudal sense.

As these Hkamti states have played an important role in Kachin affairs they are worth enumerating in detail.

a. Hkamti Long (Great Hkamti), now a confederation of 7 small Shan principalities, situated near the headwaters of the Irrawaddy (Mali Hka). Though probably colonised in the first place direct from China, Hkamti Long seems to have been a dependency of Mogaung in the 17th and 18th centuries.[7] Hkamti Long appears as Putao on Map 2; the component principalities are shown on Map 4.

b. Hukawng Valley Shans, notably those of Maingkwan, Ningbyen, Taro. These Shans are now mostly politically dependent on the neighbouring Kachins. They are said to be the residue of a once much more numerous population organised on feudal lines.[8] (Map 4.)

---

[5] See Imbault-Huart (1878), where Meng K'ong = Mogaung; Meng Yang = Mohnyin.
[6] Also variously spelt Kanti, Kansi, Khampti, Khamti, etc.
[7] Barnard (1925); MacGregor (1894).   [8] Kawlu Ma Nawng (1942), p. 41.

c. Singkaling Hkamti. A small Shan state on the Upper Chindwin. The bulk of the local population are Kachins and Nagas. The Shan element, including the ruling family, seem to have come from Ningbyen in the Hukawng Valley.[9] (Maps 3 and 4.)

d. The Hkamti of Assam. Located to the east of Sadiya and also on the Dihing near Ledo (Map 4). The former derive from colonists from Hkamti Long who entered Assam about 1795. The latter stem from various groups of Shan colonists who entered Assam from the Hukawng Valley during the 18th and 19th centuries.[10] Throughout the past 120 years the Hkamti of Assam have always been much mixed up with Assamese, Mishmis, Nagas, and Kachins (Singpho).[11]

e. The jade mines which were a major factor in the original downfall of the Mogaung princes in the 18th century have, for the last 60 years at any rate, been under the control of a line of Kachin chiefs. These chiefs, though treated as Kachins by the British administration, aped the manners of the Shans and married into Shan families. They also assumed the title *Kansi* (*Kanti*) *duwa* as heirs, it would seem, of the original Shan domain.[12] (Map 2.)

From this list it will be seen that there is a confusion between the use of Hkamti to denote a particular group of people of supposedly common ethnic origin, and the use of the same term as the name of a political state. This ambiguity applies also to the more general term Shan. Nearly all the Shan states within the Kachin Hills Area include non-Shan elements of population. In a good many cases the non-Shan elements are considerably more numerous than the Shan elements. The political capital of a Shan state is in all cases a Shan township located in the vicinity of irrigated rice lands, but the feudal dependencies of such a state may include not only other communities of wet-rice growing Shans, but also a variety of hill villages with a non-Shan population and a *taungya* economy. In some cases the resulting political hierarchy is somewhat elaborate. For example, prior to 1895, the present Chinese Shan state of Möng Wan included not only the Shan villages in the Nam Wan Valley but also a number of Kachin settlements which are now regarded as being on the Burma side of

[9] *Shan States and Karenni*, pp. 75–6.   [10] Dalton (1872), p. 6.
[11] See especially Pemberton (1835); Mackenzie (1884); Michell (1883).
[12] Hertz (1912).

the frontier. The Shan villagers in the Nam Wan plain did not for the most part pay their feudal dues to the Möng Wan Saohpa direct but to one or other of several Kachin chieftains. The Kachin chiefs in turn paid dues to the Möng Wan Saohpa. The Shan villagers paid their dues in rice, while the Kachin chiefs paid their dues in gunpowder, an arrangement economically very satisfactory for all concerned.[13]

Reference to the *Shan States Gazetteer*[14] shows that in 1900 there were numerous similar instances in which Kachin political domains were integrated into a larger Shan feudal structure. The complete political separation of Kachin and Shan territory which prevailed during the latter part of the British régime in Burma was not a natural phenomenon but the product of administrative action on the part of the paramount power.

The scattered distribution of the Tai speaking, Buddhist, wet-rice growing population has frequently been a matter for comment and pseudo-historical speculation. The explanatory theory most commonly advanced seems to be that the Tibeto-Burman speaking peoples and the Tai speaking peoples repre-sent two distinct ethnic stocks. The Tibeto-Burman peoples are credited with a general tendency to migrate from north to south. According to this theory, the southward migration was temporarily interrupted between the 8th and 12th cen-turies A.D. by a westward infiltration of Tai speaking Shans. This westward migration of Shans corresponds to the political expansion of the Shan 'Empire' of Nanchao which had its capital in the vicinity of Tali. Later, with the decline of Shan political power, the Tibeto-Burman southward movement is supposed to have been resumed. On this theory the Jingh-paw-speaking Kachins are the last of the Tibeto-Burmans to arrive from the North; during the 18th and 19th centuries they are supposed to have 'overrun' the Shans, so that the North Burma Shans of today are merely scattered survivors from this heathen invasion.[15]

Such a complicated interpretation of the evidence is unneces-

---

[13] R.N.E.F. (1899), p. 3.   [14] Scott and Hardiman (1900–1).
[15] There is an extensive literature of this topic, see for example Enriquez (1933); Hanson (1913); Lowis (1919); Eickstedt (1944.)   In criticism, Green (1933; 1934) has pointed out that differences of physical type in N.E. Burma do not cor-respond at all to linguistic distributions; this invalidates the whole argument.

sary.   As Von Eickstedt has clearly recognised,[16] the very essence of Shan (Tai) culture is its association with wet-rice cultivation.   In the Kachin Hills Area with very few exceptions, wherever there is a stretch of country suitable for wet-rice cultivation, we either find Shans or we find no one at all. Only as an exception do we find any of the 'Kachin' peoples domiciled in the plains and valleys.   And *vice versa* in localities suitable only for *taungya* cultivation, we find either Kachins or no one at all.   The inference is clear: it is unlikely that the distribution of Shan settlements has ever, at any time since the original spread of Shan culture, been substantially different from what it is now.   If, as is quite possible, there was formerly a numerically larger Shan population than there is now, that does not imply that the Shans were more widely dispersed; it merely means that the present-day Shan settlements were formerly somewhat larger.   There can never have been a Shan population domiciled in the mountain areas.   It is only in those localities such as the Hukawng Valley where we encounter Kachins cultivating rice by Shan methods that we can infer with any probability that Kachins have 'overrun' or ousted a Shan population.   And for that matter, if we encounter Kachin-speaking people cultivating rice by Shan methods, it might almost be inferred that these 'Kachins' are already well on the way to 'becoming Shans'.

It may well be true that over the last thousand years or so, there have been very substantial migrations and demographic changes among the hill population throughout the Kachin Hills Area, but it needs to be remembered that these changes could take place without affecting the position of the Shan population in the plains and valleys.   Facts or inferences about the history of either segment of the total population can therefore give us few certain clues about the history of the other.

Factual history for any part of the Kachin Hills Area is fragmentary.   I give a summary of this established history in Chapter VIII along with my own guess at some of the crucial facts for which we have nothing but purely circumstantial evidence.   But in Chapter VIII I am concerned mainly with Kachin 'history' and it will be as well if I do my guessing about the Shans right away.

[16] Eickstedt (1944).

One of the facts that can be taken as established for certain is that the Chinese were familiar with various routes from Yunnan to India as early as the first century A.D. We cannot be quite certain what these routes were, but, since there are only a very limited number of passes through the main mountain ranges, routes cannot have differed very greatly from those we know of today. It is not unreasonable to see the original Shan colonisation of the river valleys as a process associated with the maintenance of these trade routes. There is evidence that communications were maintained by establishing a series of small military garrisons at suitable staging posts along the route. These garrisons would have had to maintain themselves and would therefore need to be sited in a terrain suitable for rice cultivation. The settlement thus formed would provide the nucleus of an area of sophisticated culture which would develop in time into a Shan type petty state.

The extent to which any particular state would develop would be conditioned by local circumstances. In Hkamti Long, for example, the area suitable for development as a rice plain is substantial and a much larger area seems actually to have been cultivated in the past than is now the case. The trade routes through Hkamti Long have been little used for over a century: formerly, when more trade passed this way, the population may have been larger.

In contrast, the scale of the Shan community at Sima-pa can scarcely have changed for centuries. This is a little rice plain of about three square miles situated at high altitude (about 5,400 feet above sea level). It happens to constitute one of the key passes from Yunnan into Upper Burma and lies on the route of the former jade caravans from Mogaung to Tengyuch. It is thus most strategically situated, and it has certainly been there a very long time. It is only a little place but at no time in the past can it have been any larger, for it is at least a day's march from any other Shan or Chinese community and the whole of the locally available rice land is fully taken up. (Map 2, p. 23.)

This explanation of the siting and scale of Shan communities, as determined initially by the strategy and economy of trade routes, is clearly speculative, but it fits the known facts better than those theories which explain the present day distribution of Shan settlements as the outcome of some fabulous large scale military conquest.[17] An important implication of my argument is that Shan culture, as we now know it, is not to be regarded as a complex imported into the area ready made from somewhere outside, as most of the authorities seem to have supposed. It is an indigenous growth resulting from the economic interaction of small-scale military colonies with an indigenous hill population over a long period.

The process by which Shan type development takes place is well illustrated by Davies' account of Möng Ka. The present day inhabitants of Möng Ka are Chinese speaking Lisu; their general cultural resemblance to the Shans of similar communities, such as that at Sima-pa, is very close. The place name Möng Ka is Shan. Davies wrote as follows:

'The little Möng Ka paddy plain (5,400 feet) is inhabited by Chinese and Lisus. The land is all cultivated but is not fertile and the people do not get much more than a bare living out of it. . . . The Mong Ka headman is known as the Yang-hsing-kuan which simply means 'the official whose surname is Yang'. His office is hereditary. It appears that an ancestor of his sometime or other conquered the original Lisu inhabitants for the Chinese Government and as a reward he and his men settled down there as soldier colonists and the government of the place was given to him and his descendants. The Lisus and Chinese now live together quite amicably and no doubt the original settlers took Lisu wives so that their descendants are as much Lisu by race as Chinese.'[18]

There are various other kinds of evidence which support the view that large sections of the peoples we now know as Shans are descendants of hill tribesmen who have in the recent past been assimilated into the more sophisticated ways of Buddhist-Shan culture. For example, Wilcox, the first Englishman to visit Hkamti Long, mentions that 'the mass of the labouring population is of the Khaphok tribe whose dialect is closely allied to the Singpho.'[19]

This Shan term *kha-phok* or *hka-hpaw* can be translated 'slave

---

[17] The Shans' own traditions on the subject are, needless to say, couched in terms of military conquest (cf. Elias, 1876), but such tales have no historical value.
[18] Davies (1909), pp. 37–8. Möng Ka is a staging post on the route from Sadon to Tengyueh.   [19] Wilcox (1832), p. 445.

Kachin'.[20]   Barnard, a later authority on the same area, mentions that two lower-class groups in Hkamti society are named Hsampyen (i.e. *sam hpyen*) and Share.[21]   In Jinghpaw speech these terms would mean 'Shan mercenary soldier' and 'hired soldier' respectively; the implication is that these low-class Shans are of Jinghpaw Kachin origin.   Similarly, if one examines, as I have done, the long succession of references to the Hkamti of Assam which appear in English language records, official and otherwise, between 1824 and 1940, the conclusion is unavoidable that the ancestors of many of the people now classed as Hkamti (i.e. Shan) would a century ago have been quite properly classed under some other head such as Singpho, r Nung (i.e. Kachin).

Details of such apparent change of cultural identity are given in Appendix I.   The point I want to make here is that the territorial location, the relative sophistication, and the main features of the economic organisation of what we now refer to as Shan society are to a large extent determined by the environment.   Given the requirements of a wet-rice economy in such a terrain, Shan settlements could hardly turn out to be other than what they are.   That being so I am justified in treating the Shan type social system as a relatively stable point in the total flux.

In my later theoretical chapters I discuss the Kachin type social systems—the *gumlao* type and the *gumsa* type—as intrinsically unstable, while I treat the contrasted Shan type as intrinsically stable.   The justification for this is to be found in such empirical data as I have mentioned above.   Shan culture today extends in scattered pockets from Assam to Tongking and southwards to Bangkok and Cambodia.   The hill peoples who are neighbours to the Shans are astonishingly varied in their culture; the Shans, considering their wide dispersal and their scattered form of settlement, are astonishingly uniform.   My argument is that this uniformity of Shan culture is correlated with a uniformity of Shan political organisation which is in turn largely determined by the special economic facts of the Shan situation.   My historical assumption is that the valley Shans have everywhere, for centuries past, been assimilating their hill neighbours, but the unchang-

[20] Barnard (1934), p. vii. cf. pp. 222, 238.   [21] Barnard (1925), p. 139.

ing economic factors in the situation have meant that the pattern of assimilation has everywhere been very similar. Shan culture itself has been modified relatively little.

Kachin

So much for the basic meaning of the term Shan; the category Kachin is more complicated. First the word itself. *Kachin* is a romanisation of the Burmese term ကချင်. This spelling came into use about 1890. Prior to that the usual form was *Kakhyen*.

For the Burmese the category was originally a vague one loosely applied to the barbarians of the north-east frontiers. It first appears in English around 1837.[22] It was then used as a general term for the hill tribesmen, other than Palaung, living in the Bhamo district and in North Hsenwi State. This population was then, as now, polyglot; it included speakers of the languages and dialects now known as Jinghpaw, Gauri, Maru, Atsi, Lashi and Lisu. Initially, therefore, Kachin was *not* a linguistic category.

Another Burmese population category was first romanised as *Theinbaw*. Other versions of the same word appear in the literature as Singpho, Singfo, Chingpaw, Jinghpaw, etc. It is a category applied to themselves by the people who speak the language we now call Jinghpaw. But just as in English the expression 'We Britons' can be deemed to include or exclude Scotsmen, Welshmen and Canadians more or less at the whim of the speaker, so also the expression 'We Jinghpaw' (*anhte jinghpaw ni*) is ambiguous. It commonly includes a great many people who do not themselves speak the Jinghpaw language, indeed, the word can be used so as to embrace the whole of mankind. The Burmese used Theinbaw mainly with reference to the barbarians of the Mogaung district and the Hukawng Valley. They appear to have treated it as a category distinct from Kakhyen.

The British first came into political contact with speakers of Jinghpaw and other 'Kachin' languages in Assam around 1824; the people concerned were then referred to as Singphos and Kakoos. By 1837 British military intelligence had

[22] Hannay (1837); Burney (1837); Richardson (1837); Malcom (1839).

amassed a very substantial body of information not merely concerning the Singphos of Assam but also concerning their tribal kinsmen of the Hukawng Valley and of the areas north-east of Mogaung.[23]   In these reports *Singpho* is used for the Jinghpaw speakers resident in the Hukawng Valley and their near kinsmen in Assam, while *Kakoo* includes the Jinghpaw of the Triangle and Sumprabum areas, and also the Maru, Lashi, Lisu, Nung and Duleng.   The 'Kakoo' were regarded as a variety of Singpho but of a somewhat inferior type.[24]

It seems to have been assumed at this time that the English category Singpho and the Burmese category Theinbaw were identical, but the category Kakhyen was still treated as separate.[25]   Ten years later Hannay, who had been responsible for part of the original intelligence work, published a treatise on *The Singphos or Kakhyens of Burma*,[26] thus uniting under one head the hillmen east of Bhamo, the Singpho of the Hukawng Valley and Assam, and the miscellaneous 'Kakoo' of the Mali Hka and N'mai Hka Valleys.[27]

In Hannay's scheme the whole population of Burma north of Bhamo falls under only two heads: the Shans and the Kakhyens.   Evidently what impressed Hannay most was the general cultural similarity between all the different groups of hill people.   He realised that they did not all speak the same language, but this did not strike him as particularly important.

Hannay's views were generally accepted until the end of the century.   For example, a writer in 1891[28] considered that the Gauri, who speak a dialect of Jinghpaw, and the Szi (Atsi), who speak a dialect of Maru, were 'closely related' sections of the same 'sub-tribe of Kachins'.   Kachin was thus still a cultural and not a linguistic category.

At this period, however, the expression *Kachin Hills* became part of the official administrative jargon of British Burma and led to the highly artificial notion that a Kachin was someone who lived in a particular kind of terrain rather than a person

---

[23] *Selection of Papers* (1873); Wilcox (1832); Pemberton (1835).

[24] The 'Kakoo' areas were not known at first hand but there were Lisu, Nung and Duleng villages in Assam and there were Maru settlements in the Hukawng. The term Kakoo—i.e. *Hka hku*—is Jinghpaw for 'up river (people)' and is the opposite of *hka nam* 'down river'.   The region discussed here is shown on Map 4, p. 33.   [25] Malcom, ii, 243.   [26] Hannay (1847).

[27] Burney (1842), p. 340, also makes the identification 'Kakhyens or Singphos'.

[28] George (1891).

of particular cultural characteristics. This is seen clearly if we compare two contradictory government directives issued in 1892 and 1893 respectively.

(1892)   'Kachin tribes and clans within our line of outposts and settled villages . . . must be placed in every way on the same footing as the Burmese Shans and others among whom they have settled.'

Here Kachin is a cultural category.   But

(1893)   'The Kachin Hills were to be administered in so far as they were included within the provisional area of our administration on distinct lines from the lowland tracts, where alone ordinary law and ordinary taxes were to be enforced.[29]

Here Kachin is a geographical category.

From about 1900 onwards, the ethnological ideas of the linguists began to become paramount.[30]   Grierson and other scholars put forward the view that an analysis of the present-day distribution of languages and dialects would reveal the course of the historical migrations of the sundry 'races' from which the modern population was supposed to be descended.

One consequence of this theory was that in every Burma Census between 1911 and 1941 the population was classified by 'race'—'race' being a synonym for language.[31]   Likewise in handbooks entitled *The Tribes of Burma*[32] and *The Races of Burma*[33] the population is actually classified by language.

In the Kachin area this doctrine led to paradox. The Kachins were deemed to be a 'race', therefore they must possess a special language. Thus the Jinghpaw dictionary is described as *A Dictionary of the Kachin Language*.[34] But this would imply that the hill tribesmen of the Kachin area who do not speak Jinghpaw cannot be Kachins. All official inventories of the population between 1911 and 1941, therefore, list the Maru, Lashi, Szi, Maingtha, Hpon, Nung and Lisu speakers under quite different chapter headings from the Kachin (Jinghpaw) speakers.

However logical this may appear to the linguists, it is

[29] R.N.E.F. (1893), App.; R.N.E.F. (1894), p. 3.
[30] Lowis (1903), pp. 117–18.   [31] Taylor (1923).
[32] Lowis (1919).   [33] Enriquez (1933).   [34] Hanson (1906).

ethnologically absurd. The missionaries,[35] the Army,[36] and the local administration[37] have always continued to use Kachin as a general term in Hannay's sense. I shall do the same.

Since the departure of the British, the former administrative districts of Bhamo and Myitkyina have been formed into a semi-autonomous political unit known as the Kachin State (*Jinghpaw Mungdan*), and presumably all the population of this area, who are not either Shans or Burmese, are now officially deemed Kachins (*Jinghpaw*) regardless of the language they speak. Nevertheless, within the confines of Rangoon University, a Kachin is still someone who speaks Jinghpaw! It is all rather complicated.

The sub-categories of Kachin, as I use the term, are of three kinds, (a) linguistic, (b) territorial, (c) political. From the end of this chapter onwards, almost the whole of this book is concerned with political distinctions, especially those which the Kachins themselves denote by the terms *gumsa* and *gumlao*. In this later discussion I hardly mention linguistic distinctions at all. That does not imply that I consider language differences unimportant, but only that I do not feel myself competent to discuss the subject in detail.

However, since much of the existing ethnography of the region is written in terms of linguistic categories, it is necessary that I give some indication of what these categories are. I must try also to show, at least approximately, how these linguistic categories tie in with the political differences in which I myself am mainly interested.

The total number of distinguishable dialects spoken in the Kachin Hills Area is enormous. Linguists usually distinguish four separate languages (other than Tai) with numerous subheads. The exact classification of several of these dialects— e.g. Atsi, Maingtha, and Hpon—seems to be rather optional, but the following is fairly generally accepted.

    1. *Jinghpaw*—all dialects are more or less mutually intelligible

        a. Normal Jinghpaw—as taught in the mission schools
        b. Gauri

---

[35] Hanson (1913), Chapters 1 and 2.   [36] Enriquez (1933), p. 56.
[37] Kachin Hill-tribe Regulation 1895, amended 1898, 1902, 1910, 1921, 1922, 1938.

    c. Tsasen
    d. Duleng
    e. Hkahku
    f. Htingnai

2. *Maru*—numerous dialects said to be mutually unintelligible (Maru is closer to Burmese than to Jinghpaw)
    a. Normal Maru—as taught in schools
    b. Lashi
    c. Atsi—seemingly a hybrid of Maru and Jinghpaw
    d. Maingtha (A'chang)—seemingly a hybrid of Atsi and Shan
    e. Hpon—probably a dialect of Maru

3. *Nung*—several distinct dialects. Rawang and Daru dialects said to be mutually unintelligible. Linguistically Nung is said to be nearer to Tibetan than to Jinghpaw. Southern Nung dialects probably merge with Northern Maru.[38]

4. *Lisu*—several regionally distinct dialects. This language differs widely from either Jinghpaw or Maru but the grammar is of Burmese type. Lisu speakers are marginal to the 'Kachin Hills' as discussed in this book.

In marginal areas there are important dialect groups which do not fall readily into any of these categories. In the Katha District west of the Irrawaddy, there is for example a population of some 40,000 people locally known as Kadu. They are more or less Burmese in culture, but their language seems to contain a heavy admixture of Jinghpaw and other Kachin dialects. I have no idea how far, if at all, the generalisations given later in this book apply to this Kadu population. Similarly on the western frontier of the Kachin Hills Area, Jinghpaw speech merges into Naga and Kuki dialects. Here too the confusion of language is associated with a complicated political inter-relationship between Shans, Kachins and Nagas, but all details are so far lacking.[39]

    Some Kachin dialects occur only in one distinct locality—e.g. Gauri, Tsasen, Hpon—others are widely scattered and

---

[38] Thus the literature mentions a people called Naingvaw described as Northern Maru or Black Maru; but Naingvaw is simply Maru for 'Naing (Nung) people' and is a term applied by Southern Maru to a population ordinarily described as Nung; e.g. see Pritchard (1914). For best description of Nung, see Barnard (1934).

[39] Grant Brown (1925), Chapters 2 and 8; Dewar (1933).

territorially jumbled up with other languages—e.g. Maru, Atsi, normal Jinghpaw.   In Maps 3 and 4 I have tried to state the crude facts about the language distribution so far as these are known, but this information is at best very approximate. For one thing, normal Jinghpaw is widely used as a *lingua franca* by groups which have some quite different mother tongue—this is the case for example with many Naga villages on the north-western fringe of the Kachin Hills Area; for another, the intermingling of language groups is often too fine grained to be shown on any small scale map.   To illustrate this latter point, I may mention that in 1940 in the Kachin community of Hpalang, which is the subject of detailed analysis in Chapter IV, no less than six different dialects were spoken as 'mother tongue' within a community of 130 households!

The aspect of this situation which has interested the linguists is the historical one—how did this surprising distribution come about?   The problem provides a nice exercise for the imagination.   I can think of several possibilities, but since there is no evidence to support any of them, I will let the matter rest. But another aspect of the language map has received much less attention—what does language difference signify in the lives of the present day population?   Here are populations of nearly identical culture seemingly maintaining differences of language at great inconvenience to themselves.   Why?

The linguists have assumed that the population group which, objectively considered, speaks the same language is necessarily an all important unit.   They refer to *the* Maru, *the* Lashi, *the* Jinghpaw and describe such groups as 'races'.   Now it is certainly true that *locally* the language group is always of great importance.   In a mixed community of Lisu, Atsi, Maru and Jinghpaw speakers, the Jinghpaw speakers *as a group* will certainly have some solidarity among themselves as against the rest.   This, however, is quite different from arguing that all Jinghpaw speakers throughout the Kachin Hills Area are somehow distinct as a social group from all Atsi or all Maru speakers.   Politically speaking, the Atsi are quite indistinguishable as a group from *gumsa* Jinghpaw.

The significance of language group solidarity is not something that can be determined from first principles; it is a matter

for investigation.   My own field experience convinces me that
the average Kachin, like the average Englishman, is keenly
alert to differences of dialect and even of accent; but the values
that he attaches to such differences are not those of the gram-
marian.   I think that the whole situation may perhaps be best
understood by analogy with corresponding phenomena in the
British Isles.

In this country we use language identity in several different
ways.

Firstly, unity of language can be used as a badge of social
class.   In England the 'public school accent' is a highly
sensitive criterion in this respect.   Of this English upper-
middle class speech we may note (a) that it is not localised in
any one place, (b) that though the people who use this speech
are not all acquainted with one another, they can easily
recognise each other's status by this index alone, (c) that this
élite speech form tends to be imitated by those who are not of
the élite, so that other dialect forms are gradually eliminated,
(d) that the élite, recognising this imitation, is constantly
creating new linguistic elaborations to mark itself off from the
common herd.

In North Burma, Tai and Jinghpaw can both be regarded
as 'upper-middle class' languages in this sense, though at the
present time the status of Tai is on the decline.   Historically,
Tai and Jinghpaw speaking groups have constantly tended to
assimilate their Naga, Maru and Palaung speaking neighbours.
This assimilation has not come about as the result of any active
policy of conquest, but because, in mixed language areas, the
political power has for many centuries been in the hands of
either Tai or Jinghpaw speaking aristocrats.   Thus to 'become
Tai' or 'become Jinghpaw' has had political and economic
advantages.   In reaction to this, the genuine Tai and Jinghpaw
aristocrats have in turn developed speech forms of their own.
They have done this by incorporating into their everyday talk
numerous flowery and poetical expressions drawn from the
language of religious ritual.   When two Jinghpaw-speaking
strangers meet one another, their accent and phraseology
betrays not only their place of origin but also their social
class.

Secondly, unity of language can be used as a badge of

political or 'national' solidarity. In the British Isles an ability to speak Welsh is just such a badge. It should be remarked that many of this nationalistic Welsh speaking community use English in their ordinary everyday affairs and maintain the use of their 'native tongue' only at the cost of considerable inconvenience.

In North Burma localised language groups such as Hpon, Maingtha, Gauri and Duleng (and for that matter numerous others which have escaped the notice of the linguists) have this kind of political solidarity. Such groups usually have a tradition of common origin and descent and share a wide range of common customs. Language unity here is only one cultural badge among many which serve to mark off 'we' from 'they'.

Thirdly, unity of language can be a residue from history. It is an objective fact that most Irishmen continue to speak English. The reasons for this are historical. I do not think that it can be said in this case that unity of speech denotes any deep subjective feeling of social solidarity! But also I cannot agree that the common language of the Irish and the English is an historical accident which is sociologically quite irrelevant. The historical facts which account for the Irish speaking English also account for a great deal else in present-day Irish social organisation.

In North Burma, the present distribution of languages must be regarded as an historical residue. Today Jinghpaw, Maru, Nung, Lisu and Tai speaking communities are jumbled up. There must have been a time in the past when these language groups were territorially separate. If we could discover how the present distribution has come about, it would no doubt be very relevant to our understanding of the present-day social situation. Unfortunately, historical reconstruction in such matters is very difficult. Most of the assumptions that have been commonly made in the past are quite preposterous.

As I have indicated it has usually been accepted as dogma that those who speak a particular language form a unique definable unit, and that this unit group of people has always had a particular culture and a particular history. Hence if we describe the history of a language we are describing the history of the group of people who now speak that language.

It is groups of this sort which are meant when we find reference to the 'races' and 'tribes' of Burma.

This convenient academic doctrine does not relate to the facts on the ground. It can easily be established that most of these supposedly distinct 'races' and 'tribes' intermarry with one another. Moreover it is evident that substantial bodies of population have transferred themselves from one language group to another even within the last century.[40] Language groups are not therefore hereditarily established, nor are they stable through time. This makes nonsense of the whole linguistic-historical argument. For example, by linguistic criteria Palaung is an Austro-Asiatic form of speech. Therefore according to the linguist's argument the Palaung should be the most ancient 'race' to be found within the Kachin Hills Area. On the same basis the Tai speaking Shans should be the most recent 'race' to enter the area. Therefore, since race and culture and language are supposed to coincide, one should expect the Palaung to be culturally very different from their Shan neighbours. But in fact Shans and Palaungs intermarry, and in general culture the tea-raising Palaung are far closer to the Shans than any of the other hill peoples of the area. Moreover Palaung and Shan are members of a common political system.

My own interest in the Kachin Hills language distribution map is not primarily in its value as evidence for history, but in the seeming paradox that while in some cases Kachins seem to be excessively conservative about language—so that small groups living as close neighbours and attending the same Shan market yet continue to speak totally different languages—others seem almost as willing to change their language as a man might change a suit of clothes.[41]

The two sides of this paradox both exemplify the same social fact, namely that, in my terminology, for a man to speak one language rather than another is a ritual act, it is a statement about one's personal status; to speak the same language as one's neighbours expresses solidarity with those neighbours, to speak a different language from one's neighbours expresses social distance or even hostility.

[40] For some evidence on this point, see Appendix I.
[41] Grant Brown (1925), Chapter 2; Green (1933), p. 245.

In any political system we usually find sub-groups which stand in opposition to one another as factions. Such sub-groups may be of equivalent status or they may be ranked as superior and inferior. Common language is one way in which the unity of such a sub-group may be expressed.

One explanation of the polyglot structure of the Hpalang community with its six separate dialect groups could be then that it is a community split by faction. The six linguistic groups in Hpalang are six factions which use language as a badge of group solidarity and group difference.

From this point of view, the empirical fact that in some parts of the Kachin Hills we encounter extreme examples of this sort of language factionalism, whereas in other areas the 'miscellaneous' Kachin sub-groups readily adopt Jinghpaw speech, must be seen as an index or symptom of some contrast in political ideology. This brings us to the topic of *gumsa* versus *gumlao* about which I shall have plenty to say later on. Here it will be sufficient if I generalise.

Gumsa ideology, very roughly, represents society as a large-scale feudal state. It is a system which implies a ranked hierarchy of the social world; it also implies large-scale political integration. Every group has a fixed relation to every other. Like the Roman Catholic Church it is all embracing; in theory factionalism is excluded. Now I suggest that there is an inherent inconsistency between the efficient exercise of such centralised political authority and the long-term maintenance of localised language differences. If then we find a political system which embraces several language groups and these language groups are ranked in a class hierarchy, superior and inferior, there is a prima facie probability that the language situation is unstable and that the higher ranking language groups are tending to assimilate the lower ranking groups. This is clearly true of our own experience of our own European society, and it follows from very simple economic causes. It is advantageous for the individual to identify himself linguistically with those who possess political and economic influence.

In Kachin terms this would seem to mean that where the autocratic, hierarchically ordered, *gumsa* political system works efficiently as it is theoretically supposed to work, we may expect to find a trend towards linguistic uniformity within the political domain of any single *gumsa* chief.

The contrasted Kachin political theory denoted by the term *gumlao* is, in its extreme form, one of anarchic republicanism. Each man is as good as his neighbour, there are no class differences, no chiefs; a protestant theory, in contrast to a catholic one. And of course, among the *gumlao*, factionalism is rife, each little local unit is a political entity on its own. In such conditions, I suggest, where each petty village leader is prepared to assert that he is as good as his neighbour, we may expect to find an obstinately persistent linguistic factionalism even in the face of nominally centralised political authority.

I must admit that this theory, if valid, would imply a distribution of languages and dialects different from that which actually occurs, but I shall offer some explanation for this later on.

Meanwhile these are the facts. The distribution of *gumsa* and *gumlao* political systems in relation to area and language grouping is roughly as follows (see Maps 2 and 3):

Zone A so far as the Kachins are concerned is almost entirely Jinghpaw speaking. There are one or two small pockets of population of Maru and Lisu origin, and there are substantial groups in the Hukawng Valley area which claim 'Assamese' origin. The tendency is, however, for all such groups to adopt Jinghpaw speech. The zone includes both *gumsa* and *gumlao* areas, but there is no obvious correlation between dialect and political form. Thus one of the most markedly distinct forms of Jinghpaw is that spoken by the Tsasen (Singpho) of the Northern Hukawng Valley and Assam, but Tsasen dialect speakers are partly *gumsa* and partly *gumlao*.

Zone B is linguistically highly polyglot. The Zone can be considered as consisting of three sections:

i. The Burma Northern Shan States area—here Jinghpaw, Atsi, Maru, Lashi, Lisu, Palaung, and Shan-speaking communities are mixed up in a quite fantastic way. The whole section is politically *gumsa*. Until the British created an arbitrary administrative separation, the hill villages were all, in theory, dependencies of one or other of the local Shan *saohpa*. (Map 2. Zone B. South of latitude 24° N.)

ii. The Chinese Shan States area. A similar linguistic mixture prevails. The 'Kachins' are mostly Atsi speaking. All are *gumsa* and in theory dependent upon local Shan *saohpa*. Chinese administration of the 'Kachins' seems usually to have been more indirect than was the case with the British, so that a Chinese-Shan *saohpa*, though ruthlessly taxed by his Chinese superiors, retained greater political influence over his domain than did his counterpart in British Burma. (Map 2. Zone B from lat. 24° N. to lat. 26° N.)

iii. The Nam Tamai Area. Here there is a mixture of Lisu and Nung and intermediate dialects such as Tangser and Kwinhpang. The Nung here are *gumlao* as also are certain mixed Lisu-Nung communities. The majority of Lisu villages seem to be organised in a class stratified system quite different from the Kachin *gumsa* system. For this reason I consider the main Lisu area in the Salween Valley to fall outside the Kachin Hills Area.

Zone C. The southern part of this zone comprises mainly the border area between Sadon and Namhkam. The language mixture is here similar to that found in Zone B (i) except that there are very few Palaung. I think that in 1940 all villages in the area were nominally *gumsa*, but this may have been due to the preference shown by the Administration for hereditary chiefs. Many of the 'chiefs' were not fully recognised by the Kachins themselves.

The northern part of the zone comprises the N'mai Hka Valley and the Hills to the east. The population here speaks various Maru and Lashi dialects. There are also considerable numbers of Lisu and some Chinese. There are practically no Jinghpaw speakers and no Atsi. The majority of the Maru and Lashi communities appear to be organised on *gumlao* principles. The ethnography of the area is at present very inadequate.

Only three general principles emerge from all this. Firstly, all Atsi speakers are *gumsa*, and no Atsi are found north of the N'mai-Mali Hka confluence. Secondly, the presence of Jinghpaw speakers usually implies that at least a part of the population is organised on *gumsa* principles. Thirdly, the *gumsa* system as described in this book does not occur anywhere where there are neither Jinghpaw nor Atsi speakers.

I shall return to this theme in my last chapter where I shall discuss how far the facts we have examined fit with my argument that the adoption of a new speech or the maintenance of an old one may be regarded as a kind of ritual action.

Not all Kachin sub-groupings have a linguistic basis, some are territorial categories, some are both territorial and linguistic.

Of the dialects listed on pp. 44 f., Gauri, Tsasen, Duleng, Maingtha, Hpon and the several Nung dialects are all more or less localised. Consequently to refer to a Gauri or a Tsasen or a Duleng is rather like referring to a Yorkshireman. The essence of the matter is that he comes from a particular place; he is still a Yorkshireman even if you happen to meet him in London and he fails to talk in Yorkshire dialect. What complicates the matter is that the Kachins themselves tend always to conceptualise their society in terms of kin groups. Thus categories such as Tsasen or Duleng are liable to be described as *amyu*—that is as 'clans'—with an eponymous ancestor.

In these cases where the dialect group is confined to a particular locality, and is credited with some kind of kinship solidarity, it might at first appear that we have an entity corresponding to the 'tribe' of ordinary ethnographic usage. Why then should I not be content to make a study of, say, the Gauri as a discrete ethnographic unit and leave it at that? Why make things so complicated by dragging in all the other Kachin dialects and languages? This point is best answered by taking note of the Atsi grouping. Consider the following set of facts.

Atsi as we have seen is a distinct dialect. Linguistically speaking it seems to be something of a hybrid between Maru and Jinghpaw.[42] All Atsi villages have *gumsa* organisation. Atsi speakers all live south of the Mali Hka-N'mai Hka confluence but are otherwise widely dispersed. Jinghpaw speakers recognise that the Atsi have a separate language but say that they also have many other distinct Atsi customs (*htung*). Thus an Atsi does not necessarily speak the Atsi language. The Atsi who live south of Mogaung in fact nearly all speak Jinghpaw.[43] Atsi chiefs consider themselves to be all members of one lineage, namely Lahpai-Shadan-Aura. The Lahpai-Shadan lineage of which Aura is a segment includes large numbers of very influential Jinghpaw-speaking chiefs. The Aura lineage itself includes the Gauri chiefs. Consequently the Gauri chiefs, who speak a dialect of Jinghpaw and the Atsi chiefs who speak a variant of Maru are always regarded as close lineage brothers. Moreover this link up

[42] Davies (1909), Loose Vocabularies.   [43] Enriquez (1933), p. 46.

between the Jinghpaw-speaking Gauri and the Maru-speaking Atsi does not operate only at the aristocratic level. Many of the commoner lineages also are 'the same' in both language groups, thus:

Gauri lineage name	Atsi lineage name
Dashi	Dawshi
Jangma	Jangmaw
Mahka	Mahkaw
Sumnut	Sumlut, etc. etc.

This identity is socially recognised. Dashi are lineage brothers to Dawshi. A Gauri Dashi might properly marry an Atsi Jangmaw but not an Atsi Dawshi.

If in addition we note that Gauri territory abuts onto Atsi territory and that the Gauri, though Jinghpaw speakers, are commonly in political alliance with Atsis rather than with fellow Jinghpaw, it becomes clear enough that the Gauri, despite their localisation, are in no sense a discrete ethnographic unit. Atsi and Gauri, though belonging to different language groups, cannot possibly be treated as separate societies, and therefore we cannot regard the Gauri as a separate 'tribe'.

Besides confusing matters by referring to localised language groups as if they were clans, Kachins also have a tiresome habit of referring to clans as if they were local groups! For a brief period after 1885 the British administrators were so bewildered by this practice that they actually attempted to carve up the Kachin Hills into distinct 'tribal' districts—'tribe' in this case being used to denote the Jinghpaw royal clans of Marip, Lahtaw, Lahpai, NhKum and Maran.[44] The explanation here is simply that, in the *gumsa* Kachin system, the territory of a chief is deemed to be 'owned' by the lineage of that chief and hence by his clan. Hpalang, for example, has a chief of the Maran-Nmwe lineage; it is consequently liable to be described as Maran land or Nmwe land. This does not imply that any specially large proportion of the Hpalang population are of either Nmwe or Maran descent. None of the

---

[44] Shakespear (1914) still writes as if these dispersed clans were each a discrete tribe settled in a distinct territory.

major descent groups in Kachin society (apart from Tsasen
and Duleng) are in any way localised. There are Lahpai
and Lahtaw and Nhkum in Assam and there are Lahpai and
Lahtaw and Nhkum in North Kengtung. The main framework of the kinship system extends over the whole Kachin
Hills Area and overrides all political and linguistic frontiers
except that between Kachin and Shan. It is this fact more
than any other which justifies the use of the concept Kachin
in a serious anthropological analysis of such a vast polyglot
region.

Apart from speech, the most obvious cultural variable in
different parts of the Kachin Hills is dress. The Lisu excepted,
Kachins everywhere live in much the same sort of houses, they
cultivate land in much the same sort of way, they adhere to
much the same sort of religious practices, to a substantial
extent they share a common body of myth and tradition, but
costume and the details of material culture show wide variation. These variations are more or less regional and have
only a low correlation with language differences. Costume
can undoubtedly serve very readily as a symbol of status
difference, but I do not pretend to understand the whys and
wherefores of Kachin fashion variations. Why do Nungs
wear white where other Kachins would wear black? Why do
some Kachins decorate their cloth with brocade weave and
others with plain stripes? Why do Northern (Hkahku) Kachins
wear tubular skirts and Southern Kachins rectangular skirts?
I simply have no idea. There is certainly plenty of scope here
for a student of material culture.

The zones I have given in Map 2 are climatic zones.
Kachins themselves have names for various districts. Thus
Sinpraw Ga—the eastern land—roughly the Bhamo and
Sadon districts; Sinli Ga—North Hsenwi State; Htingnai Ga
—the lowlands—the region between Mogaung and Katha;
Hkahku Ga—up river country—the region to the north of
the N'mai-Mali Hka confluence and so on. Differences of
costume such as those to which I have referred on p. 20 more
or less correspond to these different named districts; I do not
know why this should be so.

I can usefully conclude this chapter with a glossary that
summarises the rather diffuse information contained in the

foregoing pages. The following are the meanings which I attach to the terms listed:

Shan

Valley dwelling cultivators of wet-rice. Buddhist. Class stratified into aristocrats, commoners and low caste. With the exception of some low caste commoners all Shans speak some dialect of Tai. Organised politically into States (*möng*), each State having its own hereditary Prince (*saohpa*). Such *möng* sometimes exist in isolation; sometimes they are federated as units of a larger *möng*.

The most important of these larger *möng* fall into three groups (I mention only those within the Kachin Hills Area):

i. The Northern Shan States of Burma, notably North and South Hsenwi, Mongmit, Hsipaw, Manglun. (A few Kachins are found as far south as the State of Kengtung.)

ii. The Chinese Shan states, notably Möng Mao, Chefang, Mengpan, Mengting, Kengma, Mangshih, Nantien, Kangai, Luchiangpa, Möng Wan, Menglien, Chansi, Chenkang, Mengmeng, Hohsa, Lahsa, Chanta. Chinese policy has been to replace the Shan *saohpa* by a Chinese official whenever the chance occurred and several of the above States have already disappeared as separate entities. Around 1900 there are said to have been some three dozen separate *möng* in Chinese territory.

iii. The Hkamti Shan States of Upper Burma. These now include Shan settlements in Hkamti Long (Putao), the Hukawng Valley, Singkaling Hkamti (Upper Chindwin). There are also some Hkamti Shan settlements near Sadiya in Assam. Historically these Shan *möng* are associated with the once influential Shan states of Upper Burma, the most important of which were Bhamo, Mogaung, Mohnyin, Waingmaw (Myitkyina). There is still a large Shan population in these areas, and the traditions of the former power of the Mogaung Prince still play a part in North Burma politics.

Palaung

This book does not concern the Palaung, but their similarity to both Shans and Kachins needs to be noted. Typically the Palaung are the hill-dwelling population of Tawngpeng State (Burma, Northern Shan States). They cultivate rice by *taungya* (shifting cultivation) methods but depend primarily upon the cultivation of tea which is traded elsewhere for rice and cash. The Palaung speak various dialects of a common language—Palaung—which is quite unlike that of any of the other groups here considered.

Politically the organisation of Tawngpeng State is the same as that of a Shan state, but the organisation at village level differs in important respects from that of the Shan.

The Palaungs are Buddhists.

Outside Tawngpeng there are numerous Palaung settlements which form elements in different Shan states. Geographically these Palaung villages are often intermingled with Kachin villages, but intermarriage between Kachins and Palaungs is negligible. It is maintained by Lowis (1903) that Palaungs formerly occupied much of the territory now occupied by Kachins. There is no genuine evidence in support of this view.

Kachin

I use this as a general category for all the peoples of the Kachin Hills Area who are not (even in theory) Buddhists. This category Kachin includes speakers of many different dialects, the most important of which have been listed above (p. 44–5).

Kachin society includes a number of different forms of political organisation but these can be considered under two polar types *gumlao* and *gumsa*:

i. Kachin *gumlao*—a 'democratic' species of organisation in which the political entity is a single village and there is no class difference between aristocrats and commoners,

ii. Kachin *gumsa*—an 'aristocratic' species of organisation. The political entity is here a territory called a *mung* (cf. Shan *möng*) which has at its head a prince of aristocratic blood called a *duwa* who assumes the title *Zau* (cf. Shan *Sao*).

All Kachins recognise the existence of an elaborate system of patrilineal clanship elaborately segmented. The lineages of this clan system ramify throughout the Kachin Hills Area and override all frontiers of language and local custom.

Jinghpaw

I use this term strictly as a linguistic category. Jinghpaw are those Kachins who speak a dialect of the Jinghpaw language. Kachins themselves now often use the word Jinghpaw as an exact equivalent for what I here call Kachin. In this book I shall avoid this use.

Duleng

Jinghpaw-speaking Kachins inhabiting an area east of the Mali Hka (Irrawaddy) and north of the Shang Hka (Nam Tisang). They are thus the Kachins who are closest neighbours to the Shans of Hkamti Long. They have a widespread reputation as black-smiths. They are *gumlao* in organisation. (Map 4.)

Tsasen

Jinghpaw-speaking Kachins inhabiting the northern and western portions of the Hukawng Valley and occurring also in eastern Assam where they are known as Singhpo. Tsasen include both *gumsa* and *gumlao* groups. (Map 4.)

Gauri

Jinghpaw-speaking Kachins inhabiting a small but important section of the Kachin Hills, east of Bhamo. A few isolated Gauri villages occur also elsewhere. They are *gumsa* in organisation (Map 5, p. 64.)

Atsi (*Ži*)

An important sub-category of Kachins most of whom speak a language Atsi more or less intermediate between Maru and Jinghpaw. Atsi communities are widely dispersed but do not occur north of the N'mai-Mali confluence. Atsi are *gumsa* in organisation. Many Atsi lineages including those of the chiefs are 'identical' with those of the Gauri.

Maingtha (*A'chang, Möng Hsa*)

The commoner population of the Shan state of Möng Hsa in Yunnan. The organisation of the state is Shan; the population is at least nominally Buddhist. Their language is Atsi or closely related to Atsi. Some A'chang recognise kinship with the Atsi Kachins in the immediate vicinity. By a curious confusion Scott and Hardiman (1901) (Part I, Vol. I, p. 390) mix up the Maingtha with the Duleng under the name Tareng. This error has recently been perpetuated by Thomas (1950) (p. 10).

Maru

The language (comprising numerous dialects) spoken by the Kachins east of the N'mai Hka and west of the China border. There are numerous Maru speaking settlements outside this area. Some, perhaps the majority of Maru, are organised on the *gumlao* pattern. But there are also Maru chiefs (e.g. of the Dabang clan) and where intermingled with other Kachin groups Maru villages fit into the *gumsa* organisation without difficulty. They intermarry freely with other groups of Kachins.

Lashi

A dialect of Maru, spoken by certain villages in the main Maru area west of N'mai Hka and also by some settlements elsewhere. The difference between a Lashi and a Maru is similar to that between a Gauri and an Atsi—i.e. the same kinship system includes both. Most Lashi seem to be organised as *gumlao*.

Nung

A population inhabiting the high mountain country on both sides of the Upper N'mai Hka (Nam Tamai) north of the confluence of the N'mai with the Mehk. Communications in this region are very difficult and language variation is considerable. To the south Nung merge gradually with Maru; to the north with various little known 'tribes' of the Upper Salween and Tibetan frontier. Nungs within the Kachin Hills Area are accustomed to pay tribute to their more powerful Lisu and Lolo neighbours of the Upper Salween, the Shans of Hkamti Long, and the Jinghpaw Kachins of the North Triangle. Like the Maru the Nung resemble the Jinghpaw closely in most aspects of culture other than language. Intermarriage of Nung with other Kachins is frequent. In parts of their area Nung villages are closely mixed up with Lisu villages. Nung organisation appears to be of a *gumlao* type insofar as internal affairs are concerned, but is *gumsa* in respect to the tribute obligations rendered to eternal Shans, Jinghpaw, etc. (Map 4.)

Lisu (Yawyin)

The language spoken by the hill population of the Salween Valley to the east of the main Maru country. This main body of Lisu speakers, and also a related population known as Lisaw occurring far to the south, fall outside the Kachin Hills Area. Their mode of political organisation follows principles of class stratification but differs radically from the Kachin *gumsa* pattern.

Along the whole eastern frontier of the Kachin Hills Area there are small pockets of Lisu speakers. Such communities are usually in political relation with neighbouring Kachin groups with whom they intermarry. For purposes of such marriage Lisu clans are, by a fiction, identified with Kachin clans and lineages so that the Kachin kinship network is extended to embrace these Lisu speakers.

In this book I only discuss Lisu speakers in so far as they fall within the orbit of Kachin kinship organisation.

Chinese

The Chinese mentioned in this book are mostly of Yunnanese stock from the highland country east of the Shweli. Some are nominally moslem by religion. Ethnically they are not very different from the rest of the population and might well be called Min Chia or Chinese-Lisu. Most of the Chinese villages in the Kachin Hills have their origin in the caravan trade between Burma and Yunnan which, before the coming of lorries, was all carried on Chinese mules with Chinese muleteers. The Chinese villages in question are staging posts for the mule caravans. Intermarriage between Chinese and their Kachin neighbours is unusual but not rare.

The problem then that presents itself is this. In the Kachin Hills Area as a whole we find a considerable number of named groups culturally distinct or partly distinct. In places these groups are segregated into fairly well-defined areas, in other places they are all jumbled up. A study of Kachin social organisation cannot therefore proceed in the classical manner which treated culture groups as social isolates.

This classical manner in ethnography may be summarised thus: It is assumed that within a somewhat arbitrary geographical area a social system exists; the population involved in this social system is of one culture; the social system is uniform. Hence the anthropologist can choose for himself a locality 'of any convenient size' and examine in detail what goes on in this locality; from this examination he will hope to reach conclusions about the principles of organisation operating in this particular locality. He then generalises from these conclusions and writes a book about the organisation of the society considered as a whole.

It is quite clear that in the Kachin case, generalisation of this kind would be invalid. The social system is not uniform. The conclusions of the anthropologist would vary very greatly according to what sort—of several possible sorts—of locality he happened to examine in detail. The method of exposition I myself propose to follow is therefore as follows.

I assume that within a somewhat arbitrarily defined area—namely the Kachin Hills Area—a social system exists. The valleys between the hills are included in this area so that Shan and Kachin are, at this level, part of a single social system. Within this major social system there are, at any given time, a number of significantly different sub-systems which are interdependent. Three such sub-systems might be typed as Shan, Kachin *gumsa*, Kachin *gumlao*. Considered simply as patterns of organisation these sub-systems may be thought of as variations on a theme. The Kachin *gumsa* organisation modified in one direction would be indistinguishable from the Shan; modified in another direction it would be indistinguishable from Kachin *gumlao*. Viewed historically such modifications actually occur and it is legitimate to speak of Kachins becoming Shans or of Shans becoming Kachins. When therefore I, as an anthropologist, examine a particular Kachin or Shan locality I need to recognise that any such equilibrium as may appear to exist may in fact be of a very transient and unstable kind. Further I need to be constantly aware of the interdependence of the social sub-systems. In particular, if I examine a Kachin *gumsa* community, I must expect that much of what I find may be unintelligible except by reference to other related patterns of organisation, e.g. Shan or Kachin *gumlao*.

PART II

THE STRUCTURE OF
KACHIN GUMSA SOCIETY

CHAPTER IV

HPALANG—AN UNSTABLE
KACHIN GUMSA COMMUNITY[1]

My total problem might now be stated thus: Within the somewhat arbitrarily defined area which I call the Kachin Hills Area the population is culturally diverse and the political organisation is structurally diverse. The variations of culture do not fit with the variations of structure, nor do the variations of either culture or structure fit consistently with variations in ecological background. How then are these three factors Culture, Structure, Ecology, related in this Kachin Hills Area?

Unlike most ethnographers and social anthropologists I assume that the system of variation as we now observe it has *no* stability through time. What can be observed now is just a momentary configuration of a totality existing in a state of flux. Yet I agree that in order to describe this totality it is necessary to represent the system *as if* it were stable and coherent.

In Part II of this book (Chapters IV and V) I try to explain how Kachins of the *gumsa* persuasion suppose that their society actually functions; I also try to explain why this pattern is necessarily a fiction. In Part III (Chapters VI–X) I discuss the implications of this fiction for an understanding of the total system of variation which I have briefly outlined in Part I (Chapters I–III).

Accordingly, before attempting to examine further the structural interrelations between Shan and Kachin types of

[1] Many of the individuals named in this and the next chapter are still living. For reasons explained in Appendix VII I may in some cases have recorded their names incorrectly. In one or two cases I have intentionally confused the record. This makes no difference to the ordinary reader, it is merely that I write of John Doe of London instead of Richard Roe of Edinburgh.

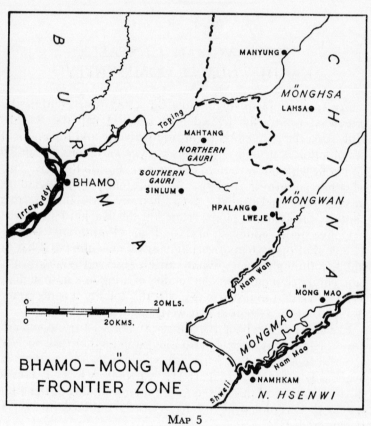

BHAMO – MÖNG MAO
FRONTIER ZONE

MAP 5

HPALANG

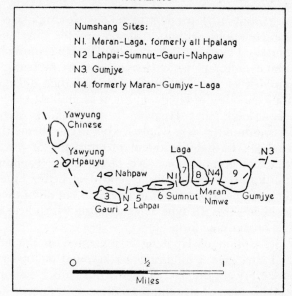

Numshang Sites:

N1. Maran-Laga, formerly all Hpalang
N2 Lahpai-Sumnut-Gauri-Nahpaw
N3. Gumjye
N4. formerly Maran-Gumjye-Laga

Yawyung Chinese

Yawyung Hpauyu

Laga   N3

Nahpaw

N1 7 8 N4 9

Maran Nmwe   Gumjye

3 N 5   6 Sumnut

Gauri 2 Lahpai

0   ½   1
Miles

MAP 6A

HPALANG AND NEIGHBOURHOOD
VILLAGE SITES

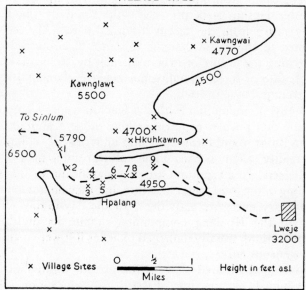

×Kawngwai
4770

4500

Kawnglawt
5500

To Sinlum

×4700×
×Hkuhkawng

5790
×1

6500

×2   4 6 78 9

3 5   4950

Hpalang

Lweje
3200

× Village Sites

0   ½   1
Miles

Height in feet asl

MAP 6B

social organisation, I propose to take a close up view of the structural relations within a single specific Kachin *gumsa* community. I cite the evidence from Hpalang simply because this is the community which I happen to know best. It will be apparent that the rules of *gumsa* organisation did not function at all smoothly in Hpalang, but it should not be supposed on that account that Hpalang is particularly atypical of Kachin communities as a whole. One major theme throughout this book is that functional inconsistency is intrinsic to Kachin social organisation. No doubt many Kachin *gumsa* communities are superficially a good deal better 'integrated' than the example I am about to describe, but all of them have a tendency towards the type of factionalism which here appears in rather an extreme form.

My description of Hpalang is presented in the following order. I first give a minimum background of topographical and bare ethnographic fact; I follow this with a description of the formal system of structural relations in the form in which it was most commonly described by the Hpalang Kachins themselves, namely as a system of persisting affinal links between small groups of patrilineal kinsmen; finally I explain how this kinship structure was rationalised by the Kachins as derivative from the recent historical past. My account is designed to emphasise that the existence of an agreed dogma concerning the nature of structural rules by no means excludes a high rate of social mobility nor even fundamental shifts in the structural system itself.

To anyone unfamiliar with the Kachin scene, a community of some 500 people, comprising nine villages and six dialect groups, must sound formidably and unnecessarily complicated. The reality is not so bad. The cultural differences of which the dialects are a symptom are very significant for our understanding of the total social structure, but they do not loom large in ordinary everyday activities. In the day-to-day affairs of 1939–40 the Hpalang community, despite its multiple linguistic factions, usually managed to act as if it were a culturally homogeneous entity.

Hpalang is situated close to the present frontier of Burma and China.[2] At the time of the British annexation (1885) it

---

[2] See Maps 5, 6a, 6b.

was a part of the neighbouring Shan state of Möng Wan (Lungchwan) in Yunnan. It was not formally recognised as being within the Burma frontier until 1896; effective British administration dates from 1898.

The Hpalang community in 1940 included sub-groups speaking Jinghpaw, Gauri, Atsi, Maru, Lisu, Chinese. Thus, in a sense, this community of 500 people considered in conjunction with the Shan villages in its immediate vicinity, provides a model of the total social system of the Kachin Hills. In the previous chapter I argued that in this area cultural differences do not denote significant major structural frontiers in the social system. Hpalang with its numerous dialect groups provides admirable material for demonstrating this assertion.

In 1940 Hpalang was a community of 130 households. The settlement was very dispersed, most of the buildings being sited near the crest of a ridge about two miles long which slopes down towards the valley of the Nam Wan and the Shan community of Lweje (Map 6). At the western end the altitude is about 5,800 feet a.s.l.; between here and the eastern end of the community there is a fall of about 800 feet; thereafter the ridge falls away very steeply to Lweje which is only about 3,200 a.s.l. The sides of the ridge at its upper (westerly) end are precipitous and covered with secondary rain forest. These areas are felled in rotation for monsoon *taungya* cultivation. At the lower end of the ridge (to the east), where it sheers away towards Lweje, the former forest has been replaced by grassland. This also is used for shifting cultivation, but by the grassland *taungya* technique. The flat alluvial plain of the Nam Wan in the valley below is laid out in irrigated rice plots of the familiar kind. In 1940 most of these were worked by Shans. Members of the Hpalang community, however, worked some and owned others.

The adjacent hill communities, though mostly smaller than Hpalang, were similar in other respects. Being sited on other ridges, they were more difficult to reach than the Shan settlement of Lweje down in the valley. At Lweje there was a market every five days and this was the general meeting-place for all the Kachins and Shans of the neighbourhood. Kachins from Hpalang went down to the Lweje market, not merely to trade with the Shans and itinerant Chinese pedlars, but also to meet friends and exchange gossip from other parts of the hill country.

The Kachins described Hpalang as a *mare*, a term I shall translate as 'village cluster', and they recognised it as containing nine sub-divisions of unequal size and importance. These subdivisions were called *kahtawng*, which I shall translate as 'village'. In Hpalang the smallest village contained only one house; the largest had thirty-one houses. The households in any one village all spoke the same language as mother tongue.

Each village had an hereditary headman, whose lineage surname was in most cases the same as that of his village. This does not imply that everyone in the village was of the same lineage as the headman. Most villages contained members of half a dozen or more different lineages. Usually everyone living in a village was related to everyone else, but by affinal ties rather than common clanship.

The following is a list of the villages with the headman's lineage of each. The map numbers refer to Maps 6a and 6b.

Map No.	Village name	Headman's lineage	Language group	No. of separate families
1.	Yawyung (Chinese)	?	Chinese	14 (16)
2.	Yawyung (Maru) or Hpauyu	Hpauyu	Maru	4 (6)
3.	Gauri (Dashi)	Dashi	Gauri	17 (29)
4.	Lahpai	Lahpai-Aura	Atsi	1 (3)
5.	Nahpaw	Ngaw Hpa	Lisu	3 (5)
6.	Sumnut	Sumnut	Atsi	20 (18)
7.	Laga	N'hkum-Laga	Jinghpaw	22 (27)
8.	Maran	Maran-Nmwe	Jinghpaw	18 (25)
9.	Gumjye	Maran-Gumjye	Jinghpaw	31 (26)

The figures given in brackets in the last column are derived from the tables of the 1921 Census (*Burma Gazetteer*, Bhamo District, Volume B, No. 28, p. 51). It looks as if a substantial section of Gauri village may have left Hpalang between 1920 and 1940 but otherwise the changes are not very significant.

Formally Hpalang was a *gumsa* community. In theory this should have implied that it was the domain (*mung*[3]) of a

---

[3] *Mung*. This is the Jinghpaw form of the Shan term *möng*. The romanised Burmese form of the same term is *maing*. This and other concepts mentioned here are more fully discussed in Chapter V.

specific aristocratic lineage and that this lineage should regularly provide the territorial chief (*mung duwa*). In theory there can only be one such chief in any one domain. Thus, while the chief is *ipso facto* headman in his own village, the headmen of all other villages are, as it were, tenants of the chief. Or, to put it another way, land title is vested in lineages rather than in individuals. The total territory of the domain is 'owned' by a single aristocratic lineage; this lineage is represented in the person of the chief. Other lineages have tenancy rights in the domain established by historical precedent; these subordinate lineages are represented in the persons of the various village headmen. Within each village again there are minor lineages which have rights of tenancy in relation to the rights of the lineage of the headman.

But in Hpalang, *gumsa* theory did not work very well. Of the nine village headmen only four could lay any plausible sort of claim to being considered 'aristocratic' (*du baw amyu*), but of these no less than three claimed the title of chief (*duwa*). To make matters worse the Administration recognised as chief a fourth man who, in the local view, had no rights in the matter whatsoever. Moreover, it was not simply a rivalry between persons of more or less equal standing. The main alignment of faction was as between the Jinghpaw group led by the headman (chief) of Maran village (Maran-Nmwe lineage) and the Atsi group led (nominally) by the headman (chief) of Lahpai village. But the Lahpai chief was in fact an imbecile and functioned merely as the puppet of the headman of Sumnut village. The latter being a commoner knew that he had little hope of advancing claims to chieftainship, but rather than co-operate with the Maran group he proclaimed his allegiance to the Lahpai chief and acted as his spokesman (*bawmung*).[4]

The various village headmen of Hpalang were related to one another by ties of clanship and affinity. Thus the Gumjye headman and the Maran headman were clan brothers, Gumjye and Nmwe being regarded as segments of the same Maran clan. The Laga headman was a brother-in-law (*dama*) to the Maran headman and also brother-in-law (*mayu*) to the

---

[4] From Shan *pawmöng* (Hanson, 1913, p. 63). In its Burmese form *pawmaing*, the word appears frequently in the 19th-century literature of the Kachin Hills; also written *pawmine*. Cf. pp. 124, 188 f.

Hpauyu headman; the Nahpaw headman was brother-in-law (*dama*) to the Dashi headman of Gauri village and so on. The network of kinship relations thus crossed the barriers of language grouping very freely. As will be seen in a moment, factionalism in Hpalang was to some extent aligned in terms of language groups and rival factions did not intermarry, but there is nothing in general Kachin theory or practice to suggest that members of one language group should not intermarry with members of another language group.

Although political factionalism inside the community was often intense, the populace usually presented a solid front to outsiders such as the Shans of Lweje or representatives of the Administration; indeed I had lived in Hpalang for over four months before I realised that the feuds so lovingly described to me were not, as everyone pretended, matters of past history but bitter issues of the present-day situation. Down in the market all inhabitants of Hpalang were treated as one group, they were *Hpalang bu ni*, 'people of Hpalang', no distinction was made between Atsi and Jinghpaw, Nmwe or Gumjye. In the paddy plain where Kachin fields were mixed up with those of the Shans, the Sumnut headman and his mortal enemy the Nmwe chief worked neighbouring fields and even loaned one another plough cattle. The Kachins who worked wet paddy land were constantly squabbling with one another over water rights. Usually these were matters settled by the arbitration of village headmen. But when a similar row blew up, which involved not only Kachins but also some of the Lweje Shans, the Administration's Native Officer held an enquiry. The Hpalang people then dropped their differences and all told the same lies for the common good.

Hpalang was neither exceptionally prosperous nor exceptionally poor. They tended of course to boast of a golden age before the coming of the British. In those days it would seem the Kachin chiefs had owed a due of gunpowder to the Shan prince of Möng Wan, but the Shans of the Lweje plain had been the tenants of the Kachins and had paid rent in paddy, an arrangement economically satisfactory to all concerned. The British, with an arbitrary disregard for established custom, had given most of the wet paddy land in the valley to the Shans. For a while this must have seriously upset the economy of Hpalang, but later there were compensations for the frustrations of British rule. From about 1915 onwards service with the Army and the Military Police became increasingly popular.[5] The effects of military service upon individual Kachins were very varied, but the system as a whole provided an important source of cash income for the hill districts. But besides this, Hpalang was right on the China-Burma border. The more efficient the British administration became, the higher went the price of contraband such as opium and liquor. In 1940 smuggling was certainly a major source of revenue for most inhabitants of Hpalang.

I have already mentioned that the official Government-recognised chief was not locally recognised at all. The circumstances were these. The Administration (in 1940) considered that Hpalang was Maran-Nmwe territory; they therefore considered that the Nmwe lineage should provide the chief. The legitimate head of the Nmwe lineage, though in some ways a rather ineffective personality, was extremely acceptable to the people of Hpalang for he was notorious as one of the most competent smugglers in the district. The Administration, however, also regarded him as a highly competent smuggler, and on the death of his father some years previously had refused to recognise the succession; instead they had imported from another part of the Kachin Hills a distant lineage brother (actually a second cousin) and appointed him chief of Hpalang. This latter unfortunate individual (Zau Li) had no social function except that of collecting the house tax and submitting reports to the Administration Office. As far as the people of Hpalang were concerned the local head of the Nmwe lineage was Zau Naw, the son of the previous chief. In this book, when I refer to the Nmwe chief, I shall always mean this Zau Naw unless I specifically state the contrary.

'Rich men' owned two or three water buffalo and several hump-backed cattle and one or more plots of wet paddy land in the valley. 'Poor men' cultivated only a plot in the hillside *taungya* clearing, they had no cattle, but probably a pig or two and several chickens. Very little money currency circulated in the ordinary way; in the Lweje market most transactions were by barter. Apart from animals and wet-rice land the

[5] cf. Enriquez (1923), pp. 108–17.

indications of wealth were mainly symbolic. 'Rich men' had large houses, they owned antique gongs and shotguns, their womenfolk had a store of fine jewellery for show occasions. But the ordinary standards of life were virtually the same for rich and poor alike. Cooked rice and vegetables twice a day was the normal staple for all, eked out by forest roots and maize in the months before harvest. Hunting apart, meat was only eaten as the sequel to a religious sacrifice, but such sacrifices were frequent since they formed part of the routine treatment for all illness. Since sacrificial meat was widely shared, rich and poor had virtually the same diet. The rich had more liquor.

The rhythm of the year was determined by the monsoon. Rice was planted in May at the break of the rains; it was harvested from October to December at the beginning of the dry weather. January to April was an agricultural off season devoted to house-building, marriages, funerals, and, in the old days, war.

In 1940, about one-fifth of the Hpalang community were nominally Christians, more or less equally divided between Roman Catholics and American Baptists. Sectarian affiliation served admirably as a banner for faction, but missionary activity had not had as much effect upon the structural organisation of the community as might perhaps have been expected. The cleavages between the Catholics and the Baptists and the Pagans were certainly very marked, but exactly the same groups of people had been involved in fratricidal bickering before the coming of Christianity.

Apart from the regular routine of religious ceremonials connected with medical treatments, marriages, deaths, etc., the pagan part of the community held two major communal festivals—one at sowing time and the other towards the end of August before the rice came to ear. These major festivals were the occasions on which, according to orthodox *gumsa* practice, the formal status of the chief ought to have been made visibly manifest. What was actually made manifest was the intensity of the factional hostility and it was on these occasions that rival claims to the chieftainship were asserted and emphasised. At other times the rivals were mostly on fairly amicable terms.

The mayu-dama *system in Hpalang*

In this chapter I shall not examine the structural principles underlying Kachin society in any great detail, but one such principle at least must be made clear if we are to understand the workings of the Hpalang community, namely that which is implied by the Jinghpaw terms *mayu-dama*.

All Kachins trace descent patrilineally. Each individual, male or female, inherits one or more lineage surnames from the father, none from the mother. Such surnames are not always used, but everyone knows what they are. In a Kachin community, family names such as Dashi, Laga, Hpunrau, Hpauyu and so on, correspond to English surnames such as Smith, Brown, Robinson, and are inherited in the same way.

In any one community the individuals who share such a surname (*htinggaw amying*—'household name') are considered to be close patrilineal kin, they are of one 'household' (*htinggaw*), though in practice this does not necessarily mean that they normally all live in one house. Though the Kachin usage is not always quite consistent, the meaning of the term *htinggaw* in the sense which we are now considering can be taken as being 'exogamous patrilineage of small span'. The size of such a lineage is not precisely defined. In any one village there are not likely to be more than ten family heads who are members of the same *htinggaw* lineage and these are likely to have a common male ancestor not more remote than great-great-grandfather. On the other hand a *htinggaw* group is often represented in a village by just a single family.

In all social activities a Kachin individual identifies himself very closely with his *htinggaw* group. In the context of rights and obligations one seldom hears a Kachin claiming anything as exclusive to himself; it is always a case of 'we' (*anhte*). This 'we' normally refers to the individual's *htinggaw* group.

Much the most important set of relationships in any Kachin community are those which establish the mutual status relations between the various *htinggaw* groups that exist in that community. From the individual's point of view every *htinggaw* group within the community falls into one or other of four categories:

i. *kahpu-kanau ni* (*hpu-nau ni*) are lineages which are treated as being of the same clan as Ego's own and are near enough related to form an exogamous group with Ego's own lineage.

ii. *mayu ni* are lineages from which males of Ego's lineage have recently taken brides.

iii. *dama ni* are lineages into which females of Ego's lineage have recently married.

iv. *lawu-lahta ni* (*hpu nau lawu lahta*) are lineages which are recognised as relatives, and on that account are friends and not foes, but with which the relationship is distant or indefinite. A member of Ego's lineage may marry a *lawu lahta* relative but in that event the lineage in question would cease to be *lawu lahta*. It would become *mayu* or *dama* as the case may be.

The essential feature of the system is that the three categories (i) *kahpu kanau ni*, (ii) *mayu ni*, and (iii) *dama ni* are distinct. A man may not marry into his *dama*, a woman may not marry into her *mayu*. From an analytical point of view the system is one of matrilateral cross cousin marriage,[6] but it needs to be stressed that a Kachin, in marrying a girl from his *mayu ni*, does not normally marry a true matrilateral cross cousin but only a classificatory cross cousin.

To explain the practical implications of these formal rules it is necessary first to say something of the nature of Kachin 'marriage'.

The Jinghpaw word *num* (woman) may mean either 'legal wife' or 'concubine', and ordinarily Kachins are not very sensitive about the difference between these two legal statuses. There is nothing particularly disgraceful about a man and woman living together and raising a family when they are not legally married. 'Legal marriage' in this sense implies that the woman should have gone through the ceremony of *num shalai*. This ceremony will normally only be undertaken when the details of the bride price have been finally agreed and at least a substantial part of the total actually paid over to the bride's relatives. The effect of the *num shalai* is to legitimise the status of the offspring of the woman into the lineage of the man paying the bride price; it is not in itself directly concerned with the sexual relations between husband and wife. A couple may be married while they are still children; in the Gauri

[6] See Leach (1952); Lévi-Strauss (1949), also below, Appendix IV.

country it is contrary to custom for even a grown woman to join her husband until several years after she has been 'married'.[7]

It is tacitly accepted that a 'married' girl living at home with her parents may sleep with men other than her husband, but the children of any such liaison are regarded as legitimate offspring of the legal husband even when there is no possibility that he could have been the physiological genitor.[8] It is, however, rather a disgraceful matter and if it is notorious these misbegotten children will have lower status than their more respectably born siblings. The blame in sexual offences is usually deemed to lie with the man, so that adultery (*num shaw*) is an offence by the adulterer against the husband. The wife's status is not necessarily affected.

If, on the other hand, a woman who has *not* been through the *num shalai* bears children, they will be illegitimate (*n-gyi*) even if the genitor is the woman's potential husband. Such children can be legitimised into the lineage of the father either individually by payment of a fine called *sumrai hka*, or collectively by payment of the bride price and completion of the *num shalai* ceremony. Once a woman has been through the *num shalai*, all previous illegitimate children and all future offspring automatically become members of the husband's lineage.

This *sumrai hka* system, whereby a genitor can legitimize one of his offspring without marrying the mother, can lead to somewhat curious results which have an important bearing on the working of the social structure. Many Kachin families are in a sort of ambiguous social status, neither married nor unmarried. A man can live with a woman who for most practical purposes is recognised as his wife and who is mother of his legal children, yet in a formal sense the couple may be unmarried and in a strict sense the lineage of the woman are not *mayu* to the lineage of the man, which means that affinal obligations, if not freely fulfilled, cannot be enforced.

A case from Hpalang will illustrate this point. One family group consisted of a man and a woman and five of her six children.[9] It was only by accident that I discovered that the

[7] Gilhodes (1922), pp. 221 f.

[8] Gilhodes, op. cit., p. 224, states the contrary.

[9] Most family groups are smaller, the average being less than three children per household.

couple were not 'married' (i.e. the woman had not been through *num shalai*).   Enquiry eventually revealed the following:

1st child, male.   Born illegitimate to a genitor in another village who paid *sumrai*.   Now living with father (genitor) in Kawnglawt.

2nd and 3rd children, one male, one female.   Born illegitimate to a genitor now serving in the army.   This genitor had paid *sumrai* for the elder but not the younger child.   The elder was now therefore legitimate, the younger illegitimate.   Both children now living with the mother and her present paramour whom they address as 'father'.

4th, 5th, 6th children, one male, two female.   Born illegitimate to present paramour who is a lineage cousin of the genitor of the 2nd and 3rd child.   No *sumrai* paid as yet.

It was said that the present paramour was working for the bride's father[10] and that eventually the girl would be officially married and the children made legitimate in the lineage of the present paramour.   Whether this legitimisation would apply to the third child I am uncertain, but I think it would.   The second child, it will be noted, is already a member of this lineage.

In the case of Christians, a Christian marriage rite replaces the *num shalai* as the crucial criterion of the complete marriage, but 'respectably unmarried married couples' are, I think, as common among Christian Kachins as among Pagans.

The implications of this kind of ambiguity about the married state are considerable.   The Kachin *mayu-dama* system if described as a formal structure appears extremely rigid and complex, so rigid in fact that it might appear unworkable[11]; but, in practice, there are two important elements of flexibility which makes it possible for Kachins to talk *as if* they were conforming to *mayu-dama* regulations while in fact they are doing something quite different.   In theory, the *mayu-dama* relationship established between two lineages by a marriage persists in time and must be perpetuated by further marriages, and this would seem to restrict very severely the choice of mates for any one individual.   In practice, the possibility of legally marrying a *lawu-lahta* relative coupled with the widespread

---

[10] In lieu of bride price payment.   This is a recognised Kachin procedure. Barnard quoted in Carrapiett (1929), p. 35.   [11] Lévi-Strauss (1949), p. 325.

occurrence of what amounts to a 'trial marriage' system removes this limitation. It is really only persons of high status, such as the sons of chiefs and the sons of lineage heads, who need to conform strictly to the *mayu-dama* rules. Their marriages become thereby marriages of state. In the Hpalang situation, when the Nmwe and the Laga lineages declared that they were *mayu-dama*, this implied a relationship which in theory should continue indefinitely. But it did not imply an exclusive relationship such that all Laga males must marry Nmwe females. The relationship was adequately preserved as long as, in each generation, there was at least one marriage which conformed to the formal rule.

In Hpalang, genealogies when considered in conjunction with miscellaneous documentary evidence such as court records indicated that the pattern of *mayu-dama* relationships generally recognised in the community had been almost stable for at least 40 years. Any elder of the community could state immediately what were the formal *mayu-dama* relations existing between any particular pair of lineages. As far as the principal lineages were concerned, it was a verifiable fact that throughout the forty-year period there had been repeated marriages which conformed to the stated pattern. But there had also been numerous other incidental marriages which were the affair of a single pair of individuals, which had not resulted in any long-term sequence of marriages, and which therefore had not permanently affected the formal structural relationship between kin groups.

The Hpalang community as a whole was in 1940 divided into two main factions of long standing. Both factions claimed to be *gumsa*, but recognised different chiefs. On the one side were the villages of Maran, Laga, Gumjye, Yawyung (Maru), and Yawyung (Chinese); on the other were Lahpai, Sumnut, Gauri, Nahpaw. Except for the fact that the Hpauyu lineage of Yawyung (Maru) had intermarried with Sumnut as well as Laga, there appeared to have been no marriage across this division for many years. Shortly before I left Hpalang, a marriage was arranged between a Catholic Jangmaw of Sumnut village and a Catholic Gumjye of Gumjye village; this caused considerable excitement and there was much discussion as to whether the marriage would ever actually take place and what would be its implications for local rivalries if it did. This betrothal was itself a reflection of internal rivalries within Sumnut village between the headman's lineage who were Baptists and the Jangmaw lineage who were Catholics.[12]

The cleavage between the Maran group of villages on the one hand and the Lahpai group of villages on the other was the residue of a feud which was in progress before ever the British appeared on the scene at all.   That community fission had persisted in this form for so long was at least partly the result of the ineptitude of a particular British administrator. In 1900 in adjudicating on the feud he had ruled that both sides were in the wrong and that two rival chiefs, a Maran and a Lahpai, were both equally entitled to hold office.[13]   This historical incident provided the immediate charter for the fact that in 1940, in the nominally *gumsa* community of Hpalang, there were several rival claimants to the chieftainship.   In ordinary *gumsa* theory there could only be one chief in any one village cluster, and ordinarily all the principal lineages within such a cluster would intermarry.

I no longer have the data to provide a complete analysis of the total *mayu-dama* network resulting from marriage either for Hpalang as a whole or for any part of it.   But the table opposite shows the constituent *htinggaw* lineage groups of Laga village with their *principal* affiliations.   This gives a good indication of the overall pattern of the structure.

Although in a great many cases there is no significant difference in the rank status of a *mayu* lineage and that of their *dama*, there is always implicit in the *mayu-dama* relationship a suggestion that within any one community the *dama* are the vassals of the *mayu*.   *Mayu* and *dama* can assert claims on one another on all kinds of occasions, at marriages, at deaths, in economic activities, in warfare.   But in economic terms the

---

[12] The Sumnut headman, an ex-sergeant major from the army, was on the face of it an ardent Christian.   As has already been remarked, he claimed allegiance to the imbecile Lahpai chief who was really his puppet.   He took care that the imbecile chief remained a pagan so that the Atsi group of villages, though nominally largely Christian (Baptist and Catholic), should have an excuse to go on celebrating the annual pagan agricultural rites!

[13] Had this story been mere hearsay I might have doubted the evidence but both sides to the dispute had preserved copies of a signed memorandum from the officer concerned to justify their case.   The affair was evidently of some importance as it is mentioned in several administration reports of the period.   See p. 125 and Appendix II.

The *mayu-dama* network between lineages in
Laga Village (Hpalang) in 1940

Dama *lineage outside Laga village. (Name in brackets is village of residence)*	Dama *lineage within Laga Village*	*Lineage Name (No. of houses in Laga Village)*	Mayu *lineage within Laga Village*	Mayu *lineage outside Laga Village (Village of residence)*
Gumjye (Gumjye) Hpauyu (Hpauyu) and others outside Hpalang	Lahtaw Mahkaw Pasi Kareng	LAGA (7)	Hpukawn	Nmwe (Maran) Hpukawn (Hkuhkawng) and others outside Hpalang
Two minor lineages in Gumjye Village	Kareng	MAHKAW (4)	Laga	Nmwe (Maran) Gumjye (Gumjye)
		JAUJI (2)	Kareng	
	Pasi Jauji Htingrin	KARENG (4)	Mahkaw Laga	Lineage in Gumjye Village
		PASI (2)	Kareng Laga	
		LAHTAW (1)	Laga	
Gumjye (Gumjye) (marriage pending)		HTINGRIN (1)	Kareng	
	Laga	HPUKAWN (1)		Hpauyu (Hpauyu)

The reading of this table is thus:
Laga lineage in Laga Village comprises 7 households; it has as
   dama within Laga Village—Lahtaw, Mahkaw, Pasi, Kareng and as
   dama elsewhere—Gumjye in Gumjye Village, Hpauyu in Hpauyu Village
      and others outside Hpalang
Laga lineage also has as
   mayu within Laga Village—Hpukawn and as
   mayu elsewhere—Nmwe of Maran Village, Hpukawn of Hkuhkawng
      Village and others outside Hpalang

goods of real value go from the *dama* to the *mayu* rather than vice versa. Within any one village therefore the *mayu-dama* links of the dominant lineage reflect the status superiority of that lineage.[14]

In this case the Laga are the dominant lineage. Lahtaw, Mahkaw, Pasi, Kareng are their vassals. The *mayu* lineages of the Laga (implicitly their superiors) are mostly to be found in other villages where they do not affect the status of the Laga headman within his own village. It is definitely embarrassing for a village headman to have to deal with a villager who stands in *mayu* (i.e. superiority) relationship to himself. In Laga there was only one such, namely the Hpukawn household. The Hpukawn being a Maran lineage were distant clan brothers of the Maran chiefs of Nmwe and Kawngwai and thus had some claim to be considered superior to the Laga in any case.

The history of Laga village as recounted to me was that it had been founded by the Laga and that the Mahkaw had come with them as their vassals. Later the Kareng had joined

---

[14] Leach (1952). Where matters of sex and kinship are concerned Kachins make great use of elaborate verbal punning, consequently the homonyms of the key terms *mayu-dama* and of the corresponding terms *mayu-shayi*, used by Northern Kachins, are of considerable interest. *Mayu* has several meanings, thus:

 a. mayu—'the throat' or 'to swallow'. The *mayu ni* 'swallow' the bride price.

 b. mayu—associates with ideas of witchcraft. This aspect is discussed at pp. 180 f.

 c. mayu—'usual'. The *mayu ni* are the 'usual' affines.

 d. mayu—'to choose' in the sense of 'decide whether to do a thing or not'. In a marriage decision rests with the *mayu ni*. Thus proverbially: *mayu hpu tsun ma ai; dama ni bau gun ma ai* 'the *mayu ni* decide the price, the *dama ni* carry the gong (as bride price)'.

 e. mayu—'to descend'. The *mayu ni* are 'higher' than the *dama ni* so that the *mayu ni* in marriage are 'those who descend'. Ideologically the *mayu ni* live at the top of the hill, the *dama ni* at the bottom, they are linked by a river (*hka*, that is by a 'debt' see pp. 144f), and the water of the river (*nam*) runs down the hill to join the *dama* (*nam* is the relative whom a man marries, see Appendix IV). If a man breaks the usual conventions and goes to live with his father in law, it is said that the *dama* 'climbs the hill' (*dama lung*).

 f. mayu—'growing paddy', 'the green rice field before it comes to ear'. The *mayu ni* are the potential bearers of our children just as the *mayu* paddy is the potential bearer of the harvest.

 Dama means 'the permanent children'. The term expresses the fact that the *mayu/dama* relationship resembles in many ways that of father to son. It also emphasises the inferior status of the *dama* towards their *mayu*.

 Shayi, the Northern alternative to *dama*, means simply 'the females', the *shayi ni* being the households where the married women of 'our group' reside. But there is also a pun with *shari*—'the harvested rice field'—which makes the term an appropriate counterpart symbol to *mayu* in the sense of 'growing paddy' (see *f* above).

the Mahkaw to whom they were *dama*; the Kareng then became *dama* to Laga also. Jauji, clan brothers to Mahkaw, had come in from the Gauri country and later intermarried with Kareng. The Hpukawn household which included a former wife's brother of the Laga headman had originally come from Hkuhkawng on the next ridge. Why they lived in Laga I don't know. The Lahtaw household was that of an illegitimate son of a distant Lahtaw chief married to the Laga headman's sister. The Htingrin household were *dama* to Kareng and therefore nominally their subordinates.

One point that needs perhaps to be stressed is that the *mayu-dama* relationship is effective as between lineages of *htinggaw* group scale; it does not operate consistently at the clan level although Kachins sometimes talk as if it should. Thus in the Laga case Gumjye, Nmwe and Hpukawn are, at the clan level, 'brothers' (*kahpu kanau ni*), they are all Maran; but whereas Nmwe and Hpukawn are *mayu* to Laga, Gumjye is *dama* to Laga. Similarly Mahkaw and Jauji considered themselves 'brothers', but in Laga village Mahkaw were *mayu* to Kareng while Jauji were *dama* to Kareng.

This account of Laga village has brought out the fact that within the village the more permanent *mayu-dama* links serve to display the formal political status relations between different *htinggaw* lineage groups. In this formal system it is assumed that the *dama* are the political subordinates of the *mayu*; but let it be stressed that even within the village this subordination may be theoretical rather than actual. Any nominal inferiority can, in practice, be largely compensated by strategic marriages outside the village. In the case cited above the Htingrin household were recent arrivals and had no direct affinal link with the dominant Laga group. Their formal status position in Laga village was thus low. But in practice Htingrin Gam, the householder in question, was very prominent in village affairs and clearly a person of influence; this was not unconnected with the fact that his daughter was living in Gumjye village with a cousin (father's brother's son) of the Gumjye headman. Assuming that the marriage payments were eventually completed Htingrin would become *mayu* to the Gumjye and their formal status would be considerably enhanced—at any rate as long as this marriage continued.

In a formal sense the interrelationships between the constituent villages of a village cluster are analogous to the interrelationships between the constituent lineage (*htinggaw*) groups of a village. In theory the status of the village as a whole, in relation to the village cluster as a whole, depends upon the formal relationship between the principal lineage of the village and the lineage of the chief of the village cluster.

In the case of Hpalang the circumstances were rather peculiar since there were several persons who claimed the title of chief. At a simple level of analysis the total community fell into two hierarchically ordered sections.

In one section the chief (*duwa*) was the headman of Maran

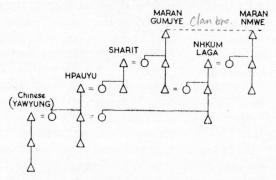

FIG. 1. Diagram to show formal structural relations between principal lineages of the five villages of the Maran sector of Hpalang.

village and a member of the Maran-Nmwe lineage. Nhkum-Laga of Laga village were *dama* to Nmwe and *mayu* to Gumjye and Hpauyu. Maran-Gumjye of Gumjye village were 'brothers' (*hpu nau*) to Nmwe, *dama* to Laga and *mayu* to Hpauyu. Hpauyu of Hpauyu village were *dama* to both Laga and Gumjye and *mayu* to the headman of the Chinese village of Yawyung.

The formal pattern of these relationships can be shown on a diagram (Fig. 1) from which it will readily be seen that even at this abstract level the *mayu-dama* system does not suffice to define precisely the mutual status of the different lineages concerned. The position defined by the rules leaves plenty of room for argument. Thus, in this case, Laga claimed to be second only to Nmwe, being senior to Gumjye because the

latter were *dama* to Laga.   But Gumjye maintained that as they
were clan brothers to Nmwe they were necessarily senior to
Laga who were *dama* to the Maran.   By an elaboration of this
argument the Gumjye headman claimed the title of chief,
asserting that the Gumjye is a youngest son branch of the
Maran clan while Nmwe are only an eldest son line (*ma gam
amyu*).[15]   Nmwe of course strongly repudiated this suggestion
though they admitted that the Gumjye were their 'brothers'.

The other section of the community comprised the villages
of Lahpai, Sumnut, Gauri, Nahpaw.   Here Lahpai-Aura of
Lahpai village provided the chief.   Sumnut were *dama* to
Lahpai-Aura; Dashi of Gauri village were *dama* to Sumnut;
Ngaw Hpa (a Lisu lineage) were *dama* to Dashi.   The formal
structure of authority was here unambiguous but was complicated in practice by the fact that the Lahpai 'chief' was an
imbecile who was really only a puppet of the commoner headman of Sumnut.   The Dashi group, though they would have
been willing enough to accept a genuine Lahpai chief, were
by no means willing serfs to the Sumnut, and in 1940 there
were some indications that the *mayu-dama* relationship between
the Sumnut and the Dashi would soon come to an end.   It
was significant that while the majority of the Sumnut were
Baptist Christians, a number of leading Dashi had recently
become Catholics.

The formal seniority of the *mayu* to the *dama* in such cases
provides the basis for claims to prior land title on the part of
the *mayu*.   Some affinal links are associated with land tenure
while others are not, but it is always the former which are given
emphasis and which are the most enduring.   The basis of the
dama inferiority seems to lie in the fact that where *mayu* and
dama are members of one territorial unit the *dama* must, by
implication, have broken the normal rule of patrilocal residence.
The fact that the *dama* are settled alongside the *mayu* implies
that the founder of the *dama htinggaw* must have settled matri-
locally with his father-in-law, and it is thus a token of inferior
status.[16]   In orthodox marriages where residence is patrilocal
and bride price is paid in full, there is not the same emphasis

---

[15] *Gumsa* Kachins normally hold that the youngest son line is politically the
senior.   The matter is discussed in detail in later chapters.
[16] Hanson (1906), p. 103.   cf. p. 80, n. 14, above.

on the political inferiority of the *dama*. The Hpauyu for example had originally come to Hpalang because they were *dama* to a minor lineage in Gumjye village and because their relatives, the Yawyung Chinese, had already moved there. By settling in Hpalang they made themselves dependents of the Maran. Later they became *mayu* to Sumnut and *dama* to Laga, but these later marriages did not involve any change of residence and the Hpauyu were not politically subordinate to Laga or superior to Sumnut. Similarly the Sumnut were originally *dama* to Lahpai and they explained their political fealty to the Lahpai chiefs in these terms. In 1940 they were also *dama* to Hpauyu, but they were in no sense the political dependents of the latter.

The formal principle by which *mayu* stand in superior status to *dama* has a logical extension in that the '*mayu* of the *mayu*' are formally senior to the *mayu*, while the '*dama* of the *dama*' are formally inferior to the *dama*. This comes out clearly in the kinship terminology. The literal meaning of *dama* is 'permanent children'. The '*dama* of the *dama*' are *shu*, that is to say they are classed as grandchildren; reciprocally the '*mayu* of the *mayu*' are *ji* and are classed as grandfathers.[17]

But again there is considerable discrepancy between theory and practice. These 'grandchildren' and 'grandfathers' are not true clan brothers of Ego but only 'brothers below and above' (*hpu nau lawu lahta*).[18] Marriage with such relatives is permitted and approved. Consequently a man's *lawu lahta* relatives are mostly resident in communities distant from his own; with the *htinggaw* groups within his own community he usually has an alternative closer connection either as *hpu-nau*, *mayu* or *dama*. The sort of situation in which the status implication of the *lawu lahta* relationship might come in would be the following. The wife of Dashi Gam, the headman of Gauri village, was Lamai Kaw, a Gauri girl whose mother's brother was the Lahpai-Aura chief of Mahtang, an important community some 30 miles from Hpalang. There was no sort of collateral kinship connection between Dashi Gam and the Mahtang chief, but in *lawu lahta* terms the latter was *ji* ('grandfather') to the former. On the strength of this relationship Dashi Gam could count on the friendship and protection of

[17] Leach (1945). cf. Appendix IV.   [18] See above, p. 74.

the chief in any dealings that he might have with persons in Mahtang territory.

But for the time being we are concerned only with the system of relationships within the Hpalang community and here *lawu-lahta* relationship was of little moment. What mattered was the formal pattern of the *mayu-dama* structure since it was this that was used as a justification for ranking the different *htinggaw* groups in the *gumsa* political hierarchy.

The Story of the Hpalang Feud

This formal pattern of *mayu-dama* relationships between principal lineage groups—of which I obtained a number of different versions—was always presented to me in the form of a myth which I will now attempt to expound. The myth was not referred to the distant past but purported to be an historical account of events reputed to have occurred during the last 30 years of the 19th century. If the details of this story are to be understood in terms of what has gone before, I must first elaborate my theoretical position regarding the structural significance of stories of this type.

The 'myth' in question is not a myth in the generally accepted sense. It is not a sacred tale hedged about by taboo. I call it a myth simply because, as will be apparent, the truth or untruth of the tale or any particular part of it is quite irrelevant; the tale exists and is preserved in order to justify present-day attitudes and actions. But even here the implications of the story are not categorical and definite. Many anthropologists have tended to write of myth as being 'a sanction for socially approved behaviour'; the sort of myth with which we are now concerned is perhaps better described as 'a language in which to maintain social controversy'.

Basic to my interpretation is the argument that the ideas which different groups within the Hpalang community hold about the social structure as a whole are intrinsically inconsistent. This inconsistency ultimately derives from the fact that the 'language' in terms of which Kachins can make statements about their own social structure is a non-scientific language. The social anthropologist can, if he chooses, develop a purely abstract terminology with no affective content. If he observes two distinct yet similar groups of people in relation, which at times act independently and at times act as a unity, it may be useful to describe these groups as 'complementary homologous segments'. Technical language of this kind is often cumbrous and uncouth but it has the advantage that, given suitable definitions, abstract description becomes precise and unambiguous. With a technical language, properly used, inconsistent statements should always be self-evident. My thesis is that in ritual action and in myth the actor is 'making statements' concerning the same abstract order of reality as that with which the anthropologist is concerned when he uses technical jargon to describe some feature of social structure. But whereas the anthropologist's language is (or should be) precise, the actor's language is intrinsically poetic and ambiguous. And just as two readers of a poem may agree about its quality and yet derive from it totally different meanings, so, in the context of ritual action, two individuals or groups of individuals may accept the validity of a set of ritual actions without agreeing at all as to what is expressed in those actions.

Thus where the anthropologist talks about 'being in relation' the actor must symbolise his meaning through concepts associated with the everyday facts of kinship behaviour and friendship; similarly 'being distinct' tends to be represented in images of hostility and contrast. But in abstract technical language relationship and distinction are merely two aspects of the same thing; the mental operation of classifying A and B as similars is the same as the mental operation of distinguishing A plus B from C. In the language of ritual this identity introduces an element of paradox. Very similar social situations may be described at one moment as systems of social solidity and the next as systems of mutual hostility. Indeed it must be so, for every social group that is to continue as a group must at one and the same time emphasise its difference from other like groups and yet maintain alliances with these other contrasted parties.[19]

This complementary role of hostility and friendship has been stressed repeatedly by recent writers on African materials, and it is certainly a feature that appears prominently in my account of Hpalang. But my interpretation differs from that of the Africanists in one very important respect. For Evans-Pritchard

[19] Durkheim (1947), p. 177.

and Fortes in particular, hostility and friendship, social solidarity and social opposition necessarily balance out to form a system which, regarded as a whole in long term, is a system in structural equilibrium. At no point in my studies did Hpalang give me the impression of being part of a system that tended towards equilibrium; equilibrium of a kind existed but it was an essentially unstable equilibrium. My argument is that this state of affairs is always to be expected in Kachin *gumsa* communities. It seemed to me that every influential leader in Hpalang would have preferred the structural arrangements to be other than they were and accepted the *status quo* only perforce as a compromise for want of anything better.

It is important that this contrast with the African material should be understood. In the African situation, faction is ultimately resolved by a process of fission, but the new social structure that results is merely a duplicate of the old with the segments arranged in a rather different way. In the Kachin situation faction may be resolved in several different ways but the most typical of these lead not merely to a regrouping of segmentary elements but to the emergence of new social structures of a fundamentally different type.

Hpalang in 1940, in my view, was probably in process of changing from a *gumsa* to a *gumlao* type of organisation. It was restrained from completing the change over only by the arbitrary dictates of the paramount power whose officers objected to the *gumlao* system as a matter of principle.

It is also necessary before proceeding, to say something of the concept of structural continuity. What are the entities which Kachins themselves consider to endure from generation to generation?

I suggest that three concepts are here of particular importance. Firstly, there is the idea of a territorial locality with which people are associated. In this case the locality is the mountain ridge called Hpalang. The residents of Hpalang for the time being are 'the people of Hpalang' (*Hpalang bu ni*), but Hpalang has a continuity independent of what particular kin groups are resident there or in political control.

Secondly, there is the idea of a village (*kahtawng*). The inhabitants of a village are not all of one lineage, but the village was founded by members of a particular lineage, and the headman of the village is a member of that lineage. The actual site of a village may be changed but the land rights—that is to say the rights of cultivation—are normally defined in perpetuity by the circumstances associated with the foundation of the village. Great importance therefore attaches to stories associated with the foundation of a village and these stories assume a partly mythological character even when the events related purport to be quite recent.

Thirdly, there is the localised lineage segment—the *htinggaw* group which has already been discussed. As we have seen this is in practice a small group seldom comprising more than half a dozen or so independent simple families. Empirically, in my experience, all such localised lineages act with very striking solidarity in all matters of public concern. In what follows I write as if all the members of any one such lineage held virtually identical rights and identical opinions and as if the lineage was personified in the person of the lineage head. This is a distortion, but at the first level of analysis not a very grave one.

The reader will do well at this point to remind himself of the general topography of Hpalang as already described. In the story which follows the headman's lineages in the several villages concerned are the characters of the play. To recapitulate briefly they are:

A. *The Maran and their allies*

    i. The Nmwe lineage (Maran clan) (Jinghpaw speaking) (aristocrats)

    ii. The Laga lineage (Nhkum clan) (Jinghpaw speaking) (possibly aristocrats)

    iii. The Gumjye lineage (Maran clan) (Jinghpaw speaking) (aristocrats)

    iv. The Hpauyu lineage (Maru-speaking) (commoners)

    v. The Chinese of Yawyung village.

B. *The Sumnut and their allies*

    i. The Aura lineage (Lahpai clan) (Now represented by a solitary imbecile treated as a chief) (Atsi-speaking) (aristocrats)

    ii. The Sumnut lineage (Atsi-speaking) (commoners)

    iii. The Dashi lineage (Gauri-speaking) (commoners)

    iv. The Nahpaw lineage (Lisu-speaking (commoners)

The land title of these several village communities was intimately associated with stories concerning a feud reputed to have occurred towards the end of the 19th century. Each of the principals had its own version of these events. The only document in the case was consistent with all or any of the rival versions.

To avoid reduplication I will recount a consolidated version of the story, noting the deviations of the rival versions as we go along.

In the old days Hpalang was acknowledged by all as being Atsi-Lahpai territory. There had been no Jinghpaw speaking villages on the ridge though there were several other Atsi villages besides those that are there now. The ruling chief had been an ancestor of the present imbecile Lahpai chief. The neighbouring ridge to the north on which is today situated the village cluster of Kawngwai was even then Jinghpaw territory, the chiefs being of the Maran-Nmwe lineage which now rules in the Jinghpaw portion of Hpalang.

At some unspecified date a feud developed between the Lahpai chiefs of Hpalang and the Maran chiefs of Kawngwai. This led to a prolonged 'war' (*majan*) and the ultimate defeat of the Lahpai chiefs.[20] In the outcome the Maran-Nmwe chiefs became lords of Hpalang.

At least two quite different stories are now current as to the origin of this feud. The Maran version is that the Lahpai and the Maran were *mayu-dama*; the daughter of the Maran chief was seduced by the son of the Lahpai chief.[21] The Maran girl became pregnant and named the son of the Lahpai chief as the father of her child; the Lahpai chief's son denied responsibility and refused either to pay *sumrai hka* or marry the girl. To make matters worse he accompanied his denial with an oath. 'If the child be mine, let it be born harelipped.'[22] The girl in fact died in childbirth. In order to establish responsibility an autopsy was performed and the augurs duly declared that the stillborn child was harelipped. A state of blood feud (*ndang bunglat*) thereafter ensued.

This story is ingeniously constructed so that from a Kachin

[20] The Jinghpaw word *majan* here translated as 'war' also means 'a love song'. Its literal significance seems to be 'woman business'.
[21] In Kachin theory this is incest—*jaiwawng*. See p. 137.
[22] See p. 139 E.

point of view it would be almost impossible to think of arbitrating the feud. It needs to be remembered that the present Maran-Nmwe chiefs admit to having purloined their land from the former Lahpai chiefs; this could only be justified if the feud had originated in circumstances of the most serious possible kind.

For a Kachin every kind of offence is a debt (*hka*) which can be settled by a process of arbitration and compensation, but a certain class of offences known as *bunglat* (feud) call for exceedingly heavy penalties and are considered to justify the offended person in taking violent reprisals. Homicide, unjustified enslavement, and accidental wounding of a chief are all justifications for a feud, but the most usual and most typical Kachin feud is the *ndang bunglat* which arises when an unmarried girl dies in childbirth.[23] Furthermore, a feud against a person of chiefly lineage is twice as serious as one against a commoner.[24] For the offence to be committed by one person of chiefly blood against another, and between persons in *mayu-dama* relationship at that, makes settlement all the more difficult. The addition of self-evident perjury would in the Kachin view make compromise virtually impossible. The force of the Nmwe version of the feud origin is therefore not merely to put the blame on the Lahpai chiefs. It also makes it quite clear to all that compromise and settlement was out of the question.

The Sumnut version is entirely different. According to this there was an Atsi lineage Hpukawn[25] living under the ægis

---

[23] Kawlu Ma Nawng and Leyden, who may be considered the most reliable of several authorities, recognise four categories of *bunglat*. (*a*) for intentional homicide, (*b*) for accidental homicide, (*c*) for the death of a woman in childbirth (*ndang bunglat*), (*d*) for wounding or accidental injury to a chief (*hkrung bunglat*—'feud of a living man'). Hertz also mentions unjustified enslavement as a cause of *hkrung bunglat*. Kawlu Ma Nawng (1942), pp. 53, 67; Hertz (1943), p. 153.

[24] Kawlu Ma Nawng (1942), p. 54; Hertz (1943), p. 153. *Du bunglat hpaga lasa, zaw bunglat manga shi*—'100 *hpaga* must be paid in compensation for a chief's *bunglat*, only 50 for a commoner'. For the significance of the term *hpaga*, see Chapter V, pp. 144 f.

[25] Unfortunately I failed to obtain any Hpukawn version of this story. The Hpukawn lineage provide a fascinating example of the way language group and lineage affiliation overlap in this area. In 1940 the Hpukawn household living in Laga village (p. 80) were Jinghpaw speakers, they were regarded by the Laga as being of the Maran clan but were also said to be of Maru origin. Their relatives living on the next ridge at Hkuhkawng were sometimes referred to as chiefs (*duni*) but I do not know whether their title was good. The lineage has been mentioned by several previous Kachin authorities; George (1891) gives it as **an**

of the Maran chiefs of Kawngwai. These Hpukawn of
Kawngwai were *dama* to the Sumnut of Hpalang. There was
a woman of the Sumnut lineage living as a widow among her
deceased husband's people the Hpukawn of Kawngwai.
According to custom this widow should have been cared for
by her husband's people, that is to say she should have been
taken as levirate wife by one of her husband's male relatives.
For some unexplained reason this procedure of 'picking up
the widow' (*gaida kahkyin*) had not operated and the woman
was living alone. In returning from the fields, the widow
spiked her foot on a *panji* (a fire hardened spike of bamboo)
which formed part of a trap for wild pig set by a member of
the Maran (Nmwe) chief's household. Of this wound the
widow died. Whereupon the Hpukawn refused to give the
widow proper obsequies and the Nmwe refused to contribute
the appropriate animals with which to make a mortuary
sacrifice and a sacrifice to the *maraw* spirit of misfortune. The
Lahpai chiefs supported the claims of their adherents the
Sumnut; the Maran and Hpukawn proved adamant and a
feud ensued.

This story seems unnecessarily complicated and the circumstances improbable. Also it seems to me rather unlikely that
such events, even if they occurred, would lead to a major feud.
Indeed perhaps that is the point of the story. It clearly makes
the main dispute one between the Sumnut and the Maran-
Nmwe and puts all the blame on the Maran side; but further
than that, since the initial quarrel is between commoners, the
dispute ought to have been arbitrated by the chiefs. That
a feud developed was due to the arrogance of the chiefs.

The nature of the resultant 'war' was difficult even for my
informants to visualise. When pressed to elaborate any particularly unlikely detail they would usually merely say that in
the days before the British came things were different from what
they are now. The first phase of the 'war' seemed to be
thought of as having gone on for about 20 years; fighting, by
tacit agreement, being confined to the off-season period between harvest and sowing (December–May). No one claimed

---

Atsi lineage; Hanson (1906) gives it as a Maran lineage; Enriquez (1933) says they
are 'Atsi of Chinese origin'. In Hpalang they were claimed as Atsi by the Sumnut,
as Maru by the Hpauyu, as Maran by the Maran. Such claims are not necessarily
contradictory.

any substantial number of human casualties; active hostilities took the form of raids, the main purpose of which was to steal cattle and burn and plunder houses. It may seem odd that in such a prolonged and fabulous war the slayings should be slight, but it needs to be remembered that all Kachin blood feuds can, in the last resort, only be settled by compensation. Feud policy is thus often directed to making life so generally unpleasant for the enemy that he finally agrees to pay compensation. Additional human casualties merely make such settlement all the more difficult. In this particular case the rival parties were, in 1940, living more or less amicably in the same community and it would have been hardly practicable for either side to maintain that there were large blood debts outstanding.

The outcome of the war was that the Lahpai chiefs abandoned Hpalang and the Maran-Nmwe assumed the chiefship. I was given several rival versions of the events leading up to this Maran victory.

The Maran-Nmwe merely said that they and their allies were so powerful that the Lahpai fled (*hprawng mat sai*). They claimed further that at the conclusion of hostilities they had held a victory feast (*padang manau*) and that the enemy Lahpai had joined in a formal ceremony closing the feud (*nat hpungdun jaw*).[26] In evidence they pointed out that the grave site of the first Hpalang Nmwe chief had a completed circular ditch round it. If the feud had still been outstanding this ditch would have been left incomplete. Overtly this was put forward simply as proof of victory and the formal closing of the feud. Its covert implication is that it validates the Nmwe claim to be the 'owners' of Hpalang, for only members of the land owning lineage are entitled to make circular ditches round their graves at all.[27]

The Laga, the allies of the Nmwe, supplemented this version somewhat. They said that at first the Nmwe suffered serious reverses at the hands of the Lahpai chiefs so that they were forced to call to their aid their *dama*, the Nhkum-Laga chiefs who held territory far away to the north. These Laga chiefs were powerful and influential. The eldest son of the Laga chief himself formed a war party and called to his aid the

[26] cf. Hertz (1943), p. 155.   [27] Kawlu Ma Nawng (1942), p. 58.

Gumjye-Maran (his *dama*) as well as various other affinal relatives from a wide area. By the aid of this powerful army the Nmwe were finally victorious. In recognition of the aid provided, the Laga and their *dama* the Gumjye were both allocated village sites in the conquered territory of Hpalang. This would imply that the land title of the Laga and the Gumjye was *regau ga*[28] and inalienable.

The point of this version is firstly to assert that the Laga lineage, although *dama* (and therefore subordinate) to the Nmwe, is really of aristocratic descent. It further asserts that since the Gumjye only came on the scene as *dama* to the Laga, therefore the present-day Gumjye are the subordinates of the Laga in social rank and land title.

The Gumjye scornfully rejected this last argument. They agreed that at the outset of the feud the Nmwe were no match for the Atsi Lahpai chiefs and their allies. They said that after a while the Nmwe sent round messages to all the Maran chiefs far and wide calling for a general war against the Lahpai. To this call the Gumjye responded. This settled the issue and the Lahpai chiefs were quickly routed. In reward for their services the Gumjye were allocated a village site on Hpalang. The Gumjye claimed that their lineage status in the Maran clan ranked as high as or higher than that of the Nmwe and they therefore considered themselves joint owners of Hpalang along with the Nmwe. Hpalang, they said, is Maran territory not merely Nmwe territory. In recognition that the status of the Gumjye on Hpalang was just as good as that of the Nmwe, the Nmwe chiefs had never attempted to claim from the Gumjye the usual hind leg (*magyi*) of slaughtered animals which is the normal tributary due of *gumsa* chiefs (*magyi sha ai du ni*—'thigh-eating chiefs').[29]

A Lahpai version of the story is lacking since the only surviving Lahpai was an imbecile. But the Sumnut did not agree with any of the foregoing. The Sumnut said that as long as they (the Sumnut) supported the Lahpai chiefs the latter were consistently victorious, but there came a time when their former *dama*, the Hpukawn, were ready to admit their error and the Kawngwai Nmwe agreed to pay up the disputed sacrificial cattle (*maraw nga*). Indeed the Nmwe went even further and

---

[28] ibid.; also see below p. 158.   [29] See Chapter V, p. 155.

offered a bride to the Sumnut. The latter thereby became *dama* to the Nmwe. This should have settled the war, but the Lahpai chief by this time had become arrogant and claimed on the Nmwe for all sorts of 'war damages' which the Nmwe refused to accept. The Sumnut therefore changed sides and allied themselves with the Nmwe. The Lahpai chiefs then fled.

The Dashi (Gauri village) version was a sort of counterpart to that of Laga. The Dashi were not very specific as to whether their land rights ante-dated 'the war', but they pointed out that all Gauri chiefs are members of the Lahpai-Aura lineage and that they (the Dashi) had joined in the hostilities as loyal supporters (*zaw*) of this lineage. Moreover unlike their *mayu* the Sumnut, who had proved treacherous, Dashi had remained loyal to their chiefs, and when the Lahpai chiefs had left Hpalang they had left too. They had only returned when the Lahpai chiefs were restored to office in 1900.

There were a number of other ways in which the Dashi group managed to emphasise their factional hostility to their allies the Sumnut. I have already remarked on their tendency, in 1940, to become Catholic as against the Sumnut who were turning Baptist. But it was also very significant that they bothered to insist on being regarded as Gauri. The Sumnut and their Lahpai chiefs were Atsi speakers. In Gauri village it was claimed that their normal speech was Gauri (i.e. a dialect of Jinghpaw) though everyone also spoke Atsi. Among the lineage names which occurred in Gauri village were Dashi, Malang, Jangma. All these have their Atsi equivalents (Dawshi, Malang, Jangmaw) which are considered to be not merely related but identical lineages. All are commoner lineages. But if the inhabitants of Gauri village had allowed themselves simply to be considered Atsis, Dashi must rate as the inferiors of their *mayu* group, the Sumnut. By stressing their remote Gauri connection Dashi emphasised that in ancestry their lineage is more distinguished than that of the Sumnut, for the Gauri Dashi claim that their ancestors were formerly aristocrats in the Lahtaw clan (Jinghpaw), whereas Sumnut can at best claim connection with commoner Maru lineages.

This is a fairly clear instance of cultural and linguistic

difference being maintained simply for reasons of group prestige.

But to return to the Hpalang feud. All were agreed that, with the Lahpai vanquished, the Nmwe ruled as chiefs in Hpalang. At this point the constituent villages appear to have been Nmwe, Laga, Gumjye, Sumnut. These all shared a common *numshang* (sacred grove). All reports agreed that the Sumnut headman of this period was an aggressive and dominating personality. The Sumnut themselves said that he was the recognised *bawmung*[30] of the whole community, and that the Nmwe chief though harmless enough was only a figurehead. The Maran said that this Sumnut headman was a bandit (*damya*) who made a living from cattle raids and extorting 'blackmail' (protection money) from the Shan villages in the valley below and that a quarrel finally broke out between the Nmwe and the Sumnut over the disposal of some cattle.

Tradition here was at first somewhat bowdlerised for my benefit but the Maran grievance seemed really to be that Maran had themselves purloined, in dubious circumstances, some pack animals belonging to a passing Chinese caravan and that the Sumnut had then seized the animals and sold them over the border, thus making it impossible for the Maran to extort the ransom that had been intended.

The Sumnut on the other hand said that the new quarrel was again about a woman. Since the Sumnut were now *dama* to the Nmwe, the latter were not entitled to dispose of their women to other lineages except by agreement of the Sumnut. The Sumnut wished to maintain the *mayu-dama* relationship and negotiated for a further marriage, but the Nmwe insultingly refused to accept the bride-price offered.

Consequent upon this renewed quarrel between the Nmwe and the Sumnut, the Sumnut appealed to the British for justice and the great *Ri duwa* (D. W. Rae, the first British Civil Officer, Sinlum) arbitrated the dispute. This part of the story at least is historical. In 1900 D. W. Rae did arbitrate a major Hpalang feud and gave a surprising ruling. He ruled that the Lahpai chiefs should again rule over the upper (western) end of the Hpalang ridge, while the Nmwe chiefs should rule over the lower (eastern) end. I think it is fairly certain that no Kachin

[30] cf. above, p. 69.

could have expected such a 'judgement of Solomon' and that this was the very last sort of decision that anyone wanted. However, today the leaders of the Nmwe and the Sumnut each carefully preserve their respective copies of *Ri duwa's* vital judgement. My copy of this intriguing document has not survived but the published record of the affair is given in Appendix II.

I collected no 'Hpalang stories' from members of the three remaining groups of the present-day community—the 'Chinese' of Yawyung, the Maru-Hpauyu of Yawyung, and the Lisu of Nahpaw, but some historical facts are available. The Chinese considered themselves adherents of the Nmwe and not the Lahpai. They were related to a similar Chinese group at Kawnglawt, also in Maran territory. They were already established in Hpalang at the time of the 1911 census.[31] The Maru-Hpauyu group were then at Pangyao,[32] close to Kawnglawt but had moved to Yawyung by 1913.[33] They were *mayu* to the Chinese headman's family, and *dama* to a minor lineage (Sharit) in Gumjye village. Soon after their arrival they became *dama* to the Laga. The Nahpaw group were already in Hpalang in 1911 when they were counted as part of Gauri village.[34] They are similar in status to a large number of small Lisu settlements in the area each of which is attached in a *dama* status to a neighbouring Kachin group.

For a number of years the community seems to have continued as a simple dichotomy. The Lahpai, Sumnut and Gauri formed one section and had one *numshang*, while Nmwe, Laga and Gumjye formed another section and had a separate *numshang*. Then sometime around 1930 the old Nmwe chief died.

As already explained Zau Naw, the old chief's son, was unacceptable to Government because of a smuggling incident and a distant second cousin Zau Li was appointed official chief. In 1940, though Zau Li only functioned as a Government agent, lack of official recognition had certainly reduced Zau Naw's status and correspondingly increased the relative status of his subordinate headmen. The headman of Gumjye had now somehow managed to get himself recognised by

[31] *Burma Gazetteer Bhamo District, Vol. B,* 1913 edition.   [32] ibid., 1925 edition.
[33] **Carrapiett** (1929), p. 107, Case 9.   [34] *Gazetteer,* op. cit., 1913.

Government as an 'independent' headman and he now called himself a chief (*duwa*).[35]   Gumjye had ceased to share a *numshang* with Maran and Laga and now had one of their own.

In 1940 therefore the ritual situation was that Gumjye had one *numshang*; Maran and Laga had another to which the Hpauyu lineage of Yawyung also contributed; Lahpai, Sumnut and Gauri shared a third *numshang* to which the Lisu of Nahpaw were entitled to contribute.   The Chinese of Yawyung did not ordinarily participate in any ritual proceedings though their headman was frequently present at major celebrations, especially those of the Nmwe group.   We see then that claims to the title of chief (*duwa*) and to the possession of a ritual grove (*numshang*) corresponded to the main political cleavages within the community.[36]

We see also that while the kinship composition of the community had remained more or less unaltered over the past 40 years, there had been radical changes in the internal authority structure.   The leaders of the community still used *gumsa* categories to describe the respective status of groups and persons; they attached importance to the notion of aristocracy, to the title of chief (*duwa*), and to the rights of chiefs (such as the rights to meat tribute, ditched graves, large houseposts and so on); they insisted vigorously on the obligations of *dama* towards their *mayu*; they stressed the importance of large and spectacular sacrifices at the *numshang*.   But all this was largely pretence.   Had the community been organised on *gumlao* principles with no aristocrats, no chiefs and no tributary dues, the de facto situation would have been almost the same.   This is an illustration of the fact that the contrast between *gumsa* and *gumlao* is a difference of ideal order rather than empirical fact.

One feature of the foregoing stories that is worth mention is that the Hpalang feud, as it was recounted to me and as I have recounted it, differs strikingly from all Kachin feuds of which we have any historical record.   In the telling of the tale there

[35] Village headmen were issued with certificates of office by the Administration and the Kachins themselves attached great importance to these.   In 1940 the Laga headman's certificate stated that he was subordinate to the Nmwe chief of Maran village; the Gumjye headman's certificate contained no such clause.
[36] The positions of the various *numshang* sites to which I have referred are indicated on Map 6a, p. 65.

was always much boasting about fighting (*gasat*—lit. killing) and the suggestion of pitched battles and resounding victories. In actual Kachin feuds, vengeance seems always to have been achieved by guile rather than by valour. The normal procedure in a blood feud was to hire one or more 'braves' (*share*) who would ingratiate themselves into the favour of the enemy and then assassinate a member of the enemy lineage at the first favourable opportunity. Any member of the lineage in question would do. For obvious reasons the braves thus hired were not normally closely related to either of the principals, since, if they had been, their activities in the enemy camp would be suspect. An assassin hired in this way was not deemed personally guilty of his crimes; all responsibility rested with the principal who hired him.

Now in the Hpalang stories, there was no reference to any 'braves', nor did anyone claim that important principals had been killed. Such deaths as had occurred seemed to be accidental. The reprisals engaged in by the disputing parties were represented as having consisted of house burning, cattle theft and the like instead of the purposive assassination which is typical of genuine Kachin feuds. One possible explanation is that the historical event which everyone now remembers as a blood feud and a 'war', was really a somewhat minor quarrel over land rights and village boundaries. In that case it is likely that the Sumnut version comes nearest to the historical facts in that the Lahpai chiefs ceased to be chiefs of Hpalang simply because their own followers, the Sumnut, turned them out and invited the Nmwe to take their place. Our real interest, however, is not in what actually occurred but in the reasons for the very diverse stories of the event which are now reported.

Obviously each lineage head tells a version which puts himself and his group in the most favourable possible light and I have already pointed out some of the more obvious instances of this. But while the different versions stress quite different elements, they are not actually contradictory. They could all be equally true or equally false. Indeed I never found that the rival story-tellers would deny the truth of an opponent's version, they merely said it was unimportant or disorientated. It was as if each version was the property of one particular group and that there was tacit recognition that rival groups were entitled to own other stories.   This fits with my general thesis that though these tales purported to relate to events of the 1890's, their content was mythological rather than historical.

The stories I have described purport to be the account of a war between the Atsis on the one hand and the Maran-Jinghpaw on the other, but what is represented is not simply a straightforward cleavage of the community into two moieties. Every principal lineage used these stories as the basis for faction against all the others.   Dashi and Sumnut, though allies, did not tell the same tale.

The best instances of this last point was the manner in which the feud stories showed up the latent hostility between Nmwe and Laga.   The two closest and most consistent allies in the whole Hpalang system were always the Nmwe and their *dama*, the Laga.   From the way the Laga headman, Laga Naw, and the Nmwe headman, Zau Naw, usually behaved, one would have supposed them to be the closest possible personal friends as well as brothers-in-law and traditional allies.   When Zau Naw told me his version of the feud story, Laga Naw was present and confirmed Zau Naw throughout, but the next day Laga Naw came to me with his own supplementary account in which he included a long list of debts (*hka*) owed by the Nmwe to the Laga—these included such things as the lives of one man and one slave killed in the hostilities but not compensated for, various cattle sacrifices to the spirits on different occasions, several viss of gunpowder, a horse stolen by the enemy, various ritual gifts offered to allies but not recouped by the Nmwe and so on.   It was obvious of course that Laga Naw had no expectation that these 'debts' of half a century ago would ever be paid; they were remembered simply as a kind of ammunition for argument.   No doubt when any issue arises upon which the interests of Laga and of Nmwe tend to conflict, these debts are brought to the fore and used to whip up sympathy for the Laga case among the elders and others upon whom the judicial decision rests.

Argument of this kind rests on the assumption that the hearer of the story will be familiar with the general range of Kachin ideas about land tenure, rank, affinal relationship and so on.

Thus when Kachin talks about 'debts' (*hka*) he is using a concept which has associations over the whole range of his social life. If then we are to understand the full range of what is represented in myths concerning 'debt', we need to examine such key verbal concepts in considerable detail. Already in the present chapter I have made an analysis of what Kachins mean by the antithesis *mayu-dama*; in the next chapter I carry the analysis of Jinghpaw verbal concepts a good deal further.

CHAPTER V

THE STRUCTURAL CATEGORIES OF KACHIN *GUMSA* SOCIETY

I

Introduction

In this chapter we are concerned with the elements which go to make up Kachin ritual actions and the meanings that can be attached to them.

It is an obvious truism that you can only carry on an argument with a man who understands what you say. The Kachins of Hpalang understood one another's arguments very well; the language in which they expressed these arguments was the language of ritual and of mythology. Although in matters of rank and prestige and authority there was scarcely a single point of fact upon which all the people of Hpalang were in agreement, they were in complete agreement about the theoretical principles by which rank should be assessed. All the Hpalang Kachins, whether speakers of Jinghpaw, Atsi or Maru considered themselves members of a *gumsa* system; they agreed that the chief (*duwa*) of Hpalang should have the rights and titles of a *gumsa* chief and that the status and obligations of everyone else in the community should fit into a hierarchy dependent on that chief. The major disagreements simply centred round the question of what particular individual was entitled to be treated as chief and why.

In Chapter IV the interest centred in the kind of details which were used as banners for factional disagreements. In this present chapter our task is to understand those fundamental principles of Kachin ritual expression which constitute, as it were, the 'grammar' of ritual action and about which *gumsa* Kachins are in agreement.

According to the functionalist tenets of much recent British anthropology it is impossible to approach an analysis of this kind without first describing in detail 'the whole of Kachin culture'. In that case my task would indeed be hopeless for the 'whole of Kachin culture' is a mere welter of variations.

I agree of course that there are an enormous variety of different kinds of cultural activity which can have ritual significance and that ideally it would be very nice if one could describe and analyse them all. In practice this is clearly an impossibility. In the Kachin case, as it seems to me, the basic elements of ritual expression are not very numerous and can be described without much difficulty. That this should be so is perhaps a by-product of the complexity of the cultural situation. From a strictly cultural point of view the various linguistic sections of Kachin society are distinct; their integration is at a political, not a cultural, level. In a cultural sense the Hpalang community comprised Jinghpaw, Atsi, Maru, Lisu and Chinese, and each of these sectors had its own special body of customary behaviour. But in discussing the principles of *Kachin* social structure we are not concerned with the details of such variations, but only with that part of the culture which is common to all of them. Since the members of the Hpalang community were all part of one political system, they had to be able to communicate with one another about political status, and they did so in the language of ritual action. Precisely because Kachin society as a whole is made up of numerous sub-groups speaking diverse spoken languages we may expect that at a ritual level there is a rather simple stereotyped ritual 'language' which is understood by all sub-groups and in which issues of status are constantly represented in much the same way. Kachin ritual expression is relatively simple precisely because Kachin culture is complex.

But granted that I can interpret and understand the ritual actions of the Kachins of Hpalang, what grounds have I for claiming that this ritual language is in any sense 'typically Kachin'? I have repudiated the notion of a uniform Kachin culture; what grounds have I now for claiming the existence of a uniform Kachin system of ritual expression?

Clearly this is a very difficult matter to prove one way or the other, but it seems to me that one very significant piece of evidence is provided by Kawlu Ma Nawng's *History of the Kachins of the Hukawng Valley*.[1] Kawlu Ma Nawng was himself a Gauri Kachin from the Sinlum area; he was thus brought up in a cultural climate very similar to that of Hpalang.

[1] Kawlu Ma Nawng (1942).

But his book relates to the northern part of the Kachin Hills Area and was written in consultation with various eminent Jinghpaw and Tsasen chiefs and saga-tellers (*jaiwa*) from the Hukawng Valley and the North Triangle. The book, as published, is in English, but it is a faithful translation of an original Jinghpaw text. The argument is still couched in Kachin terms. The subject-matter relates mainly to feuds and factions between rival groups of *gumsa* and *gumlao* Kachins now resident in the Hukawng Valley. As with the Hpalang stories, the content is in part historical, but the history is twisted into mythological shape to justify present-day conditions. What strikes me very forcibly in reading this book is that though the material relates to the Kachins of the Hukawng Valley, practically every detail would be strictly comprehensible if it had in fact related to the Kachins of Hpalang and their neighbours. This must mean that despite the very considerable cultural differences between the Kachins of the Sinlum area and the Kachins of the Hukawng Valley, Kawlu Ma Nawng and his informants understood one another. They were in agreement about the significance that ought to be attached to the incidental details recorded in mythological tales.

I therefore infer that, despite all cultural and geographical variations, Kachins throughout the Kachin Hills Area use essentially the same rather limited set of ritual symbols to make statements about what an anthropologist regards as 'structural' relationships.

Let me recapitulate once more what I consider to be the essential difference between the ritual description of structural relations and the anthropologist's scientific description.

The social anthropologist in establishing his academic theories of social structure endeavours to employ a terminology which is completely unambiguous. He therefore adopts the normal scientific procedure of inventing a language of special terms which have no meaning at all other than that with which the scientist endows them. Such expressions as *exogamy*, *patrilineage*, *status*, *role*, etc., which are used by anthropologists to describe a system of structural relationships *mean* just what the anthropologist says they mean, neither more nor less. Consequently structural systems as described by anthropologists are always static systems.

But the ordinary member of a social system is not equipped with mental tools of this precision. The Kachin is made aware of structural relationship through the performance of ritual acts and the recitation of tales which have ritual implications. But the symbolic elements of which ritual is composed are far from being precise scientific categories. The components of symbolism may have a 'ritual meaning' but they also at the same time have a 'practical (technical) meaning' and the two types of meaning are never wholly distinct. If then we are to understand the nature of Kachin social structure, we must examine the practical meaning of those verbal expressions which a Kachin uses when making statements about the subject matter which I, as anthropologist, call social structure. For example, before we can understand the ritual implications of '*owning* a *debt* of 5 *wealth* objects', we must be able to comprehend something about the practical applications, in their Kachin context, of *ownership, debt* and *wealth.*

Anthropologists usually conceive of social structure as being the formal system of relationships existing between persons and groups of persons within a social system. Any society contains a large number of groups of varying degrees of formality and permanence and it is convenient to classify such groups according to the principles in terms of which they are aggregated. One such scheme of classification which is often used is that in which the groups within a given population are defined by reference to locality, kinship, sex, age, rank and professional occupation. The analysis which follows is not precisely along these lines for I am concerned to explain not only the principles of grouping in Kachin society but also the basis of the Kachin scheme of values, particularly in relation to property, rank and religious belief. The concepts with which I deal are arranged according to topic, thus:

> *a.* Territorial division
> *b.* Grouping of persons
> *c.* Affinal relationship
> *d.* Property and land tenure
> *e.* Rank and social class
> *f.* Belief in the supernatural
> *g.* Political and religious office

The aspects of these matters with which I am primarily

concerned are the ritual aspects, the way in which the categories I mention are used as symbols in arguments about status and obligation. Ethnographically therefore my account is distorted. For example, in talking of houses I stress only those features which denote prestige and try to explain the background of ideas associated with the Kachin notion of a 'palace'; I do not give an ethnographic description of a Kachin house. Similarly when discussing villages I say much more about such matters as the place of religious sacrifice than I do about basic means of subsistence.

Most of the Kachin expressions which I discuss do not readily translate into exact English equivalents but throughout this book I use English and not Kachin terms as a normal rule. Thus I normally write 'village' and 'village cluster', not *kahtawng* and *mare*. To assist the reader who may want to remind himself from time to time as to just what a 'village cluster' really is, I have crossheaded the more important definitions so as to simplify reference. Despite this itemisation the argument of this chapter is intended to be consecutive. The 'definitions' of concepts given in Section VIII are not meaningful except in the light of those given in Sections II–VII.

There is one particular characteristic which all the concepts here discussed have in common which seems to me to be of fundamental importance. In every case the meaning of the Kachin concept, when translated into English, appears in some degree vague and ambiguous. In English, for example, it may seem unsatisfactory that a single term which I translate as 'village' should denote an aggregate of any number of houses from one upwards. It is important to understand that although the ambiguity is a real one, a Kachin does not necessarily notice the ambiguity, it is simply that in the field of ideas with which we are here dealing, Kachins habitually use much broader verbal categories than we do. Needless to say this is not to be taken as implying any mental incompetence upon the part of Kachins. In matters which seem to him really important, such as rice agriculture, the Kachin has a vocabulary of the utmost precision, whereas English has practically no vocabulary at all. But in matters social, it is English which is usually the more precise language.

This broadness of indigenous social categories can be important and should be respected. It is a feature which is probably very common in the study of primitive societies and may be irritating to a research worker with a tidy mind. Some anthropologists, to judge from recent work in Africa, have been tempted by vagueness of this kind to introduce new more specific categories of their own which have no equivalents in the native language. In my view this is methodologically a mistake. If one attempts to interpret a social structure by means of analytical categories which are more precise than those which the people use themselves, one injects into the system a specious rigidity and symmetry which may be lacking in the real life situation.

In my view the ambiguity of the native categories is absolutely fundamental to the operation of the Kachin social system. It is easy enough to produce a neat paradigm of the Kachin kinship system and demonstrate its beautiful structural symmetries; indeed Granet and Hodson have both done this,[2] and in one myth the Kachins even seem to do it themselves. But if we translate the Kachin categories into rigidly defined English terms, such a paradigm has scarcely any relevance to the Kachin actuality. It is only because the meaning of his sundry structural categories is, for a Kachin, extremely elastic that he is able to interpret the actuality of his social life as conforming to the formal pattern of the traditional, mythically defined, structural system.

If then my categories seem very imprecise in such dimensions as numerical scale, physical size and geographical concentration, this imprecision is intended. It is just this imprecision which makes real Kachin society very flexible in form despite the fact that the ideal structure of society is both elaborate and rigid.

The categories as here described are the categories of the *gumsa* Kachin ideology. *Gumlao* Kachins share most of the ideology but evaluate the items of it differently. For example, *gumsa* and *gumlao* alike agree that to pay 'thighs' to a chief is to recognise him as your lord; but *gumlao* Kachins recognise no chiefs and therefore pay no thighs.

Some of the ideology is common also to both Kachins and

[2] Hodson (1925); Granet (1939).

Shans.   Later chapters of this book are devoted to explaining more precisely what these common features are and for the present I will only take note of the relevance of Shan ideas in a few instances.

In the present chapter I am trying to demonstrate the system of *gumsa* Kachin ideology *as if* it were an integrated coherent set of ideas.   I am talking about an ideal system.   But the relevance of this ideal system for the main theme of my book had best be understood.   This main theme is fundamentally: What is the difference between a Kachin and a Shan?

From one point of view the contrast between Kachin and Shan organisation corresponds precisely to the difference which Morgan[3] had in mind when he distinguished *social* organisation from *political* organisation.   The first is a segmentary organisation based in the balanced opposition of lineage groups: the second is a feudal type system based in the rights of property. It is then of great interest that Shans and Kachins alike express their ideas about the political order by making use of identical or closely related concepts.   They manage to do this by emphasising different aspects of particular ideas.   For example, neither in the Kachin system nor in the Shan system are notions of local grouping and kinship grouping wholly separable, but whereas a Kachin identifies himself in the first place by giving his lineage, a Shan starts by giving his place of birth.[4] Or again, 'trade'—that is the exchange of goods and services —plays a very important part in the attainment of status in both systems; but whereas Shan 'trade' is mainly trade as we understand it—that is the bartering of goods of ordinary economic value to achieve a profit—Kachin 'trade' is carried on largely, though not wholly, in goods which have no ordinary economic value at all.   I shall emphasise distinctions of this kind as we proceed.

[3] Morgan (1877), Part II, Chapter 2.   'The experience of mankind has developed but two plans of government . . . the first and most ancient was a social organization founded upon gentes phratries and tribes.   The second and latest in time was a political organization founded upon territory and upon property.'
[4] Harvey and Barton (1930), *passim*.

II

Concepts of Territorial Division

(*a*) *nta*—'a house'; (*b*) *htingnu*—'a chief's house'

Kachins in certain circumstances distinguish verbally between the dwelling-houses of ordinary people and the dwelling-house of a chief. The fundamental difference between the two is not in any feature of design but in the fact that the house of the chief contains a special compartment known as the *madai-dap* which is a shrine dedicated to the Madai *nat*, the chief of the Sky Spirits (*mu nat*), who is looked upon as an affinal relative of one of the chief's remote ancestors.

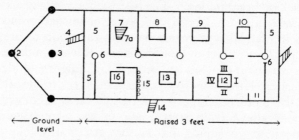

FIG. 2.   Ground Plan of a Kachin Chief's House.

1. Covered porch and stable—*n'pan*.   2. Front house post—*jun shadaw*. 3. Porch house post—*n'hpu daw*.   4. Entrance ladder—*lakang*.   5. Verandah—*n'tawt*.   6. Door—*chyinghka*.   7. Madai nat shrine room—*madai dap*.   7A. Madai shrine—*karap tawn*.   8, 9, 10, 12, 13, 16. Hearths—*dap*. 8. Hearth of married son's family—*lapran dap*.   9. Hearth of householder's young children and servants.   10. Sleeping quarters of householder—*n'bang dap*.   11. Shrine of household *nat*—*nat tawn*.   12. Guest hearth—*manam dap, lup daw dap*. There is an order of precedence as to seating position indicated by the figures I, II, III, IV.   13. Cooking hearth—*shat shadu dap*. 14. Side entrance—*hkuwawt hku*.   15. Rack for water tubes—*ntsin n'dum*. 16. Private room of unmarried adolescent girls—*n-la dap*.

All Kachin dwelling-houses are rectangular shed-like structures with the flooring of the living-rooms raised several feet above the ground. Fig. 2 shows the ground plan of a typical Kachin chief's house (*htingnu*). In the case of an important chief it would include more hearths than are shown here and in an extreme case might be as much as 100 yards long. The great size of chief's houses is probably responsible for the theory that Kachins have a typical 'long house' organisation analogous

to that of the peoples of Borneo.   A recently published ethnographic handbook asserts that Kachin houses 'are often over
100 feet in length in which the members of an extended family
reside . . . a (separate) fireplace for each biological family'.[5]
This is erroneous though it might seem to be a reasonable inference from statements of good authority.[6]   A better
generalisation is that 'the Kachin household usually consists
of father, mother, sons and daughters; sometimes needy relatives
and very frequently visitors'.[7]   There is nothing in principle
to prevent several married brothers sharing a house after the
death of the father, but this is not now the general pattern.
Moreover since the tradition is strong that the succession should
properly pass to the youngest son (the *uma* of a chief; the
hpungdim of a commoner) it is unlikely that there is any real
expectation that brothers should live together.   Elder sons
today usually either move to another village or set up a house
of their own adjacent to the old one.   I suspect that this was
also the normal pattern in the past.   That residence on the
joint family pattern is exceptional is also indicated by the fact
that there is a special Jinghpaw term (*htingyan*) to denote households of this kind.   From certain areas, notably Assam, a
succession rule of primogeniture instead of ultimogeniture is
reported.[8]   Here the residence pattern may be different;
alternatively the ethnography may be incorrect.

The majority of present-day Kachins live in small houses
that cannot comfortably house more than a single family.
Prestige, however, attaches to large houses and those who can
afford it will build larger houses than they actually need.
The huge barrack-like *htingnu* of the chief is today often largely
empty space.   However, the size of this particular building
does have some justification besides that of prestige.   Though
polygamy is, on average, rare, a chief may often have more
than one wife, and each wife has her own hearth or hearths.
Formerly the chief's household would nearly always include a
number of 'slaves' (*mayam*) (see p. 160) and other personal
adherents.   Furthermore, the chief's house commonly serves
as a general guest-house for passing travellers.

---

[5] Thomas (1950), p. 20.   [6] Anderson (1871), p. 122.
[7] Carapiett (1929), p. 13.
[8] Neufville (1828), p. 341; also see below, pp. 156, 261.

The layout of an ordinary man's house is similar to that of the chief but smaller and contains fewer hearths. A poor man's house would lack altogether the porch and stable area in front of the house (*npan*). The house of a village headman, who is not also a chief, might in some cases be as large as that of his chief but would always lack the oversize porch posts (*nhpu daw*) which are a special mark of chiefly rank. As already remarked, the *madai dap* occurs only in chief's houses, but a shrine to the ancestor spirit of the householder is to be found in every dwelling house. This is usually an unobtrusive affair consisting of nothing more than a shelf fitted to a side wall near either the front or back entrance of the house.

An important part of the paraphernalia associated with this shrine are two small bamboo liquor tubes known as *nat htawt*. They are undistinguished objects and kept tucked away under the eaves. Swords (*nhtu*) and spears (*ri*) which have been received from affinal relatives as part of the contract for a debt (*hka*, see p. 144 f.) are similarly kept in the rafters close to the household shrine.

The ancestor spirit in question, normally referred to simply as *masha nat* (human spirit) or *gumgun nat* (protecting spirit), receives offerings rather frequently, since every misfortune, illness, minor ailment or risky undertaking of any member of the household is the occasion for a *masha nat* sacrifice. Such offerings, however, are always on a very small scale. If, for one reason or another, a householder wishes to give a feast on a large scale, he will invoke other deities besides his own ancestor spirit. The *masha nat*, as a human individual, seems usually to be a quite recent ancestor—e.g. a great grandfather. This cult is important for an understanding of the lineage system (cf. p. 175 f.). The householder and his wife are both referred to as 'owners' (*madu ni*) of the house, but the *masha nat* of the house is an ancestor of the husband not of the wife. Close agnatic kin living in adjacent houses usually have household shrines dedicated to the same *masha nat* but this is not necessarily the case. Some houses contain shrines to more than one ancestor.

It should perhaps be stressed that the material of the house itself is not very valuable, most of the construction is of bamboo, thatch and soft woods, all of which need to be replaced at frequent intervals.   The most permanent feature about a house is the site (*htingra*) on which it stands.   The right to build a house is allocated in the first place by the village headman, but the decision as to where exactly it should be built is governed by geomancy and thus rests with the diviner (*nwawt wa*, p. 192).   One consequence of this is that the houses of most Kachin villages are scattered haphazard without any systematic alignment; where the contrary is true, it is usually the recent result of arbitrary decrees by the Administration. The lack of orderly arrangement makes Kachin villages strikingly different in appearance from those of the Naga and Chin areas further to the west.   Kachin ideas about house site orientation probably derive initially from the Chinese concept of *feng-shui* but are also shared with the Shans.[9]

The household—i.e. those who live in one *nta*—is the primary unit of economic cooperation.   Plots (*yi*) in the annual village clearing (*yinwa*) are worked by households.   Each house normally has associated with it a temporary hut (*wa*) located in the rice field and some members of the household may sleep and eat in this hut for large parts of the year, but this does not make the field hut a separate residential unit.   There may also be, adjacent to the *nta*, another separate hut (*dum*) which serves as a granary.   This hut may have social as well as economic functions.   The compartment marked *n-la dap* (woman-man hearth) in Fig. 2 is the room of the unmarried girls of the *nta* and they may here entertain their lovers without parental restraint; indeed they are expected to do so.   The granary may serve a similar social purpose.   In Hpalang in 1940, in deference to mission criticism, the institution of the *n-la dap* had been suppressed, but so-called granaries, which were in fact sleeping quarters for the young people survived.

In some areas every *nta* has attached to it a small fenced garden (*sun*).   This area is kept in permanent cultivation.   It is private property in a sense that the field plot (*yi*) is not. The crops grown in the garden (*sun*) are vegetables, herbs used for secret semi-magical concoctions, and valuable (and/or illicit) products, such as opium.   In 1939 a well-meaning British administrator pointed out that the garden system involved the construction of a most unnecessary amount of

[9] Milne and Cochrane (1910), p. 99.

fencing and suggested that households should pool their gardens so as to work a sort of allotment system. Hpalang comments on this suggestion were most unfavourable; it seemed clear that the whole point of a *sun* was that it was immediately adjacent to the house (*nta*) and private to the members of that house.

From the point of view of ritual expression the most important detail to be noticed in all this is, I think, the verbal distinction between *nta*—a house, and *htingnu*—a chief's house. Chiefs' houses are also referred to by other names. *Hkaw* is simply the Shan word *haw*—a palace. Royal persons such as Kings and Emperors are referred to as *hkaw-hkam* (palace of gold) or *hkaw-seng* (palace of precious stone), here again the usage seems to be pure Shan. *Htingsang*—'the paddy store'—another poetical term for Chief, refers presumably to the fact that while a chief's followers pay a due in paddy to the chief, he gives most of the paddy back again in contributions to feasts. *Htingnu* itself means either 'the house of the mother' or 'the mother house'. Two ideas seem to be involved. One is that the chief's house is the parent house from which other houses of the village have segmented off; the other that the house of the chief is *mayu* to the houses of his followers (see Chapter IV, pp. 78 ff.). More figuratively, the chief's house may be referred to as *baren lungpu*, an expression usually translated as 'the cave of the alligator' (Hanson, 1906, p. 73). Whether Kachins have ever had the opportunity to meet alligators in the flesh I am not quite sure. *Baren(g)* is some sort of fabulous monster, a *nat* spirit of the valley rivers and marshy places, and 'alligator' will serve as a translation. These 'alligators' crop up frequently in Kachin mythology, usually as ancestors of the Kachin race.[10] The term is also applied by the Kachins of the Sinlum Area to the Maingtha Shans of Möng Hsa.

I shall refer to this symbol again. Meanwhile I would say only that *baren* stands for (i) the notion of a Shan *saopha*—the Lord of the paddy plains, and (ii) the male phallic principle which the chief (Shan or Kachin) represents. The sky spirit (*mu nat Madai*), with whom the chief is also associated, likewise represents the male principle in contrast to the female element

---

[10] Carrapiett (1929), Chapter 1; also see p. 201 and Chapter IX below.

in the productive earth (*ga*).   Both Chinese and Shan-Buddhist ideas are here relevant.

In the first place *baren*, as a symbol, bears a striking resemblance to the Chinese 'dragon' (*lung*), which is similarly associated with water, maleness (*yang*) and kingly state.   And secondly there are close parallels of ritual behaviour.   Thus the Temple of Heaven at Peking was formerly the site of important annual rituals undertaken by the Chinese Emperor in person and designed to ensure the well-being of the Chinese nation and the fertility of the crops.   The Temple of Heaven consists of two parts.   The part dedicated to the sky is a roofed building, while the part dedicated to the Earth is an open circular platform.   In the Kachin *gumsa* system the religious functions of the chief include the obligation to make offerings to *Madai*—the chief of the sky spirits.   This being controls wealth and general prosperity.   The offerings are made at the *madai* shrine in the chief's own house.   But the chief also makes offerings to the earth spirit (*ga-Shadip*), a bisexual being more or less synonymous with the concept of 'creation', who controls the fertility of the soil and of human beings.   These latter offerings are made at a circular open space in the sacred area known as the *numshang* (see p. 117).   The Kachin chief's role in these matters thus has a definitely Chinese flavour. The chief's house is more than a dwelling-house, more than a palace, it is also a kind of temple to the *Madai nat*.

But it may also be noted that it has been characteristic of all the Buddhist kingdoms and principalities of South East Asia ever since the 4th century A.D. that the King has assumed many of the attributes of a living Buddha and Divine King. It is highly typical of all these societies that the King and his Court and his very numerous wives and concubines live a life cut off from that of the secular world in a walled palace which is conceptually a model of the sacred Mount Meru.   The Burmese royal palaces of Amarapura, Ava and Mandalay can be included in this general category, and so also the 'palaces' (*haw*) of modern Shan princes.[11]   A Kachin chief's house (*htingnu*) is not normally separated off from the rest of the

[11] cf. Scott and Hardiman (1900), Part I, Vol. II, p. 154. 'The palace was called *myenan* because it stood, like the Myinmo Mount (Mount Meru), in the centre of the four islands which first appeared on the earth.   It symbolizes the Bawdibin Shwepalin, the birthplace of the Buddha——'

community.   In the past, however, several of the Kachin chiefs who have been most successful in achieving recognition as having a *saohpa* (Shan prince) status have demonstrated this fact by surrounding their houses with elaborate stone walls.[12]

> *kahtawng* (*gahtawng*), *ga*—'a village'
>
> *mare, mareng*—'a village cluster'
>
> *mung* (cf. Shan *möng*)—'a chief's domain'

The distinction which I draw between the terms village, village cluster and domain has already been partly explained in Chapter IV.   Village and village cluster have primarily a territorial significance; domain is primarily political.   Thus while we sometimes find Kachin domains (*mung*) which contain several village clusters (*mare*), each of which contains a number of villages (*kahtawng*), we also find domains which consist of only one village cluster (as for example at Hpalang) or even of only a solitary village.

Kahtawng strictly speaking denotes the buildings of a village, *ga* the land which it controls, but the concepts seem almost identical.   *Kahtawng* is normal usage in the south, *ga* in the north.

A village may contain any number of households from one upwards.   In practice the majority contain between 10 to 20 households.   A village is usually sited on or close to the ridge of a hill.   The buildings are likely to be scattered about irregularly 10 to 20 yards apart, the crest of the ridge forming a rough central roadway (*lam*).   In some areas each house has adjacent to it a small fenced garden (*sun*) used for cultivating opium and other specialties.   The territory (*ga*) over which the members of a village as a whole have cultivation rights— i.e. rights of jungle clearance—is, in all but the most thinly populated areas, clearly defined in terms of landmarks such as streams, mountain tops, prominent rocks and so on.

The actual site of the village (i.e. the buildings) is not necessarily fixed.   Some villages have been on their present sites for over a century; in other cases the entire site has been abandoned after only a few years residence.   The reasons given for such movement are sometimes quite practical—e.g. that

[12] Enriquez (1923), p. 129; cf. Kawlu Ma Nawng (1942), p. 39.

the water supply turned out to be defective—but more usually magical. Disease or bad crops or a fire or other calamity is attributed to the evil influence of the locality, usually simply referred to as *bum nat*—'spirits of the mountain'. If sacrifices fail to bring about any improvement, the diviners (*nwawt*) may decide that the best course is to move the village altogether. Such a change of village site does not normally have any immediate bearing on the cultivation rights of the villagers. The theory frequently propounded by British Administrative officers that the Kachins move their villages simply because, having exhausted the fertility of one mountain side, they want to go on and destroy another, is seldom, if ever, justifiable. In all the cases where I made enquiries land rights appeared to be regarded as inalienable except in one of two circumstances. If the 'principal lineage' (see below) of the village becomes extinct (*dawm mat sai*), the land reverts to the control of the lineage of the chief; alternatively, if a village in the domain of chief A is moved right away into the domain of some other chief B, then the villagers lose their land rights in the domain of chief A. Actually of course they seldom do this; in the ordinary way when a village moves, it moves to another site in the domain of the same chief as before.

These principles of land tenure were almost wholly misunderstood by the earlier British administrators and most of the statements in the literature on this subject are quite misleading. For the most part there was a failure to realise that the technique of shifting cultivation requires a long fallow period and that 'fallowing' in such circumstances amounts to letting the jungle grow up again on once cleared land. It was generally assumed that when land was fallowed in this way it was *abandoned*—i.e. that land rights were given up. Thus the literature suggests that the lands of a village are simply the land which is under cultivation at any one time;[13] actually the land which a village headman will claim as being 'our land' is normally an area of anything from 10 to 20 times that which is actually being cultivated. There is good evidence that rights in such land have a long-term survival value whether or not they are used for cultivation. For example, soon after the Administrative Post of Sinlum was founded in

[13] e.g. Scott and Hardiman (1900), Part I, Vol. II, p. 355.

1900, a large tract of jungle, formerly farmed by the Kachin villages of Sinlum and Lawdan, was classed as reserved forest and earmarked as a fuel reserve for use of the civil station. In 1940 the Sinlum and Lawdan villagers maintained that the land still belonged to them despite the artificial government embargo and despite the fact that the sites of both villages had been moved in the interval.

Usually, in any one year, the members of a village combine to clear a single area of jungle, though sometimes it is only a section of a village group that combines to make a clearing. Once felling, burning and fencing is completed, communal activity ceases. Within the total clearing (*yin wa*) each household cultivates its own independent plot (*yi*) and there is no communal ownership of produce. As explained in Chapter II, some villages work 'grassland *taungya*' (*hkaibang*)[14] instead of *taungya* of the ordinary jungle type but the principle by which each household works its own plot within the common field is the same. Where irrigated rice land exists, the paddy plots (*hkauna*)[15] are worked strictly on a household basis though there is necessarily some group cooperation between the households using the same set of water channels. In theory *hkauna* cannot be sold outright though there are systems of mortgage which approximate closely to outright sale.

The members of a village are likely to belong to a number of different patrilineages, but one of these lineages 'owns' (*madu ai*) the village. The headman of the village is always a member of the lineage owning it. Usually the name of the village indicates the lineage of the owners: e.g. Pasi *ga*—is owned by the Pasi lineage; Laga *kahtawng* is owned by the Laga lineage, etc. I call the lineage which owns a village the 'principal lineage' of the village. The village headman is thus *ipso facto* head of the principal lineage. The significance of 'ownership' in this context is explained later (see p. 155 f.)

The village headman under the British régime was known officially as the *agyiwa* (big man) but it is not clear whether this term was in use in pre-British times. The term may have been of *gumlao* origin.[16] The ordinary *gumsa* term is *salang wa*.[17]

[14] This word is of Shan derivation and is equivalent to Shan *hai*.
[15] Another Shan term.   [16] Scott and Hardiman (1900), Part II, Vol. II, p. 559.
[17] The derivation is doubtful. It probably signifies 'standard bearer'. On ceremonial occasions a chief is properly preceded by one of his *salang* carrying a spear.

Most Kachin villages contain no public building which can be regarded as the corporate property of the village as a whole, though in recent years the households of a village have sometimes contributed jointly to the construction of a school. The house of the chief or of the village headman normally serves as a public guest-house at which any casual traveller is entitled to hospitality. The maintenance of the chief's and/or the headman's house is thus to some extent a public responsibility. Villagers have an obligation to assist in the building and repair of the chief's house.

At the entrance to most villages is to be found a sacred area, the *numshang* (*lamshang*, *mashang*). In this area certain important rituals are performed annually. At most times of the year the place presents a desolate appearance. The shrines that are erected on ceremonial occasions are very elaborate affairs but mainly of bamboo construction; once used they are abandoned, a new set being erected the following year. The only permanent shrine is that dedicated to the earth spirit (*ga nat*, *shadip*); this is normally marked by a circle of stones and occasionally a fence. In a few very prosperous communities it becomes a stone platform decorated in Chinese style.[18] The trees in the *numshang* commonly include a banyan tree (*ficus retusa*). This tree has sacred associations throughout Buddhist and Hindu India. The stories associated with this tree are very various but throughout Burma and the Shan States it is common to find the shrine of the founder ancestor of a village group associated with a tree of this type.

The trees in the area of the *numshang* are never felled. The sacredness of the area is emphasised also in other ways. For example, it was formerly regarded as a sanctuary even for persons known to be hostile to the village. Thus the traditional somewhat fantastic method of enforcing the settlement of a debt, once the settlement had been properly adjudicated, was to 'sit on the debt' (*hka dung ai*). One method of doing this was simply to send unwanted guests to exploit the hospitality of one's opponents indefinitely; less risky was the procedure of camping in one's opponent's *numshang* and killing off his livestock as opportunity offered. No reprisals could be

---

[18] cf. Anderson (1871), p. 383.

taken for none dare risk the anger of the gods by committing violence within the sacred precincts of the *numshang*.[19]

Kachin religious rituals are not confined to those which take place at the *numshang* and at household ancestor shrines. Decaying bamboo altars (*hkungri*), superficially very similar to those in the *numshang*, are to be seen in front of nearly every house in the village. The more important the householder the more substantial these indices of past celebration. To the initiated the design of the shrine or the style of the sacrificial post (*wudang*) indicates immediately the deity to whom the sacrifice was made and the nature of what was sacrificed. Since sacrifices—whatever their immediate purpose—are an important element of conspicuous consumption the latter point is particularly important. If a man can afford to sacrifice a large buffalo, he is always anxious that his neighbours should remember the fact. Consequently the skulls of the slain animals are hung up on the decaying *hkungri* and *wudang*. When the latter fall to pieces, the more impressive skulls are transferred to the houseposts of the sacrificer where they form a permanent decoration surviving sometimes for several generations. Slain chickens leave no residue that will serve as a memento but when there has been a major holocaust of sacrificial fowls a high bamboo pole is erected to which are attached chicken baskets corresponding to the number of chickens killed. The effect is rather like a naval flag-pole mounting a string of signal flags. It is worth noting that the Buddhist Shans, though they kill no chickens, also erect tall 'flag poles' decorated with streamers and baskets to mark their celebrations.[20]

Most *wudang* are of rough hewn soft wood and these decay away to nothing in a season or two; here and there, however, usually outside the house of a chief, one may see a more elaborate *wudang* cut from hardwood and decorated with what might at first appear to be cabbalistic signs. Posts with similar markings (*laban*) are erected outside the *numshang* on the occasion of an important festival. These signs are intended to be drawings of wealth objects (*hpaga*) (see p. 144) which are in the gift of the sky spirits, especially the *Madai nat*. A decorated *wudang* of this sort commemorates the sacrifice of a buffalo to Madai. Such sacrifices are the occasion of large-

[19] cf. Carrapiett (1929), p. 98.   [20] Milne and Cochrane (1910), pp. 121–4.

scale celebration known as *manau*, the performance of which has implications rather similar to those of the Feasts of Merit which have been described for the Nagas and Chins.[21]

The right to sacrifice to Madai and hence to hold a *manau* is a special perquisite of the chief. Other rich and influential men do sometimes hold *manau* but in order to do so they must first purchase permission from the chief by means of an appropriate exchange of gifts.[22]

When a *manau* is to be held a circular earthen dancing floor (*naura*) about 15 to 20 yards across is constructed outside the house of the giver of the *manau*. The posts and boards (*shadung dingnai*) which are erected at the centre of this dancing floor, though not exceptionally distinguished, represent the peak of Kachin artistic endeavour so far as the plastic arts are concerned. By tradition the posts and the dancing floor must be destroyed twelve months after giving the feast; thereafter only the *wudang* remain as symbols of past glory. Consequently it is only occasionally that one will come across a village with a *manau* dancing floor actually in existence.[23]

Burial sites are not very prominent in Kachin villages. A Kachin is usually buried fairly close to his village of residence but there are no cemeteries; the site of each grave is selected individually by divination. As in most societies funerals are an occasion for ostentation. An elaborate structure of bamboo and thatch is erected over a grave, but it is normally an impermanent affair which decays away to nothing in six months or a year;[24] thereafter the site of the grave is of no importance. In the case of chiefs only, the grave site is surrounded by a deep ditch and this survives long after the bamboo furnishings of the grave itself have disappeared. Where a chief dies with an unrequited blood feud outstanding, the ditch is left incomplete. It is completed ceremonially when final settlement is achieved.

[21] See especially Stevenson (1943).

[22] See Leonard cited in Carrapiett (1929), p. 14.

[23] The symbolism of a *manau* would clearly be of the greatest relevance for this study. Unfortunately I have never had the opportunity to see a genuine example; the only *manau* I was able to see were severely bowdlerised versions put on as a spectacle for the benefit of visiting Government officers. Existing accounts of *manau* (e.g. in Carrapiett, 1929) are more or less meaningless.

[24] Green (1934) suggests that the design of these structures is associated with that of a Shan Buddhist pagoda. I would agree.

In the foregoing account of the stereotype of a Kachin village I have stressed in particular those material features which serve to draw attention to a man's status; large houses, numerous altars (*hkungri*), carved sacrificial posts (*wudang*), graves with ditches and so on.   It is possible to generalise here.   The most characteristic way for a Kachin to assert his status is to be ostentatious in the scale of his religious sacrifices.   Quite apart from the cost of the animals sacrificed, the grass and bamboo furnishings which provide the background for such perform-ances can be extremely elaborate.   A man clearly gains esteem, as well as aesthetic satisfaction, from the manner in which such 'ritual equipment' is constructed.   But the value is transi-tory.   No altar can be used twice; everything is made afresh on the day of the sacrifice; as soon as the sacrifice is over the whole contrivance is allowed to fall into decay.   Thus it is only the symbols of chieftainship which have the quality of permanence—the great porch posts of teak or other hardwood, the ditches round the grave, the decorated *wudang* of sacrifices to the *Madai nat*.   Everything else is evanescent—the altars and the grave furnishings of bamboo, the softwood *wudang* of ordinary sacrifices, the carved *manau* poles which must be cere-monially destroyed.   It is as if anyone might be king for a day, but only the chief rules on for ever.

There is an interesting contrast here between Kachin custom and that of the Nagas and Chins further to the west.   In the Naga world prestige once established is apparently established for ever and the occasion marked by the erection of a stone menhir; the corresponding symbols in the Kachin system are perishable.

Only very seldom do Kachins put up any kind of stone monument and then it is only the chiefs who do so.   The Gauri chief of Hutung, for example, formerly erected stone menhirs to commemorate his *manau*,[25] and other chiefs of the same area had their graves decorated in Chinese fashion by Chinese craftsmen.[26]   But in the ordinary way stonework of any kind is remarkable for its absence.[27]   It is difficult to

---

[25] Anderson (1871), p. 383.   Where Hutung is spelt Hoetone.

[26] Enriquez (1923), p. 128; Green (1934) records a stone grave of pagoda shape.

[27] Here and there in the literature there are shocked references to phallus shaped stones which seem formerly to have been prominent in certain villages.   I have no reliable data about such objects though they may have been connected with

explain this in diffusionist terms; a sociological explanation might be that perhaps stone is altogether too permanent a substance to be used for the expression of status symbols in a society as flexible as that of the Kachin.

mare or *mareng*—'a village cluster'

Kachin villages may be independent political units but it is more usual, in the *gumsa* system especially, to find that the villages clustered around a particular peak or lying along a particular ridge recognise themselves as a single political entity. The component villages of a 'village cluster' may be physically adjacent (as at Hpalang) so that the 'villages' then appear simply as wards of a single settlement; alternatively they may be scattered about over an area of several square miles.

The political relationship between the component villages of a village cluster is virtually homologous to the relations that exist between the lineage groups of a single village. This point has I think been made clear in my account of Hpalang (Chapter IV) and it partly explains why the Kachins themselves often make no very clear or consistent distinction between the two concepts village (*kahtawng*) and village cluster (*mare*).

The component villages of a cluster are normally 'owned' by different lineages, sometimes of the same clan, sometimes of different clans. One of the villages is nearly always considered senior to the others. The principal lineage of this senior village can be said to 'own' (*madu ai*) all the territory (the sky and earth—*lamu ga*) of the village cluster. The headman of the senior village is thus chief (*duwa*) of the village cluster. If the chief is politically independent he is entitled to receive, from all persons not of his own lineage, a hind leg of every four-footed animal killed within his territory either in sacrifice or in hunting. He is also entitled to have certain work done on his rice plot without incurring any reciprocal obligation. In many cases he is even entitled to a tributary due of one or two baskets of paddy per household per year. Chiefs with tribute rights of this kind are called 'thigh-eating chief' (*magyi sha*

the cult of the *Madai nat*. They appear to have been owned by particular chiefly lineages. The Nhkum-Ngalang chiefs of the North Triangle are said to have such a stone. It has the property of moving of its own volition when any calamity is impending for the family. Two examples of such phallic stones are illustrated in Green (1934).

ai du). Some village headmen in virtue of their alleged aristocratic descent assume the title of chief (*duwa*) but they are not
on that account entitled to 'eat thighs'; such people I call petty
chiefs. In theory a petty chief is always the subordinate of a
thigh-eating chief, but this is hardly the case in practice. In
strict theory it would appear that only a thigh-eating chief
can perform the crucial rituals at a *numshang* so that there
should be only one *numshang* for each village cluster. In
practice petty chiefs can assert themselves by operating their
own *numshang* as we saw happening at Hpalang where the
Maran-Nmwe and Maran-Gumjye headmen both styled themselves chief and each had their own *numshang*. Such procedures
can be rationalised by saying that the ritual powers of a thigh-
eating chief can be delegated to petty chiefs.

>   *mung*—'a domain or tract', 'a township' (cf. Shan *möng*,
>   Burmese *myo*)

The political domain of a thigh-eating chief may then be
either a single village (*kehtawng*) or a cluster of villages (*mare*),
or even in some cases a number of village clusters. The territory of any such domain is a *mung*, a term borrowed directly
from the Shan *möng*. The title *mung duwa* (domain chief)
could then properly be applied to any thigh-eating chief. In
practice it is usually reserved for the paramount chief of a large
area. Within such a domain all the thigh-eating chiefs are
of the same lineage, but the 'domain chief' is the senior by
virtue of heading the 'youngest son line' of the lineage. Such
a domain chief is thus also called an *uma du* (youngest son chief)
(cf. p. 129).

In the community of Hpalang the 'domain' and the 'village
cluster' coincide. The 'village cluster' contains nine separate
'villages'.

The aggregation of villages into clusters of varying density,
and the further aggregation of village clusters into 'tracts' or
'domains', is a general characteristic of the North Burma area.
The difficulty of translating the various terms involved derives
from the fact that the Kachins, Shans and Burmese attach no
idea of particular size either to the concepts *mung*, *möng* and
myo (township) or to the concepts *kahtawng*, *man* and *yua*
(village). The English mind expects to use a different set of

categories to describe a population living in closely packed settlements from those used to describe a similar population living scattered about at low density over a wide area. The Burmese and their neighbours do not do this. The Burmese word *myo* for example can mean either a town or a district comprising a number of scattered villages. What interests the Burmese is not so much the nature of the administrative entity as the rank of the officer in charge of it. In a similar way the modern English system balances off 'urban districts' of small size and high population density against 'rural districts' of large size and low population density.[28]

Kachin usage is not quite the same as the Burmese and Shan but equally flexible. As between Burmese and Shan, *myo* and *möng* are almost exact equivalents. Both terms denote either a town or a township—that is an administrative area associated with, or comparable to, a town. Thus when, in the past, the Burmese have eliminated one or other of the Northern Shan States the tributary functions of the chief of the *möng* (*saohpa*) have been replaced by those of an official called a *myo-sa* ('eater of the *myo*'). Kachins on the other hand, who have no towns of their own, see a distinction between the Burmese term *myo* in the sense of town and *myo* in the sense of township. The former they translate as *mare* ('a village cluster'—e.g. Bhamo is a *mare*), while the latter is thought of as a *mung* (domain).

This flexibility of the scale dimension in the concepts village, village cluster, domain is of some importance. To most Englishmen it would not appear that what a Shan calls a *möng* or a Burmese calls a *myo* could be 'the same thing' as the politically much less significant entity which a Kachin calls a *mung*. Yet in the Kachin view these three categories are, in their political sense, identical; the Kachin chief (*duwa*) of a successful and prosperous *mung* undoubtedly sees himself as a Shan prince (*saohpa*) ruling over a *möng*.

[28] cf. R.N.E.F. (1908), para. 17: 'In Myitkyina and Bhamo there is, in each group of villages, one *duwa*, and, in each of the hamlets under him in which he does not reside, a man called an *akyiwa*. . . . This is the (Burmese) *ywathugyi* system. The *duwa* is the *ywathugyi*, the *akyiwa* is the *ywagaung*. In Katha each tract is what would be called a *daing* (circle); the head of the tract is a *daing thugyi* or *myo thugyi*, and in each village is the *ywathugyi*. It is in fact the (Burmese) *myothugyi* system. In Katha the head of each hamlet is a *duwa* or *thugyi* . . . and the head of the group (of hamlets) is the superior *duwa* or *myothugyi*. . . .'

This is not mere vanity on the part of the Kachin. At an earlier period the Burmese themselves—and even for that matter the British too—recognised that the political status of a Kachin chief was that of a Shan *saohpa* on a smaller scale. Thus in the 19th-century literature of the Kachin Hills Area Kachin officials are nearly always referred to as either Tsawbwa (*saohpa*) or as Pawmaing (*pawmöng*),[29] terms which the authors learnt from their Burmese interpreters. This literature contains clear evidence that, at any rate in the mid-19th century, the more important Kachin chiefs were treated by the Burmese Court exactly as if they were Shan princes.[30] Similarly *Paw-möng*, a Shan title meaning literally 'father of the *möng*' denotes, it would seem, the senior *amat* (counsellor) in a *saohpa's* court. The corresponding Kachin term is *bawmung* ('head of the *mung*'). The typical *bawmung* is a village headman (*salang*) who is a commoner by birth and cannot therefore claim the title chief (*duwa*) but who, through force of personality or other circumstance, actually dominates his legitimate overlord. In Hpalang for example the Sumnut headman was *bawmung* of the Atsi section of the community though the imbecile Lahpai headman was the chief.

These sundry parallel terms provide a good example of what I mean when I assert that although the scale of Kachin *gumsa* society is usually very petty compared with Shan society, the political structure of the former is nevertheless, in important respects, modelled on that of the latter.

With Shans and *gumsa* Kachins the term *möng* (*mung*) has the very definite connotation of political unity, the *möng* is the domain of one particular chief who is overlord of all other title holders within that territory. *Gumlao* Kachins also use the term *mung* but in a different sense. A *gumlao mung* is a district or contiguous area where the *gumlao* rule prevails. Thus the Duleng area to the east of Hkamti Long and north of the Triangle is 'Duleng *mung*'. It is now all *gumlao* territory. Each village is politically independent but by a rather palpable fiction all Duleng claim to be members of a single clan, namely the Duleng clan. The mythical founder ancestor of the Duleng

[29] Both words appear in various spellings.
[30] See especially Williams (1863); Sladen (1868); Anderson (1871), (1876); Strettell (1876).

clan is treated as the patron saint of the area and sacrifices are made to him as *mung nat* by each village on an equal basis. (Map 4, p. 33.)

The same concept is met with in *gumsa* territory but the *mung nat* in this case turns out to be a founder ancestor in the lineage of the paramount chief. The right to make sacrifices to the *mung nat* in *gumsa* territory is therefore in the gift of this chief.

I should perhaps emphasise again that the arbitrary boundaries drawn between Shan and Kachin territory under the British régime had no relevance at all to conditions in the pre-British period. A Shan *möng* normally included hill territory occupied by Kachins as well as valley territory occupied by Shans. Similarly in a number of cases Kachin *mung* included valleys occupied by Shans as well as hills occupied by Kachins. The *mung nat* as guardian deity presided over both.

The major concepts we have so far considered are all categories of place. We have now to consider categories of persons, that is to say the words Kachins themselves use to denote human groups of different kinds. In Kachin thinking these are not fully separable from the place categories we have already considered. This point will be elaborated as we proceed.

III

Concepts concerning Aggregates of Persons

   htinggaw—'family', 'extended family'

When I write of 'family' I mean the biological family of husband, wife and children, and by 'extended family' I mean a group of males and unmarried females all of the same patrilineage and all living in one village plus the wives of the former. Neither of these terms has an exact equivalent in Kachin. A Kachin may speak of his family as *nta masha* ('people of the house'), while the extended family is covered by such elaborations as *nu wa ni nau ni hpu ni yawng*—'mothers, fathers, younger brothers and sisters, elder brothers all'. The Kachin word *htinggaw*—a 'household'—can have either meaning. Literally it means 'the people under one roof'; a man who gets married *htinggaw rawn*—'extends the roof'.   *Htinggaw gade nga a ta?* can mean 'how many individual families are there?'   But usually *htinggaw* seems to mean 'the people who worship the same set of household spirits'.   In this latter sense. it may indeed imply a single household, but it may cover several houses standing close together in which the men are all of the same patrilineage, or it may even include houses in several entirely different localities.   The distinction will depend simply upon whether the ritual of 'splitting the lineage' by dividing the household shrine regalia (*nat htawt daw*) has or has not been completed.

In Chapter IV I have referred to *htinggaw* as if it were equivalent to what anthropologists mean by a localised patrilineage of small span.   The use of *htinggaw* in this latter sense is explained below.

amyu, lakung, dap, htinggaw—'a lineage', 'a clan'

A Kachin will usually talk about a local group of kinsfolk from its lineage rather than from its family aspect.   Both sexes acquire patronymic surnames which they retain throughout life.[31]   Persons of the same surname are therefore of the same patrilineage.   The lineage system, however, is segmentary and any individual is entitled to be known by several different surnames.   The different surnames denote lineages of differing span.   For example, the lineage Hpunrau is a segment of a larger lineage Layawng which is a segment of a larger lineage Kadaw which is a segment of a major clan Lahtaw.   Hence an individual entitled to call himself Hpunrau Tang could equally well call himself Layawng Tang, Kadaw Tang or Lahtaw Tang.   Similarly the headman of Laga village in Hpalang who, to avoid confusion, was referred to in Chapter IV as Laga Naw was, in point of fact, usually known as NhKum Naw, Laga being a lineage of the NhKum clan.

People of the same lineage, whatever the scale, may be described as 'brothers' (*kahpu-kanau ni*), or as of the same 'sort' (*amyu*), or of the same 'branch' (*lakung*), or of the same 'hearth'

---

[31] The early Kachin literature contains an assertion that women change their clan affiliation on marriage.   Though erroneous, this statement has several times been repeated.   True, a woman N'Du Kai who marries Htingnan Tang will thereafter be known as Htingnan Jan (Mrs. Htingnan) but she does not on that account cease to be N'Du Kai.

(*dap*). These words, however, are used interchangeably and one cannot distinguish consistently the degree of segmentation by such expressions as 'maximal lineage', 'medial lineage', 'minimal lineage' and the like.   Nor is there any clear distinction between exogamous and non-exogamous levels of segmentation.   There is certainly a theory of clan and lineage exogamy and at the lowest levels of lineage segmentation this is rigidly applied, but it is not difficult to arrange a marriage with someone of the same clan provided there is no common male line ancestor within the last five or six generations.   Finally, one cannot distinguish between actual and putative descent. Every Kachin chief is prepared to trace his descent back to Ninggawn Wa, the Creator.   To do this some groups are prepared to put forward genealogies of forty or more generations. It is quite impossible to assert at what point such descent lines become purely fictional.

My own point of view is that Kachin genealogies are maintained almost exclusively for structural reasons and have no value at all as evidence of historical fact.   Commoners are only interested in genealogy as a means of establishing correct relations with their immediate neighbours in the same community; the genealogies of commoners are consequently usually quite short, four or five remembered generations at the most. Chiefs on the other hand are concerned to establish their legitimacy as members of a 'youngest son lineage' and also to establish their seniority relative to other chiefs over a wide area. In the heart of the Kachin Area (e.g. the Triangle) the political associations of an important chief can be very numerous, consequently chiefly genealogies in this region are extremely long; in fringe areas such as North Hsenwi and the Hukawn Valley, a chief's Jinghpaw political associates are fewer in number and his genealogy correspondingly less extensive.[32]

Other writers have argued that the relative shortness of Kachin chiefly genealogies in the 'fringe' areas is evidence for the theory that Kachin culture has only recently spread into these zones,[33] but it seems to me that all Kachin genealogies must be regarded as equally fictional.   Undoubtedly they have

[32] The suggestion that genealogy may represent structural distance rather than historical time was, I think, first expressly made by Evans-Pritchard (1939).
[33] Enriquez (1923), p. 240.

some historical content but no one can say how much or how little.

I use the word *clan* to denote a lineage (*amyu*) of maximal scale. The Kachins themselves undoubtedly tend to think of their total society as being composed of some seven or eight major groupings of this type.[34] Every ordinary local lineage (*htinggaw*) is felt to be affiliated in one way or another to one or other of these major groupings. This applies even to Lisu and Chinese households when they live in a Kachin community. A Kachin 'clan' is therefore a patrilineage which is not thought of as being a segment of any other patrilineage of greater depth or span. I use 'lineage' for all other grades of *amyu*, i.e. for all segments of clans or segments of lineages whatever their scale. Such lineages are *not* necessarily exogamous.

The smallest type of lineage is the group which shares a common 'household name' (*htinggaw amying*) by virtue of the fact that its members worship the same set of household ancestor spirits (see p. 110 above). At this 'household name level' the lineage is very definitely exogamous. An individual would normally be personally acquainted with all others of the same 'household name'. Relatively speaking, it is a localised, corporate group, identified with one particular village.

The fact that lineages other than those of narrow span are not exogamous makes the affiliation of lineages to clans a rather arbitrary matter. It is not uncommon to find persons with the same lineage name living in different communities who claim to be members of different clans. This may sometimes be due to the accident that the same lineage name has come into use independently on two different occasions, but more often I think the explanation is simply that the ordinary commoner is only interested in his *local* lineage (*htinggaw*). He does not much care whether that lineage is or is not affiliated to any particular major clan.

What is at first sight more surprising is that the clan affiliation of chiefly lineages of the highest standing can also be in

---

[34] Marip, Lahpai, Lahtaw, NhKum, Maran, Kareng, Hpauwi, Tsasen are the names usually given. The first five of these are generally regarded as being of superior status, and are recognised throughout the Kachin Hills Area but views as to the names and status of minor clans differ widely. In this book I write NhKum for N'hKum.

doubt. Thus I believe that the Mashaw chiefs of the Triangle regard themselves as of Marip clan and 'youngest son' (*uma*) Marip at that, but Kawlu Ma Nawng seems to regard them as NhKum clan,[35] and I have heard them described as Lahtaw clan. Numerous similar instances could be cited. There is no right or wrong in such matters. If at the present time the Mashaw chiefs say they are Marip and their fellow Marip chiefs accept them as such, then clearly they are *at present* Marip, but that does not mean they have always been Marip in the past, or will always be Marip in the future.

It seems to me likely that, over the years, the network of lineage affiliations gets considerably reshuffled, but this is difficult to prove. It so happens that we have fairly detailed accounts of the principal lineages of the Tsasen clan as they stood in 1835[36] and as they were in 1940.[37] The discrepancies are considerable but this is not conclusive evidence of change since Hannay in 1835 may have been misled as to the facts. The operative factor seems to be that when a particular lineage acquires influence, relationship with that lineage becomes advantageous. Then, if the clan affiliation is at all vague, a number of rival versions may become current, any one of which has as much validity as any other. There is no *correct* version.

A matter of great structural importance but for which I can only provide hearsay evidence is the procedure adopted for splitting a 'royal' lineage. Commoners, I fancy, hardly bother about this. A commoner household which moves to a new village automatically becomes the potential nucleus of a new local lineage of *htinggaw* scale. For thigh-eating chiefs things are much more complicated.

The chief's political authority is based, ideologically, on his ability to preserve the prosperity of his domain by making sacrifices to the sky spirit, Madai, and to the earth spirit Shadip. He has this ability by virtue of his descent from a remote clan ancestor who married a female sky spirit—usually a daughter of Madai.[38] This ritual power is inherited automatically only by the youngest son of a thigh-eating chief. It can pass to

[35] Kawlu Ma Nawng (1942), p. 3.
[36] Hannay (1847); Mackenzie (1884), p. 62.
[37] Kawlu Ma Nawng (1942).   [38] See Chapter IX.

another line—say that of the eldest son—only if the eldest son makes a ritual purchase from the youngest son.   Assuming that this is agreed upon, the division of ritual powers constitutes a splitting of the royal lineage.   It is said to be accomplished in the following manner.[39]

The *nat htawt* (liquor tubes) of the ancestor spirit have already been mentioned.   They are kept in the roof above the ancestral shrine.   The two brothers who have agreed to divide their ritual powers between them are supposed to take these tubes to the house of the *uma du* (senior chief) of their lineage —who may live far away.   Having arrived there, and evidence having been produced that the correct gifts from elder brother to younger brother and vice versa have been exchanged, a religious ritual is performed at the shrine of the *uma nat*—the ancestral spirit of the lineage whose first home is in the house of the *uma du*.   The outcome of this ritual is that the two original liquor tubes which the brothers have brought with them are split (*daw*) into halves and are replaced by four new tubes, two of which are given to the elder brother and two to the younger.   The wives of the two brothers then carry back their tubes to their respective houses.   The tubes are carried on the back wrapped up in a silk shawl as one might carry a baby.   The elder brother and the younger brother can now both claim the status of thigh-eating chief.   The *nat htawt* tubes must be carefully preserved.   The symbolism of the whole performance is extremely plain.   The ceremony amounts to a public recognition of the equivalent status of the two newly constituted lineages.

Even at the end of all this, however, the ritual status of the youngest son chief and his descendants is deemed to be higher than that of the eldest son chief and his descendants.   Moreover it is the youngest son chief who 'stays put' on the originally chiefly domain while the eldest son chief has to go off and be a chief somewhere else.   If one accepts this construction of how lineages are supposed to segment it follows that where today we find any royal lineage *d* associated with a locality *D*, it is likely to have segmented in the past from a lineage *c* associated

---

[39] This account was given to me by a chief of high status from the Triangle area; Gilhodes (1922), pp. 280–2, gives a similar account derived from a Gauri informant. Evidently there is a clear stereotype of what constitutes orthodox procedure.

with a locality *C* which in turn segmented from lineage *b* associated with a locality *B* and so on until lineage *a* is one or other of the eight primary clans already mentioned.

It follows that if the lineage members of *d* admit that their lineage is a segment of *c*, they also admit that the lineage head of *c* who still lives at *C* is their superior in rank.

To take an example. All members of the Hpunrau lineage recognise that they are a section of the Layawn lineage; they therefore recognise the chief of Layawn Ga as their overlord so far as lineage affairs are concerned. But the Layawn are

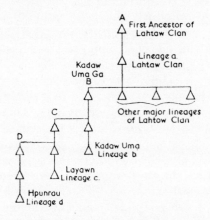

Fig. 3. Diagram to show theory of lineage segmentation and the senior status of the *uma du*.

a segment of Kadaw and on some matters the Layawn chief will have to refer to the head of the Kadaw lineage who lives far away at Kadaw Uma Ga in the central Triangle. The Kadaw, being a segment of the Lahtaw clan, ought of course to pay deference to the senior chief of the whole clan, but in fact there is no such chief. Instead there are a half-dozen or so senior Lahtaw lineages each of which claims to be superior to all the others; Kadaw is one of these.

This deference to lineage heads who reside at a distance applies almost exclusively to members of chiefly and aristocratic lineages but is of considerable importance in the total 'balance of power'. As we have already seen, the headman of a village is normally of aristocratic (*ma gam amyu*) rank (see

p. 83).   In most matters his political obligations are towards his domain chief (*mung duwa*) who is usually of quite different clan to himself.   His obligations towards this domain chief are essentially the dues of a feudal tenant towards his Lord of the Manor.[40]   But in addition, where lineage matters are concerned, the village headman owes deference not to his own territorial chief but to the *uma du* who is head of the youngest son branch of his own lineage, and through him to one or more further *uma du*, geographically even more remote.   The retention of lineage affiliations thus serves as a check upon the powers of the local territorial chief.

The practical authority which the ultimate senior lineage head (*uma da*) can in fact exercise over the scattered junior branches of his lineage is certainly extremely slight, but the notion that this kind of hierarchy exists fosters a sense of what might perhaps be called 'tribal solidarity' among the totality of the Kachin population.   An important theoretical function of a lineage head is that of arbitrator.   Disputes between persons who are members of different local lineages but of the same senior lineage should properly be referred to the head of the senior lineage which embraces both parties.   It seems doubtful whether this ever happens at the present time and I have no data on how far it really happened in the past.

In defining a village (p. 114) I described the headman as head of the principal lineage (p. 116).   Such lineages are corporate localised lineages in the sense here implied, and the members of such a lineage will all have the same 'household name'.   That, however, does not exclude the possibility that there may be one or more scattered households in other localities having the same household name, but settled for one reason or another in a foreign country.

bu ni—'villagers'

The importance of this category is that it cuts across all kinship rivalries and denotes explicitly loyalty to a place and not to a lineage.   The village cluster of Hpalang was in 1940 split into factions of the most diverse kind but all the inhabitants alike claimed to be *Hpalang bu ni*—Hpalang villagers—and spoke of Hpalang as their *bu ga*—'home land'.   Normally all

[40] Leach (1952), p. 41.

those who recognise themselves as *bu ni* of the same locality will share a common *numshang* (sacred grove) and will thus participate in the same ritual offerings to the local earth spirit, but this is not invariably the case.   It was not so, for example, at Hpalang. *Bu ni* as an aggregate of persons is the counterpart of *mare* (village cluster) as a category of place.

> *Informal groupings and categories*
> *mani*—'children'; *shabrang ni*—'youths';
> *mahkawn ni*—'maidens'; *madu ni*—'married couples';
> *ga ni*—'labourers'

From the point of view of structural analysis the most significant types of grouping in Kachin society are certainly the lineage and locality categories I have now described, together with 'class' categories considered below (p. 162).   Paradoxically groups of this kind play little part in ordinary day to day affairs though they become prominent at every formal ritual occasion.

The informal groups which are listed in this section cut across both kin group and locality affiliations.   They are based mainly on age.   Kachins have no formalised system of age grading such as occurs in some of the Naga groups.[41]   Children start learning their household crafts from a very early age, but they are not at first distinguished into separate social categories. They are simply children (*mani*).   As they attain an age approaching puberty (*sek*) they begin to separate out as youths (*shabrang ni*) and maidens (*mahkawn ni*).   By the time they have reached puberty (*ram*) youth and maiden are regularly sleeping together, but courtship and flirtation is carried on in groups rather than by individuals.   A youth of sixteen or so spends most of his time in the company of an informal gang of four or five of his male age mates not necessarily all from one village. They work together as a team in the fields or on tasks like housebuilding, and in the evenings meet their girl friends for sing song and flirtation (*nchyun ga*) at some prearranged rendezvous.   Once he has attained puberty a young man seldom sleeps at home (see p. 111: *nla dap*).

These groups of young men have no formal organisation, but the corresponding groups of young women are to some extent

[41] e.g. the Ao.   See Mills (1926).

organised. The moon is regarded as a female *nat* who looks after the welfare of young women and there is a rite at which only women can be present at which the 'moon maiden' (*shata mahkawn*) is invoked. How far older women participate in or organise such seances is not known to me.

Young men are mostly married by the time they are 20; young women somewhat earlier. At marriage both sexes attain the status of full adults. The youth becomes simply a man, *la*; the maiden a woman, *num*. For the married there is no informal, sex-based grouping corresponding to that of the youths and maidens. On marriage husband and wife become householders—they are the 'owners' or 'lords' (*madu ni*) of their house.

It is, I think, worth remarking that the householder 'owns' his house in the same sense as a chief (*duwa*) 'owns' his domain (*mung*). The verb *madu ai* serves in both contexts.

Changes in social status such as these are indicated mainly by changes of dress. Boys do not go through any form of ritual initiation but when a lad begins regularly to carry a sword (*nhtu*) and bag (*nhpye*) he expects to be treated as a youth rather than a child. Thereafter these two items of personal equipment will scarcely ever be out of arms reach. There is no difference in the attire of a youth and that of a young married man. As he gets older he will take increasing pride in his skill at handling his sword—which is a general purpose tool serving equally well for felling trees and paring finger-nails; elders of the community (*myit su ni*) can usually be distinguished by the fact that they carry a sword of particularly fine quality.

Women's dress is distinctively Kachin and varies in different parts of the country, but everywhere hair style betrays a Kachin woman's social status. As a maiden she has her head bare with her hair cut in a bob. At marriage she assumes a turban; in old age she wears a turban of outsize dimensions.

The categories of persons I have listed here, namely the children, the youths, the maidens, the married men, the married women, the old men, the old women are the categories among which labour tasks are allocated.

For example at a housebuilding, youths do the thatching, maidens fetch the thatch, married women prepare the beer, married men fetch the wood and bamboo, old men sit splitting bamboo to make tie cords (*pali*), while the old women carry on with their usual tasks of looking after the pigs and the geese and the chickens. And so it is with all activities which call for organised team work. Labour teams may be variously constituted but tasks are always allocated according to age status.

Most ordinary economic activities are carried out by individuals acting simply as members of their own individual households. Outside the field of religious ritual there are few technical tasks that call for a professional specialist. Communal labour, however, is employed for certain set types of task, particularly housebuilding and sowing. The labour is then recruited from married and unmarried alike; the labourers are referred to as *ga ni*. The principle is that the householder hiring the labour supplies beer and food but does no work himself. In hiring labour in this way the hirer incurs a debt of one day's labour towards each of his labourers. Such debts are normally worked off on a reciprocal basis during the course of the year. Labourers are not necessarily kinsmen or near neighbours of the hirer. A chief or a village headman acting in his official capacity can call on his followers to supply labour for certain communal purposes without incurring any obligation to repay the debt—such purposes include the clearing of paths and the clearing and fencing of the annual village rice field (*yin wa*). The chief can also summon labour to carry out free services for himself. Thus the chief's field hut is built and his field sown as a communal duty and not as part of a system of reciprocal labour service.

The generalisations I have made here apply equally to *gumsa* and *gumlao* Kachins and the great majority of them apply also to Shans. The transition from childhood to adolescence is more formal for a Shan than for a Kachin. It is normally marked by a period of residence in a Buddhist monastery in the status of monk novitiate and by the assumption of elaborate tattooing on the thighs.[42]

Among the Chinese Shans age status is further formalised by a system of ceremonials of the Feast of Merit type.[43] This

---

[42] Milne and Cochrane (1910), pp. 54, 66. Both practices are now much less regularly observed than in the past. Burmese custom was similar.

[43] See T'ien (1949).

increased formalism attached to age status in Shan society correlates with a relative absence of emphasis upon lineage.

IV

Concepts of Affinal Relationship and Incest

mayu-dama—'affinal relationship'

The meaning of this fundamental Kachin concept has already been discussed at some length in Chapter IV and also in two previous publications.[44]   Here I need only to recapitulate the main argument.

When a marriage has occurred *mayu* denotes the relationship of the wife's lineage to that of the husband, *dama* denotes the relationship of the husband's lineage to that of the wife.

The rule of exogamy is that, at the *htinggaw* level of lineage, a man shall not marry into his own lineage or that of his *dama*; a woman shall not marry into her own lineage or that of her *mayu*.   There is a preferred marriage for a man to marry into his *mayu* and for a woman to marry into her *dama*.

The following points need to be emphasised:

a. The *mayu-dama* relationship is one between lineages rather than individuals.

b. It is thought of as a persisting institution.   One marriage gives the *dama* the right to open negotiations for another one, and they are expected to do so, indeed they can be penalised if they do not.

c. If *mayu* and *dama* are of different social class, *mayu* almost certainly rank the higher within any one village.

d. Within a local community lineages of lower social class tend to be related affinally to those of higher social class.   Those of higher social class being *mayu*.

e. In some communities three or more lineages may be linked in a formal circle—*hkau wang hku* ('cousin circle path').   The existence of a closed circle of marriage arrangements such that e.g. A are *mayu* to B who are *mayu* to C who are *mayu* to A always implies that all the lineages in this circle are of the same social class, and, very probably, have common political interests.

[44] Leach (1945), (1952).

Concepts of Incest and Illicit Sex Relations

a. *jaiwawng*—sex relations between a man and a woman of his own lineage (*moi, na, nau* or *sha*) or with a woman of his *dama* lineage (*hkri*).[45]

b. *shut hpyit*—sex relations with a female *mayu* relative of superior status, e.g. *nu* (mother), *rat* (elder brother's wife).

c. *num shaw*—adultery with a married woman, the husband not being a lineage brother or a *dama* relative of the adulterer.

Kachins distinguish several varieties of heterosexual offence, the main distinction being between adultery with a married woman (*num shaw, num shut, shut hpyit*) and sex relations with an unmarried woman excluded by rules of exogamy—i.e. an unmarried woman of the *hpu-nau* or *dama* categories. *Jaiwawng*, the dictionary term for 'incest', seems properly to apply only to the latter type of offence. *Jaiwawng* would thus include sex relations between a man and his sister and between a man and his daughter, but relations between a son and his own mother would be classed, I think, as *shut hpyit*. As I understand the position, offences classed as *shut hpyit* are of a sacrilegious nature, they constitute an outrage to morals rather than a legal offence. Thus in a wartime case where Japanese soldiery were alleged to have destroyed a village and assaulted the women, the unmarried girls were said to have been 'raped' (*roi*), while the married women and the widows had been 'outraged' (*shut hpyit*). Both terms can mean 'to insult' but *hpyit* seems to associate with *hpyi*—'a witch'.[46] *Shut hpyit* in the sense of adultery with a *mayu* relative of senior status cannot result in legal penalties (*hka*—'debts')[47] because the offended husband is by definition of the same lineage as the adulterer. Ideologically the sanction against this type of offence is supernatural punishment of the witchcraft type. I have no case histories of how Kachins actually react in this type of situation. Offences classed as *num shaw* ('common adultery') are ordinary civil offences. Here the adulterer is not closely related to either the woman or her husband, and the adultery establishes a 'debt' between the two males which must be worked out by feud or compensation.

[45] See Appendix IV.   [46] See pp. 179 f.
[47] See pp. 144 f.

Jaiwawng is conceptually an offence of quite a different kind. It may be translated as 'sex relations between two individuals who stand in such a relation that if the girl were to marry the man as her first husband it would be a breach of the ordinary rules of exogamy'. These formal rules of exogamy are that a man shall not marry a woman born of his own lineage—e.g. *moi*—'father's sister', *na*—'elder sister', *nau*—'younger sister', *sha*—'daughter', or a woman born of a *dama* lineage, *hkri*. The formal rules, however, are frequently broken. Classificatory 'brothers' and 'sisters' who are in *lawu-lahta* status[48] frequently marry. Marriages between classificatory 'father's sister's daughter' (*hkri*) and classificatory 'mother's brother's son' (*tsa*) also occur although in theory such relationship is incestuous (*jaiwawng*). The rule in this case is linked up with the residence pattern. Within any one community there is likely to be a status difference between any two households in *mayu-dama* relationship; the ban on marriage between *tsa* and *hkri* avoids the incompatible obligations that must result if a man were simultaneously *mayu* and *dama* to the same household. Kachin, especially Jinghpaw, society as it at present exists simply could not function at all if the *mayu* and *dama* relatives among a man's near neighbours were not clearly distinguished. A marriage between a *tsa* and a *hkri* who come from the same local community is thus intolerable. But as far as affinal relationships outside the local community are concerned, the rules are much less stringent. It does not really matter much if some geographically remote *dama* relatives are suddenly switched over into the status of *mayu*.

So much for exogamy; the theory and practice of what is allowable in the way of extra-marital sex relations is even more vaguely defined. In theory a man should not sleep with a girl whom he is prohibited to marry, yet unquestionably many men do so without getting into serious trouble. In flirtatious poetry of the kind called *nchyun ga*[49] it is normal for lovers to address one another as *hkri* and *tsa*. Although, in the context of the poem, this is partly mockery, there is no reason to suppose that the titles are always inappropriate. It is, I think, considered rather smart to have an affair with a forbidden relative of this category; there is added spice in what is formally for-

[48] See p. 74.   [49] Hanson (1906), p. xxvii.

bidden; a love-affair with a girl of the marriageable category (*nam*) who has anyway to pay respect to her prospective husbands is hardly worth while.[50]

But young people are allowed so much freedom in their sexual affairs that the parents have little chance of enforcing the formal rules.   If anyone looks after a girl's morals it will be her unmarried elder brother, and if he is on good terms with her lover (who is probably his *hkau*) she is not likely to suffer many restrictions.   Unless and until the girl becomes pregnant, 'incest' (*jaiwawng*) creates no legal debts.   If a girl does become pregnant by her *tsa* then the ensuing 'pregnancy debt' (*sumrai hka*) is doubly heinous and is known as a *mayu hka*. It may easily blow up into a serious feud or.involve accusations of witchcraft.   The Maran version of the origin of the Hpalang feud[51] turns on this point.   The fact that the child was (allegedly) 'harelipped' was proof that the *tsa* (the Lahpai chief's son) had brought witchcraft on to his *hkri* (the Maran chief's daughter).   As a matter of fact one of the reasons most commonly given by Kachins in explanation of the ban on marriage between *tsa* and *hkri* is that such unions result only in stillborn or malformed children.[52]   The English theory that marriage between first cousins results in mentally defective offspring is very similar.

While the *jaiwawng* concept is most frequently invoked with reference to sex relations between *tsa* and *hkri* the term also applies to sex relations between siblings of opposite sex. Kachins would certainly regard sex relations between true siblings or closely related lineage relatives with the strongest disapproval.   I have no data as to whether scandals of this nature are frequent or as to the nature of the expected public reaction.   If the sibling relationship is distant so that the relationship is one that falls into the *lawu-lahta* category the incest is purely theoretical.

Formally speaking, the heterosexual relations between the younger members of a household fall into several distinct categories all of which are illicit.

[50] One might compare the Kachin romantic ideal of having affairs with the forbidden *hkri* with the ideal of 'courtly love' in medieval Europe, where the loved one was always another man's wife.   See Lewis (1936), Chapter 1.

[51] See p. 89.

[52] Sema Naga theory is exactly comparable; see Hutton (1921), (b) p. 131.

1. *hpu-nau*—'elder brother—younger sister'. The elder brother has the role of guardian of his younger sister's morals in the sense of seeing that she does not carry her affairs beyond the (very elastic) limits of Kachin propriety. The *nla dap* institution[53] implies that a girl conducts her love-affairs with considerable publicity. This perhaps to some extent acts as a safeguard against incest between close siblings, but I have no real evidence on this point.

2. *na-nau*—'elder sister—younger brother'. It is probably significant that the same phoneme *na* which means 'elder sister' also means 'remote in time', 'disease', 'tabooed holiday'. The elder sister is a tabooed person with the power to curse. Many anthropological parallels come to mind immediately.[54] But though the formally correct behaviour towards an elder sister may be one of respect bordering on avoidance the nature of the real relationship seems to depend very much upon individual temperament and the respective ages of the parties. *Na* are usually married and living elsewhere by the time a young man starts having love-affairs, so tacit avoidance is not difficult.

3. *rat-rat*—'elder brother's wife—husband's younger brother'. Sex relations in this case would be adulterous (*shut hpyit*) rather than incestuous (*jaiwawng*) but I am far from clear how Kachins deal with such situations when they arise. If a husband is away for a long period Kachins do not expect the wife to maintain an onerous chastity. The husband's brother is then the proper substitute bedfellow, but what happens when a brother exceeds his rights in such matters I do not know. It needs to be remembered that Kachins practice the levirate and a man's widow or widows will ordinarily be taken over as wife by a lineage brother or son. A man may therefore ultimately become husband to his *rat*.

4. *gu-nam* — 'husband's elder brother — younger brother's wife'. Terminologically speaking this relationship is the same as that between a man and his potential spouse (e.g. 'mother's brother's daughter' (younger than Ego)). In theory, I fancy, the husband's elder brother (*gu*) can take much greater liberties with his sister-in-law than can the husband's younger brother (*rat*). What this difference amounts to in real life I cannot say.

[53] See p. 111.   [54] Firth (1936), pp. 222 f.

V

Concepts of Property and Ownership

The concepts which are discussed in the present section are of the utmost importance for my general argument, for they provide the categories in terms of which social relations are linked with economic facts. In the last analysis the power relations in any society must be based upon the control of real goods and the primary sources of production, but this Marxist generalisation does not carry us very far. The way in which particular goods and services are evaluated one against another is a cultural phenomenon which cannot be deduced from first principles.

An anthropologist perceives a social system as a structure of persisting relations between persons and groups of persons; objectively these 'relations' are rights and obligations over things and individuals. The Kachin word *hka* which is normally translated as 'debt', contains aspects of meaning which correspond closely to this abstract notion of sociological relation. When a Kachin talks about the 'debts' which he owes and which are due to himself, he is talking about what an anthropologist means by 'social structure'. What follows should make this clear.

sut—'wealth'

Kachins, along with most of their neighbours, distinguish and even contrast two aspects of 'ownership'. Sovereignty, that is to say the rights of a ruler, is expressed by the word *madu*. A chief owns (*madu*) his domain in the sense that he is the final authority, there is no one higher. Similarly the house-holder is owner (*madu wa*) in respect to his house. But usufruct, that is the right 'to make use of and to enjoy for the time being' is expressed by *lu* (to drink)[55] and *sha* (to eat). Thus to 'eat

[55] Of the numerous possible meanings of *lu*, 'to drink' seems to me primary. If I drink a thing, I enjoy it, I 'have' it.   If I have the doing of a thing, I 'can' do it, or I 'must' do it.   If I drink a thing to excess, I 'exhaust' it, I 'ruin' it, I 'steal' it.   Hence paradoxically *u lu ai wa* is 'a man who possesses chickens', but *u lu lu ai wa* is 'a man who steals chickens'! The individual who is in physical possession of a thing, who has it and 'drinks' (*lu*) it, may also own (*madu*) it in a more absolute sense, but frequently this is not the case. Although a speaker may make a tonal distinction between *lu*—'to drink' and *u*—'to have', I don't think we are dealing here with two different words.

a hill field' (*yi sha*) means simply to make a livelihood by cultivating a hill field.

This kind of thinking is not peculiar to Kachins but is shared also by Shans and Burmese. Thus in pre-British Burma the *myo-sa* ('the eater of the township') was an individual who enjoyed the fruits of taxation at the King's pleasure. He did not on that account necessarily have sovereignty over the territory in question. The most typical *myo-sa* were the King's own supernumerary wives;[56] they enjoyed the fruits of the territory, they did not rule it.

This distinction between owning in the sense of 'having, and therefore being able to enjoy for the time being' (*lu, sha*), and owning in the sense of 'having rights over something or some person' (*madu*) has many ramifications. A very significant example is:

hka madu ai wa: the owner of a debt—the *petitioner* in a lawsuit (i.e. he who has rights over someone or something).

hka lu ai wa: the owner of a debt—the *defendant* in a lawsuit (i.e. he who has whatever is in dispute, enjoys it for the time being but owes it to someone else).

It is this link-up between notions of legal process and concepts of rights over property which I now want to pursue in some detail.

Kachins do not look upon movable property as capital for investment, they regard it rather as an adornment to the person. The word *sut* which is used to denote riches can also be used adjectivally to mean 'smart' in the sense of 'a smart coat'. Wealth objects other than ordinary perishable foodstuffs have value primarily as items of display. The best way to acquire notoriety as the owner (ruler) of an object is publicly to give possession of it to someone else. The recipient, it is true, then has the object, but you retain sovereignty over it since you make yourself the owner (*madu*) of a debt.[57] In sum, the possessor of wealth objects gains merit and prestige

[56] Scott and Hardiman, Part I, Vol. II, p. 89: 'These minor ladies were called *myo sa* or *ywa-sa mibuya* (i.e. town eating or village eating queens) according to the towns or villages assigned to them as pin money by His Majesty.' King Mindon had at least 45 such queens, 'probably there were a good many more'.

[57] Kachins make a nice distinction between *myit madu kumhpa*, 'mind ruling gifts' and *lata madu kumhpa*, 'hand ruling gifts'. The former are economically useless objects which nevertheless put the recipient under an obligation to the giver.

mainly through the publicity he achieves in getting rid of them.

This explains the fact that among Kachins, as indeed in most societies, the ritual value of wealth objects often seems inversely proportional to their practical utility. Swords (*nhtu*) and spears (*ri*) are objects of everyday use in Kachin society, but the swords and spears which count as ritual wealth objects (*hpaga*) in the settlement of a legal dispute are seldom genuine weapons; they are far more likely to be exotically shaped blunt-edged models of no practical utility. So too the athletic challenge cups of our own society seldom even approximate to a practical drinking mug.

In practice, Kachins distinguish fairly consistently between three types of movable property (*sut*):

a. Ordinary perishable foodstuffs (shahpa) *and forest products.*

Goods of this kind are the object of trade (*hpaga*), that is of speculative buying and selling. They may form part of the tributary dues from a political inferior to a superior but they are not ordinarily used in ritual exchanges between equals. Thus they do not constitute items in a bride price, nor are they likely to be used as compensation in the settlement of a legal offence.

b. Livestock, especially cattle (nga).

Four types of livestock are commonly met with in a Kachin village, namely water buffalo, humped cattle, pigs and chickens. The cattle may be used sometimes for ploughing or for pack transport but the anticipated destiny of all such animals is to provide meat for a sacrificial feast. Livestock are usually the most important item in any ritual exchange but they never stand alone. For example, the bride price of a well-to-do commoner might be 4 cattle, plus a substantial list of other items (*hpaga*) such as gongs, swords, spears, cooking pots, coats, blankets. It is, however, the cattle that set the value of the bride price and such a man would normally simply say that the price was '4 cattle' (*nga mali*) without specifying the other items.

In the stereotyped traditional lists which record the 'correct' gifts to be given in specified ritual and legal situations, the only animal mentioned is the water buffalo (*uloi*). Other kinds of animal have no proper ritual status. Pigs and chickens and humped cattle are regularly used for sacrifice but only for offerings to minor deities. Sacrifices to the Madai nat, as controller of wealth, should always be buffalo. Consequently, it is the ownership of buffalo rather than any other single factor which is the mark of a rich man (*sut lu ai wa*).[58]

c. Goods and objects used in ritual exchanges other than livestock.

Roughly speaking these are non-perishable valuables of certain traditional types which are listed below.   When used as items of ritual exchange (*hpaga*) the *number* of objects is usually more important than the quality.   In classifying *hpaga*, a Kachin distinguishes large gongs from small ones and breech-loading guns from muzzle loaders, but the fact that a gong is cracked or a gun rusty and unusable does not necessarily reduce its value as an item of exchange.   The value of *hpaga* in this context is definitely not the ordinary economic value of the open market.

The distinction between these three categories is not absolute because the notion of *hpaga*, in the sense of 'ritual wealth object', includes, not only all the items in category *c*, but also the water buffalo in category *b* and certain items (such as opium, slaves and bullion) which in the past were extensively traded on the open market under category *a*.   It is not true therefore to assert that ritual wealth objects have no ordinary commercial value.   What is true is that some types of ritual wealth object have no ordinary commercial value, and that the value of a wealth object used in ritual exchanges is not in any case wholly determined by its ordinary commercial value in the open market.

I have already used the term *hpaga* in the double sense of 'trade' and 'ritual wealth object'.   To explain this concept further we must discuss it in asociation with another very important Kachin notion, that of *hka* (debt).

hpaga—'trade'; 'ritual wealth object'

hka—'debt'

Almost any kind of legal obligation that exists between two Kachins is likely to be described as a debt (*hka*).   If one pursues the matter further and tries to discover what this 'debt' really implies, one's informant will probably convert it into a list of so and so many *hpaga*.

At first sight this does not seem very difficult.   The statement

---

[58] In the extreme north in the Nung country mithan take the place of buffalo in this respect.   In the south riding ponies rate as orthodox *hpaga*; they are not sacrificed.

that the penalty for getting an unmarried woman with child is a fine of 8 *hpaga* suggests that *hpaga* denotes a currency. But the fine in question bears little resemblance to a cash fine of 8 shillings or 8 pounds. The 8 *hpaga* are not interchangeable; in detail they are:

1. a calf 'small enough to enter the pig pen'
2. one gong
3. one paso (a length of Burmese silk)
4. one small iron cooking pot
5. one sword
6. one necklace—to 'wash the woman's face'
7. one paso—'in which to wrap the child'
8. one cow buffalo—'for the milk for the child'

Items 1–5 go to the girl's parents; 6, 7 and 8 go to the girl herself and are only paid if the child is claimed as a member of the father's lineage.[59]

When such a matter is being brought to settlement the principals do not appear; the argument is carried on by agents (*kasa*). The agents arrive on the scene equipped with bundles of small bamboo tally sticks which they proceed to lay out on the ground as 'representing' the various *hpaga*—this large stick represents a buffalo, that little one over there is a calf and so on. Then the bargaining begins. Items are substituted. Everyone knows that the defendant in the case cannot really produce a buffalo for *hpaga* no. 8. In the end the agents may settle for a pig. The pig in question is then 'the pig that is substitute for a buffalo' (*uloi sang ai wa*); it is still represented by the original large tally stick, and in reckoning out the settlement it is counted as if it were actually a buffalo. The doctrine that pigs do not rate as ritual wealth objects is not infringed.

This is all rather confusing and we had better go back and consider the verbal concepts.

The word roots *ga* (*ka*) and *hka* differ only by an aspirate and over a considerable range of meanings the two terms appear to be related. *Ga* is the static impermeable fact, *hka* the active fluid principle that emerges from the fact. For example:

ga is the dry cracked earth: *hka* is water from the spring
mam ka is dry paddy: *sahka* is cooked food

[59] Kawlu Ma Nawng (1942), p. 62.

The relationship between *hpaga* the material fact, and *hka* the immaterial debt is rather similar.

In one sense *hpaga* simply means trade. This use perhaps derives from the method of recording trading transactions. In the less sophisticated areas, away from Shan markets, a travelling trader has his regular partners with each of whom he runs a credit account. Debts (*hka*) are recorded by making notches (*hka*) in a tally stick of bamboo which is then split in half (*ga*), each partner retaining one half as a record. What is peculiar, and to a European very confusing, about this system is that each notch represents a particular transaction (*hpaga*) and is not equivalent to any other notch. For example, in the case of a complicated affair between a Chinese trader and a Lisu in the Nam Tamai country in 1943, the notches represented respectively:

a. 2 goats
b. one piece of cotton cloth
c. one jar of liquor
d. one cow
e. 6 viss of *numrin*
f. 7 viss of *numrin*
g. 6 rupees cash
h. a quill full of gold dust

The settlement of this set of debts took the best part of a day. The problem of how to equate viss of *numrin*[60] with goats and cows was eventually solved but at no point was there any attempt to reduce all values to a common medium. Each debt or notch (*hka*) had to be settled on its own merits.

Hpaga may therefore be translated as 'the items which are specified in a statement of claim'. In this instance the 'claim' related to transactions of an ordinary trading type; in the earlier instance it was a 'claim' relating to a civil offence. For the Kachin, legal claims and commercial claims are alike *hka* (debts). The only difference is that with commercial claims the items may be anything, depending on the circumstances of trade, while, with legal claims, the items are stereotyped according to a traditional pattern. Leyden specifies the following types of *hpaga* as traditionally orthodox: (1) a buffalo, (2) a gong (several different types), (3) silver bullion, (4) a slave, (5) a cooking tripod, (6) *n'ba* (several types of shaped cloth which serve as male skirts, blankets and shawls), (7) an iron cooking pot, (8) a sword (usually a dummy blunt edged

---

[60] A root *coptis teeta* used in Chinese medicine.

one), (9) a spear (also usually a dummy), (10) a sheepskin coat, (11) a silver pipe, (12) opium, (13) a Chinese embroidered silk coat, (14) bead necklaces of a special type.[61]

Nowadays a good many other objects are regularly used. Guns and pistols, usable or unusable are always popular and also lengths of silk cloth (*paso*). Ordinary cash frequently appears as a *hpaga* in a settlement but it is always a substitute for some item which circumstances make unobtainable, e.g. a slave, bullion, opium.

As already remarked, a few of these items are sometimes dealt with in the open market but, in the ordinary way, ritual wealth objects of this kind only change hands on certain set occasions. The principal occasions are: (*a*) marriages, (*b*) funerals, (*c*) in payment of ritual services by priests or agents, (*d*) on the occasion of a transfer of residence or the building of a new house, (*e*) as judicial compensation in settlement of any kind of dispute or crime.

The formal payments due on any particular occasion are defined by an agreed tradition.[62]   For each kind of settlement the tradition specifies a number of *hpaga* and gives a title to each *hpaga*.   For example, if a commoner has a claim against another commoner for the theft of a buffalo, the complainant is entitled to

a. the return of his buffalo
b. another buffalo in compensation
c. 3 *hpaga*

The three *hpaga* in this instance are:

i. 'a gong big enough to cover the tracks of the buffalo' (*nga hkang magap bau*)
ii. 'a hundred bead necklace as a halter for the buffalo' (*sumri matu hkachyi latsa*)
iii. 'a sword to clear the path on the way home' (*lam hkyen nhtu*)[63]

It is typical of such titles that they carry a double meaning, referring simultaneously to the context of the offence and to the settlement of the quarrel as such.   Thus in this case *hkang*

---

[61] Kawlu Ma Nawng (1942), pp. iv, 68.
[62] The details of what are the correct *hpaga* for particular types of claim vary somewhat in different districts.
[63] Hertz (1943), p. 154.

is a pun on *hka* and the gong is 'to cover the debt of the buffalo'; *sumri*, a halter, is figuratively a cord of friendship, so the necklace is 'to restore friendship'; *lam hkyen* is not only to clear a path, it is 'to set everything in order'.

In some cases the list of titled *hpaga* is a very long one. The settlement of a chief's blood feud, for example, involves payment of 100 *hpaga* which are memorised in a series of poetic stanzas. Kawlu Ma Nawng gives the full list of *hpaga* but not the poetic titles. The type of symbolism is apparent even in the abbreviated form thus—

1 *hpaga* for the skull—a gong
1 *hpaga* for the spine—a gun
1 *hpaga* for the finger-nails of the left hand—5 cowries
1 *hpaga* for the finger-nails of the right hand—5 cowries and so on.[64]

But although the theoretical form of each *hpaga* is meticulously detailed, greater stress is laid on the number and title of the *hpaga* than on its outward form. The real payment is always a matter for agreement between the parties and here the principle of substitution (*sang ai*) is all important. An item listed as 'for the eyes—2 meteoric stones' sounds very well in poetry but is not easy to fulfil in practice; this item in the final reckoning may turn out to be a couple of beans.

What is of especial importance here is the flexibility of the system. By manipulating the principle of substitution to its limits a poor man owning only a few pigs and chickens, and a rich man owning many buffalo can both appear to conform to the same formal code of gift giving. Although they do not in fact contribute goods of the same economic value, they do, by a fiction, contribute the same *hpaga*.

This is important for our understanding of class differences. In theory, gift obligations are scaled according to class. For example, the theoretical penalty for giving a woman a bastard is

between aristocrats 50 *hpaga*
   ,, commoners 10 ,, (8 in Bhamo district)
   ,, slaves 3 ,,

[64] Kawlu Ma Nawng (1942), pp. 55–7.

In practice the payment depends on the economic standing of the defaulter not on his class status by birth. As we shall see, 'being an aristocrat' is not really a question of being born into the right kind of lineage. What matters is that a man should be able to validate any claim to aristocracy that he may care to make. Now the validation of class status depends more than anything else on an ability to fulfil correctly the gift-giving obligations that are proper to a member of that class. An aristocrat will be accepted as an aristocrat so long as he carries out an aristocrat's obligations. And it is precisely here that the individual is faced with choice.

Tradition sets the standard of what is proper. But the principle of substitution makes it possible for any man to avoid fulfilling the letter of his obligations if he so choses; yet if a man fails to pay what is proper he loses face and risks a general loss of class status. Paradoxically therefore it is often true, especially of the more enterprising individuals, that they pay as much as they can afford rather than as little as they can haggle for.

An important implication of this is that in bride price payments the scale of the payment tends to be determined by the class status of the man rather than that of the woman. Thus if a chief's daughter marries a follower of the chief, who is of aristocratic but not chiefly lineage, the bride price received by the chief's lineage will be much less than will have to be paid out in order to secure a bride of chiefly lineage for the chief's youngest son, who is his heir. In theory of course the same list of *hpaga* is payable in each case.[65]

A set of concrete examples will illustrate this point. In 1943 I had much to do with Hpunrau Tang, a young man 18 years of age who was by birth the senior chief (*uma du*) of the Layawng lineage of the Kadaw branch of the Lahtaw clan. He was still unmarried and his position was complicated by the fact that, as he had been only a child when his father had died, the Administration had recognised his eldest brother, Zau Ra, as regent during Hpunrau Tang's minority. Zau Ra had consolidated his position and now shared a joint

[65] A man marrying a girl of higher social class than himself will normally pay more than he would otherwise have done but not as much as would be paid by a suitor of the girls' own class.

household with the large family of an intermediate brother. Though Hpunrau Tang was now, in theory, old enough to assume his rights as chief, he was not sanguine about his prospects of being able to do so. He clearly understood that he would never be able to operate effectively as chief unless he could somehow persuade his brother to break up the extended family and move elsewhere.

The family consisted of the following members:

Males

Eldest brother (Zau Ra) married to a chief's daughter A
Second brother deceased
Third brother (La Hpri), formerly in the army, had had seven
    children by six different women before finally he married the
    last one B.   Now a rich man trading in opium (*kani laoban*)
Fourth brother deceased.
Fifth and youngest brother (Tang Nyeng, Hpunrau Tang), the *uma*
    and potential chief.   Still unmarried.

Females

Eldest sister (Ja Kawn) married to a village headman X subordinate
    to the Hpunrau chiefs
Second sister (Ja Lu) married to a Maran chief Y, neighbours to
    the Hpunrau but less influential
Third sister (Aja) married to a Maran commoner Z from the south
    who had settled in the Hpunrau domain.

The total marriage exchanges in each of the five cases A, B, X, Y and Z was elaborate.   To take A as an instance.   The bride's relatives received:

10 cattle
7 *hpaga*, namely one Chinese coat, one embroidered blanket, 6
Burmese skirts, one large gong, one small gong, 140 rupees cash in
lieu of one viss of silver, one gun.

The bridegroom's relatives received, at least:

6 *hpaga*, namely a cooking tripod, an iron cooking pot, a Chinese
carpet, a ten-span gong, a pair of silver ear tubes, a bracelet, a
necklace of old beads (these were presumably additional to the
2 spears, 2 swords, 2 baskets, 2 skirts and the collection of gardening
seeds which are almost standard equipment for the young bride).

In this instance the various *hpaga*, *other than* the cattle, more or less balance out, and this is commonly the case. In other words, the real economic cost of a bride price is in the item specified as cattle. Here the rating was as follows:

Marriage A   Zau Ra paid 10 cattle
    ,,   B   La Hpri paid 2 cattle[66]
Marriage X   Hpunrau received 3 cattle
    ,,   Y   ,,   ,,   6 cattle
    ,,   Z   ,,   ,,   2 cattle

Hpunrau Tang explained that because of his status as *uma*, it was quite essential that he should pay at least 10 cattle for his bride. In theory of course the two older brothers ought to have helped to provide the cattle, in practice it seemed they were being very unco-operative (naturally enough since once Hpunrau Tang was married he would have to be recognised as chief).

It will be seen that in every case the scale of the bride price, as measured by the number of cattle, corresponds to the ranking status of the bridegroom and not that of the bride. The importance of this fact is considerable. We have seen that a crucial element in the structure of *gumsa* society is that when an individual marries out of his or her own social class it is normally the man who marries up and the woman who marries down. If bride price in such cases were fixed according to the status of the bride, the system would break down, for the men of junior status would seldom be able to raise the necessary quantity of cattle and *hpaga*. Nevertheless, despite what happens in practice, Kachin formal theory is that bride price is adjusted to the standing of the *bride*. It is a theory which permits a powerful chief to pick and choose among potential suitors for his daughters and to use their marriage as direct instruments of political alliance. The following example illustrates this very well.

The leading Marip chiefs of the North Triangle have long had a circular marriage system (*hkau wang hku*). Girls of the Um lineage marry boys of the Mashaw lineage; girls of the Mashaw lineage marry boys of the N'Ding lineage; girls of the N'Ding lineage marry boys of the Um lineage. Some of

[66] The agreed bride price for marriage B was 2 cattle, one viss of silver, one viss of opium, 2 guns; actually, according to my informant, the whole transaction **was** carried out in terms of opium.

these girls also no doubt from time to time marry persons of
lower rank who are political subordinates to their fathers; in
that case the bride price would be quite moderate.   In the late
1930's the Governmental post of Native Officer (*taungok*) of
the North Triangle area was held by a well educated Kachin
from the Sinlum area, a man who by birth was a commoner
and in origin a stranger.   In the administrative hierarchy the
taungok was superior to any of the chiefs; in the theory of the
gumsa class system he was their inferior.   The *taungok* married
a daughter of one of the Marip chiefs and paid a bride price
of staggering dimensions.   The Marip chiefs justified this by
saying that a commoner must pay heavily for the honour of
marrying a chief's daughter.   Actually the reverse was true.
It was politically advantageous for the chief to be related
affinally to a *taungok*, and the high bride price paid corresponded to the *de facto* high status of the *taungok*.

We see then from all this that the concept of *hpaga* is of great
significance, for it permits structural rules which have all the
appearance of rigidity to be interpreted very freely, thus
opening the way for social mobility in a system which pur-
ports to be a caste-like hierarchy.   The related concept of
hka (debt) is equally important.   As the following examples
show, Kachins tend to perceive every kind of mutual relationship that may grow up between a pair of individuals as being
part of a system of debts.   I have chosen these particular
instances to show the bearing of the debt concept on the
Hpalang situation described in Chapter IV.

a. If A borrows money from B: B owns (*madu*) the debt; A drinks
(has) (*lu*) the debt.

b. If A steals anything from B: B owns a debt against A.

c. If A gets B with child: B's lineage owns a debt against A's
lineage.

d. If A kills B either intentionally or unintentionally: B's lineage
owns a debt against A's lineage.

e. If A has an accident, fatal or otherwise, while employed by
B: A's lineage owns a debt against B's lineage.

f. If A fails to complete the stipulated terms of a contract (such
as a bride price agreement) with B: B's lineage owns a debt against
A's lineage.

g. If A, not being a fellow clansman of the chief, fails to pay to his 'thigh-eating chief' B tribute of the hind leg (*magyi*) of an animal he has slaughtered, B owns a debt against A.

h. If lineage A and lineage B are *mayu-dama* and a boy of lineage B marries a girl of lineage C without first informing A and paying token compensation, then lineage A owns a debt against lineage B.

i. If a man of lineage A dies leaving a widow of lineage B, and no other male of lineage A 'picks her up' as a levirate wife; lineage B owns a debt against lineage A.

If the two parties in a debt relationship come within the jurisdiction of a single chief, then it is up to the chief to see that they come to some agreement about the terms of compensation. The compensation when it is agreed will amount to so and so many *hpaga*, in the manner we have seen.

Settlement when it is achieved is always the result of negotiations by third parties (*kasa*) who are usually persons superior in social standing to the principals. Where two chiefs are in dispute, it may be difficult to find anyone senior enough to act as *kasa*, and it is cases of this kind that are most likely to degenerate into feud.

In principle any outstanding debt, no matter what its origin, is potentially a source of feud. For a Kachin, feud and debt are the same thing—*hka*. It is especially debts between strangers that must be settled quickly otherwise the owner of the debt has a legitimate excuse for resorting to violence; in contrast, debts between relatives, especially affinal relatives, are not urgent matters. Indeed as between *mayu* and *dama* some debts are always left outstanding almost as a matter of principle; the debt is a kind of credit account which ensures the continuity of the relationship. There is thus a kind of paradox that the existence of a debt may signify not only a state of hostility but also a state of dependence and friendship. To the Kachin way of thinking co-operation and hostility are not very different.[67]   I shall refer to this point again when we come to examine the Kachin concept of witchcraft.

It is to be noted that with few exceptions debts are deemed to exist between lineages rather than between individuals. Any unpaid debt may be carried on from generation to

[67] cf. Wilson (1945), p. 26n.

generation.   Indeed a major feud is most unlikely to be finally settled within the lifetime of any of those who saw it start.

The close correspondence between the Kachin concept of debts and the anthropologist's concept of social structure should now be apparent.   Kachin tradition and ritual lays down what are the proper relations between individuals, that is to say, it specifies what obligations A has towards B and B towards A.   Debts come into existence whenever anyone feels that these formal obligations have not been adequately fulfilled.

Hpaga (wealth objects), which are the medium through which debts are settled, are thus a kind of currency of social obligations.   Ordinary money such as is used in a market is a medium for the exchange of goods; any one kind of goods can be converted into any other through the medium.   So also in the Kachin system of social obligations, any one kind of obligation can be balanced off against any other through the medium of *hpaga*.   Marriages are legitimised, blood feuds settled, land titles transferred, all in terms of this single species of currency.   The units of the currency are formalised objects which are not directly interchangeable with one another.

In some ways *hpaga* can be thought of as analogous to the individual cards used in a game of poker.   One ritual context calls for the production of four aces, another for a royal flush —the cards are valuable only in their context.   Thus the acquisition of *hpaga* is not really an end in itself.   *Hpaga* are a device for manipulating social status and they are used in a game which proceeds according to set rules; but as with poker, a mere understanding of the rules gives very little idea of how the game is really played!   In the theoretical system the value of any particular *hpaga* is ritualistic and symbolic; in real life the actual *hpaga* are only substitutes for the traditional objects. The real *hpaga* have both ritual and economic significance at one and the same time.

It should now be easier to understand why, as we saw earlier in this section, the difference between owning goods (which can be given away) and owning land (over which one merely asserts sovereignty) is felt by Kachins to be the same sort of difference as that between debtor and creditor in a commercial transaction or between defendant and petitioner in a lawsuit.

Land Tenure

Some of the distinctions that are to be drawn between different types of Kachin land tenure have already been noted. Individual villagers only have rights of usufruct in the land: they 'eat it' (*sha*). Chiefs and village headmen on the other hand own the land (*madu*) or rule it (*up*). This latter kind of ownership implies claims of sovereignty over the land rather than rights over its products. The claims are of value as status symbols; from a strictly economic point of view their value is, if anything negative, since they involve the owner in expense.

Rights of usufruct and tenancy can be freely disposed of. Thus when Kachins clear a stretch of jungle to make a hill field it has, in most cases, been cleared before, and each plot 'belongs' to the lineage which first cleared the virgin jungle. But when the land is cleared the second time it is not necessarily used by the same lineage. Some other lineage may use it, sometimes just by 'borrowing' it, sometimes on payment of a token rent. The same applies to land under permanent cultivation. The land is 'owned' by the chief; the individual farmer has a right of permanent tenancy, which he can dispose of to another without affecting the chief's overlordship.

In contrast the rights of ownership that pertain to a chief cannot readily be disposed of. They are ritually defined rights which rest with the members of a particular lineage. They cannot be casually bought and sold. If disposed of at all, the transfer must be carried through in ritual fashion with an appropriate exchange of *hpaga*.

In this latter sense the fullest type of ownership (*madu*) is that possessed by a 'thigh-eating chief' (p. 121 f.). The meat that he receives from his tribute of 'thighs' has little economic value; the importance of the thigh payment from the Kachin point of view is that it betokens recognition of the chief's claims to other rights—and these other rights are all symbols of status. They are: the right to commit violence on the land, the right to make offerings to the Madai *nat*, the right to dig out ditches round the larger graves which are the prerogative of those of chief's blood, the right to erect the large main house post (*nhpu daw*) (characteristic of chiefs' houses), the right to hold a *manau* (p. 119).[68]

Thus besides the contrast and opposition between ownership as sovereignty and ownership as right of usufruct, we have the fact that sovereignty itself is a bundle of rights each of which can be separately enjoyed. A review of the various ways in which sovereignty may be acquired or partly acquired will demonstrate this.

a. The ordinary way in which a thigh-eating chief acquires his title is by direct inheritance either from his father or (if the old chief has no sons) from a lineage kinsman. The heir should be the youngest son. It seems probable that even in the absence of intervention by a paramount power the youngest brother will in fact often not be in a position to retain power against the opposition of his brothers. De facto succession is not always to the youngest son.[69] Retrospectively succession through a line other than that of the youngest son may be used to disparage the validity of a chief's title. 'Youngest son' should, I think, be interpreted as being the youngest son living at the time of the father's death, but this too leaves room for equivocation. It is recognised that the next senior in the line of succession after the youngest son is the eldest son.

b. In the absence of a paramount power the son of a ruling chief (especially the eldest son) can collect personal followers (*zaw*) from his own lineage and establish a village in previously unclaimed territory giving himself the title of chief. If he is a strong character his title will be tacitly recognised but if a dispute were to arise outsiders will say that he is only a 'boasting chief' (*gumrawng gumsa du*). In particular, outside arbitrators would repudiate such a man's claim to be a 'thigh-eating chief' unless he had publicly gone through a formal ceremony (*nat htawt daw*) for the purchase of ritual powers over the Madai *nat* from his youngest brother. The main sanction preserving the rights of the youngest brother against his older siblings is that 'thigh-eating' rights cannot be transferred away from the youngest son line without the formal and public agreement of the youngest son himself. It may be worth remarking here that a high proportion of the village headmen who, under the British

---

[68] Kawlu Ma Nawng (1942), p. 58.

[69] According to Neufville (1828), p. 341, succession among the Assam Singpho is avowedly to the eldest son while the youngest son inherits only the moveable property. Later authorities (e.g. Dalton (1872)) repeat this statement. Green (1934) makes similar statements regarding the Kachins of the North Triangle. See below, p. 261.

régime, styled themselves chief (*duwa*) were not 'thigh-eating chiefs' from the Kachin point of view; they were not the holders of a legitimate title formally purchased from the youngest son line of their lineage.

c. In the absence of a paramount power warfare can take place leading ultimately to transfer of chieftainship title by right of conquest (as at Hpalang). This does not seem to have happened very often even in pre-British days. What was more common was that a major feud between rival chiefs would at last be brought to arbitration and, in the settlement, one side would cede land while the other side would give a daughter in marriage.[70] The new chief would thus be *dama* to the old one who would thus retain a kind of distant sovereignty over his former land. The Layawng marriages given on p. 150 are an example of this. Hpunrau-Layawng claim to have acquired their land by conquest from a Lahpai lineage some three generations ago. The Lahpai lineage in question had been their *mayu* before the feud and they became their *mayu* again after the feud. The girl A was a member of this Lahpai lineage. In Hpalang the Nmwe chiefs would no doubt have become *dama* to the Lahpai chiefs if the British had not insisted that the Lahpai chiefs actually reside within the boundaries of the disputed territory.

The cession of land from one lineage to another is marked by the celebration of a 'victory *manau*' (*padang manau*) to which both parties contribute. Thereafter the validity of the new chief's claim to be a thigh-eating chief will rest on the acknowledged fact that this *padang manau* took place.

d. If a chief's lineage dies out so that there are no male heirs and if the members of closely related lineages of the same clan agree, then succession may pass through a daughter instead of a son. The land is treated as if it were one of the *hpaga* of the girl's dowry and her husband and his lineage heirs become the title holders. Land transferred in this way is called *kungdawn ga*. Such transfer is rare.[71] The mode of transfer resembles that in (*c*) above; the new chief is *dama* to the old one.

e. The son of a ruling chief can collect followers (as in *b*) and establish a new village within the domain of some other chief. To do this he must purchase the rights of tenancy from his new chief. According to circumstances and the nature and number of *hpaga* that are transferred, his status may be either that of *salang wa* or petty chief, *duwa*. If, for example, he is recognised as a petty chief he may be entitled to put up a chief's houseposts and have a ditch dug round his grave, and have a *Madai dap* shrine in his house, and

[70] Kawlu Ma Nawng (1942), p. 55.   [71] Kawlu Ma Nawng (1942), p. 58.

have a separate *numshang* for his village, but he would still not be a thigh-eating chief, he would not be entitled to claim 'thighs' from his followers or hold a *manau* without permission from his superior chief.

Partial transfer of sovereignty of this kind is a matter which concerns the whole of the lineage of each chief and the matter is arranged by agents (*kasa*) just as with a marriage. Indeed the transaction itself closely resembles a marriage. The 'price' of the land includes a 100 bead necklace just as the bride price of a chief's daughter includes a 100 bead necklace, and the return gift from sellers to buyers includes a sword and a spear; the sword is retained as evidence of the legality of the land transfer just as the bride's sword is retained as evidence of the legality of the marriage.[72]   As has been explained already, it would be normal in such circumstances if the subordinate tenant chief became in fact son-in-law (*dama*) to the superior chief.

f. It was explained in Chapter IV that the orthodox method of pursuing a blood feud was not in fact to resort to open warfare but to hire braves (*share*) to carry out assassinations among the enemy.   Such braves need not be (and usually were not) closely related to their employers.   Such braves might be paid for their services by means of *hpaga* in the usual way, but could also be rewarded by a grant of land.   Such land is called *regau ga*.   I think the title in such land is similar to that held by a petty chief (see *e*) but I am not clear about this.   When a chief was at feud he had a legal right to demand assistance (i) from his fellow clansmen and (ii) from his *dama*.   The reward for services rendered would be less if based on kinship than if it was simply the service of a hired *share*. In Hpalang one of the issues in dispute was just why the Laga and the Gumjye had originally come to the aid of the Nmwe.   The point at issue was whether the land in Laga and Gumjye villages was held as *regau ga* or simply in feudal dependance on the Nmwe.[73]

From all this we can see that householders, village headmen, petty chiefs and chiefs who claim to 'own' land (*madu*) actually lay claim to a variety of different rights.   The differences

---

[72] Kawlu Ma Nawng (1942), pp. 57–8.   The sword is said to symbolise the 'cutting off' of the land (and/or the bride?) from the original lineage, the spear denotes the right of the new owners to do violence on the land (or to the bride?). But again there is multiple symbolism.   The spear is phallic; the spear denotes the transference of the bride's male offspring; but *ri*, a spear, is also a pun on *ri* a cord, the cord of friendship which links *mayu* and *dama* together.

[73] See p. 93; cf. Kawlu Ma Nawng (1942), p. 58.

between these rights are in the first instance of ritual rather than economic significance and serve as symbols of status for the different grades of 'owner'.   To proceed further therefore we must examine the Kachin ideology with regard to concepts of rank and class difference.

VI

Concepts of Rank and Class

What makes the Kachins particularly interesting from an anthropological point of view is that they have a society which is simultaneously segmentary and class stratified.   In most types of lineage system that have so far been described in any detail, the process of lineage segmentation leads to a 'balanced opposition' between the resulting segments rather than to a status ranking, superior and inferior.   For this reason, among others, the interesting typology of political systems which Fortes and Evans-Pritchard have suggested for African societies[74] would not cover Kachin *gumsa* society.

The Tikopia, as described by Firth,[75] have indeed what may be considered a 'pure' lineage system associated with notions of a class hierarchy, but here the whole scale of social activities is on such a minute scale that analogy is not very useful.   I think that there are plenty of societies in the world of the Kachin *gumsa* type, but it so happens that social anthropologists have not yet got round to looking at them.   That makes it all the more difficult for me to achieve lucidity.

In what I am going to say now, I repeat to some extent what I have said already, but I am arguing from a different point of view.   In the previous sections we have been concerned mainly with the nature of lineage segments and the status relations between them.   Now we are concerned with how these same status relations are fitted into the Kachin's own notion that his society is stratified into classes of almost caste-like rigidity.

To be frank, Kachin *gumsa* theory about class differences is almost totally inconsistent with Kachin practice.   I want then to explain not only what the Kachin theory is but also how

---

[74] Fortes and Evans-Pritchard (1940), Introduction.   Southern Bantu lineages are often ranked; cf. e.g. Hilda Kuper *An African Aristocracy* (1947).
[75] Firth (1939), Chapter 6.

the inconsistencies in actual behaviour affect the total social structure.

In theory rank depends strictly upon birth status; all legal rules are framed as if the hierarchy of aristocrats, commoners and slaves had a caste-like rigidity and exclusiveness. In Kachin theory rank is an attribute of lineage and every individual acquires his rank once and for all through the lineage into which he happens to be born. It is easy to see that this theory is a fiction, but less easy to understand just what kind of fiction is involved.

It would appear that in pre-British days a very high proportion of the total population—in places nearly half[76]—were classed as *mayam*, a term which the dictionary translates as 'slaves'. The British disapproved of slavery and suppressed the institution of *mayam*. It is therefore difficult to discover the exact nature of the original institution or to discover whether 'slavery' was an adequate description of it.[77]

What evidence there is suggests that Kachin slavery had a good deal of resemblance to the *tefa* system of the Central Chins,[78] the *sei* system of the Lakher,[79] the *boi* (*bawi*) system of the Lushai,[80] and the *mughemi* system of the Sema,[81] or for that matter the 'slavery' of pre-British Burma.[82]

Nearly all slaves were owned by the chief or village headman. In most cases the status of slave amounted to that of permanent debtor. But, as we have seen, the role of debtor in Kachin society is not necessarily one of disadvantage. The slave might be in debt bondage to his master; but he also had claims on his master. His overall position resembled that of an adopted son or bastard (*n-gyi*) of the chief, or even more perhaps that of a poor son-in-law (*dama*) working to earn his bride. Thus by a kind of paradox the 'slave' though reckoned to be the lowest social stratum stood nearer to the chief than the members of any other named class.

The chief disposed of the marriages of his slaves just as he did those of his real children. Where slave married slave the

[76] Barnard (1930), p. 182.
[77] The most detailed account available seems to be that given by Green (1934), pp. 86–91. It is quoted here with Col. Green's permission in Appendix III.
[78] Stevenson (1943), pp. 176 f.   [79] Parry (1932), pp. 223 f.
[80] Hutton (1921*b*), App. IV; Shakespear (1912), pp. 46 f.
[81] Hutton (1921*b*), pp. 145 f.
[82] Sangermano (1893), pp. 156; 261 f.; Richardson (1912); Lasker (1950).

children were slaves to the father's master (since he had paid the bride price).   Similarly even if a male slave married a free woman the children were slaves to the master who paid the bride price.   But if a free man married a slave woman, the bride price was paid to the slave's master and served to redeem the children.

During the 19th century most Kachin slaves seem to have been of Assamese origin.   Assamese were captured in large numbers in the period of Burmese ascendancy in Assam just prior to 1824 and these captives and their descendants were traded all over the Kachin Hills.   Thus in 1868 Anderson found that most of the Kachin and Shan slaves in the Bhamo area were of Assamese origin;[83] in 1910 Grant Brown found on the Upper Chindwin whole villages of Kachin speakers directly descended from Assamese slaves.[84]   Even when the Hukawng Valley Kachin slaves were released in 1926 it was still to be noted that of the total 3,466 released, 2,051 were of Assamese origin.[85]   But slaves of this type do not seem to have been treated any differently from bond 'slaves' who were themselves Kachins.   Neufville writing in 1828 is interesting on this point.

'When in their own country and before the plunder of Assam furnished them with slaves they appear to have cultivated their lands and carried on all other purposes of domestic life by means of a species of voluntary servitude entered into by the poorer and more destitute individuals of their own people who, when reduced to want, were in the habit of selling themselves into bondage either temporarily or for life to their chiefs or more prosperous neighbours. They sometimes resorted to this step in order to secure wives of the daughters and in either case were incorporated into the family performing domestic and agricultural service but under no obligation.   Singphos in this state were called gumlao.'[86]

Neglecting for the moment the description of these 'slaves' as *gumlao*, it is evident that Neufville's informants regarded the status of 'slave' as close to that of adopted son or poor *dama*.

Formal rules about the payment of *hpaga* such as are given above in section IV of this chapter usually differentiate only

[83] Anderson (1871).   [84] Grant Brown (1925), p. 16.   [85] Barnard (1930), p. 182.
[86] Neufville (1828), p. 240.   This is the first reference to the term *gumlao*. cf. p. 199.

three classes, namely the chiefs (*du*); the free-born commoners (*darat*); the slaves (*mayam*). But there are also intermediate classes which blur the distinction between these categories. *Ma gam amyu* (eldest son lineage) denotes an aristocracy. Aristocratic lineages in this sense are not the lineages of chiefs but lineages sufficiently close to those of chiefs for their members to be able to claim that they are descended from chiefs and to feel that their descendants might one day become chiefs again. Similarly there is a category *surawng*[87] which comprises (in theory) the children of slave women by free-born men—a category which blurs the distinction between free and not-free. The commoners (*darat daroi, mayu maya*) are simply a residual category, the 'ordinary' lineages which are not aristocrats and not slaves.

Kachin class is not directly correlated with economic status, either in a ritual or an objective sense. The Kachin 'rich man' (*sut lu ai wa*) is, as we have seen, the man who possesses many *hpaga*, but this does not necessarily mean that he is wealthy in terms of ordinary economic goods. There is no suggestion in Kachin ideology that a 'rich' man is necessarily an aristocrat or that an aristocrat is necessarily 'rich'. There are rich chiefs and poor chiefs; though it is true that a powerful chief is also a rich one. Within any one domain there is no substantial difference in standard of living between the aristocrats and the commoners—members of both classes eat the same food, wear the same clothes, practise the same skills. Master and slave live in the same house under almost the same conditions.

In theory Kachin class difference has attributes of caste—that is to say it is a ritual distinction. Individuals are born great. Persons of higher class than oneself are deserving of honour (*hkungga*)—and this is true even if the individual in question is poverty stricken and an imbecile. Honour is expressed through deference, notably by offering gifts and by the use of an appropriate florid or poetical style of speech.

[87] cf. Barnard cited in Carrapiett (1929), p. 99. I have never heard the term used myself. Presumably with the abolition of slavery it has lost its utility. Green (1934) makes the interesting point that *surawng* were usually the bastards (*n-gyi*) of a slave woman by aristocratic fathers of the owner's household. Their descendants were no doubt well placed to receive recognition as aristocrats themselves.

In theory then people of superior class receive gifts from their inferiors. But no permanent economic advantage accrues from this. Anyone who receives a gift is thereby placed in debt (*hka*) to the giver. The receiver for a while enjoys the debt (he has it, he drinks it: *lu*) but it is the giver who owns the debt (rules it: *madu*). Paradoxically therefore although an individual of high-class status is defined as one who receives gifts (e.g. 'thigh-eating chief') he is all the time under a social compulsion to give away more than he receives. Otherwise he would be reckoned mean and a mean man runs the danger of losing status. For though Kachins hold that a man is born to high rank and do not acknowledge that social climbing is possible, they readily admit that it is possible 'to go downhill' (*gumyu yu*)—i.e. lose class status.

In practice it would appear to be equally possible to gain status. Since, in theory, rank is acquired at birth, it is clear that class is an attribute of whole lineages not of individuals. Therefore an individual who wishes to be recognised as of high birth must strive not simply for personal recognition, but for the recognition of his whole lineage. Usually this is not very difficult. Most commoner lineages can claim some sort of aristocratic connection, and in all such cases there is room for manœuvre and social improvement. However, a few lineages are notoriously 'common'—i.e. they have no connection whatever with the royal 'chiefly' clans;—for these the *gumsa* system has nothing much to offer;—the leaders of such lineages aim to be recognised as *bawmung* or as priests rather than as chiefs.[88]

Where a commoner lineage has remote claims to aristocracy an ambitious individual can work his way up the social scale by repeatedly validating these claims. Such a man in Kachin terminology possesses *hpaji*. *Hpaji* is the counterpart of *sut* (riches), it is manifested by lavishness in hospitality and feast-giving. It can be translated as 'wisdom' or 'cunning'. Only the rich can afford to give feasts; only the wise and cunning

---

[88] The question whether a commoner lineage can assert a claim to aristocracy is largely a matter of names. In the same way our College of Heralds can usually provide a family tree for anyone with a name like Howorth, or Howarth, or Howard, but may be hard put to it if the applicant's name is Smith. I fancy that a really influential commoner family would always come to be recognised as of chiefly (*du baw*) origin if they maintained their position long enough. cf. p. 273 Kareng-Hpauwi. For status of priests see p. 189.

know how to get rich.   Wisdom in itself does not necessarily imply aristocracy but when it comes to social climbing, the cunning ones are at an advantage.

We have then a situation in which the class hierarchy is supposed to be rigid, but in fact is not.   In such a situation great store will be set by the symbols which attach to rank, and the rights to use such symbols will be jealously guarded. We have already seen this process at work in our discussion of land tenure.   We have seen, for example, that the political status of any lineage within a village is specified by the links of clanship and affinity that relate that lineage to the 'principal lineage'—that is to say the lineage of the founder ancestor of the village.   For this reason the exact status relationships that originally existed between the different founder ancestors of the various lineages which now compose the village or village cluster are matters of paramount importance.

Great ingenuity is devoted to garbling the evidence upon this crucial matter.   The Hpalang feud stories given in Chapter IV are an excellent example.   It is clear that in each generation each rival faction within a group reinterprets the traditions of the past to its own liking.   How far any one individual realises that this process of 're-writing history' is going on, it is impossible to say.

Social climbing then is the product of a dual process. Prestige is first acquired by an individual by lavishness in fulfilling ritual obligations.   This prestige is then converted into recognised status by validating retrospectively the rank of the individual's lineage.   This last is largely a matter of manipulating the genealogical tradition.   The complicated nature of Kachin rules of succession makes such manipulation particularly easy.

We have seen that by natural right the youngest son succeeds the father in his rights to make sacrifices to the ancestral deities of the lineage, and that though other members of the father's lineage may on occasion succeed, they must first 'purchase' the rights of office from the youngest son by making the appropriate ritual gifts.   In course of time therefore the total lineage of a chief includes a number of collateral branches tracing descent from the elder brothers of chiefs.   In such a case only the 'youngest son line' is, strictly speaking, *du baw amyu*—'of chiefly sort'; the collateral lines are inferior, they are *ma gam amyu*—'eldest son sort'.

Let me emphasise, however, that the next senior line after that of the *youngest* son is that of the *eldest* son. In the fictitious instance in the diagram, A_1, A_2 and A_3 are youngest sons and each succeeds in turn by right of birth. But if A_3 dies without issue, his *eldest* brother B_3 is the next in line and not C_3. Moreover this cannot be obviated by adoption as in some other societies. A_3 may adopt a son, but that will not affect the succession of ritual office. Going back a generation, the descendants of B_2 and C_2 will in time come to consider themselves separate lineages. Then in order of ranking, the descendants of B_2 will be senior to those of C_2. But of B_2's descendants, the line from D_3 will be senior to that from E_3.

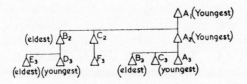

Fig. 4. Diagram to illustrate principle of succession.

The rank order of the individuals shown in the third generation is thus: A_3, B_3, C_3, D_3, E_3, F_3.

To complicate things still further several additional criteria can be used to demonstrate that lineage A is decisively senior to lineage B or vice versa.

a. In a situation of polygamy, the children of a chief wife (*latung num*) all rank superior to those of a second wife (*lashi num*) who in turn all rank superior to those of a third wife (*labai num*).

b. A wife is not a wife until she has gone through the ceremony of *num shalai*. This can have important consequences. An important Kachin chief will not infrequently 'marry' a Shan princess but by Buddhist rites. It may then be contended that her offspring are illegitimate.

c. Kachins practise levirate marriage. If a man dies, his widow is 'collected' by a lineage brother. It is sometimes contended that any offspring the woman has by this second marriage all rank lower than those by her first husband.

d. Children born out of wedlock or as the result of adultery within wedlock are in the one case the legal offspring of the man paying the bastardy penalty (*sumrai hka*), and in the other of the legal husband of the mother.   But such children, even when their status has been legitimised, rank lower than children of the same father born legitimate.   E.g., if a man A has illegitimate children by a woman B and then marries her (*num shalai*), the children born after marriage rank higher than the children born before marriage, though all are legitimate.

It follows therefore that the offspring of a man may fall into a considerable number of different categories; the heir (*uma*) of a chief is not simply his youngest son but 'the youngest son of the first wife with whom he went through the ceremony of *num shalai*', and that may easily be a matter of dispute.[89]

These elaborate rules not only allow for much controversy, they also make it relatively easy for any influential aristocrat to reconstruct remote sections of his genealogy in his own favour.   For example, to return to the hypothetical example given in Fig. 4.   As described above, F_3 and his descendants are in the junior line of the six lineages originating in A_1, B_2, C_2, E_3, B_3, C_3.   They will thus soon be far removed from any chance of chiefly office.   In a few generations they will come to form a lineage which no one will recognise as aristocratic, even if they themselves continue to boast of their chiefly connections.   The Kachins say of such a lineage that it has 'gone downhill'—*gumyu yu*.[90]

But if an individual in this F_3 line were by good fortune or strong personality to work himself and his family into a position of influence, he might well begin to assume the titles of a chief. It would then no doubt turn out that his ancestor A_1 had more than one wife and that of A_1's several children, only C_2 was the child of his chief wife, so that, after all, the real *uma* line

---

[89] It is interesting to note that in the Tallensi lineage system studied by Fortes the usual form of lineage fission is for the descendants of a senior wife to hive off from the descendants of a junior wife, so that, in this very patrilineal society, the critical founder ancestor of a lineage is usually a woman.   This is sometimes the case also with the Kachins, for it is frequently the marital status of the mother of the lineage founder which determines the rank of the lineage.   Numerous examples of this can be seen in Kawlu Ma Nawng (1942), pp. 2–10.   cf. Fortes (1945), pp. 198 ff.

[90] cf. Hanson (1906), p. 103.   *Dashi ni shawng e Lahtaw du rai ma ai dai hpang e gumyu yu mat ai:* 'formerly the Dashi were chiefs of the Lahtaw clan but afterwards they lost caste'.

passed through F_3! In Hpalang I found that there could be disagreements of this kind even with regard to persons as near as the great grandfather's generation. When it is realised that some chiefly genealogies purport to record history for the last forty generations or more, it will be appreciated that although a man's rank is in theory precisely defined by his birth, there is an almost infinite flexibility in the system as actually applied.

So far in this discussion I have been emphasising that practice often deviates a long way from the structural ideal, and yet because of the flexibility of the native concepts Kachins can persuade themselves that they are keeping to the rules. I now want to make a different point—namely, that the structural ideal can itself be inconsistent, so that two or more quite different courses of action can both be equally 'right' (or 'wrong').

Inconsistency arises from the association of a rule of patrilocal residence and a rule of succession by ultimogeniture.

The ideal of patrilocal residence is consistent with the notion that class is an attribute of whole lineage groups. The lineage is conceived of as a localised group identified with one particular place and having a special ranking status in respect to that place. Ultimogeniture cuts clean across this theory, being based on the assumption that the youngest son is the residual heir, the older brothers having gone off to seek their fortune elsewhere. If the older brothers stay at home an intolerable psychological situation is likely to arise. In our own society, the stereotype of a jealousy situation is with the mother-in-law or 'the lodger'. This stereotype is a reflection of the inconsistency between the ideal that each biological family should form a separate household and the economic necessity of dependence on other people. The Kachin stereotype of a jealousy situation is between elder and younger brother. Slander and jealous speech (*nsu nnawn*) is thought of as a kind of sorcery which can bring misfortune to the person slandered, and where illness is diagnosed as being due to this cause, offerings are made to the *nsu nat*—'the spirit of jealousy'. The mythical sanction supporting this offering is a tale about a quarrel between two brothers. In one version the elder brother at first uses his greater strength and knowledge of the world to deprive the younger brother of his rightful inheritance; then supernatural beings come to the aid of the younger brother who kills his elder brother by a trick and himself survives to become a rich chief.[91] The shades of the two brothers now constitute the *nsu nat*.

In other words, although Kachins maintain theoretically that an elder brother should live at home under the political suzerainty of his youngest brother, they recognise clearly enough that trouble is likely to ensue if he does.

The most obvious alternative to patrilocal residence is matrilocal (uxorilocal) residence. I have stressed already that in point of fact such residence is common. But if a married couple settle with the bride's parents (*dama lung*: 'the son-in-law climbs the hill') it is deemed a disgrace. The son-in-law thereby admits his social inferiority; he is working to earn his bride; he has virtually put himself in the position of bond-slave (*mayam*) to his *mayu*. It is understandable therefore that, if questioned, Kachins will at first maintain that exceptions to the patrilocal rule are rare.

In the real situation the corporate localised lineage segment seldom includes more than half a dozen or so separate individual families. This is clear evidence that, despite the ideal of lineage solidarity, the process of lineage fission must be going on all the time. This point I have made before, but what I am now stressing is that the mechanism of lineage fission is closely linked with ideas about class status and that the process of lineage fission is at the same time a process of social mobility up and down the class hierarchy. The choice that an individual makes about his place of residence affects the class status prospects of his descendants.

This argument is important to my general analysis so I will recapitulate what has already been said on the subject of choice of residence so as to bring out the importance of this factor for class differentiation.

Choice of residence affects commoners and aristocrats rather differently. To take commoners first. Commoners really have a choice of four alternatives:

a. A man and his wife can settle in the village of the man's

---

[91] Gilhodes (1922), p. 54.   Alternative versions of this tale are considered **below, see p. 266.**

parents. This is the orthodox procedure. The bride is then regarded as the woman of the whole local lineage group. If her husband dies she will be 'picked up' (*kahkyin*) as a levirate wife by one of her deceased husband's lineage kin. All members of the local lineage have probably helped in the provision of the bride price (*hpu hpaga*) which is determined by the rank of the husband and they will all have shared in the return presents (*sharung shakau*) contributed by the bride's lineage and determined by the rank of the bride. The bridegroom's male relatives are thus interested in seeing that he makes as 'good' a marriage as possible. If the bride's lineage is of higher status than that of the bridegroom, then the status of the bridegroom's lineage is enhanced and vice versa.

b. Where a man was too poor to afford the bride price for a wife it was formerly possible for him to become a voluntary slave of some local notable; probably his own chief. He would then have the status of *ngawn mayam*.[92] His master would provide the capital to complete the bride price transactions. In return the master would have a claim on the labour of the slave and his children and would be entitled to a share of the produce of his livestock and of the bride price of his daughters. The advantage of this procedure from the slave's point of view was the security provided by the patronage of an influential chief. The slave's status *vis-à-vis* his master would appear to have been very similar to that of an illegitimate son or a poor son-in-law.[93]

c. A man and his wife can settle in the village of the bride's parents (*dama lung*). By so doing the man repudiates the support of his own lineage and makes himself dependent upon the lineage of the bride. This situation usually originates in cirumstances where the bridegroom is on bad terms with his relatives or else they are very poor. The bride's people (*mayu ni*) then agree to a reduced bride price in return for an agreed number of years personal service from the bridegroom. After working for his bride in this way a man has 'lost face' in his own village and is likely to stay on as the dependant of his *mayu ni*. An unorthodox matrilocal marriage of this kind initiates a new subordinate lineage in the village of the *mayu ni*. The *mayu-dama* relationship, it will be remembered, has continuity from one generation to another. Hence if two lineages of the same village are in *mayu-dama* relationship, the *dama* usually have an inferior status to the *mayu*. This inferiority rests on dual ground, firstly that the *mayu* 'were there first' and therefore have superior land title, and secondly that the

---

[92] See Appendix III.   Green writes *ngong mayam*.   [93] cf. p. 160.

founder of the *dama* lineage by adopting matrilocal residence admitted his inferior status.

d. A married couple can settle in an alien community. Empirically this seems to be rare. A man can only settle in an established community by permission of the village headman and since all approaches to persons of authority follow channels of kinship, it is really rather difficult to negotiate with people who are not kin at all. In Hpalang I only identified one household which had fairly certainly been complete strangers to everyone in the community when they first arrived. Although these people had only been living in Hpalang about 5 years, three of the children had already been married off or become betrothed to local families. The stranger family was thus already fully incorporated into the local kinship network of *mayu-dama* relationships. In saying that cases of this kind are rare, I am not suggesting that the total residential pattern of Kachin villages is stable. Individual families move frequently from one community to another, but the family head usually already has either agnatic or affinal kinsmen living in the community to which he moves.

In sum then the ordinary commoner has to choose between 'being orthodox' in which case he remains at home but comes under the ritual jurisdiction of his youngest brother, or 'being unorthodox' in which case he goes to live somewhere else but must then accept the position of an affinal relative (*dama*) in a subordinate position in the new community. A poor man can avoid this latter choice only by adopting the very similar course of making himself a voluntary bond slave.

The choices that face the elder sons of chiefs are rather different. There are again several alternatives but all of these are respectable and orthodox. We have already considered these alternatives under the heading of Land Tenure (p. 156 f.).

a. He may stay at home and submit to the overlordship of his youngest brother.

b. He may collect a group of followers (*zaw*) and then go out to uninhabited country and carve out for himself a new territory. If he does this he may later purchase from his youngest brother the right to make offerings to the ancestral nats, etc., so that he may assume the status of a 'thigh-eating chief' in his new territory.

c. He may, together with his followers, apply to the chief of an established domain for a village site. If this is granted he will have to purchase the 'ownership' rights in the manner already indicated and will thereafter be recognised as headman or petty chief of the new village as the case may be. In either case he is subordinate in certain respects to the chief from whom he purchases his rights. In consequence, the lineage segment of which he is the founder loses status slightly and becomes *ma gam amyu* as opposed to the *du baw amyu* of the parent stem. In describing this alternative under the head of Land Tenure I pointed out that the 'price' paid for the village land is similar to the bride price of a chief's daughter. It would be normal for a *ma gam amyu* petty chief to become *dama* to his overlord at the first opportunity if he were not already a clan brother. Here again we see that within the context of the one community the *mayu-dama* relationship implies the subordination of the latter to the former.

Empirically it would seem that the second of these alternatives has great attractions for Kachin aristocrats. In the Kachin Hills Area west of the Irrawaddy and north of Myitkyina, and also in many other areas of notably low population density, there is a large preponderance of very small independent villages; the headman of each village claims to be an independent chief of full *du baw* status. This fact has been noted repeatedly and is the more remarkable in that the British administration was consistently opposed to such fragmented settlement. Such tiny settlements of three to a dozen households are clearly very weak both politically and economically; it would therefore seem that the prestige attaching to independent status is commonly valued more highly than economic prosperity.

In more densely settled areas there is no room for chiefs' sons to set up independent domains without infringing upon some other chief's existing rights. Therefore a chief's son, who is not content to stay at home, has no choice but to settle down in some subordinate capacity in the domain of a relative, asserting for himself as high a status as circumstances will permit.

In Hpalang, as we have seen, every village headman seemed excessively anxious to claim for himself the maximum possible degree of political independence to which some tortuous reinterpretation of tradition might seem to make him entitled. Such claims had very little real effect upon the political or economic power of the individuals concerned so that here again one must suppose that the issue at stake is purely one of prestige; recognition of one's class status by others being considered all important. So long as a petty chief or village headman can persuade other people to refer to him as a chief (*duwa*) and to credit his sons and daughters with the honorific Shan titles of Prince (*Zau*) and Princess (*Nang*), his lineage can still rank as chiefly (*du baw*), but once these titles are omitted the status of the lineage starts to go downhill and all will before long be rated simply as commoners.

VII

Concepts of the Supernatural

Earlier in this book I advanced the view that it is nonsensical to discuss the actions or qualities of supernatural beings except in terms of human action. Myth, I argued, is not so much a justification for ritual as a description of it. I hope that my meaning will become clearer as a result of what follows.

Kachins make use of concepts concerning the supernatural for practical (technical) as well as ritual ends. The illnesses of men and the diseases of crops and animals are alike attributed to the malicious attack of supernatural beings. There are many different categories of such supernatural beings, each thought to be responsible for different classes of symptoms. Treatment consists of a preliminary diagnosis to discover the type responsible, followed by a sacrificial offering to the spirit concerned. This is an essentially practical procedure no different in principle from our routine of taking one kind of pill for a headache and another for a stomach ache. With us, if one course of treatment fails, we try another; Kachins do likewise.

Offerings to the spirits have another practical aspect in that Kachins do not kill their domestic livestock except for sacrifice. A 'spirit making' (*nat galaw*) is therefore a feast for all who attend it. Since rich people make larger sacrifices than poor people, sacrifices have the effect of equalising consumer distribution. It therefore does not greatly matter who owns the livestock; when they are finally killed, meat will always be shared around the whole village.[94]   This emphasises what has been said already to the effect that the value of property (e.g. livestock) to the individual is as a prestige symbol rather than as an economic good.

It is, however, the ritual rather than the practical aspects of 'spirit making' that mainly concern us in this book.   Conceptually Kachin spirits (*nat*) are, in Lang's famous phrase, 'magnified non-natural men'.   They simply extend the human class hierarchy to a higher level and are continuous with it.   In the *nat* world, as in the human world, there are chiefs, aristocrats, commoners and slaves.   The commoners of the *nat* world are simply the deceased ancestors of the commoners of the human world; the aristocrats of the *nat* world are deceased human chiefs.   In order to obtain concessions from a human superior, a man starts proceedings by making a gift which thereby puts the superior person in his debt.   To obtain concessions from the spirits one does likewise—one 'gives them honour' (*hkungga jaw*) which, in this case, means making a sacrifice.   In accepting the gift, the spirit only takes the 'breath' or 'essence' (*nsa*) of the offering, so that, conveniently, human beings are able to consume the carcase.

The ordered hierarchy of the spirits also reflects other ideas already familiar in the real world.   In the real world if a poor commoner wishes to approach his chief, he will first approach a superior commoner (e.g. a village headman) to intercede on his behalf as agent (*kasa*).   So too with the spirits; one must approach great deities by way of lesser ones.

Let me illustrate this.   In Hpalang, as in most Kachin communities, an important religious ceremonial is held about the beginning of September.   Its avowed purpose is to bring supernatural protection upon the crops which are just then coming into ear.   It is a time when food stocks are very low so that it is not such a gay performance as the festivities that take place at harvest and at the time of sowing, but from the ritual point of view it is perhaps the most sacred of all regular annual ceremonials: the time is one of anxiety; will the crop flourish or fail?

Every household has a part to play in this ceremonial which

[94] The argument does not apply in the case of Christian or partly Christian villages.

ordinarily lasts three days and is then followed by four days tabooed holiday.[95]   On the first day each household makes an offering to its own ancestral spirits at home.   These are small offerings; probably only chickens.[96]   On the second day offerings are made in the *numshang*; in this case pigs are offered and the ritual is in two parts, first there is an offering to the ancestors of the various village headmen other than the chief, and then an offering to the chief's ancestors.   The pig given to the chief's ancestors will be a larger and better pig than that offered to the headmen's ancestors.   On the third day, at the *numshang*, offerings are made to various sky nats on behalf of the commoners—usually the sky nats Musheng and his daughter Bunghpoi.   Here probably Bunghpoi gets a pig and her father a buffalo.   Then in the evening of the third day, in a ceremony from which everyone except the chief and his priests is excluded, an offering is made to the earth spirit Shadip.   The offering is probably only a small pig, but it is a genuine sacrifice, the whole animal is buried; in all the previous cases the gift to the gods is only symbolic, the meat is eaten by the human participants.   The proceedings close with a small offering to the luck spirits (*maraw*) which serves to de-sanctify the chief, the priests and the *numshang*.

This is but the skeleton of very long and intricate proceedings, but it suffices to show how the pattern of ritual 'represents' or describes the status relations within the community.   Rank is here represented in two ways, firstly by sequence—the order of sacrifice is: commoner ancestors, headmen's ancestors, chief's ancestors, junior sky spirit, senior sky spirit, earth spirit; secondly by the scale of offering: chicken, small pig, big pig, buffalo.   Finally the exclusion of everyone except the chief and the priests from the final part of the ceremony sets off the chief as a person apart, possessed of spiritual powers distinct from those of ordinary mortals.[97]

The argument will perhaps be easier to understand if I

[95] The rituals mentioned by Gilhodes (1922), p. 124, and Hertz (1943), p. 135 (fifth), are of the type here described.

[96] At the end of the festival the 'flag pole' loaded with chicken baskets which I have mentioned in section 1 of this chapter is erected in the *numshang* to show the number of chickens killed.

[97] Distinctions in the degree of sanctity attaching to different nats is indicated also in various other ways such as the kind of costume worn by the officiating priest, the length of the priest's incantation and so on.

specify more precisely the various categories of Kachin supernatural beings.

nat—'a spirit', 'a supernatural being'

In common with other writers on the Kachins, I anglicise this word and write of nat(s).

Individual nats are legion, but they fall into a limited number of clearly defined classes of different status and function; nats of any one class are all of one *amyu* and are therefore thought of as being of one lineage. We may distinguish the following:

ga nat—'earth spirit'

These are at the top of the class hierarchy. Their chief is Shadip who is regarded as a 'reincarnation' of Chyanun-Woishun, the bisexual progenitor-progenetrix of everything.

mu nat—'sky spirit'

These are the chiefs (*du ni*) among the nats. They are the children of Shadip or rather of Chyanun-Woishun. The youngest of the *mu nat*, and therefore the senior in status, is Madai. Madai's daughter Madai Jan Hpraw Nga married a human being, the first ancestor of all Kachin chiefs. Hence the Kachin chiefs are *dama* to the Madai nat and only they can make gifts to Madai and through him to the supreme earth nat Shadip. In the same way the daughter of another *mu nat*, Musheng (thunder), married an orphan commoner. Hence commoner Kachins are *dama* to Musheng and when commoners make sacrifices to the *mu nat* they must approach Musheng by way of preliminary offerings to his daughter, Bunghpoi (storm).[98]

gumgun nat, masha nat—'ancestor nats'

As already mentioned every household (*htinggaw*) has its own shrine, situated within the house, at which offerings are made to the ancestors of the lineage concerned. We have seen that the effective depth of a commoner's lineage is often very small, so that the principal deity of a household shrine may be a very recent ancestor, often an actual grandfather of someone still living. Hence the approach to the *masha nat* is a very personal one; they are scolded as often as supplicated.

[98] See also Chapter IX.

Masha nat are not thought of as having great power in themselves, but they serve as a medium of intercession. In particular, one approaches *mu nat* by way of preliminary offerings to the *masha nat*.

uma nat

The *masha nat* of a 'thigh-eating chief' are of a special category. The house of such a chief contains two shrines, one devoted to the chief's own ancestors, the other to the *mu nat* Madai, who is *mayu* to the chief's ancestors (cf. house plan, Fig. 2, p. 108). The chief is chief because he represents the 'youngest son line', he is the *uma*. The chief therefore can trace his lineage back to the founder ancestor of his chiefly line, the *uma nat*, who is *dama* to Madai. Hence, ritually speaking, the status of the 'thigh-eating chief' as owner of a domain rests on the fact that he alone can make offerings to the *uma nat* of his lineage. Through the *uma nat* he can approach Madai. Through Madai he can approach Shadip. Shadip controls the fortunes and fertility of all things. Hence the prosperity of the domain depends upon the proper ritual observances of the chief. Hence the chief is entitled to the ritual tribute of thighs (*magyi*) which he receives from his adherents.

This is the general pattern of the ideology; when it comes to details we find that very similar stories are frequently duplicated with different human characters. A single chiefly lineage may control more than one *uma nat*. The stories associated with these different nats serve to distinguish one lineage branch from another. Thus in the Lahtaw clan, chiefs of the Sana major lineage include Ngaw Gam and Ngaw Nawng among their *uma nats*. Ngaw Gam married a daughter of a *mu nat* and Ngaw Nawng was her son.[99] But Lahtaw clan chiefs of the Kadaw major lineage have Hkintang Nien and Kasang Nawng as their *uma nats* whom they support with a rival mythology.[100]

The *uma nat* is often referred to as the *mung nat* (domain nat), the idea being that this nat is the ultimate ruler of the

---

[99] See Carrapiett (1929), pp. 79–80. Carrapiett is incorrect in saying that these nats are shared by the whole of the Lahtaw clan.

[100] I have lost my record of the mythology of the Kadaw *uma nats*. One or other of them was married to a female *mu nat*.

political domain. *Gumlao* Kachins also frequently recognise a *mung nat, gumlao* Kachins, however, have no *uma nat* since they have no chiefs (see p. 124).

jahtung, sawn, lasa—'evil spirits, spooks'

All the nats so far discussed are potentially benevolent. If they punish mankind, it is because men have failed to fulfill their ritual obligations. But there are other inferior classes of nats who are generally ill intentioned. *Jahtung* confuses the best laid plans of hunters and fishermen, *sawn* causes misfortune to women in childbirth, *lasa* causes fatal accidents of all kinds. Conversely women who die in childbirth become *sawn*, people who die by accident become *lasa*. Significantly, origin myths make two of these inferior classes of nat the *dama* of human beings. The Jahtung are the offspring of a human girl and 'the heart of a deer'; the Sawn are the offspring of a human girl and a monkey. Hence these spooks are *dama* to the human race and their inferiors. The offerings made to them are of inferior type (pigs, dogs, chickens, rats, never cattle). They are treated with scant respect as troublesome vermin rather than as gods.[101]

maraw—'luck'

Kachins have no separate category of performances which can be regarded as magical rather than religious. The explanation of all types of ritual activity is that offerings are being made to nats. Some types of nats, however, represent what in other cultural contexts anthropologists have described as witchcraft substance. Particularly significant here are the *nsu nat*, which might be described as the 'spirit of jealousy', and the *maraw* which are a concept not unlike that of the classical furies (*erinyes, eumenides*). I translate *maraw* as 'luck' or 'luck spirit'.

From some points of view the ideas involved are close to those covered by the concept of Jahtung. An offering to Jahtung protects the hunter from ill luck from unknown sources, an offering to Nsu protects from ill luck arising from slander or jealousy; an offering to Maraw does much the same. Indeed, according to Gilhodes, Kachin fishermen identify the

[101] See Gilhodes (1922), pp. 56 f.

Nsu nat as being the chief Jahtung of the rivers and they make offerings jointly to Jahtung-Nsu, Sawn and Maraw.[102]   But Nsu and Maraw have other more subtle aspects.

Raw (maraw) means 'to untie', 'to cancel'.   When a legal dispute has been finally dealt with, the 'debt is cancelled' (*hka raw*).   The basic notion of the Maraw as nats is that they are beings who, despite their very lowly origin,[103] have the power of cancelling even the gifts of the highest gods.   They function therefore as a defence mechanism for the system of diagnosis practised by the priests and diviners.   If, in the last resort, things do not turn out as was predicted, it must be the fault of the Maraw.   Consequently sacrifices to the ordinary nats are always supplemented by an additional sacrifice to the Maraw.   There are many Maraw and each has its own ritual; one must be careful to propitiate the right one—there is a Maraw of birth, a Maraw of death, a Maraw of *manau*, a Maraw of ordinary feasts, a Maraw of clandestine love-making, a Maraw of the new harvest and so on.   The offerings are small (pigs, dogs, chickens, etc.) but important.   The Maraw sacrifice is always the final action in a ritual sequence; it closes the performance and de-sanctifies the performers. In Van Gennep's terminology a Maraw sacrifice is a rite of 'aggregation'.[104]

The Maraw also serve as witnesses or guarantors that a legal dispute is finally settled.   No case can be considered finished without the ceremony of *nat hpungdun jaw* ('the libation to the nat').   The nat in this instance is the Maraw.

Many types of legal fine include a *hpaga* entitled the *maraw nga* (*Maraw buffalo*), which is the last and crucial item to be paid before the formal offering to the Maraw can be made. The *maraw nga* is not, I think, itself sacrificed to the Maraw.[105] *Maraw nga* figure particularly in fines for breach of contract

[102] Gilhodes (1922), p. 59.

[103] Gilhodes (1922), p. 66, makes the Maraw the offspring of maggots feeding on the corpse of a mad slave.   Other traditions give the Maraw the status of original beings, as in Fig. 6, p. 269.   The term *maraw* seems to be an alternative form of *numraw* (monster) which is an epithet often applied to the semi-mythical *baren* (alligator-dragon) mentioned on pp. 112, 200.   The Kachin attitude to Maraw seems highly ambivalent.   They are despised, feared, and respected all at once.

[104] Van Gennep (1909).

[105] Hanson (1906), p. 434, says cattle are never sacrificed to Maraw; Carrapiett (1929), pp. 116-17, conflicts with this but is, I think, in error.

—as, for example, where a woman has been promised to one man but is then married to another.[106]   The idea is that any failure to carry out a ritual contract will invite supernatural penalties from the Maraw until appropriate compensation has been given to the offended party.

The Maraw most frequently specified as individuals are Kajai Maraw ('the Maraw of gossip or notoriety') and Matsa Maraw ('the Maraw of curses').   The ideas involved here are very close to that of Nsu nat ('the nat of jealousy or malicious thought').   These Maraw are 'the mother of accidents' (*sa wa nu*) and hence the Lasa nats (p. 177) derive from them.

The idea here is virtually that of sorcery.   The 'sorcerer' does not necessarily have to go through any magical performance; he can bring evil upon his enemy merely by uttering imprecations, spreading malicious gossip or simply harbouring evil thoughts.   But to guarantee success he must actually invoke the Maraw.   In theory the Matsa Maraw are courted by both sides.   The sorcerer makes offerings so as to induce Matsa Maraw to bring evil on his enemy; the victim makes offerings to induce the Matsa Maraw to leave him alone.[107] In practice these Maraw are suspected of causing harm far more often than they are actually invoked.

The practice of direct magical sorcery as opposed to the invocation of evil spirits seems to be very rare.[108]

hpyi—'witch spirits'.[109]

Kachins believe that people can be possessed by witch spirits even though they themselves are unaware of this malady.   The taint is hereditary and there is no effective cure.   Witches may cause all manner of sickness and misfortune; not to the person harbouring the witch spirit but to others.   It is sometimes possible to treat the victim by exorcism, but the harbourer of a witch spirit is incurable.   The only treatment is to destroy the human host and his or her family.   The witch concept is thus a 'scape-goat mechanism'.   Illness and misfortune is

[106] For examples of fines including *maraw nga* see Hertz (1943), pp. 154–5; Kawlu Ma Nawng (1942), pp. 59, 60, 63; Carrapiett (1929), pp. 116–17.
[107] Gilhodes (1922), pp. 293–4; Carrapiett (1929), p. 79; Hanson (1913), p. 145 f.
[108] Gilhodes (1922), p. 295; Hanson (1913), p. 147.
[109] In Shan *hpyi* has more or less the same significance as *nat* in Burmese and Jinghpaw.

usually first diagnosed as due to punishment or attack by one or other category of nat; appropriate sacrifices follow. If these prove of no avail, another diagnosis may be tried, followed by further sacrifices. One possible form of diagnosis is to say that the cause of misfortune[110] is a witch and to take appropriate vengeance.

Under the British régime it was illegal to accuse specific individuals of being witches and details are consequently unsatisfactory. In 1940 the concept of withcraft was very much alive but distorted. Certain practitioners declared that they had acquired (from the Shans) techniques for exorcising witches from the victim without being too specific as to who was the human host of the witch spirit. My own cook was an expert at this kind of exorcism; but though I witnessed several spectacular cures of 'witchcraft disease', I failed to identify any individual witch. From an anthropological point of view this is a pity, for the main interest in a witchcraft situation turns on techniques of divination and the relationship between witch and bewitched.

It seems reasonably clear, however, who the witch is expected to be. A witch is not a lineage kinsman; for witchcraft is hereditary and if my lineage brother is tainted, so am I. Quarrels between lineage kinsmen lead to invocation of the Nsu nat (p. 167) but not to witchcraft in the sense we are now discussing. The typical witch is an affinal relative—a *mayu*. Witch spirits are supposed to infest their victim in the shape of a small rodent (*lasawp*) gnawing at the vitals; by a euphemism witch spirits are therefore referred to as rats (*yu*) or as secret things (*mayun*). That *yu* (rat) is the symbolic equivalent for *mayu* (affinal relative) is certain from other contexts. For example, when family A is seeking a bride from family B, A sends to B an opening gift containing (*a*) *yu ma yawn*—a packet of dried rat, (*b*) *nga ma yawn*—a packet of dried fish. *Yu* (rat) here stands for *mayu* affinal relative; *nga* (fish) stands for *nga*, the cattle of the offered bride price.

In fact the real menace of witchcraft is not so much that there is a risk of becoming ill through an attack by witches,

---

[110] 'Misfortune' in such a context is *yubak* which has the implication 'punishment for sin'. Literally it means 'full of rats (*yu*)'. *Yu* here stands for witchcraft as indicated below.

as that one may oneself become an unconscious witch through contagion from one's wife. The person possessed by a *hpyi* communicates it to his partner and all his children.[111] Here paradoxically the ideology serves only to strengthen the *mayu-dama* ideal. If I am married to a 'new' *mayu* family—that is a family previously unrelated—I am likely to be suspicious of them and may well suspect them of witchcraft; but if I am married to an 'old' *mayu* family, in particular to my mother's brother's daughter, the chance of a taint is slight, for my mother's brother is at least as free from witchcraft as my own mother. Consequently marriage to the mother's brother's daughter is a partial insurance against witchcraft infection. This ties in with the fact that when a new *mayu-dama* link is under consideration, one of the details most anxiously discussed by both parties is whether there is any trace of witchcraft in the ancestry of the other.[112]

In former times families accused of witchcraft could be expelled from the village or even killed off. There is inadequate evidence as to how an accusation of witchcraft could be established or what sanctions could be invoked to achieve vengeance. This much, however, seems clear—one looks for witches in one's own community, not far afield. This has a bearing upon the stability of structural relationships within the local community.

We have already seen that, as between lineage groups of different communities which are related by ties of affinity, the friendly debt relationship, in which the groups are *mayu-dama*, and the hostile debt relationship, in which the groups are at feud, are recognised by the Kachins themselves as alternatives. The groups that make feud are, in the long run, the same groups that are *mayu-dama*. But where the affinal relatives are members of the same community this cannot apply, for open feud between near neighbours is intolerable. Witchcraft accusations within the local community are thus the equivalent of feuds outside the local community.

If my analysis is correct it is normally a *mayu* relative that is accused of witchcraft by his *dama*; that is to say the accusation comes from a person of formally low status against a person of formally higher status. I think this is easily understood.

---

[111] Gilhodes (1922), p. 296.   [112] Hanson (1913), pp. 183–4.

In theory local *mayu* should be the equals of or higher in status than their *dama*. So long as this theory corresponds to the palpable *de facto* situation the demands of the *mayu* on their *dama* are likely to be met without resentment. But if the *de facto* situation becomes reversed, (i.e. if the *mayu* relatives are in fact people of no status), the *dama* will be able to vent their spleen without restraint, for public opinion will support the influential *dama* rather than their low status *mayu*. The outcome of such a situation will be that the *mayu* will be accused of witchcraft and expelled from the community, thus restoring the total status system to its formally correct pattern.

From all this it becomes clear that the various nats of Kachin religious ideology are, in the last analysis, nothing more than ways of describing the formal relationships that exist between real persons and real groups in ordinary human Kachin society.

The gods denote the good relationships which carry honour and respect, the spooks and the witches denote the bad relationships of jealousy, malice and suspicion. Witchcraft becomes manifest when the moral constraints of the ideally correct social order lose their force.[113]

VIII

Concepts of Authority: Political and Religious Office

But if we have reduced the gods and the witches to mere manifestations of the human emotions, what becomes of the chief and the priests who derive their authority from their supposed power to control the gods?

Much of the difficulty in understanding the real status of these men springs from the loaded meaning which we in English attach to the word 'chief', and the ethnocentric difficulty of believing that an office which seems highly disadvantageous can be the goal of every man's endeavour. Frazer, by implication, notes this very point in the opening paragraphs of *The Golden Bough*. He asks in effect: Why on earth were there ever candidates for the precarious office of King of

[113] cf. Durkheim's argument regarding anomic suicide. Durkheim (1951), Chapter 5.

Nemi?   We might well ask the same of the chiefs and priests of Kachin society.

In this section I shall review what we have so far learnt about the rank and office of chief (*duwa*) and shall compare with this the power that attaches to various offices in the hierarchy of professional Kachin priests.   The results are very relevant to the issues discussed in the last part of the book.

In the literature of the Kachins it is implied that the 'officials' in a Kachin community are always the holders of either secular or religious office.   On the secular side are ranged the chief (*duwa*), and the elders (*salang*); on the religious side we have the priests of various grades (*jaiwa, dumsa, hkinjawng, hpunglum*) the diviners (*nwawt*) and the spirit mediums (*myihtoi*). But in fact the matter is not as simple as that.   The chief, it is true, holds no priestly office; yet his power derives from a religious role; the diviner has no formal political power, yet he is in a position of considerable political influence.

duwa—'chief'

Throughout this chapter I have stressed that the status of the individuals whom I describe as chief (*duwa*) is primarily defined in terms of prestige symbols.   One can say then that the office of chief is a ritual though not a priestly office in the sense, for example, that the Lord Mayor of London has a ritual though not a priestly office.   But how far is the Kachin chief's office also a political office of real power? Here the empirical situation (in 1940) was greatly confused by the fact that the British Administration had always taken it for granted that a Kachin chief *ought* to be an autocrat.   He was expected to execute without question all instructions received from the British District Officer ('Assistant Superintendent') by way of the Government Native Officer (*taungok*);' furthermore he was made responsible for the collection of house tax and he was entitled to a commission on his collection; he was also responsible for the law and order of his community and for adjudicating upon matters of native law and custom.   Nearly all these functions are quite alien to the traditional role of a *duwa*, and most chiefs under the British found themselves in an awkwardly ambiguous position.   In Hpalang, as it happened, the individual whom the Government treated as chief was not recognised as such by any sector of the community itself, and it was thus relatively easy for me to sort out the 'proper traditional' attributes of a chief from those which were purely Government-inspired.

The role of the chief *vis-à-vis* other office holders can be best appreciated if we break down the concept of authority into a number of separate functional categories. What then is the chief's role in (*a*) judicial affairs, (*b*) military affairs, (*c*) economic affairs, (*d*) day-to-day executive decisions, (*e*) religious affairs? In each of these fields the chief has a role to play, but usually it is a minor one.

a. Judicial Leadership. Kachins have no native concept of a judge. The phrases which are nowadays used to denote this idea would mean, if translated literally, 'one who understands about Burmese lawsuits'.[114] The native Kachin idea is that disputes are settled by arbitration rather than arbitrary judgement. A lawsuit involves a debt (*hka*) and the settlement of the debt is a matter for the agents (*kasa*) of the disputing parties. The judicial body of a village cluster or domain is thus a body of arbitrators rather than a bench of magistrates; its function is to give a ruling as to what would be a fit and proper settlement of the issue in dispute. Before the coming of the British, such a body had little power to enforce its decisions. Once a judgement had been made it was up to the winner to extract the settlement *hpaga* from his opponent as best he could.

This judicial body—if it can be called such—was known as the *salang hpawng* (council of *salang*), or sometimes *du salang ni myit su ni* (chief, *salang* and wise men). *Salang*, as we have seen, is a title given to the leaders of principal lineages other than that of the chief. *Myit su* (wise man) implies any elderly man whose experience and knowledge of custom commands respect. The chief is a member of the *salang hpawng* simply in his capacity as head of his own lineage; he has no special judicial powers. Indeed because of his central position in the kinship network, the chief himself or some member of his lineage is likely to be a party to most disputes that crop up within the domain; the chief's role in the *salang hpawng* is thus more frequently that of litigant than that of arbitrator.

In theory a dispute between commoners should be arbitrated

---

[114] e.g. *amu chyeyang ai wa; tara agyi wa. Amu* (lawsuit) and *tara* (law) are both terms borrowed from the Burmese.

by *salang* (i.e. lineage heads); a dispute between *salang* should be arbitrated by other *salang* and by chiefs from outside communities; a dispute between chiefs will probably not be resolved at all for many years but when finally settled will be arbitrated by other chiefs, especially those of higher lineage status than the disputants.

But though the chief is not a judge, he has a vested interest in law and order. Among the symbols of land ownership (cf. p. 155) is 'the right to commit violence'. The significance of this is that if A assaults B within the domain of a chief C, neither A nor B being of the same lineage as C, then not only does A incur a debt (*hka*) against B's lineage, he also incurs a debt against C's lineage on the ground that he (A) has committed sacrilege against the domain nat (*mung nat*) of C, that is to say the *uma nat* of the C chief. The chief therefore has a personal interest in seeing that disputes within his territory are settled. If it is a case of violence, then the chief himself is necessarily a party to the dispute; if it is a civil offence such as bastardy or adultery, the chief is not necessarily immediately involved, but if the debt is not arbitrated quickly violence may result and then the chief will be directly involved.

A chief therefore may be expected to interest himself in the settlement of lawsuits even though he himself may play only a very minor role in any actual judicial procedure.

b. Military leadership. There are many societies where it is possible to define the political unit as the 'largest community which considers that disputes between its members should be settled by arbitration and that it ought to combine against other communities of the same kind and against foreigners'.[115] With certain qualification it might, I think, be practical to define the Shan concept *möng* in this way. But while a Kachin chief certainly likes to represent himself as the autocratic ruler of a domain (*mung*), it is quite clear that in practice Kachin warfare was seldom organised on a territorial basis. When Kachins talk of war (*majan*), they mean nothing more than a blood feud (*bunglat hka*) in which the lineages of two chiefs are involved and which on that account is difficult to bring to any immediate settlement. Only the lineages of the two chiefs are immediately concerned, and if other groups get

[115] Evans-Pritchard in Fortes and Evans-Pritchard (1940), p. 278.

involved, they do so as lineage groups, on the basis of kinship, and not as members of a territorial community. Thus if the chief of domain A is at feud with the chief of domain B, the chief of domain A cannot necessarily raise all the people of his domain to fight on his side. No doubt some will do so on the grounds of kinship, but others, being related to both sides, will prefer to take no part.

Moreover such enmities are not habitual. Nearly all feuds start over a woman. Generally speaking, at the beginning of a feud the parties to it are in *mayu-dama* relationship, and as Kawlu Ma Nawng stresses, when the feud is finally settled 'there is no question of the feud remaining outstanding as the parties have usually exchanged women between them and have (once more) become related groups.'[116] The actual fighting in such feud wars was always on a very minor scale. As in other types of debt settlement, the principals usually took no part directly. As already explained, the usual procedure was to hire agents, called *share*, to carry out the actual raids and assassinations (see p. 98).

Open warfare (*hpyen gasat*), when it occurred at all, consisted of marauding raids and ambuscades in which the short term objective was loot and the long term objective mainly to make life so generally unpleasant for the enemy that they would be willing to settle up outstanding 'debts' or else pay handsomely for 'protection'.

On the other hand, military braves (*hpyen, share*) did not act solely on behalf of their fellow Kachins. They regularly hired out themselves and their raiding parties to contending Shan princes and even farther afield—e.g. the Burmese kings had a regiment of Kachin soldiers. Under the British this tradition was continued and Kachins were recruited in large numbers for military and police service. The economic rewards of these military mercenaries have always been important. At the present time Kachin regiments still form the backbone of the Burma Army and the Kachin state is heavily subsidised by funds from the Burma Central Government as a reward for their services.

But in all these military and para-military activities, the chiefs, even when they initiated a quarrel, did not themselves

116 Kawlu Ma Nawng (1942), p. 55.

take a leading part as soldiers.   Even today this is true.   While persons rated as *salang* (lineage head) or *myit su* (wise man) have often had a distinguished career in the Burma Army or Military Police, the actual chief and his immediate heir has probably spent all his life at home.   In Hpalang the headmen of Sumnut and Gumjye and the Government-appointed Maran chief had all had military careers and reached the rank of sergeant or higher, but the hereditary Nmwe chief had never been in the army at all.   This is very typical.   The Kachin Chief like the United States President is Commander-in-Chief. Neither of these social persons is expected to fight in battle.

   c. The Chief's Role in Economic Affairs.   We have already seen that the chief, by virtue of the fact that he is expected to give bigger and more frequent feasts than anyone else, plays an important part in the distribution of consumption goods.   Conceptually he is the receiver of tribute—he is the 'thigh-eating chief' (*magyi sha ai du*), his house is the 'paddy store' (*htingsang*). If the argument I have put forward earlier with regard to *hpaga* is correct, the right to receive meat tribute and to receive an enhanced scale of *hpaga* payments for the settlement of debts does not substantially increase the economic power of the individual chief, for his obligations increase proportionately to the increase of his receipts.   Tribute in the form of paddy (rice) is not on quite the same footing.   I have already remarked upon the intrinsic interdependence of Kachin (hill) and Shan (valley) economy.   In pre-British days a very important function of leading Kachin chiefs was to offer 'protection' to valley-dwelling wet-rice cultivators in return for tribute in rice.   The procedure was to include the valley villages within the domain of the hill chief.   Thereafter anyone who attacked the valley villages would find himself at feud with the Kachin chief.   In a large number of cases the valley villages were actually brought into existence through the Kachin chief's initiative; Shans were provided with a site on condition that they paid a regular tribute of rice.   This rice tribute, in the Kachin view, was the equivalent of the 'thighs' (*magyi*) paid by Kachin.[117]

----

[117] Being Buddhists, the Shans, in theory do not kill meat. Under the British no Shan villages were allowed to remain dependent upon Kachin chiefs, but the surviving documentary evidence suggests that the relationship between a Shan

Caravans of Chinese traders and the like passing through a chief's domain were 'protected' in a similar way in return for tribute. The evidence makes it appear that all such tribute was always a perquisite of the chief and not of village headmen, and this would fit in with the general pattern of Kachin ideas about land rights. How the tribute was further distributed among the chief's own Kachin followers (*zaw*) is not apparent. It is clear, however, that in favourable cases the role of tribute holder gave the Kachin chief a position of real economic strength, provided, that is, that the tribute consisted of cash or rice or other economically valuable goods and not merely the orthodox ritual gift of meat.

Examples of this type of leadership are recorded for the Singpho of Assam in the 1830's, the Gauri of the Sinlum area in the 1850–1870 period, and North Hsenwi and elsewhere in the 1890's. It is striking that in every case where this outside tribute had become available, the Kachin chief had quickly turned himself into a petty Shan *saohpa*. One might perhaps infer from this that in the ordinary structure of Kachin society there is no expectation that the chief will wield any substantial amount of economic power. It is only when wind-fall resources become available from outside that the chief gets into a position where he can play the part of an autocrat.

d. Executive Leadership. Paradoxically, the executive initiative in such matters as the foregoing was not, in the pre-British period, necessarily a function of the chief. It was always open for a village headman (*salang*) of outstanding ability and personality to elevate himself into the position of being the 'leader' (*bawmung*) of a domain for all everyday practical affairs (see p. 124). The existence of such a *bawmung* would not in any way affect the ritual functions of the chief, nor would it affect the chiefly succession, but the recognition of such commoner leadership by the Kachins themselves serves to stress the essentially ritual nature of the chiefly office.

It is entirely consistent with the ideas about kingship current in both Shan and Burmese society that the successful, economically powerful, leader should himself disdain to take an active

village and its Kachin domain chief differed very little from that between a Kachin village and its Kachin domain chief. See R.N.E.F., 1898–1900; Scott and Hardiman (1900).

part in day-to-day administrative affairs. Such practical matters are for underlings; the King himself should live apart in his palace surrounded by his numerous wives and concubines. Kachin chiefs seldom achieved anything even approaching this status of semi-divinity, but it is significant that—to judge from the literature—the influence of commoner *bawmung* was most pronounced in the wealthiest chiefdoms, where the chief was most obviously aping the manners of a Shan prince.[118]

Under the British, the Government-recognised chief was responsible for making a great number of day-to-day executive decisions, but he did so simply as agent of the paramount power. The executive decisions that had to be made by the Kachins themselves without waiting for orders from above concerned such matters as where to make a field clearing, when to burn the felled brushwood, when to make the first sowing, where to place a house site. The decision here rested not with the chief or with any particular individual but with the *salang hpawng* as a whole. Mostly this body of elders seems to act by precedent; where precedent gives no clear guide, resort is made to divination and soothsayers. So again there is a conflict between theory and practice. Kachin *theory* is that the chief rules (*up*) with autocratic power; in my actual field-work I seldom identified any instruction which had issued from a chief acting on his own initiative. Where he gave an order it was as mouthpiece of the Government or of the *salang hpawng* or of some oracle which he had first consulted.

e. Leadership in Religious Affairs: the functions of priests. The chief's office, I suggested earlier, is a ritual but not a priestly office. It is a ritual office not merely because it is defined in terms of prestige symbols which do not necessarily carry with them any real political or economic power, but also because the chief has a very definite role to play in the religious organisation.

Mention has already been made of the chief's control over certain nats. Because of this control he is responsible for carrying out certain annual sacrifices on behalf of the community. His role is a passive one. The chief 'gives' the sacrifice in the sense that he provides the animals for slaughter, but he is not a priest.

[118] For examples see particularly references to *pawmine* (*bawmung*) in Anderson (1871) and (1876).

The same is true even when the chief holds *manau* and makes sacrifices to his personal deities for the enhancement of his own prestige. Although the right to 'give' (*jaw*) the sacrifice is exclusive to the chief and is a valued possession, it consists merely in the right to provide the materials for the feast and to employ a priest to recite the appropriate ritual chants. A chief could never be priest (*dumsa*) at his own sacrificial feast and it is rare to find a chief who is qualified to act as priest even at other people's sacrifices. We need then to analyse the nature of the priestly office.

jaiwa—saga teller
dumsa—priest
hkinjawng—ritual butcher
hpunglum—assistant ritual butcher

The Kachin system provides a large number of priestly offices of one kind or another and entry into all of these is by apprenticeship and acquired skill. Hence they are non-hereditary. But practice of the priestly art, especially in its more elaborate forms, brings to the performer considerable perquisites and great prestige. Indeed in many ways the prestige of a great priest outshines that of a great chief.

The techniques necessary for the lower grades of the priesthood are not difficult to acquire and in most villages there are several people available who are competent to perform, let us say, the rituals of a *masha nat* sacrifice and to do the job for a quite nominal fee.[119] But learning the rituals for a major sacrifice is quite another matter; it involves literally years of arduous apprenticeship. Thus in Hpalang in 1940 there must have been dozens of people qualified to recite the chants accompanying the sacrifice of a chicken in the ritual treatment of stomach ache, but there were only two men who knew the rituals for a *ga nat* sacrifice which, among other things, called for the intoning of a traditional saga for 8 to 10 hours at a stretch. At a *manau* the recitation of sagas can go on for days on end and the priests who can accomplish this feat have a

---

[119] The carcases of sacrificed animals are cut up in a most elaborate manner somewhat after the fashion described for the Chins by Stevenson (1943). The three officiating priests each get their perquisite according to their station. For important sacrifices the priest receives a substantial fee in *hpaga* in addition to his share of the meat.

special title *jaiwa*.   In 1940 there were probably only two or three competent *jaiwa* in the whole of the Bhamo district.   If anyone in Hpalang had held *manau* they would have had to employ one of these men at a substantial fee.

There is no particular rule as to who may or may not become a priest but the career tends to attract the able or ambitious man who does not hold office by hereditary right. Thus lineage heads who sit on the *salang hpawng* by right of birth are not likely to go to the bother of becoming celebrated as priests.   But the elder brother of such a man or the illegitimate son of a chief who has, as it were, been defrauded of his natural status might have every incentive to seek the vicarious prestige attainable through priestly office.   The priestly leaders of Laga village in Hpalang illustrated this point very well. Myihtoi Gam, as his name implied, was a medium as well as a priest; he was easily the most accomplished priest (*dumsa*) in Hpalang and his services were in constant demand.   By birth he had been a distinctly frustrated character.   His birth name was NhKum Gam and he was the eldest brother of NhKum Naw (Laga Naw), the headman of Laga village.   He had a wall eye and a hare lip and looked as if he must have suffered from rickets in his childhood.   Second only to Myihtoi Gam in priestly influence was my neighbour Lahtaw Naw.   As a priest (*dumsa*) he was of only medium competence—he was a *tsu dumsa*,[120] he knew how to sacrifice pigs but not cattle—but he was immensely skilled as a ritual butcher (*hkinjawng*) and was present at almost every sacrifice to cut up the meat and see that the traditionally correct portions were allocated to the multifarious claimants both human and supernatural.   Lahtaw Naw was also outstanding as a ritual dancer; he was always dance leader at the funerals which he attended and also (so I was told) at *manau*.   Lahtaw Naw was married to the sister of Laga Naw the village headman, but he was of no status by birth.   In discussions with me he was unusually reticent about his origin; local gossip alleged that he was an illegitimate son of an important Lahtaw chief 30 miles away to the south. Both Myihtoi Gam and Lahtaw Naw sat on the Maran chief's *salang hpawng* in their capacity as 'wise men'.   It is unlikely that either would have done so had they not become ritual experts.

[120] Hanson (1913), p. 153.

nwawt—'diviner'; *myihtoi*—'medium'

Diviners (*nwawt*) and mediums (*myihtoi*) are not necessarily priests (*dumsa*), though the roles are often combined.   Divining is resorted to very frequently for all kinds of purposes:—Where shall I site my house?   Is X a suitable bride for my son Y? What has happened to the buffalo I lost last week?   Is to-morrow a propitious day to go to market?   All these and a host of similar and dissimilar questions may be answered by divina-tion.   Various techniques are practised.[121]   In theory the procedure is magical and automatic and requires no special skill.   Large numbers of people claim to know how to divine. In practice all divination procedures call for interpretation by the diviner and certain people—usually priests—are recognised as specially expert.   The office of diviner has very little prestige attached to it; in theory anyone can learn how to devine in half an hour or so.   In reality it is quite clear that the diviner wields very considerable power, for his interpretations affect economic action and within wide limits his interpretations are free from all restraint.

Two very ordinary examples will serve to illustrate this. Firstly, when a feud is to be settled, each side chooses a body of elders and chiefs to act as its agents in the arbitration. Clearly much will depend upon who is chosen, but the decision does not rest with either of the interested parties, it is a matter for divination.   Secondly, when a man is ill, it is the diviner who decides what nat is responsible and what sacrifice is called for.   Now it must be remembered that the public at large will eat the meat of the sacrifice.   It is not surprising therefore that the nats demand much bigger sacrifices from the wealthy than they do from the poor.   But it is through the diviner that this discrimination is effected.

Mediums—*myihtoi*—have a considerably higher status than diviners, though their activities are somewhat similar.   In theory mediums are born not made; mediumship is a natural faculty, not something learnt from a master.   The behaviour of mediums is, however, very stereotyped and is clearly learnt by imitation even if not by actual apprenticeship.   I never heard any suggestion that the faculty was hereditary, it is

[121] cf. Hanson (1913), p. 137.

supposed to crop up quite spasmodically. The incidence of mediums seems to be about the same as that of superior priests (*dumsa*). In Hpalang there were two mediums, one was also a senior priest. The ideology of mediumship is that the medium in a trance state is able to transport himself to the world of the nats and consult the nats in person, or alternatively that he can establish direct communication with the nats and persuade a junior nat, such as a recently deceased ancestor, to come and speak through his own human mouth.

Mediums are more expensive practitioners than ordinary diviners and they tend to be consulted when the procedures recommended by the diviner have led to no result. One very important function of the medium serves to limit the destructive implications of the religious theory. In theory, all illness is due to the persecution or displeasure of the nats. Consequently all illness is curable provided only that one can find the right sacrifice to make to the right nat. Kachins are of course perfectly well aware that death is the lot of all and that fatal illnesses may be very prolonged, but strict adherence to religious ideology would imply that the relatives of any dying man ought to be ruined in their attempts to buy off the nats by repeated sacrifices. Illnesses of important people do indeed provide the excuse for large scale sacrifices, but where an old man is obviously dying, his heirs are not usually prepared to see their whole patrimony squandered as a token of filial piety. Instead they employ a medium. In the course of a ceremony accompanied by a small sacrifice, the medium is supposed to transport himself to the nat world and make promises to the effect that, provided only the sick man is allowed to recover, much larger offerings will be made in the future. If then the sick man dies as expected, his heirs are absolved from further obligation to the nats who have not kept to their part of the bargain. The medium performs this ceremony on a bamboo platform (*hkinrawng*) some 20–30 feet high, erected for the occasion in front of the house of the sick man. After the ceremony this platform remains standing as a reminder that if the sick man recovers another sacrifice is still due.

Mediums are often credited with supernormal physical powers—they are supposed to be able to climb unscathed a ladder of upturned sword blades[122] or walk along a suspended cotton thread. This, to some extent, is an index of the high esteem which attaches to the mediumistic faculty. Saga tellers (*jaiwa*) are similarly credited with the ability to ride around on tigers. I would suspect that mediums, like priests and diviners, are usually individuals who do not hold any political office by hereditary right, but I have no clear evidence that this is always the case. One feature of the system, for which I can offer no explanation, is that, while Jinghpaw mediums are nearly always male, in certain other Kachin groups such as the Nung the mediums are usually female.[123]

This review of the forms of leadership attaching to different kinds of secular and religious office in Kachin society serves only to recapitulate the theme that has been recurrent throughout this chapter. *Gumsa* Kachins appear to think of themselves as having a very clear-cut authority system. The chief is regarded as an autocrat placed at the peak of a hierarchy of ranked classes, differentiated from one another by rules of caste-like rigidity. In this ideal structural pattern everything fits together very perfectly, each person and each group of persons has an appointed place in a clearly defined system. But the reality does not correspond to the ideal. In the reality the chiefly office is only one of many offices which contain elements of authority; prestige and status do not really depend solely on birth status; the nicely ordered ranking of lineage seniority conceals a vicious element of competition. But it is competition for prestige and reputation rather than wealth.[124]

I assume that Kachins achieve personal satisfaction from being able to influence other people. Analysis shows that such influence is wielded in different ways through different channels. On the one hand recognised prestige attaches to certain formal offices—chief, lineage head, saga teller, medium —and those who can get themselves recognised as deserving

---

[122] This idea seems to be borrowed from the Chinese, see Doolittle (1876), p. 153. Green (1934) states that he actually witnessed a Kachin medium climbing a ladder of swords.

[123] In Burma proper the mediums (*nat gadaw*) are usually female, but in this case the faculty is hereditary in the female line.

[124] It is, I think, relevant to note that Kachins share Chinese ideas about the paramount importance of reputation or 'face'. *Myi man sum*—'to lose face' corresponds precisely to the Chinese concept and has equal importance.

these titles will have power and influence accordingly.   But on the other hand there are offices such as that of diviner or junior priest or ritual butcher which carry very little prestige in themselves but which nevertheless provide channels through which influence can be exerted.   The real Kachin society is not, I suggest, a rigidly structured hierarchy of fixed classes and well-defined offices, but a system in which there is constant and at times very rapid social mobility.   The mobility is brought about in one of two ways.   Either the holders of the minor unesteemed offices use their influence to manipulate their way into positions of higher recognised authority, or alternatively they become revolutionaries and repudiate the authority of the higher offices altogether.   This in essence is the difference between *gumsa* and *gumlao* organisation which we must now consider.

CHAPTER VI

GUMLAO AND *GUMSA*

In our own western world we recognise the principles of monarchy and republicanism as contrasted theories of government, and it is reasonable to assert that a monarchy has a different type of social structure from a republic. On the other hand a change of regime from monarchy to republic or *vice versa* does not necessarily produce radical changes in the social structure overnight. Cromwell, Lord Protector, had powers and functions not very different from those of Charles I, Divine King. A modern critic of the American Constitution has remarked that the President is expected to behave like a fossilised version of George III. Even Stalin at times seemed very like the Little Father who was Tzar of all the Russians. In other words, the contrast between monarchy and republicanism is essentially one of theory; in their practical application the two systems may sometimes look very much alike. If we concentrate on ideal models we shall have to say that we are dealing with two contrasted social structures; if we concentrate on practical facts, the ideals of equalitarian republicanism and authoritarian monarchy merely represent polar types in a total system of flux.

Contrasted theories of government of this kind are current throughout the Burma–Assam frontier area. Thus Stevenson contrasts the autocratic Chins of Falam and Haka with the democratic Chins of Tiddim;[1] Hutton finds that both the Sema and the Konyak have some communities which are democratic like those of the Angami but others quite the reverse.[2] Dewar, referring to peoples right on the border of Kachin territory, contrasts Nagas, who have hereditary headmen, with those whose headmen are appointed by 'selection'.[3]

[1] Stevenson (1943). [2] Hutton (1921)b, p. 121; (1929) pp. 28, 42.
[3] Dewar (1931).

In Jinghpaw speech the contrast is represented in the words *gumsa* and *gumlao*. The purpose of this chapter is to explain just what this contrast really implies. In brief, the *gumsa* conceive of themselves as being ruled by chiefs who are members of an hereditary aristocracy; the *gumlao* repudiate all notions of hereditary class difference. *Gumsa* regard *gumlao* as commoner serfs who have revolted against their lawful masters; *gumlao* regard *gumsa* as tyrants and snobs. But while the two terms represent in Kachin thinking two fundamentally opposed modes of organisation, both are consistent with the same general set of cultural trappings which we recognise as Kachin. Of two lineages of the same clan one may be *gumsa* and another *gumlao*; *gumsa* and *gumlao* speak the same languages; both in mythological and historical time *gumsa* communities have been converted into *gumlao* communities and *vice versa*.

The opposition of ideas latent in these two concepts is used as a symbol of hostility. *Gumsa* and *gumlao* in neighbouring areas usually regard one another as traditional feud enemies and use the '*gumlao* origin story' as a justification for the feud. An enquirer will, therefore, receive a very different notion as to the virtues and vices of the rival systems according as to whether his informants are themselves *gumsa* or *gumlao*.

The informants of the first British Administrators in North Burma were all *gumsa*; moreover, Colonial Administrators have a notorious preference for autocratic chiefs. Consequently in the eyes of the Administration the *gumlao* system was tainted with rebellion and thoroughly obnoxious, as the following two quotations show.

'*a*. Formerly every Kachin village was ruled by an hereditary official called a Sawbwa [i.e. *sao-hpa*]; the villagers were obliged to cultivate his land without compensation and were subject to many other imposts. These taxes having become very onerous, a revolution was started about 20 years ago [i.e. about 1870] and spread very rapidly, chiefly in the tract between the Mali Hka and the N'mai Hka rivers, which led to the murder and deposition of a large number of Sawbwas and the appointment of certain headmen called Akyis or Salangs in their places. The villages which are now without Sawbwas are called Kamlao [*gumlao*] or rebel villages in contradistinction to the others which are Kamsa [*gumsa*] or Sawbwa-owning villages.

The difficulty of a march through the Kachin country is greatly enhanced if the people of the villages passed through have no Sawbwas and are Kamlaos and not Kamsas.   With an hereditary Sawbwa, if he is friendly, no trouble need be expected from the villagers, but in a Kamlao village, which is practically a small republic, the headman, however well meaning he may be, is quite unable to control the actions of any badly disposed villager.'[4]

'*b*. More than half a century ago, a spirit of republicanism manifested itself in the unadministered territory known as the Triangle and thence found its way to the west of the Mali Hka. Certain tribesmen who found the yoke of the Duwa irksome and were impatient of control, declared themselves Kumlaos or rebels, threw off their hereditary connection with the Duwa, and settled themselves in solitary villages of their own.   The British Government steadily set its face against this movement and has declined to recognise Kumlaos.

Villages in properly constituted tracts under a Duwa are known as Kumshas.   It will be found that there is still a tendency here and there to assert this spirit of independence, and officers should be on the alert to suppress it without delay. . . .

It will be found that in some subdivisions there have been no Duwas for years past.   Here each village will be found under its own Akyi.   The mistakes of past years cannot now be rectified, and this departure from established custom must continue.'[5]

An anthropologist naturally finds it difficult to believe that a political sub-species so widespread and persistent as that of the *gumlao* should have come into spontaneous existence as late as 1870 and as already noted (p. 161) the word *gumlao* is mentioned even in an English source as early as 1828.   Kawlu Ma Nawng has no illusions on the subject.   He places the origin of the *gumlao* movement way back in mythological time 300–400 years ago.[6]

The myth recorded by Kawlu Ma Nawng relates specifically to the *gumlao* of the Hukawng Valley.   It is long and complicated and, I must confess, not fully comprehensible.   One suspects that the author has compounded several quite

---

[4] Walker (1892), p. 164.   This was the first intelligible statement published concerning the *gumsa/gumlao* opposition, though a garbled version is recognisable in 'Alaga's' report of 1879, cf. Sandeman (1882), p. 257.

[5] Carrapiett, 81–2. This quotation comes from an official government handbook published in 1929 from a chapter specifically entitled 'Advice to Junior Officers'.   It is hardly surprising that the officers who were prepared to examine the *gumlao* system on its merits were few and far between!

[6] Kawlu Ma Nawng (1942), p. 30.

different stories and attempted to produce a consecutive 'history'. What would appear to be the crucial section can be condensed as follows:[7]

A *gumsa* girl, Tangai ma Ja In, has an illegitimate child by N'Bawn La Ja while she is betrothed to Shatan Wa. N'Bawn La Ja and Shatan Wa are both of lineage inferior in rank to that of the girl (1). Shatan Wa (lit. 'the slanderer') and his marriage agent, Loileng Wa (2), are partly to blame for this lapse as they have delayed the wedding unduly (3). The child is stolen by the alligator of Hkitmung Ningdawn who hides it in a cave in the mountain (4). Tangai ma Ja In promises the sky nat Musheng the sacrifice of a buffalo if the child is returned. Musheng splits open the mountain, exposes the alligator and returns the child (5). The priest medium Dumsa La Lawn (6) is asked to make the sacrifice. Musheng tells the priest to make the sacrifice to a superior sky nat called Sinlap (7). By his mediumistic powers the priest is transported to heaven to make the offering in person.

'While he was in the heavens Dumsa La Lawn saw a number of villages with clouds of smoke over them (8). He asked what villages they were. The heavenly spirit told him that it was *gumlao* land. He also saw villages in another place with numbers of houses very close together; on enquiry he was informed that those villages were the *gumsa* land (9). Dumsa La Lawn asked what *gumlao* and *gumsa* meant and was told that the *gumlao* were people who maintained all men were of equal rank; no customary thighs from slaughtered animals were taken and no forcible cutting of the fields was required. The *gumsa*, he was told, were people who had chiefs; these chiefs demanded a thigh of every animal killed and free labour for the cultivation of their fields; they rated as commoners even their own relatives who had not the right to collect dues and insisted on the payment of the dues, labour and otherwise, from these relatives as from other commoners' (10).

Dumsa La Lawn then asks the sky nat how humans can become *gumlao*. He is instructed to take back to earth some of the meat and liquor from the sacrifice. Anyone who refuses to partake of the sacrifice is to be overthrown. He takes back the offering and calls all to partake, the chief refuses to do so (11). The chief and Dumsa La Lawn then insult one another in various stereotyped ways. The chief hits the Dumsa on the head and calls him 'an adulterer, a slave and the illegitimate child of a monkey woman'.

[7] See Kawlu Ma Nawng (1942), pp. 11–13, 20.

The Dumsa roasts the brains of a monkey in the chief's liquor tube, and later wantonly cuts down the chief's bamboos when acting as *hpunglum* at the burial feast of one of the chief's relatives (12). Finally the chief kills a girl relative of the Dumsa who is carrying water in tubes made from the said bamboos and the Dumsa kills the chief and starts the *gumlao* rebellion.

In this war the discontented sections of the Tsasen clan are joined by members of the Pyen Dingsa N'Ding lineage of the Marip clan who have similar grounds for complaint against the Marip chiefs (13).

An adequate commentary on this story would almost require a chapter to itself, but the following notes, which connect with the numbers in the text above, will make it more meaningful.

1. Tangai, N'Bawn and Shatan are represented as three lineages of the same clan, Tsasen. Tangai are the *uma* branch. Tangai and N'Bawn are real, i.e. existing, major lineages; the Tangai are now *gumsa*; the N'Bawn are *gumlao*.

2. Loileng Wa is represented as the elder cousin of Shatan. From his name he appears to be a Shan.

3. According to Kachin customary law this mitigates the girl's offence. The penalty is that the girl's illegitimate descendants rank as serfs to her legitimate descendants. A very similar story is used to explain the theoretically inferior status of a section of the Marip clan (See Kawlu Ma Nawng, pp. 4/5; also Note 13 below).

4. See the discussion of the *baren* (alligator) symbol on p. 112 f.

5. Musheng thus approves the overthrow of the alligator (chief) in the interests of the illegitimate child and the freeing of the latter from the tyranny of the former. The general theme is a widespread one. Commoner human beings are descended from alligator-dragons (see p. 269). Compare also the Nung story given by Barnard (1934), p. 114: 'After the Flood a woman gave birth to a stone in the house of a dragon with wings and a tail. . . . This stone was broken on a big slab of rock and the remnants scattered and from them sprang all the races of men'. The form of this tale derives from the fact that the word for stone in Jinghpaw and Nung is *lung* which is Chinese for dragon.

6. The point to note here is that Dumsa La Lawn, the revolutionary leader, is a priest-medium. This individual seems to be identified by Kawlu Ma Nawng with N'Dup Nawng Dai Gawng, one of the originators of the N'Dup-Dumsa ('blacksmith-priest') lineage, the originators of the *gumlao* movement (See Kawlu Ma Nawng, pp. 10, 20).

7. The point here is that since Tangai ma Ja In is of chiefly stock the offering would ordinarily have to be made to Madai, the sky nat of the chiefs. In offering to Sinlap instead, the authority of Madai is repudiated.

8. The smoke is the smoke of continuous sacrificial feasting—i.e. the villages are very prosperous.

9. The houses of *gumsa* villages are close together for defence— i.e. the *gumsa* chiefs are always at war with one another.

10. The crux of the *gumsa-gumlao* contrast is thus seen to lie in the issue of whether, when a lineage segments, the two segments are of equal status or one is subordinate to the other.

11. Because to do so would be to recognise the superiority of Sinlap over Madai.

12. *Hpunglum* is the lowest ranking ritual office. It would be insulting to offer such a task to an esteemed priest-medium.

13. (See Note 3 above). Today only one or two minor sections of the N'Ding are *gumlao*. The remainder are *gumsa* and include a number of very influential chiefs. The latter presumably would not admit the intrinsically inferior status of the N'Ding lineage.

The other main section of Kawlu Ma Nawng's story has the same structural implications, but the *gumlao* revolt is justified on slightly different grounds. In this case one N'La La Grawng inherits, as a levirate wife from his elder brother, a woman of the N'Bawn lineage. From this levirate marriage are born two children, La N'Gam N'Dup wa Daigrau (the blacksmith) and La N'Nawng Dumsa wa Daigawng (the priest); 'the descendants of these children were treated as inferiors by the descendants of the children born of the first marriage,[8] on the grounds that they were only children born of a "collected" widow. They were rated as commoners; they had to cut *taungya* for the others; they had to surrender a thigh of every animal killed; they were generally ill used'.[9] The descendants of the 'blacksmith' and the 'priest' form a joint lineage N'Dup-Dumsa (blacksmith-priests) which significantly does not split into senior and junior sections. They are the leaders of a *gumlao* revolt against their tyrannical relatives.

---

[8] It is not clear whose first marriage is meant—that of N'La La Grawng or that of his wife.

[9] Kawlu Ma Nawng (1942), pp. 10, 20.

Both these myths emphasise what amounts to a basic inconsistency in *gumsa* ideology. The *gumsa* ideal order consists of a network of related lineages, but it is also a network of ranked lineages. As the process of lineage fission proceeds there comes a point at which choice has to be made between the primacy of the principle of rank or the principle of kinship. Rank implies an asymmetrical relationship. The overlord extorts services from his subordinate without obligations of reciprocity. Kinship implies a symmetrical relationship; a *mayu-dama* (affinal) or *hpu-nau* (lineage brother) relationship between a chief and his follower may imply one-sided obligations from the follower towards his chief, but it also implies that the chief has obligations towards his follower. The weakness of the *gumsa* system is that the successful chief is tempted to repudiate links of kinship with his followers and to treat them as if they were bond slaves (*mayam*). It is this situation which, from a *gumlao* point of view, is held to justify revolt.

Yet the *gumlao* system is equally full of inconsistencies. In *gumlao* theory there are no chiefs. All lineages are of the same rank; no one brother is ritually superior to any other. Therefore, in theory, *gumlao mayu* and *dama* rank equal and there ought to be no ban on patrilateral cross cousin marriage (marriage with the father's sister's daughter). Jinghpaw-speaking *gumlao* are thus faced with the paradox that their language separates the categories of *mayu* and *dama* relatives although there is nothing in their political system which calls for such separation.[10] I have no evidence that Jinghpaw-speaking *gumlao* would readily tolerate marriage with a father's sister's daughter. The tendency rather seems to be to develop arrangements for 'marrying in a circle' within groups of localised *gumlao* lineages. Such an arrangement can theoretically maintain equality of status between the lineages in question. In practice it does not seem to work very well. Empirically, *gumlao* groups in Jinghpaw-speaking areas seem to revert rather rapidly to class differentiation on a lineage basis. Some of the evidence for this statement is cited later.

My general proposition is then that while it is analytically

[10] This is not true of speakers of Maru dialects, and it may be the case that for *gumlao* Maru there is no ban on reciprocal cross cousin marriage. Likewise in the Naga and Chin areas, groups with a *gumlao*-type political system do not have a 'Kachin-type' marriage rule.

correct to regard the *gumsa* and *gumlao* systems as separate patterns of social structure, the two types are, in their practical application, always inter-related. Both systems are in a sense structurally defective. A *gumsa* political state tends to develop features which lead to rebellion, resulting, for a time, in a *gumlao* order. But a *gumlao* community, unless it happens to be centred around a fixed territorial centre such as a patch of irrigated rice terraces, usually lacks the means to hold its component lineages together in a status of equality. It will then either disintegrate altogether through fission, or else status differences between lineage groups will bring the system back into the *gumsa* pattern. Before I give evidence for this cyclical theory of social change, it is first necessary to be quite clear that, as *ideal* systems, *gumsa* and *gumlao* really are distinct. In Chapter V I have described at length the ideal model of *gumsa* social structure; the points at which *gumlao* theory differs from this can best be shown in a side-by-side tabulation.

Gumsa	*Gumlao*
POLITICAL DOMAIN	
A *mung* normally contains a number of villages aggregated under one chief. Only the chief is entitled to make major sacrifices.	A *mung* is a territory comprising a number of villages of equal status. No one lineage or village is innately superior to the others. Each village makes its own major sacrifices independently.
CLASS	
Lineages are ranked as the chief's lineages, aristocrats, commoners, slaves.	Lineages are all of one rank.
DEBTS (HKA)	
All those who are not in a favoured status and recognised lineage kinsmen of the chief must contribute to the chief a thigh (*magyi*) from every four-footed animal slain, and they must contribute free labour to	No tributary dues of any kind are due from villagers towards village headmen.

Gumsa	*Gumlao*
the preparation of the chief's hill field and to the building of the chief's house.	
The scale of compensation for legal offences is graduated so that the penalty for offences against persons of high rank is more expensive in terms of *hpaga* than for similar offences against persons of low rank.	The scale of compensation does not vary with the rank of the individual. All kinds of debt (*hka*) are reckoned on a much lower scale than in the case of *gumsa*.
Marriage payments vary according to the class of the bridegroom.	

MARRIAGE

The *mayu-dama* system is general. It is associated with a kind of reversed hypergamy. Women may marry into their own or lower class; men may marry into their own or higher class. Within a chief's domain one mode of expressing a rank difference between lineages is for the higher ranking lineage to be *mayu* to the lower ranking lineage. The males of a chief's lineage are always married to women of other domains. There is no marked tendency towards local group endogamy.	The *mayu-dama* system is not essential. Rank differences between *mayu* and *dama* are avoided (*a*) by keeping bride price low, (*b*) by developing local patterns in which three or more lineages 'marry in a circle' on an exclusive basis. It would seem that ideally a *gumlao* community is endogamous and consists of three or more lineages marrying in a circle, each lineage having equal rights.

SUCCESSION AND LINEAGE FISSION

Of a group of male siblings the youngest ranks highest, the rest in order of birth. This rule however is subject to the fact that all children of a chief wife rank higher than children of a second wife and so on. Lineages split at fairly frequent intervals and of the two	In theory there is no rank difference between siblings. *Gumlao* lineages appear to fragment with great rapidity. Any particular named lineage is likely to be shallow and there is no precise hierarchy connecting these segments. On the other hand all *gumlao*

SUCCESSION AND LINEAGE FISSION (*contd.*)

Gumsa	*Gumlao*
segments one ranks higher than the other, seniority depending upon the relative status of the two brothers or half-brothers who were originators of the respective segments.	within any one local area are likely to maintain a fiction of common clanship.
The ritual virtues of a chief are inherited naturally by the youngest son. Other sons, particularly the eldest, can, however, become chiefs with full ritual powers provided they purchase the appropriate rights from their youngest brother.	The most stable *gumlao* communities appear to be those in which lineage is virtually neglected and loyalty to a particular place is emphasised instead.

AUTHORITY

Judicial authority rests with the *salang hpawng*—the Council of lineage heads of whom the chief is one, though not necessarily the most influential. The role of the chief, as such, is ritual rather than political, but the perquisites of office sometimes bring control over real economic resources, and the chief can then make himself a man of real power. On the other hand one of the chief's subordinate headmen may be the focus of real authority (*bawmung*).	Judicial authority rests with a Council of Elders, who are usually representatives of lineages. *Gumlao* villages normally have a headman (*agyi*) whose position is not strictly hereditary. Whatever his theoretical status, an *agyi* often has just the same opportunities to gain power as does a *gumsa bawmung*. In practice a *gumlao* 'headman' may be hardly distinguishable from a *gumsa* 'chief'.

ORIGIN MYTHS AND LAND TITLE

Gumsa communities are usually deemed to have originated by either (*a*) original settlement, i.e. segmentation from another *gumsa* community, or (*b*) conquest from another lineage of *gumsa* chiefs. In	*Gumlao* communities are deemed to have originated either (*a*) as original settlements, in which case there are three or more 'original' houses of equal status which intermarry, or (*b*) there is a tradi-

Gumsa

either case 'original title' in the land is vested in one lineage only—that of the chief.

Gumlao

tion of revolution in which the former *gumsa* chiefs were either driven out or reduced to the status of lineage headmen having no special rights. In either case all 'original' lineages have equal title in land.

RITUAL

Among 'benevolent' spirits Commoners sacrifice to:
a. household ancestors
b. the sky nat Musheng and his daughter Bunghpoi
Chiefs sacrifice to:

a. household nats
b. the *mung nat* which is the *uma nat* of the chief's lineage

c. the sky nat Madai and his daughter Hpraw Nga
d. the earth nat Shadip

Among 'benevolent' spirits Commoners sacrifice to:
a. household ancestors
b. the sky nat Musheng and his daughter Bunghpoi
At village festivals lineage heads sacrifice to:
a. household nats
b. the *mung nat*—a spirit connected in some way with the founding of the community and often considered an ancestor of *all* the original lineages
c. some sky nat—often Sinlap *never* Madai
d. an earth nat—*ga nat*—deemed to be distinct from Shadip

The point that I have tried to emphasise in this comparison is that in the *gumlao* system, equality of status between the elements of any local community is a crucial dogma. As *de facto* equality is likely to be very difficult to maintain, we may expect from first principles that communities organised according to the ideal *gumlao* pattern will be politically unstable.

To demonstrate that this theoretical instability is an empirical fact involves the use of historical materials of very uneven quality. The following appear to be the best documented examples of *gumlao* instability through time.

1. In Kawlu Ma Nawng's account the *gumlao* of the Hukawng Valley area originated in a revolt by the N'Dup-Dumsa ('blacksmith-priest') lineage of the Tsasen clan against

their traditional chiefs. The N'Dup-Dumsa lineage today controls a large area in the north east of the Hukawng Valley; they consider themselves *gumlao* but their leaders have the power and status of chiefs—they do not 'eat thighs', they do not erect chiefs' house posts, they do not dig ditches round their graves, but they were treated as chiefs by the Burmese authorities as early as 1820[11] and were consistently referred to as chiefs by the British travellers of the 1830s[12] and by the British Administrators who finally took control of the area a century later. Kawlu Ma Nawng recording these facts comments that it is very odd that both the Burmese and the British should have issued chiefs' appointment orders to people 'who do not acknowledge the right or even the existence of chiefs'.

This evidence suggests that long before the British were in any position to interfere with things, the leading *gumlao* lineages in the Hukawng had already worked their way back to something which in practice, if not in name, closely approximated to the *gumsa* system.

2. The *gumlao* area which was regarded as the *fons et origo* of the *gumlao* movement by the English writers of the 1890s was that part of the Triangle which includes the domains of Sagri Bum and N'Gum La. This area was supposed to have become *gumlao* for the first time around 1870,[13] though another authority gives the specific date of 1858.[14] (See Map 4, p. 33).

The story, as recorded in the 1890s, was that Maran Khawle, apparently a minor lineage head of N'Gum La, killed Naw Pe, chief of N'Gum La. The clan and lineage of the latter are not stated. Simultaneously Labu Shawn, another commoner, killed the chief of Sumpawng Bum, a Lahpai. Sumhka Sinwa of Sagribum (also a Lahpai and lineage brother of the Sumpawng chief) and other neighbouring chiefs thereupon agreed to abandon all their chiefly privileges and to assume the title of *agyi* (headman) in place of *du* (chief).

In 1915 this area was still unadministered. At that date,[15]

---

[11] Kawlu Ma Nawng (1942), p. 30.
[12] Hannay (1847). N'Dup Dumsa is here spelt Undooptun Sah.
[13] Thus Walker (1892) citing Elliot; thus also Scott and Hardiman (1901), Vol. I, Part I, p. 370.
[14] Scott and Hardiman, op cit., p. 414.
[15] R.N.E.F. (1915/16), p. 15. The date is important as showing that the tendency to revert to *gumsa* form was not the outcome of pressure by the Administration.

(*a*) the headman of N'Gum La, a village of 42 houses, was one Lahpai Li. He was 'overlord of eight villages'. He was a *gumlao*. (*b*) The headman of Sagribum, Sumhka Sao Tawng, and his brother, Bumbu Sao Tawng, between them ruled over 24 villages, the two largest of which contained 65 and 32 houses. These men were both *gumlao*. It is to be noted, however, that they are both known by the Sao (*Zau*) title appropriate only to chiefs. (*c*) The headman of Sumpawng Bum, a *gumlao*, was one Labu La, evidently a lineage descendant of the Labu Shawng who was credited with killing the original Sumpawng Bum chief.

By 1943 (*a*) the headman of N'Gum La was one Mangala Uri Nawng, described to me as a Lahtaw; (*b*) the headman of Sagribum was Sumhka Zao, probably the son of the man who was headman in 1916. Neither of these individuals seemed to make any pretence at being *gumlao*. At that date they were reckoned to be two of the most influential and reliable of the *chiefs* of the Triangle area. Thus the heirs and descendants of the supposed revolutionaries of 1870 were, by 1943, the staunchest upholders of British law and order. Unfortunately, I have no data as to the scale of tribute, if any, levied by these '*gumlao*-chiefs' on their followers.

In the foregoing examples *gumlao* organisation at the present day is clearly a fiction; the so-called *gumlao* headmen behave for all practical purposes like *gumsa* chiefs. The question then arises as to whether the whole concept of a *gumlao*-type society might not be a mythological fiction used as a cover story to justify a change of dynasty in what has all the time been consistently a *gumsa*-type community.

Scepticism in this extreme form is not justified. In the majority of present day Jinghpaw-speaking *gumlao* communities, the 'republicanism' appears to be quite genuine. Thus the whole of the Duleng tract is today *gumlao*. There are no Duleng chiefs. Each small Duleng village is a strictly independent entity. Duleng lineages are small and very numerous and not clearly linked into any segmentary system. Nevertheless there is a tradition that the Duleng are all the descendants of one common ancestor, and that formerly there was a lineage of great Duleng chiefs who were the senior ranking (*uma*) line among all the Kachin chiefly lineages.

Then 'about six generations ago the people of Kinduyang'[16] revolted against their chiefs and since then all Duleng *mung* has been *gumlao*.

Actually there is historical evidence that the Duleng had chiefs much more recently than that. As late as 1893 Errol Gray, who had reached Hkamti Long from Assam, was frustrated from proceeding further east by the alleged objections of a powerful Kachin chief named Alang Chow Tong (Alang Zau Tawng) who lived at Alang Ga in the heart of the Duleng country. It is possible that Gray received exaggerated reports about the Alang chief's influence, but it is hardly probable that he did not exist at all.[17] Yet I camped in Alang Ga myself in 1943 and it is certainly *gumlao* country today.

And so also with a number of other examples; the evidence is thin but consistent. It seems to amount to this. Where today we find communities of *gumlao* type—i.e. no chiefs, each village a politically independent unit, a *mung nat* which is not exclusive to any one particular lineage—we find a tradition that 'formerly, *x* generations ago, we had chiefs', and then there was a rebellion in which the chiefs either got killed or driven out. On the other hand, if we look today at those localities which are, by tradition, the focal points of the *gumlao* system, we usually find communities of the *gumsa* type, or something extremely close to this type.

I do not claim that this evidence is sufficient to prove that over a period there is always a constant oscillation between the polar extremes of *gumsa* and *gumlao*, but I think there is a very strong suggestion that this is sometimes and indeed often the case.

I think further that this type of oscillation applies especially to Jinghpaw-speaking communities as opposed to other Kachin groups, largely because the ideas about incest which are contained in Jinghpaw linguistic categories constrain even *gumlao* Jinghpaw to conform to the *mayu-dama* rules of marriage. The

---

[16] Kinduyang—'the Kindu plain'—is the focus of a good deal of Northern Kachin mythology. The Kindu nat is *mung nat* for a large part of the Duleng area. It is interesting that the Pyisa chief in Assam (Beesa Gam) told Neufville in 1828 that his lineage had migrated twenty-one generations ago from 'Kunduyung on a branch of the Sri Lohit (Irrawaddy)'. (Neufville, 1828, p. 340). The only Kindu Ga I know of as existing today is south-west of the Duleng country and is in *gumsa* territory.   [17] Gray (1894).

asymmetry of the *mayu-dama* relationship is, as it were, inconsistent with the dogma of status equality between lineages which dominates *gumlao* theory; consequently a *gumlao* community which adheres to *mayu-dama* marriage rules rather easily slips back into practices of a *gumsa* type.

Outside the Jinghpaw speaking area the *mayu-dama* pattern does not apply with the same force and in groups marginal to the Kachin area it does not apply at all. Thus with the Lisu, the rule of preferred marriage is with the father's sister's daughter, though marriage with either cross cousin is allowed.[18] Only when a Lisu marries with a *gumsa* Kachin will he keep the *gumsa* rules.

For most of the fringe areas the ethnographic material is ambiguous. There has so far been no satisfactory study of Maru or Lashi kinship terminology, but the kinship categories do not appear to fit perfectly with those of the Jinghpaw system.[19] This would be understandable if the *mayu-dama* pattern were not adhered to in the main Maru-Lashi area, east of the N'mai Hka, most of which is, politically speaking, *gumlao*. The Rawang-Nung, as described by Barnard, adhere to Jinghpaw marriage rules but I doubt if they always do so, for these Nung are subordinate to, and intermarry with, Lisu as well as Jinghpaw. The kinship system is not identical with Jinghpaw.[20] Some groups of Palaung are said to adhere to *mayu-dama* rules but not all.[21] Data for the region to the west is equally vague. Of most Naga and Chin groups it has been recorded that there is a preference for marriage with the mother's brother's daughter, but the bar on marriage with the father's sister's daughter—which is crucial to the Jinghpaw *mayu-dama* system—is relatively unusual. It is reported of the Lahker (south-west Chin) and also of a number of 'Old Kuki' groups in Manipur.[22]

My hypothesis is that a *mayu-dama* type marriage rule will never be found associated with *stable* types of *gumlao* organisation. Where *mayu-dama* rules and *gumlao* organisation are found in association, then the latter may be regarded as a transitional phase.

[18] Geis (1911), p. 152; Fraser (1922), pp. ix, 65.
[19] Term lists are given in *Census* (1911) and in Clerk (1911), p. 51.
[20] Barnard (1934), pp. 47, 114–15.   [21] Cameron (1911).
[22] For references to evidence see Lévi-Strauss (1949), Chapter XVII.

I do not want to suggest that this process of flux is a social automatism which develops automatically without the intervention of outside influences. The ultimate 'causes' of social change are, in my view, nearly always to be found in changes in the external political and economic environment; but the form which any change takes is largely determined by the existing internal structure of a given system. In this case, the *gumlao* order and the *gumsa* order are both unstable; in situations of external disturbance the tendency is for *gumlao* systems to turn into *gumsa* and for *gumsa* systems to turn into *gumlao*. But it is nothing more than a tendency; it is the most likely possibility. I do not claim to be able to predict what will happen to any particular community in any particular circumstance.

I assert then that changes from *gumsa* to *gumlao*-type organisation and *vice versa* are responses to factors external to the immediate Kachin situation. What sort of factors? This question is discussed below in Chapter VIII. Meanwhile, having explained the distinction between *gumsa* and *gumlao*, I need to make a rather similar analysis of the relation between *gumsa* and Shan political theory.

CHAPTER VII

GUMSA AND SHAN

This is a book about Kachins, but the argument I have advanced in earlier chapters is that *gumsa* Kachin society takes the form it does because Kachin chiefs, when they have the opportunity, model their behaviour on that of Shan princes (*saopha*).

In this chapter I want to explain just what this imitation involves and why, on the whole, it is unsuccessful.

Firstly, let us be clear about the major differences between the ordinary Kachin and the ordinary Shan way of life. Shan settlements are almost invariably associated with a level stretch of ground irrigated for wet-rice cultivation. The houses vary a good deal in type of construction and pattern of grouping, but the settlements are permanent. A Shan cultivator is tied to his land; he cannot readily switch his allegiance from one territorial chief to another as can a Kachin. A Shan normally expects to marry a girl from his own village and to go on living there all his life. He identifies himself with that village, it is his home; even if circumstances compel him to live elsewhere, he will still describe himself as belonging to his home village. Where land shortage compels a village group to segment, the odds are that the new village will be given the same name as the old one. A Shan's first loyalty then is to a place not to a kin group. Indeed among the commonality there are no clear-cut kin groups. Commoner Shans have no lineage patronymics like the Kachin. There is no restriction on the marriage of cousins; consequently the local community is often, to a considerable degree, an endogamous group of kinsmen. Yet there appears to be little or no sense of kin group solidarity; marriages are arranged by individual house-holders, not by groups of kinsmen; a man must pay a cash bride-price for his wife to his wife's father and he pays it even if the girl is his own father's brother's daughter. Title to property, including land, is biased in favour of sons against daughters and in favour of elder brothers against younger brothers, but daughters too have a claim in all cases.[1] The land-owning group is conceived of as all the descendants of the first owner; the latter usually acquired his tenancy either by squatting or as the result of a grant from the ruling prince who gave right of tenure in return for services rendered.[2]

In practice, ownership is confined to those descendants of the original owner who continue to reside on and draw a livelihood from the land. Strictly speaking, rights in land cannot be sold but only mortgaged. If A mortgages his land to B, then, after three years or so, A (or any descendant of A) is entitled to redeem his land whenever he has the means; this rule is supposed to apply even up to the tenth generation.

A Kachin village community, as we have seen, is composed of a group of lineage segments linked together by ties of clanship and affinity; clan and affinal links do not play the same part in Shan local organisation, it is the land holding itself which forms the element of structural continuity. Thus where a Kachin would describe himself as being of such and such a branch of such and such a lineage, a Shan will say: 'I and my ancestors are Möng Mao people and we have tilled the same fields at Ho Nawng for as long as anyone can remember'.[3]

Leadership in a Shan village appears to depend mainly upon age and natural capacity. The headship may pass from father to son but not necessarily so. Headship is not confined to any one lineage.[4]

In place of the lineage structure of Kachin society we have an exaggerated awareness of hereditary class or caste. Omitting the former category of slaves, there are nominally three main castes in Shan society:

1. The nobility. This should in theory include everyone who can trace any kind of genealogical connection with the ruling *saohpa*. In view of the principle of bilateral descent, the total number of people who might be able to claim such a kinship connection is large and the *de facto* definition of the

[1] In theory Shan inheritance is governed by the Burmese Buddhist code laid down in the *damathat*. For inheritance regulations see Richardson (1912), pp. 227 f. and 265 f., also Lahiri (1951), *passim*.
[2] cf. the account of pre-British Burmese tenures given in Scott and Hardiman (1901), Vol. I, Part 2, pp. 434 f.
[3] Harvey and Barton (1930), p. 29.
[4] See T'ien (1949) for discussion of the relation between age and status in a Chinese-Shan community.

nobility is 'those people who can persuade their fellows to address them by title names such as Sao, Hkun, Nang, etc.' The nobility is thought of as an hereditary caste; in practice there are always some individuals on the edge of it, who claim to be noble but are not recognised as such.[5] Patrilineal connection is more important than matrilineal. Wealth is also an important factor in the maintenance of patrician status. Members of the nobility tend to hold offices about the Court or to engage in trade or silversmith work. They are not usually farmers.

2. The ordinary farming class whose main interest is in their land. Numerically these form the largest element in the population.

3. The lower class. Fishermen, butchers, liquor dealers, pig keepers, etc., i.e. all those people who perform occupations which are improper according to the strict Buddhist code. Commoner Kachins who through marriage or other cause become assimilated to the Shans occupy this caste. So do the descendants of former slaves.

Government of the domain (*möng*) is in the hands of an hereditary prince (*saohpa*) and his court of appointed officials (*amat*). Many of the latter are likely to be relatives of the prince and therefore noble, but commoners too may rise to high office and by suitable marriages ensure nobility for their descendants.

Conceptually the *saohpa* is a divine king, an absolute monarch. But here we must discriminate. The Shan *saohpa* with whom Kachins have close dealings and who therefore serve as models for the Kachin chiefly order are men such as the princes of Möng Mao and Kang Ai and the petty chiefs of Hkamti Long. Such men in the Shan scale of things are only minor figures.

The Shan ideal of a *saohpa* would seem to have been best achieved by the Kings of Burma. The monarch lives apart from the world in his sacred palace (*haw*). In this palace he lives a life of luxury and indolence surrounded by a vast harem of wives and concubines. Practical affairs of state are delegated

[5] Harvey and Barton, op. cit., p. 68, quote a Shan named Paw Lun as saying: 'I come of a well-to-do patrician family . . . now I am old and poor . . . I am entitled to the prefix Hkun but nobody gives it to me.'

to a council of ministers (*amat*). These officials receive no salary but make a lucrative living from the perquisites of office. The 'good' ruler is a man who manages to maintain a luxurious and extravagant Court while at the same time keeping the rapaciousness of his courtiers within bounds. The exaggerated polygyny practised by the ruler[6] is an important part of the system. The wives of the prince include daughters of other princes, daughters of nobles and daughters of commoners. The presence of these women at Court helps to maintain the political cohesion of the domain, and to achieve a balance of power between competing factions within the Court itself.

The size of the palace and the number of the prince's wives was (and is) more or less proportional to the political influence of the prince. King Mindon of Burma who died in 1878 reputedly had fifty-three wives.[7] The *saohpa* of South Hsenwi State, who died in 1913, had sixteen wives; his still-living successor has nine. The *saohpa* of Hsipaw State who died in 1928 had twenty-four wives.[8] These are all large states. The princes of little states like Möng Mao and Kang Ai seldom seem to run to more than two or three wives at a time.[9]

Succession to the throne is in all cases governed by patri-lineal descent, so that for royalty and royalty alone agnatic lineage becomes important. The 'royal houses' of the differ-ent states are named patrilineages with totemic titles. Thus the royal houses of Möng Mao, Chanta (Santa) and Lu Chiang Pa are three separate lineages of the Tiger clan (Hso), that of Möng Mao being the 'Golden Tigers' (Hkam Hso),[10] Chefang and Lungchwan are both Black Hornets (Taw), while Kang Ai are Red Hornets (Tao).[11] One authority states that the *saohpa* is expected to include a half-sister among his wives.[12] This was certainly a fashion of the Burmese Court,[13] but pub-lished genealogies do not support the view that it is a Shan practice.[14] On the contrary, a member of the Möng Mao

[6] Both in Burma and in the Shan States polygyny was rare outside the Palace.
[7] Stuart (1910), pp. 157 f.   [8] Shan States and Karenni (1943), p. 58.
[9] See Harvey and Barton (1930), *passim*.
[10] This explains the remark on p. 2 that the Möng Mao *saohpa* were 'members of the Hkam clan'.
[11] Harvey and Barton, op cit., p. 98 n.   [12] Milne (1910), p. 78.
[13] Scott and Hardiman (1901), Vol. I, Part 2, p. 89. This wife was the chief queen but not necessarily the mother of the heir.
[14] Shan States and Karenni (1943).

royal house has stated that the royal patrilineages are strictly exogamous and that Möng Mao royalty cannot even marry with Chanta royalty because both are members of the Tiger clan.[15] This is a point of some importance for my general thesis. It is because Northern Shan royalty conceive of themselves as belonging to exogamous patrilineages which form a segmentary system that Kachin chiefs can intermarry with Shan royal houses without contradiction to their own system of ideas.

A polygynous royal household was a political advantage in that it gave the sovereign personal ties with a large number of different groups both within and without the Court. It was a disadvantage in that it fostered rivalry over the succession. For example, King Mindon on his decease left some forty living widows, about 110 children and nearly 200 grandchildren, any one of whom might have claimed the throne. Thibaw, who actually succeeded, was, on the face of it, a most unlikely candidate since he was son of a divorced wife. His success was due to the machinations of Mindon's second wife who planned to marry her daughter Supayalat to Thibaw. As Mindon lay dying most of the rival queens and the majority of Thibaw's half siblings were placed under arrest. A year later eighty or so of the latter were massacred.[16] Thibaw's activities in this respect shocked the Western World and received much publicity, but palace murders have always been very much a part of the standard pattern both in Burmese and Shan society. The witnesses in the Möng Mao case of 1930[17] took it as a matter of course that the courtiers (*amat*) should first have urged the *saohpa* to murder his rivals, and then, when he disdained to do so, encouraged the rivals to murder the *saohpa*.

We see here a most important difference between Kachin and Shan type society. Among Kachins, feuds are typically between lineages, and the dispute typically concerns a woman —it is a feud between groups potentially in *mayu-dama* relationship. Among Shans, hostilities are typically between factions supporting rival pretenders for the same *saohpa* throne; they

---

[15] Harvey and Barton, op, cit., p. 98.
[16] Stuart (1910), pp. 157 f., gives a good account.
[17] Harvey and Barton (1930), *passim.*

are thus feuds between segments of the same royal patrilineage. In the Möng Mao succession case, the pretender Hkun Set describes himself as belonging to 'the Hseng branch of the Hkam (Gold) family of the Hso (Tiger) clan'.[18] The 'Hseng branch' is a sub-lineage of only three generations depth comprising all the descendants of the *saohpa*, Sao Hkam Hseng, this group being ranged as allies in opposition to the descendants of Sao Hkam Hseng's elder brother, Hkam Yu Yung. Similarly, in the complex succession feud in Kengtung State which developed on the death of the thirty-ninth *saohpa* in 1935, the opposing factions were ranged around (*a*) the descendants of the thirty-ninth *saohpa*'s second wife—who included the *saohpa*'s eldest son, and (*b*) the descendants of his chief wife, the *mahadevi*.[19]

Shan royalty practise no regular system of unilateral cross cousin marriage which in any way corresponds to the Kachin *mayu-dama* system, but factionalism may lead to repeated intermarriage between neighbouring royal houses. In the Möng Mao case, the Hkam Yu Yung faction repeatedly intermarried with the Kang Ai royal house; in 1930 this faction was successful because Kang Ai supported them. The 'Hseng branch' sub-lineage was closely linked in a similar way with the royal house of Chefang.

In sum, the wives of Shan royalty can be classed as of three kinds; (*a*) women who are of royal status equal to that of the husband and who are married in order to cement a political alliance with a neighbouring royal house; (*b*) women who are of commoner status (i.e. status inferior to that of the husband) and who are received as a form of tribute from political subordinates; (*c*) commoner women who are purchased as concubines. Category (*b*) calls for special comment.

It will be recollected that in the case of *gumsa* Kachins a woman normally marries a man of her own social class or else a man of a lower social class; she does not normally marry into a class above. In the relationship between landlord and tenant, the landlord is *mayu*, the tenant *dama*. In the Shan scheme of things this pattern is reversed, a woman is an appropriate object of tribute from an inferior to a superior.

[18] Harvey and Barton (1930), p. 97.
[19] Shan States and Karenni (1943), pp. 6 f.

To quote a Shan chronicle: 'Some of the people asked, "When a new chief goes into a new palace what is the custom?" The Ta Kin Möng said, "The people must bring . . . . . a drum, a sword, a spear and a beautiful maiden to be his wife. They must also bring pure gold, silver and gems, carpets, mats, hats and red coats".'[20]

Consistent with this doctrine we find that in published Shan genealogies royal males are very frequently recorded as marrying commoner females, but marriages of royal females to commoner males are either glossed over or ignored. It follows that intermarriage between Kachins and Shans has a different significance according to the class status of the parties concerned and according to whether the informant is a Kachin or a Shan.

If a Shan *saohpa* acknowledges giving a woman to a Kachin chief, it is, for the Shan, a token of alliance—he is, in effect, treating the Kachin as an equal and honouring him. It may even amount to an admission that the Kachin chief is the real political overlord. For the Kachin on the other hand it may have the significance that the Kachin is accepting the Shan as his overlord. If the Shan gives a dowry of rice land along with the woman, this is definitely the case; the Kachin chief becomes *dama* to the Shan and his territorial subordinate. The reverse situation in which a Kachin chief gives a woman to the Shan chief in whose territory he resides would be directly contradictory—it would imply to the Kachin that the Kachin was overlord, and to the Shan that the Shan was overlord. Such a marriage could therefore only occur where Kachin and Shan respect one another's status as independent monarchs of equal status.

I have no reason to think that marriages between Kachins and Shans at the aristocratic level are particularly rare, but published records of such marriages are hard to find. The following examples illustrate the points I have made above.

MARRIAGE OF KACHIN CHIEF TO SHAN PRINCESS IN TOKEN OF POLITICAL OVERLORDSHIP OF THE SHAN (OR BURMESE)

Daihpa Gam, the Kachin chief who made himself overlord of the Hukawng Valley in the 1830s and who was, to quote Kawlu Ma Nawng, 'the only Jinghpaw to aspire to build a palace and be

[20] See Milne (1924), pp. 23–4. The document quoted must be regarded as a Shan not a Palaung chronicle, (op. cit., p. 18).

a King of his people',[21] needed in 1837 to give token of his submission to the Burmese throne. He therefore married the widow
of the Burmese governor (*myowun*) of Mogaung.[22] It is not clear
whether the woman in question was Burmese or Shan.

Early in this century Hkam Yu Yung, *saohpa* of Möng Mao,
seeking a Kachin alliance, married off his widowed mother to the
Kachin chief of Hkawng Hsung (which lies within Möng Mao
territory) giving a dowry of rice land at the same time. As a result
the Kachin chief 'swore the great oath that he would come to the
help of her and her children's children for all generations'.[23] In
Kachin terminology this transaction would not have made the
Kachin *dama* to the Shans but given them the higher status of
'adoptive clan brothers' (*hpu-nau lawu lahta*).

The Kansi chiefs who are Kachin overlords of the jade-producing
area west of Kamaing have for several generations married Shan
as well as Kachin wives. The Shan women are members of the
family of the former *saohpa* of Möng Hkawm (Maingkwan,
Hukawng Valley). These women are therefore Haw Hseng
Shans; their ancestors were rulers of Mogaung and overlords of
all the Hkamti Shan states of the north-west.[24] Today the Kachin
Kansi chief is far and away richer and more influential than the
saohpa of Möng Hkawm who is no more than a petty headman.
In this case the Shan marriages seem to be maintained as a token
of loyalty to the former (now extinct) Mogaung throne from which
the Kansi chiefs derived their land title. The title Kansi is the
Jinghpaw version of Hkamti.

Marriage of Shan Aristocrat to Kachin girl of Aristocratic Status

The Kachin chief of Möng Hko (mentioned on p. 2) explained
his connection with the royal house of Möng Mao by saying that
a member of this royal house Nga Hkam had settled in Möng Hko
and become a blood brother with the Kachin chiefs; thereafter he
had married a Kachin girl and others of his lineage had done likewise. Möng Mao and Möng Hko thereby became allied territories
but were not politically interdependent.[25]

It is to be noted that in two of these examples the ambiguous

---

[21] Kawlu Ma Nawng (1943), p. 40.
[22] Bayfield (1873), p. 193. cf. also Hannay (1873), p. 97 f. See also p. 280n.
[23] Harvey and Barton (1930), pp. 81, 99, 111.
[24] See Hertz (1912) for Kansi genealogy up to that date. Marriages with the
same group of Shan *mayu* have continued since then. For status of Haw Hseng
Shans in Hukawng Valley see Kawlu Ma Nawng (1943), pp. 41, 15.
[25] Harvey and Barton (1930), p. 81.

status implications of a *mayu-dama* relationship between Shan
and Kachin are avoided by putting the contracting parties in
a 'brother' relationship.

Blood brotherhood is supplementary to marriage as a means
of establishing a permanent alliance between Shan and Kachin
aristocrats. The procedure is for the two groups to 'exchange
names'. 'Lists of the immediate parents of the two prospective
"brothers" are exchanged, memorised and included by each
amongst their own relatives (i.e. the first "brother's" son
becomes the second "brother's" nephew, etc.).'[26] The family
nats of both lineages are shared, the exogamy rules of the one
group are shared by the other, lineage feuds are shared and
so on. In effect the Shan royal lineage and the Kachin royal
lineage become one and the same.

This form of kinship alliance which avoids any implication
of status difference has attractions for both sides. The data
available on this subject are unfortunately slight. I would
expect to find that where a Kachin chief's *mung* is clearly recognised as a sub-feudatory segment of the Shan chief's *mung*, then
the Kachin chief's family will periodically obtain women from
the Shan chief's family and serve the latter as military allies in
return. On the other hand, where the Kachin chief's *mung*
is independent of any Shan overlord, military alliance between
the Kachins and Shans will be signified by blood brotherhood,
plus intermarriage with third parties allied to both. Finally,
where Shan villagers pay tribute to Kachin overlords no intermarriage at aristocratic level takes place at all.

All this, however, concerns only the relations between Shan
chiefs and Kachin chiefs. Assimilation of Kachins into the
Shan system at a commoner level follows a very different
pattern. Here the norm is that the Kachins either as
individuals or in groups enter the service of the Shans as
labourers and acquire women in recompense. In thus settling
in a Shan valley the Kachin cuts himself off altogether from his
own kinsfolk. He adopts the nats of his Shan wife—that is to
say he becomes a Buddhist—and from a Kachin point of view
he becomes a Shan (*sam tai*); but he enters the Shan system at
the bottom of the scale as a person of the lowest caste, he is
virtually a slave. The Shan terms which are used to denote

[26] Harvey and Barton (1930), p. 81.

Kachins in the mass—Kha-pok, Kha-nung, Kha-ng, etc.—all have the prefix Kha meaning 'serf' or 'slave'.[27] Within the Kachin Hills Area nearly all low class Shans are probably either of slave or commoner Kachin origin.

The reverse kind of assimilation from commoner Shan to commoner Kachin is unlikely, since life in the hills offers no attractions to the plainsman. Individual Shans or Burmans who are posted to the hills on Government duty may sometimes settle there and raise a Kachin family by a Kachin wife, but such cases are rare.

A Kachin girl will no doubt sometimes elope with a Shan whom she has met in the market, but in doing so she would cut herself off completely from her own kinsfolk. There is no recognised procedure whereby a Shan man can pay bride price *hpaga* for a Kachin girl. In effect a *mayu-dama* relationship between Kachin and Shan at commoner level cannot exist.

We must therefore distinguish clearly between the assimilation of Kachin to Shan at aristocratic and at commoner level. Aristocratic Kachins can 'become Shan' in the sense that they can become sophisticated and establish a *mayu-dama* marriage relationship with an aristocratic Shan lineage, but they do not thereby surrender their status as Kachin chiefs. On the contrary, their chiefly status as Kachins in enhanced; it is the culmination of *gumsa* ideals that the Kachin *duwa* should be treated as a *saohpa* by his Shan counterpart. Commoner Kachins on the other hand can only become Shan by ceasing to be Kachins. At commoner level the Kachin and Shan systems, though linked economically, are totally separated by barriers of kinship and religion.

It seems to me that we have reached here one explanation of why the attempts by *gumsa* Kachin chiefs to turn themselves into Shan princes have almost always ended in disaster. There are plenty of quite well documented instances; the Pyisa chief in Assam around 1825; the Daihpa chief in the Hukawng ten years later; the Gauri chiefs of Mahtang (Möng Hka) in the period 1855–70; the Möng Si chief around 1885; the Kansi

[27] The Kachins recognising the derogatory implication of *Khang* apply the term to Nagas of the Upper Chindwin and Patkoi areas whom they (the Kachins) **have largely** dominated. *Khang* is also written *hkang* and *kang*.

chiefs for the last 70 years or so.   For each of these cases there exist descriptions of individual chiefs such as the following which refers to the Mahtang chief as he was in 1868:

'a man of great intelligence and self possession, quiet in his demeanour and with manners quite as polished as any Burmese or Shan gentleman. He wears his hair in Burmese fashion, but his dress is a mixture of Shan and Chinese, a costume which accords with his perfect familiarity with the two languages in addition to his native tongue, Kakhyen.'[28]

As individuals they were temporarily successful, but more than that they were *recognised* as successful; the Burmese Kings (and even the British Government) rewarded them with gold umbrellas and honorific titles appropriate to the status of a *saohpa*.[29]

Yet the political structure that emerged in such cases was wholly precarious. Although a Kachin chief may work himself into a position in which he is treated as a *saohpa* by fellow chiefs, he cannot behave like a real *saohpa* towards his followers; for, if he does so, he deprives himself of support from his fellow Kachins.

The balance of a genuine Shan state depends upon the fact that the political alliance represented by the *saohpa's* numerous wives is stronger than any dissident faction likely to arise among the *saohpa's* own immediate kinsmen. The Kachin chief who aspires to the position of a Shan *saohpa* cannot consolidate his position in this way. He cannot accept women from his Shan adherents without prejudice to his position as a Kachin; he cannot go on giving women to his Kachin adherents (his *dama*) without prejudice to his status as a Shan prince. Or, to put it in another way, the Kachin chief can 'become a Shan' without loss of status but his commoner Kachin followers cannot. Therefore, in becoming a Shan, the Kachin chief tends to isolate himself from the roots of his power, he offends against the principles of *mayu-dama* reciprocity, and encourages the development of *gumlao* revolutionary tendencies.   Then with the first shift in the economic and political wind his power collapses altogether.   In his rise to power a Kachin chief

---

[28] Anderson (1871), p. 381.
[29] cf. Kawlu Ma Nawng (1943), p. 40; Anderson, op, cit., p. 231.

depends upon the support of his relatives; but, if over-successful he can retain his position only with the aid of external authority. The cases listed below illustrate this.

a. Pyisa. When the British took over eastern Assam in 1824, they found that the most influential Kachin (Singhpo) chief was one Pyisa Gam. He held a title from the Burmese King and during the Burmese regime in Assam had acquired, along with his fellow chiefs, vast numbers of Assamese slaves. His fellow chiefs were, like himself, mostly members of the Tangai lineage of the Tsasen clan but belonged to different sublineages, namely Wahkyet, Sharaw, Hpungin, Ningkrawp, Latao, Numbrawng, N'Gaw, Ningru, Hkawtsu, Gasheng, Daipha, etc. As soon as the Burmese withdrew from Assam, feuding broke out among these allied Tangai chiefs. Bitterness was intensified when the British deprived them of their slaves and later purloined all their best land for tea growing. The Pyisa Gam was treated as paramount chief by the British and thereby forfeited the allegiance of all his fellow Kachins. But by 1840 the British had come to the conclusion that it was unnecessary to patronise the Kachins any longer and withdrew their support of the Pyisa chief as paramount. In the upshot he died in an Assam jail, having been imprisoned for life for attempted insurrection.[30]

b. Daihpa. Daihpa Gam was a distant lineage brother of Pyisa Gam above. The two were feud enemies. When the British supported Pyisa Gam as paramount in Assam, the rest of the Tangai lineage transferred their support to Daihpa. He was extremely successful. By 1837 he had visited Ava, been loaded with presents and titles from the Burmese king, and negotiated on frontier problems with British emissaries. But at home in the Hukawng Valley he had to fight his own relatives in a *gumlao* revolt. He maintained his power for a while with the aid of Burmese troops but as soon as these were withdrawn, sometime around 1842, he ceased to be of any significance.[31]

c. Mahtang. In the early part of the 19th century much of the trade between Burma and China went by boat to Bhamo and thence by mule caravan across the Kachin Hills to Hohsa State and thence to Möng Myen (Tengyueh). The chiefs through whose territory this traffic passed profited greatly by toll charges. The 'route which from time immemorial constituted the grand highway between China and Burma'[32] passed through the Kachin centre of

[30] The necessary references will be found in Leach (1946), Chapter 6.
[31] The necessary references will be found in Leach (1946), Chapter 6.
[32] Hannay (1837), p. 97.

Loilung (E. 97 40: N. 24 20) which was in the domain of Gauri
Lahpai chiefs of the Aura lineage.   These chiefs flourished exceedingly and gave their domain the Shan title of Möng Hka, assuming
the household lineage name of Mungga (i.e. Möng Hka).   In 1868
the senior chief was living at Mahtang about 4 miles to the east.
Loilung was ruled by the Mahtang chief's elder brother.   Mahtang
and Loilung are described by Anderson as the two most thriving
Kachin villages he had seen.   At Mahtang the chief's house
'although built after the plan prevalent in these hills is enclosed by
a substantial stone and brick wall with a very Chinese-looking
gateway and is approached by a paved path which leads through
the courtyard'.[33]   The sophisticated appearance of the Mahtang
chief has been noted above (p. 223).   The graves of the Mahtang
chiefs were in keeping with all this.   They were 'built of massive
slabs of granite and handsomely ornamented and carved in Chinese
style.   The facade is like the portico of a house, with imitation
doors. . . .'[34]   But the success of the Möng Hka chiefs cost them
the hostility of their lineage brothers, the Gauri chiefs of the Sinlum
area who claim, rather dubiously, to be the *uma* branch of the Aura
lineage.[35]   The British, when they came to power, not only deprived
the Möng Hka chiefs of their tolls, but built the district head-
quarters in the territory of their rivals at Sinlum.   In 1920 the
latter had their revenge.   In a case heard 'before Gauri elders' the
Assistant Superintendent's Court at Sinlum awarded the chief of
Mahtang the trifling compensation of Rs. 30/- and 6 *hpaga* against
one of his own commoners who had got his daughter with child.[36]
A generation earlier the penalty would have been astronomical;[37]
the eclipse of Möng Hka prestige was complete.

d. *Möng Si.*   In the struggles for the control of the large Shan
State of Hsenwi which were a prominent feature of the Burmese
history between 1846 and 1887, the rival Shan factions all had their
Kachin supporters.   The Kachin chiefs of Möng Si were consistent
supporters of the legitimate *saohpa*, Hseng Naw Hpa, and, though
Naw Hpa himself was seldom successful, Möng Si prospered.
When the British took over, the Kachin chief of Möng Si had the
standing of a *myosa* and ruled over a population of some 12,000
persons including 100 Kachin, 20 Shan, 15 Palaung and 12 Chinese
villages.   The domain was divided into several sub-territories 'each
of which was ruled by a Kachin *duwa*, a relative of the *myosa*'.[38]

[33] Anderson (1871), p. 383.   [34] Enriquez (1923), p. 128.
[35] Hanson (1906), ref. *uma*. See also p. 273 f.   [36] Carrapiett (1929), p. 115.
[37] Kawlu Ma Nawng (1942), p. 63.
[38] Shan States and Karenni (1943), p. 65.   Scott and Hardiman, Vol. 2.
Entry: Möng Si.

Under the British dispensation it was an enemy of Naw Hpa that came to the throne of North Hsenwi and in any case the British refused to countenance the idea of Kachin chiefs ruling over Shans. By 1940 the former domain of Möng Si was fragmented into nearly a dozen separate chiefdoms. Several of the chiefs concerned still managed to put on a brave show of aping the manners of a Shan *saohpa*.

e. Kansi. The Kansi chief's lineage clearly came to power through the fact that they held a recognised title over the land from which jade is obtained westward from Kamaing. Through all the vicissitudes of Burmese history during the past century and a half nothing seems to have seriously damaged the jade trade and the Kansi chief still draws his royalties. Around 1940 the British Government 'bought out' the Kansi chief's rights but guaranteed him an annual income instead. This action cost the British the loyalty of the Kansi chief during the war as he suspected he had been defrauded. After the war the Kansi chief was for a while jailed for co-operation with the Japanese. Today he is almost as influential as before and is still drawing his annual subsidy from the Burmese Government. The Kansi chiefs have intermarried with Shans but they have had the good sense to keep up their *mayu-dama* connections with the leading Kachin chiefs as well.

The moral seems clear, with economic luck and plenty of relatives a Kachin chief has a chance of becoming something very close to a Shan *saohpa*. But once his status is achieved the odds are that relatives will turn hostile. Thereafter, status usually rests on the whim of some paramount power.

CHAPTER VIII

THE EVIDENCE FROM KACHIN HISTORY

I suppose that the main difficulty that every anthropologist has to face is what to do with the facts. When I read a book by one of my anthropological colleagues, I am, I must confess, frequently bored by the facts. I see no prospect of visiting either Polynesia or the Northern Territories of the Gold Coast and I cannot arouse in myself any real interest in the cultural peculiarities of either the Tikopia or the Tallensi. I read the works of Professors Firth and Fortes not from an interest in the facts but so as to learn something about the principles behind the facts. I take it for granted that the vast majority of those who read this book will be in a similar position with regard to the Kachins. How then should I dispose of the facts, the detailed evidence?

To a very considerable extent the present chapter is simply a documentation of a thesis which I have already propounded. The thesis is that, in Kachin society as a whole, *gumlao*-type communities have a general tendency to develop *gumsa*-type characteristics, while *gumsa*-type communities have a tendency to break up into sub-groups organised on *gumlao* principles. But adequate proof or disproof of any such theory would require a knowledge of historical facts concerning which there is in fact no record, and, sensibly enough, many anthropologists would maintain that it is both useless and misleading to speculate about what cannot be known. From this point of view this chapter is at best a complete waste of time.

My own position is this. Any theory about social change is necessarily a theory about historical process. I am asserting that at the present time certain 'forces' operate which are likely to lead to the modification of the organisation of particular Kachin communities; I also maintain that the same or closely similar 'forces' have also operated in the past. If this be so then the facts of Kachin history should be consistent with my theory. Here at least I am on fairly safe ground for the recorded facts of Kachin history are so fragmentary as to be capable of almost any interpretation.

But precisely because the genuine historical evidence is very thin, I need to state the facts so far as they are known. I also need to be quite clear about my interpretation of these facts, the more especially since my interpretation is completely at variance with almost everything that has previously been published on the subject.

My aim in this chapter is therefore twofold—firstly, I want to explain what are the 'forces' which lead to the instability of *gumsa* and *gumlao* systems as constituted at any particular moment; secondly, I wish to show that there is nothing in the history of the area which conflicts with my interpretation. This is a negative goal which, even when achieved, gets us no further than we started.

The chapter then contains three things. An outline of the known history of the area; a guess as to what constitutes a plausible reconstruction of the (unknown) history of the Kachins; a demonstration that my guess fits both with established history and with the ecological implications of the environment described in Chapter II. Anyone who finds the result unreadable had best get on to Chapter IX.

Before we go further let me emphasise again that I do not for a moment want to suggest that the future development of any particular Kachin community is, in any absolute sense, determined or predictable. On the contrary I hold that individuals and groups of individuals are constantly being faced with making choices between several possible correct alternatives. But circumstances may operate in such a way that particular kinds of choice are likely to appear more advantageous than others. This does not mean that the outsider can predict what choice will be made, but only that one may predict what choice is likely to be made given certain assumptions about the value system and rationality of the actors. When I refer to the 'forces' or factors in the social change process I regard them as determinants only in this strictly limited sense.

In constructing a theory of social change there are doubtless many different kinds of parameter which might be treated as significant variables. I shall deal with only three. (1) Physical Environment or Ecology—by which I mean variation in the resources and means of production which supply the basic means of subsistence. (2) Political Environment (i.e. Political History). A society, however defined, is always, from certain points of view, itself a unit of political organisation, but simultaneously it is always, from some other point of view, only a segment of a larger society, that is of a political system of larger scale. I take it as axiomatic that the stability of any political unit is necessarily affected by changes in the structure and power distribution within the political system of next larger scale of which the unit forms a part. (3) The Human Element. In part no doubt, the 'great men' of any historical story are best regarded simply as the product of their environment; but the arbitrariness of personal ambition and personal charms still needs to be considered in any analysis of social change.

PHYSICAL ENVIRONMENT

For the purposes of my analysis I propose to treat ecological factors as stable through time. Clearly a population practising *taungya* cultivation, as described in Chapter II, is capable of drastically altering its own physical environment even within a generation. It is also clear that in the course of history large parts of the Kachin Hills Area have been denuded of forest cover by human agency. But I do not know when or even precisely how this happened and I can only guess at the social consequences of such events. In trying to develop a theory of Kachin social change I shall therefore start with the (clearly false) assumption that the general ecological factors against which Kachins have had to contend in the past have always been the same as they are now. I shall also write as if the area occupied by peoples of Kachin culture had remained more or less constant through the centuries. This latter assumption implies a very different definition of 'Kachin' from that usually accepted. I am here defining Kachin as comprising the peoples who live and have lived in the hill districts of the Kachin Hills Area and who cultivate their lands by the techniques described in Chapter II and who are not Buddhists. Kachins thus defined have always been an iron age people, the use of iron cutting tools and swords being quite fundamental to the whole economic organisation of Kachin society as we now know it.   We know that at one time some parts of the Kachin Hills were occupied by a neolithic people for their tools have been found in considerable quantity.[1]   I do not know how recently the use of stone tools ceased in this area but it is certain that any stone-using population must have been very differently organised from the Kachins whom we now know. Therefore from my point of view they were not Kachins and that gives us some sort of a base line to start from.   It also implies that iron-working technique is significant for an understanding of the growth of Kachin society.

The majority of existing books about Kachins contain a categorical assertion that the Kachins, as a people, migrated into the Kachin Hills Area in the fairly recent past from Tibet or even further afield.[2]   There is no evidence for such statements.   They derive from the fact that Jinghpaw and the other Kachin languages belong to the Tibeto-Burman linguistic family, and that languages of the same general family are spoken far to the north and north-east.   According to linguistic theory Tibeto-Burman languages entered the Burma area at a much later date than the Austro-Asiatic languages, of which Mon (Talaing) and Palaung are examples.   It is accordingly assumed that the modern speakers of Tibeto-Burman languages in some way represent a later strata of population than the modern speakers of Austro-Asiatic languages.   No useful meaning can be attached to such arguments.   The linguists similarly claim that Jinghpaw is a later development of Tibeto-Burman than Maru, which is similar to Burmese.   It is therefore argued that the modern Maru, as a population, are a group 'left behind' in a southward migration of the Burmese, while the modern Jinghpaw are descendants of recent immigrants who superseded a previous Maru and/or Shan population.   In this scheme the fact that at the present time pockets of Shan population are found interspersed among Kachins is interpreted as evidence that a wave of warlike

---

[1] See for example Appendix C and Plates to Anderson (1871).

[2] e.g. Stevenson (1944b), p. 9; Hanson (1913), p. 18, puts the original home of the Kachins in 'the highlands of Mongolia or on the borderland of eastern Tibet and western Szechuan'.   It is intriguing to contemplate the discomfiture of a jungle-dwelling Kachin who reversed the journey and found himself on the edge of the Gobi desert!   cf. Luce (1940), 'Scholars are generally agreed that the ancient home of Tibeto-Burman speaking peoples was somewhere in north-west China, say Kansu, between the Gobi Desert and north-east Tibet.'

immigrant Kachins arrived from the north and overwhelmed a population of decadent Shans.

I can attach no value at all to this kind of speculation. Kachin society as we know it today is a society organised to cope with the ecological situation that exists in the Kachin Hills. Kachin culture and Kachin political organisation, as systems, must be regarded as having been developed *in situ* where we now find them. Of course technical and political ideas of every description have certainly been borrowed from elsewhere—a Kachin priest's hat is a Naga helmet, the Kachin medium's skill at climbing a ladder of sharpened swords is a dodge learnt from the Chinese, and so on *ad infinitum*, but the totality of Kachin culture is quite clearly a local complex.

But if the Kachin political complex developed in the Kachin Hills as a response to the local environment, why should we have the self contradictions of *gumsa* and *gumlao*? To seek some sort of answer to this let us consider the present day distribution of *gumsa* and *gumlao* communities in relation to ecological zones.

It was pointed out in Chapter II that from a climatical point of view the Kachin Hills Area can be roughly divided into three zones, A, B, C (Map 2) and that indigenous techniques of agriculture vary accordingly. I do not think that these ecological differences determine the local differences of political development but they do set certain limits to the political probabilities. These are the empirical facts:

Zone A. Agricultural techniques:—monsoon *taungya* in hills; wet rice in valleys. No separation of *gumlao* and *gumsa* on an ecological basis. *Gumsa* and *gumlao* both occur in the Triangle where monsoon *taungya* is practised under very favourable conditions; they both occur north of Myitkyina and west of the Irrawaddy where the same techniques are practised under unfavourable conditions; they both occur in the Hukawng Valley in areas where wet-rice cultivation is practical; the climate and general terrain of the Duleng area (*gumlao*) does not appear significantly different from the region to the south (mainly *gumsa*).

Conditions of demography and rainfall are here such that even very isolated communities have no real difficulty in maintaining a living though the standards maintained are not always high. Throughout this zone the cultivators of ordinary monsoon *taungya* can, if they choose, cut themselves off altogether from the valley-dwelling wet-rice cultivators and survive. In most places this implies a very mean standard of life; monsoon *taungya* does not ordinarily produce a crop surplus to the immediate requirements of the cultivator. There are, however, a few localities where the natural fertility of the soil is unusually high and surplus production can be counted on; this is notably the case in the North Triangle area which regularly produces a rice surplus though almost entirely dependent upon *taungya* cultivation.

In the immediate pre-British period the wet rice producing areas throughout the zone were controlled politically by Kachins but cultivated by Shans and Assamese 'slaves'. Only in Hkamti Long did the Shans maintain some degree of independence. Under the British the Kachins were deprived of their authority over practically all wet rice land south of Kamaing. Elsewhere, after 1926, they were deprived of their 'slaves' which had similar economic effects. One such effect was that the chiefs of the Triangle area, whose power was not derived from wet rice land and who retained their slaves until about 1930, gained prestige at the expense of their rivals of the Hukawng Valley and the 'Htingnai'.

By 1943 the chiefs with the greatest prestige in Zone A were nearly all from the Triangle area. Htingnan Kumja, Mashaw Uma Law, N'Ding Zau Awn (Marip clan), Ngalang La (NhKum clan), Shadan Tu (Lahpai clan) were perhaps the most influential. Some of these men exercised control over sixty or more villages. The only Kachin chief of comparable status outside the Triangle area was Kansi Sinwa Nawng (Marip clan) who controlled the jade mines area. A century ago the distribution of Kachin power within this zone was very different; between 1825 and 1840 the Kachin chiefs who were treated with the greatest respect by the British and Burmese authorities were Pyisa Gam and Daihpa Gam (Tsasen clan; western Hukawng Valley and Assam) and the Walawbum chief (Marip clan, N'Ding lineage; central Hukawng Valley). At this period these Hukawng Valley chiefs controlled large numbers of Assamese 'slaves' who worked rice land on their behalf. This shift in the power structure confirms what one would expect from first principles, namely that a politically influential *gumsa* chief must be able to dispose of real economic resources.[3]

But the existence of adequate resources does not necessarily imply a *gumsa* system of authority.   The Sagri Bum-N'Gum La area in the Triangle which is nominally *gumlao* has the same natural resources as the neighbouring *gumsa* tract of the power-ful Shadan Tu.   The tract of the influential *gumsa* chief Ngalang La includes a silver mine, but it abuts on to the terri-tory of the *gumlao* Duleng which has iron deposits as well as silver.   Duleng blacksmiths seem to have traded their swords all over the Kachin Hills for generations and though they no longer bother to smelt local ores, the smithy's craft remains important.   The Duleng appear to have been *gumsa* in the past; there seems to be nothing in the history of the trade in iron to explain why they should be *gumlao* now.

Where there is no easily accessible source of economic wealth *gumlao* and *gumsa* political forms remain alternative possibilities, but *gumsa* chiefs cannot hope to achieve real power; their status as chiefs then becomes a ritual rather than a political office.

Although climatic conditions are favourable to *taungya* culti-vation throughout Zone A some parts of the area are more

[3] The *de facto* high status of the chiefs mentioned above is rationalised by the Kachins not on the grounds that these are wealthy men but that they are affinal relatives and heads of their respective *uma* lineages.   The relationship between these lineages at present is:

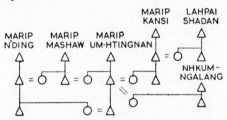

FIG. 5.   *Mayu-dama* network between leading chiefly families in the Triangle, Hukawng and Jade Mines areas.

This arrangement might suggest that the present standing of the chiefs concerned is (1) Shadan, (2) Kansi and Ngalang, (3) Um (Htingnan), Mashaw and N'Ding. This accords with the facts so far as I know them.   Any change in the prestige rating would no doubt be reflected in time by a change in the pattern of the *mayu-dama* network.   Fifty years ago Kansi were in fact *dama* to both the N'Ding and the Shadan though relations with the former were broken off for a while by a serious feud.   The Walawbum (N'Ding) chief was at that time extremely in-fluential.   (See R.N.E.F. 1900–1, p. 6.)

fertile than others. Since the average population density of the hill tracts in this Zone is everywhere very low,[4] people living in localities where the rice production is only marginal have a choice between remaining independent in a small impoverished community or moving into a dependent situation in some more prosperous area.

It is quite evident that in such contexts Kachins often value political independence more highly than economic advantage. In the area rated in the 1921 Census as Myitkyina Hills Tracts[5] no less than 94 out of 143 listed villages contained less than 10 households.   A few of these villages were possibly aggregated into village clusters under a common chief, but the majority certainly were not.   It would certainly have been to the economic advantage of this population if it had lived in larger communities in more accessible situations, but the preference was evidently for independence above all else.

These tiny communities include some that are *gumsa* in form and some that are *gumlao*.   In the case of the *gumsa* the chiefs have no authority outside their own village and are not recognised as 'thigh-eating chiefs' by their neighbours—they are *gumrawng gumsa*—'boastful *gumsa*'.   The only practical difference between *gumsa* and *gumlao* at this level is that the *gumsa* respect the 'idea' of a chief and claim that the land is the property of one particular lineage of aristocratic origin and that the village headman is a member of this lineage, while *gumlao* repudiate the idea of chieftainship and say that all lineages in the village are of equal standing.

But if the difference between *gumlao* and *gumsa* is here one of ideas rather than of fact, it is not on that account unimportant.   From the *gumlao* point of view a small isolated settlement of ten households which claims to be an independent political unit satisfies the ideal; a similar settlement claiming to be *gumsa* does not.   The *gumsa* ideal involves the notion of a hierarchy of authority—*uma* chief—domain chief—village cluster chief—village head—lineage head; the pattern of such an ideal is provided by the 'great domain chiefs' (*mung du kaba*), men such as Shadan Tu mentioned above.   When therefore

---

[4] 5-7 per sq. mile. *Census*, 1931, Vol. II, Part 2, pp. 268 f.
[5] *Burma Gazetteer*, Myitkyina District, Vol. B, No. 29.   No inference can be made from a comparison of the Census lists of different years as district boundaries were changed extensively at every Census between 1911 and 1941.

we encounter a tiny village of four or five houses which claims to be *gumsa*, we are faced with a kind of contradiction in terms. The people concerned are living in this isolation not because they must but because they choose to do so; yet the fact that they claim to be *gumsa* is an index that they would prefer to live in quite another fashion.

Zone B. Agricultural techniques:—grassland *taungya* and crop rotation in the hills; wet rice in the valleys. Tendency to grow cash crops in the hills. All political organisation *gumsa* in type.

It would appear that throughout this area the hill peoples are completely dependent upon the valley-dwelling Shans for at least a part of their rice supply. The peoples concerned are well aware of this.

For example, it was formerly a law of the Palaung hill state of Tawngpeng that no trading caravan should be allowed to enter the state to buy tea unless it brought with it a cargo of rice or salt.[6] Similarly Hkun Set, the Pretender to the throne of Möng Mao, makes the point that the only way a Shan chief can exert pressure on the Kachins is by denying them access to their valley rice lands.[7]

It follows that political organisation throughout Zone B necessarily involves close co-operation between valley areas (Shans) and hill areas (Kachins, Palaungs, Wa, etc.). Shans may be the political overlords of Kachins or *vice versa*, but the isolated hill community which repudiates all links and inter-dependence with neighbouring valley communities is not really a practical proposition. It accords with this argument that *gumlao* type communities are almost wholly absent in this area. Even communities of Maru and Lashi speakers, in this area, always, or nearly always, attach themselves to the domain of a leader who styles himself chief (*duwa*) and who is regarded as being in a minor way on a par with Shan chiefs (*saohpa*). Further north, where Maru and Lashi communities occur in Zones A and C, they are usually organised according to *gumlao* principles. This suggests that the ecological situation in Zone B, by enforcing co-operation between Kachin and Shan, precludes the possibility of the development of a Kachin *gumlao* political system. *Gumsa* communities here may be politically

[6] Scott (1925), p. 494.   [7] Harvey and Barton (1930), p. 111.

unstable but they cannot cease to be *gumsa*; if a Kachin community breaks off its relations with one set of Shans it will have to establish relations with another.

The evidence unfortunately is quite inconclusive one way or the other. The whole of Zone B (in so far as it fell within the political boundaries of Burma) was very intensively administered by the British who laid down arbitrary rules about village boundaries, separation of Shan and Kachin powers, and maintenance of the *status quo*. No tendency to political fragmentation or accretion could therefore have revealed itself even if it had existed. When the British first entered the area the Zone included a number of very powerful Kachin chiefs of the standing of the Möng Si *duwa* already mentioned. These men were nominally subordinates of the local Shan *saohpa* but in turn ruled over Shans in their capacity as *Kinmöng*. The British removed all Shan villages from the administrative control of Kachin chiefs, thus destroying the power of the more important Kachin leaders, but at the same time they approved of the principle of chieftainship and would not have countenanced the emergence of *gumlao* communities.

Zone C. Agricultural techniques:—in hills, monsoon *taungya*, grassland *taungya*, and frequently irrigated hill terraces; wet rice in valleys. *Gumsa* and *gumlao* both occur and are not readily distinguishable on an ecological basis.

Most of this country resembles Zone A more than Zone B, but the mountains are higher and steeper and the valleys seldom provide much room for irrigated paddy. Rainfall in most places is not much less than in Zone A, but the steeper slopes and higher population density (15–30 per square mile) means that *taungya* practice is far more damaging to the soil resources. Whereas communities in Zone A could survive indefinitely using monsoon *taungya* alone, in Zone C monsoon *taungya* has to be supplemented by some other technique or techniques if soil resources are not to be utterly destroyed.

As was pointed out in Chapter II, hill terracing, where it occurs, seems to have been adopted for military rather than strictly economic reasons. The hill terrace systems in the Kachin Hills are practically without exception situated on or close to important passes through the hills. The people who constructed them were clearly interested in the political control of these passes. Terracing is a device whereby relatively large permanent settlements can be maintained even at high altitudes in precipitous country. But the technique is equally appropriate to either *gumsa* or *gumlao* ideas.

Terracing is not peculiar to any one cultural sub-group or political form. The largest of these terrace-building communities is Gawlamtau (200 houses) on the Hpimaw pass, its inhabitants are Lashi (*gumlao*); but others such as Wawchon (80 houses) near Sadon are Atsi (*gumsa*), and others again such as Hutung (50 houses) near Sinlum are Gauri (*gumsa*).[8]

The distribution of *gumsa* and *gumlao* communities in Zone C cannot be clearly stated. Almost the whole of the Zone north of Sadon is inhabited by speakers of Maru and Lashi dialects. Ethnographic accounts of these people are fragmentary and the assertion that most of them have a *gumlao*-type organisation may be misleading. South of Sadon *gumlao* communities in Zone C are rare but whether this was a natural situation or due to the anti-*gumlao* policy of the British Government it is hard to say.

The relatively high population density in Zone C is probably due to a tendency for population to cluster in the vicinity of trade routes.

The trade routes through the mountain barrier covered by Zone C have been of importance for centuries and the bulk of the population has long resided on or close to these east-west tracks through the mountains. Income from tolls from transit caravans was in the past an important element in the economy of the whole zone. It was the major source of power of the leading *gumsa* chiefs in the 19th century, just as in Zone A rice land and slaves were a major source of power. At the height of their power the *gumsa* chiefs of Zone C likewise levied a rice tax on their Shan neighbours, but they never attained the level of political independence achieved by the Kachin chiefs in the Hukawng Valley. The *gumlao*-type organisation of the large Lashi settlements in the Hpimaw area is perhaps explained by the fact that these communities were able to

[8] So also in Assam among the Nagas, the 'democratic' Angami and the 'autocratic' Sema both practise terraced cultivation. The hill terrace communities in the Naga Hills are much larger than Kachin examples.

balance their economy by means of caravan tolls alone and on that account had no need to come into political alliance with the rice-growing Shan-Chinese of the valley to the east.

In sum then, this review of the ecological facts produces only negative results. Differences in the physical environment provide only a partial explanation for differences of cultural and political organisation. Ecology can to some extent explain why, if Kachins choose to live in the inhospitable terrain of the Hpimaw Pass, their technical organisation and pattern of settlement should be what it in fact is among the Lashi of that region; it does not really explain why the Lashi should choose to live there at all when there is plenty of better land elsewhere, nor does it explain why the Lashi should have a *gumlao* organisation when the Atsi of the Sadon area, practising similar techniques under somewhat similar conditions, are *gumsa*.

Political Environment

The discussion of the consequences of changes in the political environment implies a review of Kachin political history. Let me emphasise again that what follows is largely speculative.

The first references to the Kachin Hills Area occur, as might be expected, in Chinese texts. The area was initially important only as one of the possible routes from China to India and the West. There are indications that such a trade route may have been established as early as 128 B.C. and that the Chinese who founded the prefecture of Yung Ch'ang in A.D. 69 did so because it was the eastern terminus of this difficult route.[9] There is no adequate evidence as to what sort of population, if any, inhabited the Kachin Hills Area at this period.

In the period of confusion that followed the collapse of the Han dynasty the Chinese frontiers were not maintained and the administrative post at Yung Ch'ang was formally abolished in A.D. 342.

A number of early Chinese works published at various dates between A.D. 350 and A.D. 1000 make references to 'the wild and troublesome *b'uok* tribes' living apparently in the mountains to the west of Yung Ch'ang, whose land produced 'rhinoceros, elephant, tortoiseshell, jade, amber, cowries, gold, silver, salt-

[9] The evidence cited here is mainly drawn from Luce and Pe Maung Tin (1939).

wells, cinnamon and cotton trees, hill paddy and panicled millet'. This seems to be a population inhabiting the Kachin Hills Area, and though language and culture may have changed, the tribal name has stuck. Modern Maru call Jinghpaw speakers *p'ok*; the Shans of Hkamti Long used to refer to their Kachin serfs as *kha-p'ok* (serf *p'ok*)[10]; Jinghpaw itself might well be written *chying-p'ok*; modern Chinese refer to the modern Kachins as *p'u man*[11]—the *p'u* being written with the same character as the earlier *b'uok*.

During the same period there are frequent Chinese references to the P'iao, a relatively sophisticated people with a kingdom somewhere in Central Burma. These are seemingly to be identified with the Pyu concerning whom there is some archæological evidence from the Prome area. This population, though it seems to have had a Burmese-type language, was markedly Indian in culture.

In the 8th and 9th centuries the Kachin Hills Area was clearly under the political influence of Nanchao. Nanchao was a Kingdom of Shan type composed of various *möng* linked in feudal federation. The technical apparatus of Nanchao was no doubt borrowed or developed from Chinese sources, but the political pattern was definitely Shan. The Nanchao leader Ko-lo-feng (*c.* A.D. 750) opened trade routes to India and the Pyu Kingdom in Central Burma and established permanent settled garrisons at suitable staging posts on the way. The Shan settlement of Hkamti Long probably dates from this period and also perhaps the Shan settlements between Mogaung and Assam by way of the Hukawng Valley. There are descriptions of actual itineraries between China and India dating from this period, but the identification of place names is uncertain. Pelliot, who has analysed the documents in question, concludes that the northern of the two routes ran more or less due east to west—Yung Ch'ang, Teng Yueh, Sadon, Waingmaw (Myitkyina), Mogaung, Somra Tract (Naga Hills), Kohima, Dimapur, Gauhati.[12]

The chronicles mention by name numerous different tribes of barbarians inhabiting the hill districts and these appear to

---

[10] Wilcox (1832).   [11] Siguret (1937), p. 122.
[12] Pelliot (1904). This should not be taken as implying that there were settlements at all or any of these localities at this date.

have been enlisted in substantial numbers in the Nanchao armies. None of these groups can be identified with certainty with any existing Kachin sub-groups or for that matter with any other modern tribal groups. Assuming that 'Li Shui' is correctly identified as the Irrawaddy River, it would seem that Waingmaw was the centre of a gold-washing industry and that the amber deposits of the Hukawng Valley (eighteen stages west of Yung Ch'ang) were already being worked. Salt was another important product of the Waingmaw-Mogaung area and an important article of trade.

Shan (Nanchao) influence at this period did not extend further west than the present frontiers of Burma. The Assam Valley was a Hindu Kingdom—the Kamarupa of Hiuen Tsiang (c. A.D. 625).[13] Shan (Ahom) *political* control of Eastern Assam dates only from the mid-13th century.[14]

Sometime about A.D. 832 the Pyu Kingdom of Central Burma was overthrown by a Nanchao army and when we next meet records of a Burmese Kingdom (about A.D. 1050) the Kings have Nanchao titles. It was this 11th-century kingdom, originally an offshoot of Nanchao, which developed as the Burmese Kingdom of Pagan. Some authorities seem to postulate a vast southward migration of 'Burmese' at this period from some undefined location in the Kachin Hills Area.[15] This is quite unnecessary. The population of Burma under its first 'Burmese' (Nanchao) Kings could have been just the same as it was under the last 'Pyu' (Indian Kings). Both the Pyu and the Pagan peoples were Buddhist. Nanchao was not. The Shans appear to have become Buddhist only at about the end of the 16th century.

Nanchao capitulated to the Mongols in 1253[16] and was succeeded by a puppet Yunnan government subject to Peking.[17] Warfare between this government and Burma resulted in the destruction of Pagan and the collapse of the Pagan dynasty (1287). The Kings of Burma (Ava) for the next three centuries

[13] Gait (1906), p. 22.
[14] ibid., p. 74. By this time Nanchao had capitulated to the Mongols and the new military expansion of Shan power was perhaps partly an instrument of Mongol policy.   [15] Luce and Pe Maung Tin (1939), p. 273.
[16] Howorth (1876), p. 212. Nanchao surrendered without a fight. There was no massacre.
[17] The Mongol capital was at Peking (Khanbulig) from 1267, though the Mongols did not control the whole of China until 1278.

were of Shan origin.   By 1531 most of what is now Burma had become a loose federation of Shan *möng* under various more or less independent *saohpa*.   The *möng* which made up the Kachin Hills Area owed fealty to the Chinese Emperor as successor to the throne of Nanchao.   The extent to which the Chinese exercised effective control is not known, but an official Chinese administrator seems to have been posted to Mohnyin (Möng Yang) in 1296 and at various later dates.[18]

From the time that Burma became integrated as a single kingdom (*c.* 1560)[19] the *möng* of the Kachin Hills Area became objects of bitter contention between the Burmese and the Chinese.   The Burmese appear to have gained effective control of Hsenwi, Möng Mit, Bhamo and Mohnyin from about 1600 onwards, but the status of Mogaung and its tributary Hkamti States was in dispute until 1796.   The Chinese have never admitted Burmese rights over the country east of the Irrawaddy and north of Myitkyina.   Tribute taxes to Chinese authorities have been paid by Maru Kachins of the Htawgaw area, Nung of the Nam Tamai and the Shans of Hkamti Long even in very recent years.

The Ahom (Shan) Kingdom in Assam existed from 1250 until the end of the 18th century.   The Ahom Kings continued to recognise their relationship with the Princes of other Shan states, notably those of the 'Kingdom of Nora' (Mogaung) and it is evident that throughout this period routes from Hkamti Long to Assam and from Mogaung to Assam via the Hukawng Valley were regularly used.   The inhabitants of the northern part of the Kachin Hills Area were thus in closer touch with India and China than they were during a large part of the period of British domination 1885–1942.

The jade mines west of Kamaing which, until very recently, have been of major importance in Kachin politics were first extensively developed during the 18th century.   This development greatly increased the importance of the area from the Chinese point of view and doubtless led to an increase in the trade in other commodities as well.

In 1824 the Burmese clashed with the British in Assam. One outcome of the brief war that followed was the virtual

---

[18] Scott and Hardiman (1901), Vol. II, Part 2, p. 346.
[19] Under Bayinnaung.   See Harvey (1925), p. 165.

closing of the frontier between Assam and Burma. By this time the Shans had ceased to have military importance. The Burmese had destroyed many of their main centres and deposed their rulers. The remnant squabbled among themselves for empty titles, hiring Kachin mercenaries to fight their battles. In the outcome it was the Shans who became serfs to the Kachins rather than the other way about. Around 1830 the Shan element were still the masters in Hkamti Long and in the Hkamti colony at Sadiya in Assam; but in the Hukawng Valley Kachins were already the overlords and Mogaung had become a governorship under the Burmese crown.

But while the early 19th century saw the closure of the Hukawng Valley, the trade between Burma and Yunnan flourished. Most of it was canalised through either Bhamo or Hsenwi.[20] It was of such a scale that both British and French speculators envisaged opening up one or other of these routes for railway communication. The Burmese, though now masters of the Shan settlements in the valleys on the Burmese side of the frontier, made no attempt to control the Kachins directly. On the contrary, the Kachin chiefs, though described to foreigners as scoundrels and brigands, were awarded Burmese honorific titles and treated with the respects due to minor royalty.

The Annexation of Lower Burma by the British in 1852 quickly led to the economic and political disintegration of the remnant kingdom of Upper Burma. Moreover 1850–70 was a period of civil war in Yunnan between the Mohammedan rebels and supporters of the central Chinese government. Trans-border trade thus shrank to a trickle and led to a crisis in relations between the Burmese authorities and the Kachins.

A whole series of abortive attempts were made to overthrow the regime of King Thibaw in Mandalay and the Kachins were supporters of most of them. In 1883 there was a well-organised attempt to re-establish an independent Northern Area under Mogaung. The leader of this revolt—a Burmese Shan named Maung Shwe Le—claimed to be a descendant of the former Mogaung *saohpa* Haw Hseng (died 1777) and took the same title for himself.[21] The suppression of this revolt

[20] See Map 5 p. 64.
[21] The Kachins refer to the Shans of the Mogaung-Hukawng Valley area as the **Haw Hseng** (*Hkawseng*) Shans. The name would appear to be an hereditary title in the Mogaung royal house. cf. Kawlu Ma Nawng (1942), p. 41.

resulted in the destruction of most of the Shan villages in the Mogaung Myitkyina area, and when the British finally annexed Upper Burma in 1885 the whole region was in chaos. Further south the *saohpa* succession in the joint state of Möng Mit—Möng Leng was continuously in dispute from 1840–92. Rival claimants all used Kachin levies as mercenaries. One of them, Kan Hlaing, seems to have had a good claim to the throne of Möng Leng (Mohlaing) but was treated as a rebel by the British. Consequently the Kachins who supported him had their villages destroyed. Another, Saw Yan Baing, a grandson of King Mindon, who was a focus of Burmese patriotic sentiment in 1889 was similarly treated.

To the east, the story of Hsenwi is very similar. Here again in the immediate pre-British period, rival claimants to the *saohpa*'s throne used Kachin mercenaries, and here again there was an attempt to organise a patriotic revolution both against Thibaw's tyranny and against the British. In this case the leader was the Myinsaing Prince, a son of Mindon and half-brother of Thibaw.

When the British attempted to assume control in 1885 the situation was confused but British accounts of the period are certainly extremely prejudiced. As successors to the Government of Thibaw, they treated all rebels against Thibaw as rebels against themselves, and Kachin interference in local politics was ruthlessly suppressed. But though the early British administrators seem to have regarded the Kachins as mere dacoits and brigands, it is evident that the Kachins in question were strong upholders of the principle of legitimacy. They appear never to have conducted a raid except in the name of some Shan or Burmese prince or else in reprisal for injuries done to themselves.[22]

When the British first assumed control, Shan and Kachin were not only in political alliance; they were living side by side. The following, for example, describes an area near Myitkyina in 1890:

'Out of eighteen villages which were formerly Burmese Shan, six were entirely inhabited by Kachins; in eight Kachins had houses alongside the Shans, and in four only the Shans were living alone.

[22] The facts cited above are based on Scott and Hardiman (1901), especially references to Myitkyina, Mogaung, Mohnyin, Mohlaing, Möng Mit.

The Shans throughout (this area) lived under the protection of the Kachins in a condition which was not without mutual advantages. The Kachins demanded little tribute and were not hard masters otherwise, whilst the Shans were free to indulge exclusively in trade and to make as much profit out of the Kachins as they could in doing so.'[23]

This kind of thing was anathema to the tidy bureaucratic minds of British officials. One of the few continuing elements in British administrative policy towards the Kachins was the policy of treating Shan and Kachin as separate racial elements. Even to the last—in 1946!—British officials were engaged in surveying precise boundaries between Kachin and Shan territory. The political dependence of Shan on Kachin or *vice versa* was excluded by edict; economic relations between the two groups, though not prohibited, were made extremely difficult. Everything possible was done to deter the more sophisticated Kachins from settling in Shan territory in the plains. This policy originated from a desire 'to establish peace and security within the settled districts',[24] and it achieved its end, but at high cost. In 1889, in one section of the Kachin Hills alone, four punitive expeditions registered the following score in the interests of peace and security:

46 villages (639 houses) burnt
509,000 lbs. paddy destroyed
17 Kachins killed—'their losses were probably higher'
63 buffalos and 4 cows killed.[25]

Yet the stupidity of such a policy should have been obvious. In 1891 a military column was sent to Maingkwan to explore and prepare 'for our future control of the Hukong Valley'. What they found was this:

'The population of the valley is almost entirely Kachin. The Kachins of these parts are reported to lose their turbulent qualities in descending from the hills and to become lazy and peaceable like the Shans who formerly inhabited the valley and whom they have

---

[23] Scott and Hardiman (1901). Myitkyina.   [24] R.N.E.F. (1893).
[25] Hertz (1912), p. 42; R.N.E.F. (1890). It was a feature of the punitive expeditions at this period to levy huge money fines. It was quite common to fine a recalcitrant *duwa* up to Rs. 2,500 and then burn his village if he didn't pay. Protests that so much hard cash was not available were treated as frivolous evasions.

gradually ousted. The valley is almost entirely free from crime or disturbance of any kind. Each village is governed by a Sawbwa or Agyiwa. In the rare cases in which a serious crime is committed, the leading headmen combine to punish the offender. In view of the peaceful condition of the valley . . . it is proposed to postpone for the present the work of bringing the Hukong Valley under direct administration.'[26]

And indeed the Hukawng Valley was left alone in peace and prosperity until in 1926 certain British officials in Rangoon decided to enhance their political reputations in Whitehall by 'releasing the Kachin slaves'. The economic consequences of this action have already been indicated. Out of a total population of 7,903, 3,466 were found to be 'slaves'. Their release and virtual deportation merely meant that many of the rice lands of the Hukawng went out of production altogether.[27]

Once the British had established peace in the Kachin Hills their policy was one of maintaining the *status quo*. Wherever possible village boundaries were recorded and treated as fixed. This meant that in the more congested areas it ceased to be practical for a village to grow in size, for if it did so land would run short. In this way the relative status of the chiefs of different communities tended to be stabilised. *Gumlao* principles of government were disapproved of but countenanced in some cases. Chiefs were turned into agents of government; succession was supposed to follow traditional law and custom, but appointment was always subject to approval by the British administrator. By these means Kachin chiefs were reduced to a dead level of petty mediocrity. Except in the relatively unadministered areas of the north, there ceased to be great chiefs and little chiefs; they were just chiefs, who in most cases were no better than minor village headmen.

Along with the British administration came the missions; indeed the missions arrived first. The Catholics had a permanent station at Bhamo from 1874; the American Baptists from 1875. Most of the Kachin leaders of today are nominally Christians. This does not necessarily mean much more than that they have attended a Christian school. The Christian

[26] R.N.E.F. (1892), para. 32.
[27] It is reported that at the present time (1951) there is a considerable movement of Kachins from North Hsenwi to take up land in the Hukawng Valley abandoned by the freed slaves of 25 years ago.

God Karai Kasang[28] seems to have been well assimilated to Kachin ideas; he is Karai Wa and treated as a kind of superior sky nat.

In this review of the salient features of the history of the Kachin Hills Area certain elements stand out.

a. The population of the hill country has at all times been in close political relation with the population of the valley country. Until the British attempted to impose their ideas there was never any suggestion of distinct Shan and Kachin territories.

b. The material culture of the hill population may have changed a good deal over the centuries and also the distribution of language groups, but the basic economy of both hills and plains seems scarcely to have changed in the last 1600 years. There appears to be little or nothing to justify the repeated assertions that modern Kachins are the descendants of quite recent immigrants into the area.

c. While there have been frequent changes in the locus and intensity of external political power, the type of this external influence was, until the coming of the British in 1885, always of the same kind. It was Shan-Chinese influence deriving in the first place from theories of government developed by the Chinese in Han times.

What were these Shan-Chinese theories of government? It is not irrelevant, I think, that by the first century B.C. there was an extensive literature on the subject. By the end of the Han dynasty, the philosophy of Confucianism had reached its fullest development in two contrasted theories. On the one hand the school of Hsuntze maintained above all else the necessity for respecting the established order of society. In this doctrine, the five criteria—position, wealth, age, wisdom, ability—determine the amount of wealth which each man should have when due share is allotted to every man. The logical inference from this is an absolute respect for the divine authority of the hereditary ruler. Obedience to the law becomes the supreme requirement of ethics. In sharp contrast the school of Mencius took the view that the first duty of the ruler was to better the welfare of his people. Property

---

[28] As might be expected the missions maintain that the Kachins had the notion of a superior high god from the beginning and Karai Kasang is supposed to be the name of this deity. If so, he was a deity with no myth and an unintelligible name. 'Karai Kasang', I suggest, is simply a confused pronunciation of 'Christian'. cf. Gilhodes (1922), Chapter 3.

should be for the benefit of all regardless of their hereditary rank. Revolution against a tyrant was justifiable and in accordance with the wishes of Heaven.[29]   If then the Kachins borrowed their theories of government from the Chinese by way of the Shans, it might almost seem that the *gumsa-gumlao* opposition was there from the beginning.

I move on now from semi-history to pure speculation. We do not know how Kachin society grew to be what it is but I am going to guess. My guess must fit with the historical facts which I have outlined above, it must also be consistent with known facts of Asiatic ethnography. To take the latter first.

From the point of view of the student of material culture much of the present-day technology of the Kachins has a strongly 'Indonesian' flavour. The techniques and apparatus of weaving and iron-working and cultivating rice as well as a variety of household equipment ranging from fire-pistons to brass gongs are common, not only to all the hill peoples of Indo China, Burma and Assam, but also to similarly situated tribes in Western Szechuan, Formosa, the Philippines, Borneo and much of Indonesia.

It has been argued that this distribution of traits reflects a prehistoric migration of 'Indonesian' peoples.[30]   But no plausible chronology could be fitted to such a theory. The only reasonable assumption is that these widely dispersed culture groups have many similarities of material culture because they all originally borrowed them from the same source, namely China in the first millennium B.C.[31]

I assume therefore that the techniques of working iron and of working *taungya* with iron tools were not known to the hill peoples of the Kachin Hills Area much before the beginning of our era and that wet-rice cultivation first began to be practised in this region at much the same period.   Garrisons established by the Chinese and later by the Nanchao Shans to protect their trade routes became focal points of relatively sophisticated culture and formed the nuclei of what ultimately

[29] Liang Chi-chao (1930), Chapters 3, 4, 7.

[30] Smith (1925), Chapter 6.   Such well-known authorities as Henry Balfour, J. H. Hutton and Charles Hose have written in a similar sense.

[31] Heine Geldern appears now to argue along these lines having earlier postulated the migration of an Indonesian race. For bibliography see Embree and Dotson (1950), pp. 21–2.

became separate Shan *möng*.   The valley cultures and the hill cultures were thus associated from the beginning.

When the Chinese established Yung Ch'ang in A.D. 68, and for some centuries after, the population of the hill district was probably very small.   It would have tended to concentrate into the areas of greatest economic importance—e.g. near trade routes, salt wells, iron ore deposits.   Distances in the Kachin Hills are great and these localised populations would have been more or less isolated; marked dialectical differences would result.   I take the 'proto-Maru' community to have been a group associated with the exploitation of the salt deposits in the valley of the N'mai Hka; similarly the 'proto-Jinghpaw' were a group who exploited the iron ore deposits in the vicinity of Hkamti Long; there may have been many such 'tribes'— although some of these survive in modern tradition, the recorded names have no significance.

Let me follow up a single instance to illustrate this latter point.

Chinese sources of the 9th century A.D.,[32] in describing the ethnography of Yunnan and the Western Frontier, make a broad distinction between Man tribes who are apparently the ultra primitive groups; and the Mang tribes (so called because they styled their Kings Mang-Chao—i.e.? *Möng-sao*), who are more sophisticated, and might perhaps be regarded as 'proto-Shans'.   There is, however, no clear distinction between the Mang and the Man.   Modern Shans use the term Khang to mean 'primitive hill tribesman' much as the early Chinese used Man.   The Chinese category P'u (formerly pronounced *bu'ok*) was closely allied to Man and Mang.   I have already noted that the Shan prefix *kha* means 'serf'.   When then we find that the Hkamti Shan tradition records that the pre-Shan inhabitants of the area included (amongst others) Kha-mawng, Kha-man, Kha-p'ok, and Khang,[33] these are simply the old Chinese categories reduced to serf status.   Carried a stage further we find that Kachin tradition declares that the pre-Jinghpaw inhabitants of the Hukawng Valley were the 'Hkummawng Hkumman Khang (Nagas)'.[34]

[32] Cited by Luce and Pe Maung Tin (1939), mainly from the *Man-shu* of Fan Ch'o published about A.D. 865.
[33] Barnard (1925), (1934); Wilcox (1832).   See pp. 222, 239.
[34] Kawlu Ma Nawng (1942), p. 15.

All this does not tell us much about the facts of historical ethnography; what it does show very clearly is that Shan traditions are borrowed from Chinese sources, and that Kachin traditions are borrowed from Shan sources.

We cannot know for certain what sort of social organisation these 'proto-Kachin' communities possessed. I assume that generally speaking they were *gumlao* in type, that is to say they had no hereditary chiefs and no concept of land being the property of one lineage to the exclusion of others. The Lhota and Angami Nagas described by Hutton and Mills[35] give an indication of what I have in mind.

The crucial distinguishing principle of modern Kachin social structure is the *mayu-dama* marriage system. Lévi-Strauss[36] puts forward arguments which seem to imply that the basic rules of this system may have been borrowed from the Chinese at a very early date. I am not persuaded by these views and I do not think that my 'proto-Kachins' necessarily had a *mayu-dama* system of the modern type. On the other hand I do assume that the 'proto-Kachins', like the Chinese of the period, were organised in a system of exogamous patrilineal lineages.

So far as is known there have only been two areas within the Kachin Hills Area where iron-working has ever been carried on on any extensive scale, namely (*a*) in the Duleng area east of Hkamti Long, (*b*) in the Shan state of Möng Hsa. The Möng Hsa blacksmiths have to import their crude iron from elsewhere,[37] but the Duleng craftsmen can, if they choose, smelt their own ore. I assume that these latter iron-workings were already being used by 'proto-Jinghpaw' before the 8th century A.D., and that the exploitation of this iron was a crucial factor in providing an economic basis for the development of early Jinghpaw society. It is to be noted that this area is just north of the Triangle zone which, under modern climatic conditions, produces better *taungya* crops than any other part of the Kachin Hills. In an economic sense, my 'proto-Jinghpaw' were thus very well situated.

The Shan state of Hkamti Long is supposed to have been established about A.D. 750, as a military outpost of Nanchao

---

[35] Hutton (1921); Mills (1922).
[36] Lévi-Strauss (1949), Chapters XXIII and XXVIII.
[37] Anderson (1871), p. 111.

in the course of three-sided hostilities in which both the Chinese and the Tibetans were involved. [38]

The Shans of Hkamti Long are today few and decadent but the area of marshy grassland hereabouts suggests that in the past there may have been very large areas of paddy land and a large population to match. The decay of this state was probably due firstly to malaria—of which a particularly virulent form is now a local speciality—and secondly to the fact that this particular route from China to India gradually fell into disuse. Around A.D. 1000 Hkamti Long may well have been one of the principle sub-states in the whole Nanchao confederacy.

According to their own traditions, the Shans who established Hkamti Long found a state ruled over by a Tibetan Prince who had subjugated Kha-p'ok, Kha-man, etc., tribesmen. The Shans defeated the Tibetan Prince and ruled in his stead.

Broadly speaking this tradition seems acceptable. I assume that the local Kha-p'ok, etc., were my 'proto-Kachins' and that they were of the same ethnic stock as modern Kachins. Those who actually worked for the Shans in the Hkamti Long paddy plain would quickly have become assimilated as Shans. This assimilation seems to have continued until recent times. In Modern Hkamti Long there is a sharp caste distinction between the aristocrats and the 'slaves' (lok-kha). The latter include various sub-groups, some of which speak dialects of Jinghpaw[39] while others speak Shan.[40] The following quotation applies particularly to the latter:

'They were, up to the time of our (British) occupation, subordinate to the Shans and had to render them service in the way of building houses and supplying the saohpa with fuel, etc. Very little is known of these tribes and I have not been able to obtain even a small vocabulary of their language, as they have been absorbed into the Shans whose language they have completely adopted. . . . With the occupation of Hkamti the status of these tribes has improved and many try to pass themselves off as Shans, being ashamed of their low origin. The Shan does not intermarry with any of these lok-kha.'[41]

[38] Luce and Pe Maung Tin (1939), p. 270.
[39] Nogmung (Sam-hpyen); Kha-lang; N'tit; Pangsu.
[40] Kang, Langhka , Nokkyo, Yoya, Tawhawng.
[41] Barnard (1925), p. 139.

But there would have been other proto-Kachins with a more independent status.   The blacksmithing industry of the Kachins must have been very important.   In later years Duleng swords were traded all over the Kachin Hills, but the trade remained in Kachin hands.   This fact is of symbolic as well as economic importance.   Silver, as well as iron, is mined in the Hkamti Long area, but silver-working is a Shan not a Kachin craft. For the Shans, silversmithing is a profession proper and peculiar to the nobility;[42] iron-working is a task for slaves.

I infer that it was the trade in iron more than anything else which gave the early Jinghpaw power and which enabled the *gumsa* to become feudal satellites of the Shan princes rather than their serfs.

If this reconstruction were correct, one might suppose that among the proto-Kachins the blacksmith was a person of high status, and it is therefore interesting to find that in modern Kachin origin stories N'gawn Wa (who is at once the first parent of men and the creator of the earth) is unquestionably a blacksmith.   He forges (*ndup*) the earth and the terms used to describe the process are those of a Kachin smithy.[43]

It is then surely remarkable that in modern *gumsa* Kachin society the blacksmith's craft has scarcely any status at all. Outside the Duleng country, which as we have seen is today *gumlao*, Kachin blacksmiths are rare.   I attribute this largely to the fact that, despite the N'gawn Wa myth, blacksmithing has got mixed up with the *gumsa-gumlao* opposition.   Black-smithing is not respectable for aristocratic *gumsa* Kachins because it is not respectable for Shan aristocrats either.   Here we may recall that in the myth concerning the origin of the *gumlao* movement, as it concerns the Hukawng Valley, the leaders of the *gumlao* movement are members of a lineage called N'Dup-Dumsa—'the blacksmith priests'.

My suggestion is that Jinghpaw culture spread over the Kachin Hills Area at the expense of the culture of the other miscellaneous tribal cultures because the Jinghpaw achieved a relatively superior political status *vis-à-vis* their Shan over-lords.   When the Shans of Hkamti Long went to war, the

---

[42] Wilcox (1832) notes that the Hkamti Long chiefs were expert silversmiths; Anderson (1871) reports that in the Sanda Valley silversmithing was a profession of the Shan Buddhist priests.   [43] cf. Gilhodes (1922), p. 14.

Jinghpaw went with them, but as feudal allies rather than as slaves. Thereafter Jinghpaw-speaking *gumsa* Kachins attached themselves in similar fashion to the Shan princes of other states—Mogaung, Mohnyin, Maingkwan, Waingmaw, Bhamo and the rest. The net result was that the area in which *gumsa* organisation and Jinghpaw speech prevailed gradually spread south and west from Hkamti Long. We need not suppose that there was any large scale migration of Kachins. It was rather that *gumsa* organisation, as first developed by the Hkamti Long Jinghpaw, was adapted to fit with Shan political ideas, so that Shan princes who wanted to employ Kachins as mercenaries employed only *gumsa* Kachins and this led to the absorption of the lesser hill tribes into the *gumsa* system. It is, for instance, evident that the Gauri and Atsi groups of today are composed of populations whose ancestors were speakers of some Maru dialect.[44] The fact that they became incorporated into the *gumsa* political system, so that their chiefs are now reckoned to be the lineage kinsman of Jinghpaw chiefs, has led the Gauri to adopt Jinghpaw speech while their relatives the Atsi have developed a language about half-way between Maru and Jinghpaw. Indeed, as noted already, there are some places where the Atsi have dropped their own language altogether in favour of Jinghpaw.

Gumsa organisation as developed in the Hkamti Long area was, I insist, a kind of imitation of the Shan political order. There is nothing very mysterious about this. In our own age we are familiar with the phenomenon of subject colonial peoples who, in achieving independence, carry on with a political system imitated and modified from that of their former rulers. Burma, India, Jamaica, the Gold Coast, provide examples. The early Jinghpaw achieved some degree of freedom from their Shan masters but retained Shan ideas about the nature of political society. It is because of this that, both in modern behaviour and in traditional tale, Kachins and Shans alike take it for granted that Kachin chief and Shan chief are persons of the same kind. Evidence on this point from Möng Mao has already been given. The following is a Kachin account of how the Hkamti Shans and Kachins entered Assam:

'After this the descendants of Jihkawp Tang went over to Assam

[44] cf. p. 54.

by way of Hkamti Long and the Chyaukan Pass. They were the
following lineages (a) Gasheng-Daihpa, (b) Pyisa, (c) Hkamti Shan
Namsun Wa. Hkamti Shan Namsun Wa and Gasheng Wa joined
forces and on their way to Assam . . . fought with the Hkumman
people[45] . . . After defeating the Hkumman people Namsun Wa
and Gasheng Wa inflicted a yearly due of 10 baskets of paddy from
each household of the Hkumman tribe; of this ten baskets the Shan
Namsun Wa was to get six and Gasheng Wa four. After the subjugation of the Hkumman people the Gasheng Wa became dissatisfied with his share of four baskets and demanded more; the
Shan refused to allow him more so the two parted. The Shan left
for Assam; Gasheng Wa remained at the Tayun river. After the
Shan's departure the Hkumman people utterly refused to pay this
paddy due; they hit the Gasheng Wa over the head with a tobacco
pipe and by this insult indicated that he had merely become as the
dust which is thrown away after the smoker has finished the tobacco
in his pipe; as he had thus been robbed of all prestige the Gasheng
Wa could no longer remain in the Tayun country and so followed
the Namsun Wa to Assam, living under the Assamese.'[46]

In this story 'the descendants of Jihkawp Tang' stand for all
the Tsasen *gumsa*, who are represented as one major lineage
opposed to all the Tsasen *gumlao*, who compose another major
lineage, namely 'the descendants of Jihkawp Tu (the elder
brother of Jihkawp Tang)'. The *gumsa* lineage is for the purposes of this tale divided into three segments, descendants of
three brothers Gasheng Wa, Pyisa Wa, Namsun Wa. The
eldest and second brother are Kachin; the youngest brother
(i.e. the *uma*) is Shan. In accordance with orthodox *gumsa*
principles the youngest brother ranks highest and the eldest
brother next. The feudal supremacy of Shan over Kachin is
thus represented as the relationship between youngest brother
and eldest brother; which is strictly in accordance with the
principles of Kachin *gumsa* social structure already described.

The same authority gives a rather similar story about the
entry of the *gumsa* Kachins into the Hukawng Valley which
again shows how the Kachins are thought of as fitting in to a
feudal hierarchy dominated by Shans.

The story runs that Laisai Nawng, an ancestor of the Marip-
N'Ding lineage captured Hkumman Wa and from him learnt

[45] In this case Hkumman stands for the Mishmi.
[46] Kawlu Ma Nawng (1942), p. 13.

of the virtues of the Hukawng Valley. Laisai Nawng makes a pact with Hkumman Wa and after sundry incidents the latter leads Laisai Nawng to the Hukawng Valley. He takes him to the Kang village of Singgai. The Kang chief takes him to the Hkansawng *saohpa*; the Pangsang *saohpa* takes him to the Hpaknaw *saohpa*; the Hpaknaw *saohpa* takes him to the *saohpa* of Mung Kawm (*Maingkwan*) who is the senior Shan chief in the valley.[47]

Kawlu Ma Nawng makes a very shrewd analysis of how, from this legendary beginning, the relationship of Shan and Kachin was ultimately inverted.

'Four hundred years ago the six (Shan) chiefs (of the Hukawng Valley) had 7,000 households in their tracts. The Kachins followed the Shans by a slow infiltration which subsequently led to them inducing a *gumlao* mode of thought amongst the Shans. In the fighting consequent upon this *gumlao* movement, Kachins were employed as fighting men on both sides. The people on the losing side of this fight ran away from the Hukawng and had their land taken over by Kachins. As more and more Shans ran away, more and more Kachins entered into their land; finally the Kachins were in complete possession of the valley. . .   After the great exodus the only places where Shans remained in the Hukawng Valley were Kangdau, Mainghkwan and Ningbyen. . . .   The Shans formerly at Kangdau were so badly treated by the Kachins that they finally moved to the Dalu area. The Ningbyen Shans are still in the valley as they accepted the overlordship of the Ningbyen Kachin chief. They remain subordinate to him even now. The Mainghkwan Shans are looked after by the Walawbum chiefs so no one dare ill-treat them. . . .'[48]

The Hukawng Valley story was unusual because in this area the Kachins to a considerable extent ousted the Shans altogether, replacing their labour by Assamese slaves. Elsewhere even at their most influential moments the Kachins seem to have been satisfied with the status of political parasite rather than acknowledged overlord. In the latter part of the 19th

[47] Kawlu Ma Nawng (1942), p. 15, but cf. p. 41 where the Mung Kawm *saohpa* is said to owe allegiance to the Hkawseng *saohpa*. The latter title originally denoted the *saohpa* of Mogaung. The implication is that the Shans of the Hukawng Valley had 'Naga' (Hkumman, Kang) adherents before the Kachins arrived there.

[48] Kawlu Ma Nawng (1942), p. 41.

century the Kachins in the Northern Shan States were everywhere the 'Kingmakers', but the *saohpa* whom they supported were always Shan not Kachin.

For purposes of political alliance it is evident that a Kachin chief could be treated 'as if' he were a Shan chief, and a Kachin *mung* could be treated 'as if' it were a Shan *möng*. But the differences between Kachin *gumsa* and Shan structure must also be stressed.

As we have seen, the requirements of *taungya* agriculture dictate a dispersed settlement pattern; in contrast, a Shan *möng* can be closely settled. A Shan petty *saohpa* controls directly the community of which he is lord. A Kachin chief playing at being a Shan *saohpa* on a comparable scale needs to control villages scattered over a wide area. Moreover in the Shan case the villagers are tied to their land; the rice fields represent capital investment. Kachins have no investment in the *taungya*. If a Kachin doesn't like his chief he can go somewhere else. The Kachin chief therefore, whether he likes it or not, must have much closer personal ties with his followers than does his Shan counterpart; for if he does not his followers will disappear. Granted this, and granted a pre-existing organisation based on patrilineal exogamous lineages, the use of marriage as a device for establishing political links becomes obvious.

The *mayu-dama* system is thus the natural counterpart of an attempt to imitate Shan political relations through the medium of Kachin culture.

Yet paradoxically the *mayu-dama* relationship is itself directly antithetical to Shan ideas. The status of the Shan *saohpa* is in theory that of the absolutely superior chief, the divine King. He marries, as superior wives, women from other *saohpa* families of status equal to his own; he marries, as inferior wives, women who have been given to him as tribute. Such women can be thought of as a part of the rent which the feudal tenant pays for his land.

The relationship of the Kachin chief to his 'tenants' is far more precarious. The tribute he receives is largely token tribute (e.g. the gift of 'thigh meat'); if he wants to obtain real goods from his landlordship he must give women in exchange.

It seems to be precisely this paradox which leads to the breakdown of the *gumsa* system. The mythological justification of *gumlao* revolt concerns rebellion against chiefs who 'rated as commoners even their own relatives who had not the right to collect dues and insisted on the payment of dues, labour and otherwise, from these relatives as from other commoners'.[49] *Gumsa* principles logically result in a chief being in either *hpunau* (lineage brother) or *mayu-dama* (affinal) relationship with a large proportion of his feudal dependants. The obligations of the tenant to his lord are tempered by the fact that the lord is the tenants' relative and by the fact that the *mayu-dama* network has a long-term continuity. The obligations of a Shan *saohpa* towards his wives' relatives are of a much more temporary nature. The influential Kachin *gumsa* chief is tempted to rely on the support of his immediate (non-kin) dependants, that is to say on his 'slaves' (*mayam*), and to ignore obligations of kinship towards his subordinates. If he succeeds in this he gets very near to the status of a true Shan *saohpa*; if he fails, it is his lineage relatives and *dama* kinsmen who lead the *gumlao* revolt.

It is also obvious that if marriage is used to express differences of political status, then the marriage rule must be asymmetrical. If lineage A give wives to lineage B, and marriage expresses the fact that lineage A are the overlords of lineage B, then clearly lineage B cannot give wives back to lineage A. Matrilateral cross cousin marriage is thus a correlate of a system of patrilineal lineages rigged into a class hierarchy.[50] It does not necessarily follow that the bride-givers (*mayu*) should rank higher than the bride-receivers (*dama*); but it does follow that if class difference is expressed by marriage, then *mayu* and *dama* must be exclusive and one of the two must rank above the other.

In Kachin idealogy the *mayu* rank above the *dama* and, as I have shown, this fact is tied up with the nature of Kachin ideas about property. It seems to me therefore that the characteristic Kachin *mayu-dama* system would have developed automatically as a result of Kachin assimilation of Shan ideas about class difference.

The crux of the difference between the *gumsa* Kachin and the Shan systems of political relationship is that whereas in

---

[49] Kawlu Ma Nawng (1942), p. 12. See p. 200.
[50] This whole theory has been elaborated at length in Leach (1952).

the former the relationship between landlord and tenant is 'expressed' in the affinal status *mayu-dama*, in the latter the lord is conceptually the absolute master and the tenants are his serfs.

It follows that, from one point of view, the process by which a Kachin *gumsa* chief tries to give himself the status of Shan *saohpa* involves reducing his subordinate tenants from the status of son-in-law (*dama*) to that of serf or bond slave (*mayam*).

I have mentioned earlier (see p. 161) that the first historical reference to *gumlao* seems to make the word mean 'slave' in the sense of *mayam*. This is now understandable. Neufville's informants were *gumsa*, the *gumlao* against whom they were at feud were their relatives. But before they had become *gumlao*, they had been relatives in a status approaching that of *mayam*. From the *gumsa* point of view the *gumlao* had formerly been their 'slaves'.

We do not know how often *gumlao* rebellions have upset the *gumsa* hierarchy, but I think we can see the political conditions which would favour such occurrences. So long as the Shan system flourished, the *gumsa* system could flourish too, but in a subordinate status. In such conditions we should not expect *gumlao* rebellions. Difficulties would arise only when external factors led to a decay of Shan power. It is then that Kachin chiefs would get the chance to assume powers close to that of a *saohpa*, and it is only then that a *gumlao* revolt is likely to ensue.

Now the historical records indicate that Mogaung reached the height of its power under the Möng Mao *saohpa* Sao Ka Hpa around 1500. But half a century later his successor Sao Peng was overthrown by a Burmese army under Bayinnaung; from then on the Mogaung State was seldom wholly independent of the Burmese.[51] Everywhere in North Burma the political status of the Shans has been declining steadily ever since the mid 16th century until it has now reached nadir. The whole period of this decline up to the coming of the British in 1885 was one which was favourable to the development of *gumlao* movements among the Kachins, and I think they may have been of frequent occurrence.

The same set of circumstances often led to a situation in

[51] Scott and Hardiman (1901), reference *Mogaung*. Mogaung (Möng Kawng) and Mohnyin (Möngyang), though different places, appear to have been the same political entity. Thohanbwa, King of Ava 1527–43, was son of the *saohpa* of Mohnyin. (See Harvey, 1925, pp. 107, 165, 323).

which ultimately the Shan chief's power was derived entirely from the military support of his Kachin feudal dependants. This was generally the state of affairs in 1885. British policy altered all this. The British prevented by force any further trend towards *gumlao* organisation; they encouraged existing *gumlao* headmen to behave as if they were *gumsa* chiefs; they endeavoured to isolate Kachins from Shans and thus deprived the Shan chiefs of their Kachin military support; at the same time they kept their own nominees on the various *saohpa* thrones by force. The outcome of this was seen in 1947 when the British finally left Burma.

Most of the Kachin Hills Area now (1952) falls into two administrative areas. The south-eastern section falls into the Shan States area. In this area it is reported that the *saohpa* chiefs have lost their authority and are faced with a communist movement which receives considerable Kachin support. The north-western section on the other hand—the former Bhamo and Myitkyina subdivisions—now constitutes the Kachin State (*Jinghpaw Mungdan*). Political power is almost wholly in the hands of Kachins. The Head of the State—a Kachin—sits as a cabinet minister in Rangoon. The finances of the Kachin State are heavily subsidised from Central Government funds. In the initial phases power has been exclusively in the hands of orthodox aristocratic *gumsa* elements. Commoner Kachins who had achieved high military rank under the British appear to wield little influence. The Head of the State, Sima Sinwa Nawng, is a *gumsa* chief turned Buddhist. He comes from the Kamaing area. His kinship connections are not known to me though it seems possible that he is related to the Kansi *duwa*, owner of the jade mines. The Kansi chief who has been somewhat in eclipse since the war seems now to be recovering his influence, and at a recent parliamentary election stood as opponent of Sima. Kansi was defeated. There are hints that the chiefs of the North Triangle may have resumed control of their former 'slaves'. These chiefs and most other Kachin notables now spend much of their time away from the hills, living in the vicinity of Myitkyina. Thus it appears that, with British restraints removed, the *gumsa* chiefs are playing true to form. Having got the power, they are trying to act the part of Shan princes. In the process they tend to isolate themselves from their hill kinsmen. My prognosis is a new *gumlao* movement at an early date though it may not appear under that title.

Factions in the Kachin Hills Area now appear in the guise of political parties. The A.F.P.F.L., an all-Burma party, appears to represent, in the Kachin area, the special interests of the plains people (Shans and Burmese) against the Kachins. The two principal Kachin parties are the Kachin National Congress and the Kachin Youth League. There is also an Independence Party. This last is local to the Kamaing area and appears to consist of personal adherents of Sima Sinwa Nawng. At the present time (1952) the parliamentary representatives of both the National Congress and the Youth League are alike mostly aristocrats of moderate standing. I do not know what issues of policy are supposed to distinguish the two groups. It would appear that the National Congress has the support of a high proportion of the better known *gumsa* leaders. It is alleged that National Congress members refer to Youth League members as 'riff-raff and town loafers'. So also in the past *gumsa* were wont to describe *gumlao* as 'good-for-nothing slaves' (*mayam*).

Another feature of the present day Kachin situation which is certainly important but which I cannot assess, is that most of the Kachins now in positions of authority were educated in mission schools. In the past, factionalism between different varieties of Christian (Roman Catholic, Baptist, Bible Churchmen, etc.) has been pronounced; how far it is relevant in the present situation I do not know.

THE HUMAN ELEMENT

This review of Kachin history has emphasised that the swing from *gumsa* to *gumlao* organisation or back again is heavily influenced by political factors external to the Kachin situation itself; but I must insist again that Kachin destiny is in no sense determined by these external factors. The social analyst may be able to reach a point where he can see what is likely to happen next but he can never be sure. The environment in its largest sense creates the context in which choice is made, but the choice is made by individuals. The breakdown of a *gumsa* system into *gumlao* fragments has to be initiated by some individual, a leader, a revolutionary. What are the attributes of such men?

Let us be quite clear as to what is involved. A *gumsa* domain is properly the 'property' of a particular royal lineage. That lineage will in the ordinary course of time segment into superior and inferior sub-lineages. Ordinarily the superior sub-lineage will continue to 'own' the original domain; the inferior sub-lineage will in most cases lose caste and acquire a subordinate status in some other domain altogether, but in other cases it may come to 'own' a domain of its own and its leaders may come to be recognised as 'thigh-eating chiefs'. Fission of this kind is normal and necessary for the survival of the *gumsa* system and does not involve any idea of a *gumlao* revolution.

The *gumlao* concept is something quite different, it is the total repudiation of the idea that the lineages of chiefs are any different from commoner lineages and hence a repudiation of the theory that tributary dues must be paid to the owners of the soil. It involves also a repudiation of the *gumsa* theory that special ritual powers are automatically inherited by the youngest son so that inheritance rules become not only equalitarian but vague.[52]

Let us examine the ordinary *gumsa* rule of ultimogeniture a little further.

Ultimogeniture as a general topic was made the subject of an exhaustive comparative study by Frazer in 1918.[53] His argument is extensively documented with materials relating to the Kachins and their neighbours. His conclusion is that the legal rule is intimately connected with the practice of *taungya* cultivation.

'The migratory system of agriculture which many of the tribes follow is wasteful and requires an extent of territory large out of all proportion to the population which it supports. As the sons of a family grow up, they successively quit the parental abode and clear for themselves fresh fields in the forest and jungle, till only the youngest is left at home with his parents; he is therefore the natural support and guardian of his parents in their old age. This seems to be the simplest and most probable explanation of ultimogeniture.'[54]

The evidence that Frazer marshalls on this point seems to me

---

[52] The Angami Nagas provide a good example of this. See Hutton (1921), pp. 135 f.   [53] Frazer (1918), Vol. I, Chapter 2.   [54] ibid., p. 481.

quite convincing especially so far as the Kachins and their neighbours are concerned.

As we have seen already the Kachin *gumsa* situation is roughly that both the eldest and the youngest son are privileged in relation to their other brothers. The eldest brother is ideally a warrior who goes out with a group of followers drawn from his father's relatives and supporters and carves for himself a new domain; the youngest brother stays at home and inherits the ritual function of guardian of the shrine of the household ancestors and, in the case of a chief, of the *madai nat*. In practice, under the British regime, administration insistence upon having a responsible adult headman in charge of every village, coupled with the administration's equally strong objections to the repeated fragmentation of villages, frequently resulted in succession passing through the eldest son instead of the youngest. The Kachins themselves were seldom greatly disturbed by such a development.

Indeed the earliest account of Kachin inheritance is as follows:

'In the succession to patrimonial property the mode of division as described by them appears most singular, the eldest and youngest sons dividing everything between them, the eldest taking the landed estate or place of settlement with the title, the latter the personals while the intermediate brethren, where any exist, are entirely excluded from all participation and remain with their families attached to the chief as during the lifetime of the father.'[55]

Such a rule is of course the precise reverse of ordinary Kachin ultimogeniture and would appear to be not only improbable but also quite impractical. But I do not think that Neufville misunderstood his informants. These informants were, as he himself says, the chiefs of Satao (Latao) and Bisa (Pyisa). They were the two most influential Kachin chiefs living in Assam at the time and on that account they naturally claimed to be the natural heads of their respective lineages. Both considered themselves members of the Tangai branch of the Tsasen clan. The Tangai major lineage has a great many segments, the exact affiliation between which is obscure. Neufville's own informants and modern tradition agree how-ever that the 'youngest son branch' are the Wahkyet[56] with

[55] Neufville (1828), p. 341. See above, pp. 109, 156.
[56] Neufville, op. cit.; Hannay (1847), p. 10; Kawlu Ma Nawng (1942).

whom as it happened the Pyisa chief of Neufville's day was at feud.[57] This Pyisa chief was also at feud with Daihpa Gam, whose lineage appears to have been 'the youngest son line' of the Maiaw section of the Tangai, Latao being another section of the Maiaw.[58] In the circumstances the Pyisa and Latao chiefs rather naturally combined to tell Neufville that youngest sons had no intrinsic superiority. I fancy that Green's statement that Kachin succession in the North Triangle area is normally to the eldest son is to be explained in a similar way.[59]

In any case there seems to be evidence that even in pre-British days the ultimogeniture rule was far from sacrosanct and that, as an alternative to manipulating genealogies, an influential chief of a (theoretically) junior line would sometimes simply repudiate the *uma* principle altogether. But if it is conceptually possible to a Kachin to repudiate the notion of the natural sacredness of youngest sons, it is equally easy to repudiate the notion of chieftainship itself since, in theory, tribute is paid to the chief only as recompense for his ritual services as controller of the Madai and Shadip nats. If the youngest sons have no innate spiritual grace (*tsam*)[60] why bother to respect them?

The whole system of succession and inheritance is thus full of paradoxes and contradictions. The argument can be summarised as follows:

a. gumsa theory presupposes a *taungya* system of agriculture and the necessity for constant segmentation of the local group.

b. gumsa theory supposes that authority over land is derived from birth status only.

c. These two postulates together provide the basis for succession by ultimogeniture.

d. But local group segmentation is unfavourable for the development of any large scale stable political state.

e. Thus when a Kachin chief in fact becomes economically and politically powerful he is tempted to ignore *gumsa* principles—especially with regard to ultimogeniture.

f. Such a man may also be influenced in the same direction by the fact that Shan succession, while confined to the ruling patrilineage, is not limited by any rule of ultimogeniture. Shan succes-

---

[57] Kawlu Ma Nawng (1942), p. 37.
[58] Hannay (1847), p. 10.   [59] Green (1934), p. 110.
[60] *tsam* is a concept resembling the classical anthropologist's *mana*.

sion rules, though somewhat vague, appear to favour primogeniture
—at least in theory.

g. Thus although, from certain aspects, the *gumsa* system can be
regarded as modelled after a Shan pattern, the *gumsa* chief whose
status and power begins to approach that of a Shan *saohpa* is led
to repudiate principles which are fundamental to the *gumsa* system.

h. He will be led to repudiate in particular the doctrine of succession by ultimogeniture and the doctrine that the ties between a lord
and his followers are based in affinal relationship.

Now I have already argued that the circumstances most
favourable for the development of a *gumlao* revolt are those in
which a Kachin chief comes most near to approaching the
status of a Shan *saohpa*. What my present argument displays
is that a *gumlao* revolutionary, in refusing to pay tributary dues
to his chief and in refusing to accept the class difference implications of the *mayu-dama* system, is merely imitating the
behaviour of his chief. *Gumlao* revolt emerges at precisely that
point in the political cycle at which the *gumsa* chiefs themselves
have been led to infringe the formal rules of their system.

It seems to me therefore that the *gumlao* revolutionary leader
is in no sense an aberration from the Kachin norm. As a
character he is just the same kind of person as the chief against
whom he revolts, an ambitious seeker after power who treats
economic facts with greater respect than ritual theories.

Myth as we have seen makes the archetype *gumlao* leader a
priest (*dumsa*), a blacksmith (*n-dup*), and the child of a levirate
wife of an elder brother in a chiefly lineage. In Chapter V
I made the point that while anyone can become a priest, it is
typically the enterprising elder sons of chiefs and village headmen who fill this role; individuals, that is, whom the rule of
ultimogeniture somewhat defrauds. Similarly, although black-
smithing has high status in archaic Kachin myth, it is not a
trade appropriate to persons of *saohpa* status; the blacksmith as a
type is a professional expert but not a chief. The children that
a woman may bear after she has been 'picked up' as a levirate
widow rank lower than their half-siblings.

In brief, the mythical archetype of the *gumlao* leader is that
of minor aristocrat of ambition and ability who might himself
have been a chief if the accident of birth order had not dictated
otherwise. The myth is a description of the real man.

CHAPTER IX

MYTH AS A JUSTIFICATION FOR FACTION AND SOCIAL CHANGE

I will now leave off the discussion of the varieties of Shan and Kachin organisation and their interchangeability and take up my main theme from a different angle.

In Chapter I I argued that in the language employed in this book, myth and ritual are essentially one and the same. Both are modes of making statements about structural relationships. In Chapter V, where I describe a number of the leading concepts which occur in *gumsa* Kachin ideology, I have elaborated this theme. What I describe are culturally defined objects, actions and ideas; what I am interested in is their implication for the formal relationships that exist between social persons. So far I have tried to keep the emphasis on ritual rather than on myth—that is on actions rather than on verbal statements which are counterparts to the action, but already in a number of instances, particularly when attempting to explain the conceptual difference between *gumsa* and *gumlao*, I have had to explain by means of myth.

This raises issues of theoretical importance, the most important of which is 'How can mythology be held to justify change, in the social structure?' Isn't it almost a contradiction in terms to suggest such a possibility?

Within the general Kachin-Shan complex we have, I claim, a number of unstable sub-systems. Particular communities are capable of changing from one sub-system into another. Let us assume for the moment that this analysis is correct from the sociological point of view. We must then ask ourselves how do such changes and alternative forms of organisation present themselves to the participant Kachins and Shans?

I have asserted that the social structure is 'represented' in ritual. But if the social structures with which we are here dealing are unstable, this instability must also be 'represented' in the ritual system. Yet ritual, being backed by tradition, is surely always the most rigid and conservative element in social organisation?

I think it is fair to say that most British social anthropologists commonly look upon myth from much the same point of view as that adopted by Malinowski in his well-known essay *Myth in Primitive Psychology*.[1] According to this view myth and tradition are to be thought of primarily as a sanction or charter for ritual action. Ritual action reflects the social structure, but it is also a dramatic recapitulation of the myth. Myth and ritual are thus complementary and serve to perpetuate one another. It is no part of this doctrine that the myths of any one culture should be mutually consistent, but adherence to the rest of Malinowski's functionalist theory leads to the assumption that they must be. In the Malinowskian scheme the various aspects of a culture are necessarily integrated to form a coherent whole; hence the myths of a people must be mutually consistent—for any one group of people there is only one culture, one structural system, one mutually consistent set of myths.

Now in my view it is unnecessary to postulate this kind of consistency. I think social anthropologists only tend to think of myth systems as internally consistent because they retain something of the ethnologist's notion that myth is a kind of history. Because of this prejudice they come to be selective in their analysis of myth and tend to discriminate between 'correct' and 'incorrect' versions of the same tale.

In the case of Kachin mythology there can be no possibility of eliminating the contradictions and inconsistencies. They are fundamental. Where there are rival versions of the same story, no one version is 'more correct' than any other. On the contrary, I hold that the contradictions are more significant than the uniformities.

Kachins recount their traditions on set occasions, to justify a quarrel, to validate a social custom, to accompany a religious performance. The story-telling therefore has a purpose; it serves to validate the status of the individual who tells the story, or rather of the individual who hires a bard to tell the story, for among Kachins the telling of traditional tales is a professional occupation carried out by priests and bards of

[1] Malinowski (1926).

various grades (*jaiwa, dumsa, laika*). But if the status of one individual is validated, that almost always means that the status of someone else is denigrated. One might then infer almost from first principles that every traditional tale will occur in several different versions, each tending to uphold the claims of a different vested interest.

And that is the case. There is no 'authentic version' of Kachin tradition to which all Kachins would agree, there are merely a number of stories which concern more or less the same set of mythological characters and which make use of the same kinds of structural symbolism (e.g. the marriage of a man with the daughter of a nat), but which differ from one another in crucial details according to who is telling the tale.

A good example of this kind of adaptation is to be seen in the two published versions of the story of the origin of the Nsu nat —the spirit of jealousy—to which reference has already been made. The Kachin stereotype of a jealousy situation is the relation between elder and younger brother. Two Kachin ethnographers, Hanson and Gilhodes, recount very nearly the same myth but the one is the reverse of the other.[2] In Gilhodes' story the eldest brother is jealous of the younger brother, who is favoured by the nats. In the end the elder brother is drowned in a coffin he has prepared for the younger brother and the younger brother lives on to become a rich chief. In Hanson's story the roles are reversed and the younger brother, having long defrauded the elder, is finally drowned in the coffin he has prepared for his elder brother.

Neither of these versions can be said to be more correct than the other. It is simply that where bad blood exists between an elder and a younger brother either party may suspect the other of bringing on misfortune by jealous thoughts; either party may then make an offering to the Nsu nat. If the younger brother makes the offering, Gilhodes' version will figure as the mythical sanction; if the elder brother makes the offering Hanson's version will serve the same purpose. The bard-priest (*dumsa*) will adapt his stories to suit the audience which hires him.

---

[2] Gilhodes, 52–4; Hanson, 126–8. The whole story is a long one. All the incidents in Hanson's version occur (reversed) in Gilhodes' version, but the latter has some features missing in the former. See also p. 168 above.

Now, in the past, Kachin ethnographers have never appreciated this point. They have regarded tradition as a species of badly recorded history. Where they have found inconsistencies in the record, they have felt justified in selecting that version which seemed most likely to be 'true' or even in inventing parts of the story which appeared to be missing.

Such an approach to the data makes it possible to represent the basic structure of Kachin society as very simple. Confusions of practice are regarded as due to the fact that the stupid Kachins fail to understand their own society or to obey their own rules. Enriquez, for example, has reduced the whole structural system to a couple of paragraphs.

'There is a common misconception amongst Europeans with regard to the existence of Kachin tribes. There is, as a matter of fact, hardly any tribal feeling amongst the Kachins, except in connection with property and boundaries, and the reason for this is that they consider themselves divided into families rather than into tribes. The so-called five main tribes (Marip, Lahtaw, Lahpai, N'Hkum and Maran) are really five aristocratic families descended from the five eldest sons of Wahkyet Wa, the reputed father of the Kachin race. Their order of precedence is as given above, the Marips being the senior family. Any man with one or other of these names may be regarded as well born; and *Duwas* or 'chiefs' always belong to these families. Other clans are subsections of the five main ones, or are in some degree related to them. A man may not marry into a family bearing the same family name.

Every Kachin family knows exactly with what families it may intermarry. Amongst the five aristocratic families Marips take their brides from Marans, Marans from N'Hkums, N'Hkums from Lahpais, Lahpais from Lahtaws, and Lahtaws from Marips. This, however, is only a very broad statement. The subsections of nearly every clan have modifications of the marriage rules peculiar to themselves. No European, as far as I know, has ever understood them, and certainly no Kachin does. A discussion of marriage laws usually becomes heated. In the case of *Duwas* the rule is further modified, because there are no longer any Marip *Duwas*;[3] and with commoners there are many minor exceptions amongst individual families. The rules are, however, not as rigidly enforced now as they used to be.'[4]

[3] This is not true, although it is generally believed to be the case among Kachins in the Bhamo area.   [4] Enriquez (1923), pp. 26–7.

If mythological inconsistencies are eliminated on the grounds that there could after all be only one set of historical facts, inconsistencies in traditional law and custom are also necessarily eliminated and the whole scheme becomes rigid and simple. If, however, we regard Kachin mythology as expressing a system of *ideas* instead of a systems of *rules* or a set of historical events, the need for internal consistency in the various traditions disappears. The contradictions between rival versions of the same story then take on a new significance.

My argument here can be well illustrated by a comparison between the various published versions of the Kachin stories concerning the relationship between the first men and the nats, and the relationship between the ancestors of the principal aristocratic clans.

The saga-teller's (*jaiwa*) account of a Kachin chief's genealogy 'from the beginning' (*ahtik labau gawn*) normally falls into several sections corresponding to the system of 'branches' or segments in terms of which the family tree is conceived. The first section takes the tale from the creation to the birth of Shapawng Yawng—the first Kachin; the second section proceeds from Shapawng Yawng to the sons of Wahkyet Wa— who, as noted by Enriquez, are regarded as clan founders; the story then splits up and pursues the fortunes of each clan independently, noting the various points of segmentation.

Only one authority (Kawlu Ma Nawng) has provided us with extensive material of the third type, but for the first two sections of the story we have rival versions from George, Wehrli, Hertz, Gilhodes, Hanson, Carrapiett, Kawlu Ma Nawng. Although in some respects these rival authorities are derivative from one another, their mutual contradictions are sufficient to illustrate my argument.

The first section of the story is really concerned only with establishing the fact that the Shadip nat is the Supreme Being and that the first humans were *dama* to the sky nats (*mu nat*) and that the chiefs alone are *dama* to Madai nat. The rival versions differ from one another only in the degree of condensation, i.e. in the number of generations intervening between two events. That part of the story which concerns us here can be reduced to the following precis: (Fig. 6)

In the beginning there was a female-male creator spirit which gave birth to the various elements of the universe. This being, Chyanun-Woishun, a sort of personification of earth and sky is now worshipped in the form of Shadip (Ga Nat)—the Earth Spirit of the chiefs.

From Chyanun-Woishun are descended:

    a. Ninggawn Wa, a half-human half-divine creator who 'forges'

THE RELATIONSHIP OF HUMANS TO GODS

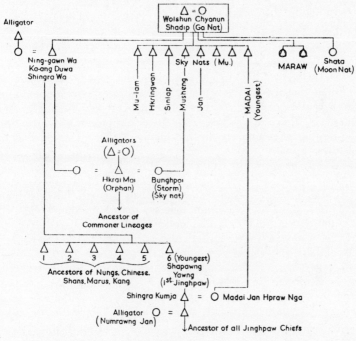

FIG. 6.

the Earth. He later assumes a more human form and is known as the Ka-ang Duwa, chief of the *middle* land, a title with a strongly Chinese flavour.

The Ka-ang Duwa marries an alligator (*baren*) and has six sons who are the progenitors of the Nungs, Chinese, Shans, Maru, Nagas (*Kang*), and Jinghpaw.

It is the youngest of these sons Shapawng Yawng who is first parent to the Jinghpaw.

b. The Mu Nat—the sky nats who control general prosperity and wealth. The principal Mu Nat are a series of 7, 8 or 9 brothers. Although there is agreement about the names of most of them, there is a significant disagreement about their order of birth. The chief of the Mu Nat is La N'Roi Madai and it is this Madai Nat which can only be approached by chiefs. The Madai Nat is the youngest of the Mu Nat.

c. The Maraw—these beings have been described on p. 177 f.

Shapawng Yawng, the first Jinghpaw, founds a lineage called Shingra who are lords of Shingra Ga (original land). A scion of this house marries a daughter of the Madai Nat named Madai Hpraw Nga (Madai White Buffalo). Other descendants continue to marry alligators (*baren numraw*). Madai Hpraw Nga's marriage constituted the first *manau*. All aristocratic Jinghpaw are descended from Madai Hpraw Nga.

Nearly all lineages in *gumsa* society can make out a case for claiming that they have aristocratic connections, but it is maintained by present day aristocrats that commoners are wholly and innately inferior. There are consequently a variety of stories which trace the descent of commoners from orphans (*hkrai*). The descendants of these orphans (who are again sometimes the children of alligators) are given a status *vis-à-vis* the minor sky nats, similar to that of the chiefs *vis-à-vis* the chief of the sky nats, Madai.

In one account Hkrai Mai, the orphan, marries Bunghpoi, the daughter of Musheng, in another he marries a daughter of the Ka-ang Duwa. The commoners are thus *dama* to the sky nat Musheng but not to Madai ; they are also *dama* to the line of chiefs descended from the Ka-ang Duwa.

I have, in a previous chapter, pointed out that the affinal status of the commoners in relation to the chiefs is a kind of paradox in the *gumsa* structure. It is symptomatic of this that alongside stories which make the commoners *dama* to the chiefs and/or the minor sky nats we find other stories which make the commoners descend from a pair of orphans who are sole survivors of the Flood and who have no connection with the chiefs or the nats.[5]

[5] My account is based mainly on the following sources:
Carrapiett (1929), pp. 12, 75, 76, 79.
Gilhodes (1922), pp. 9, 10, 13, 44, 51, 70–5, 79–83, 126.
George (1891).
Hanson (1913), pp. 110, 121, 165.
Hertz (1943), pp. 135, 156.
Anderson (1876), Appendix.
Kawlu Ma Nawng (1942), pp. 1 f.
Bayfield (1873), p. 223.
There is greater consistency between the various versions than might at first appear. For instance, while the alligators (*baren*) are missing in some, they are

The story now enters its second section. Here the discrepancies between different versions become more serious. The skeleton of the story is given above in the quotation from Enriquez. Shapawng Yawng has a descendant, Wahkyet Wa, whose sons are the founders of major clans. The birth order of these sons should, as Enriquez perceives, affect the rank order of the clans, but the different clans have very different ideas about what this rank order is. Without seriously altering the structure of the mythological story each of the five clans named—as well as several others—can put forward a case to be regarded as the senior group. First as to the agreed part of the story. This is represented in diagram form in Fig. 7.

There is agreement that the male line of descent from Shingra Kumja and Madai Jan Hpraw Nga leads eventually to Wahkyet Wa Ma Gam who is father to a series of sons. There is agreement that the first three sons are respectively the ancestors of Marip, Lahtaw and Lahpai. Other clans are said to be descended either from the younger brothers of these three or else from an ancestor of Wahkyet Wa by a collateral line. Wahkyet Wa is usually in the 'youngest son' line of descent. Kawlu Ma Nawng's version, which makes him a member of an eldest son branch, makes his principal wife Magawn Kabang Jan, a member of the 'youngest son' lineage. Now for the variations put forward by different clans.

Clan Marip: Wahkyet Wa had seven sons. The eldest was Marip Wa Kumja, ancestor of the royal Marip. The youngest and *uma* was La N'Hka Hkashu Hkasha. But apart from a few elements who have become absorbed into the Marip, the Hkashu Hkasha have died out. Therefore the Marip are the senior clan (Kawlu Ma Nawng (1942), pp. 2, 3, 7).

Clan Lahtaw: Wahkyet Wa had seven sons. The second son was ancestor of the Lahtaw. The youngest and *uma* was La N'Hka Hkashu Hkasha. The latter have largely died out but have become absorbed with the main branch of the Lahtaw. Apart from this a descendant of the Lahtaw Wa (second son of Wahkyet Wa) named Ngaw Wa married a daughter of the sky nat Musheng.

replaced by females of the Numrang or Numrawng lineage. But allegators are often described as *baren numraw(ng)*—'monstrous alligator'—so the stories are really the same. As has been pointed out on p. 178n. the mythological concepts of *baren numraw* and *maraw* are closely associated. Also, as noted before, the notion of *baren* resembles the Chinese notion of 'dragon' (*lung*).

Furthermore the claims of the Marip chiefs are bogus as all the 'true' Marips died out long ago and modern Marip chiefs are mere pretenders (Enriquez (1923), p. 27; Carrapiett (1929), p. 80; Gilhodes (1922), p. 84; Hanson (1913), p. 14).

Clan Lahpai: Wahkyet Wa had numerous sons of whom the third

THE RANK ORDER OF CLAN ANCESTORS

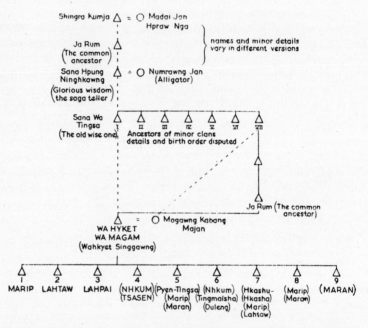

FIG. 7. The nine sons of Wahkyet Wa Ma Gam in the bottom line of the genealogy are the ancestors of the major clans. Only the clan affiliation of the first three sons is generally agreed. For the rest both the number of sons and the order of birth is disputed. Hkashu-Hkasha (7) ('the descendants') is a fictitious clan but it is mythologically important since it is usually regarded as the youngest line and hence *uma*.

was ancestor of the Lahpai. Wahkyet Wa had numerous wives but only the first three sons were born to his chief wife Magawng Kabang. Therefore the third son was the true *uma* and the Lahpai are the senior clan. (There is no printed version of this; it was the first version which I recorded myself).

Clan Nhkum: Most people say that the Nhkum are descended

from one of the younger sons of Wahkyet Wa—the fourth or the sixth. This is incorrect. The first Nhkum was Mahtum Hkum, identified as II in Fig. 7. He married Madai Jan, a daughter of the Madai nat and had a son Tsinghkum Tu (Matsaw Wa Tsinghkum) who married a daughter of the sun nat (Jan Jan). The Nhkum thus have better connections with the nat world than any of the descendants of Wahkyet Wa (Kawlu Ma Nawng (1942), pp. 1–6; cf. Hanson (1913), p. 14).

Clan Maran: Wahkyet Wa had eight or nine sons not seven. The youngest was La N'Kying Maran Wa Kying Nang and the *uma*. The Maran are therefore the senior clan. Alternatively in areas where the Lahpai maintain that only a few of Wahkyet Wa's sons were the offspring of his first wife, the argument becomes: Wahkyet Wa had five sons by his first wife, of these the youngest, an *uma*, was La N'Tang Maran Wa Ning Shawng (Kawlu Ma Nawng (1942), pp. 2–3; Hanson (1913), p. 14; Gilhodes (1922), p. 84).

Clan Kareng-Hpauwi: Some allege that the Kareng are not of royal blood at all. This is most insulting. The Kareng are descended from III in Fig. 7. Their claims are then similar to those of the Nhkum (Carrapiett (1929), p. 2; Kawlu Ma Nawng (1942), p. 1; Enriquez (1923), p. 27).

and so on.

The above variants all represent claims to seniority by different major *gumsa* clans. The same kind of rivalry and conflicting interpretation of myth is also noticeable at lower levels of clan segmentation, as between different lineages of the same clan. For example:

Aura branch of Shadan lineage of Lahpai clan. The Lahpai chiefs of the Gauri and Atsi all consider themselves Lahpai-Shadan-Aura. The Aura are further divided into various minor segments.

The 19th-century feud between the Gauri chiefs of the Mahtang area and their neighbours of the Sinlum–Lawdan group of villages has already been mentioned (Chapter VII). The latter group are now in the ascendancy; they are mainly Baptists while most of their rivals are Catholics. It is the Sinlum version which the Baptist missionary Hanson thus reports:

'The division of the Gauri territory into two sections took place after a feast of a certain Jauhpa Hkun Wa[6] who made a double

---

[6] Jauhpa Hkun Wa (Saohpa Hkun) is a particucularly blatant Shan title. See Map 5, p. 64, for Gauri location.

dance (*hting htang manau*) for his twin sons, the last-born of which was an *uma*; the first-born of the two sought a country of his own, that is he went to "another country" (*mung kaga*) and therefore called his territory Mung Ga, while the country of the younger twin was called Uma Ga.'⁷ This account needs to be compared with the historical evidence which I have cited on p. 225.

The story is nicely designed to denigrate the undoubted high status of the former chiefs of Mung Ga (Möng Hka). In this connection it has to be remembered when reading Kawlu Ma Nawng's usually excellent account that his own lineage (Kawlu) is commonly considered a subordinate branch of this same Aura lineage. In Kawlu Ma Nawng's story a crucial Lahpai ancestor is Numtin La Jawng who has five wives and a large number of sons who are specified as ancestors of different Lahpai lineages. Aura are given as the *uma* line— the offspring of the fifth son of the first wife.

Here is another example in which rival parties cite different myths to justify the same facts. In the Duleng country south of Putao the empirical situation is that the Duleng are now *gumlao*. Their immediate neighbours to the south are *gumsa*.

The first version is one recorded by myself from Duleng *gumlao* elders:

The Duleng claim that they are all descendants of one Duleng Hkawp Gumwa, the eldest son of Duleng Yawng Nang, sixth son of Wahkyet Wa. This Duleng Hkawp Gumwa had a younger brother Duleng Nawng Dungmai who was driven out of the Duleng country and went to live in the Hukawng Valley. The descendants of Duleng Hkawp Gumwa (unlawfully) assumed the chieftainship. At a time when there were two chiefs with the ominous names Maju Kinji and Hpyi, the chiefs were driven out. Since then the Duleng country has been governed on the *gumlao* system without chiefs.

The second version is that given by Kawlu Ma Nawng and clearly derived from *gumsa* sources:

The sixth son of Wahkyet Wa (the ancestor of the Duleng) was Tingmaisha Dawng Yawng (N'Dawng Wa). From him are

⁷ See Hanson (1906), p. 46. cf. also the myth which links up the Gauri chiefs (Lahpai-Aura) with the Atsi chiefs and the Hpunggan chiefs (Scott and Hardiman (1901), Part I, Vol. I, p. 378). This also exists in several rival versions.

descended the Tingmaisha or N'Dawng clan, which includes the Duleng.

At the great *manau* at which the precedence of the clans was decided and at which the Hkashu Hkasha were recognised as the senior line, the N'Dawng arrived late after all the feasting was over. 'They knew that they had arrived too late for meat so they decided to collect the scattered bamboos in which meat had been cooked and lick out the insides.' The N'Dawng are thus classed by the *gumsa* as of the status of pariah dogs. 'To this day people quarrelling with the N'Dawngs can insult and annoy them by saying, "You N'Dawngs who licked bamboos at the head waters of the Punghkang." '[8]

In all the foregoing examples the rivals for precedence all agree as to what the principles of seniority are, they merely disagree about the crucial mythological incidents which are supposed to sanction present day status. A slightly different kind of conflict arises when the rival parties disagree about the 'ethic' of the myth itself, as for instance in the rivalry between the *gumsa* and *gumlao* sections of the Tsasen clan reported by Kawlu Ma Nawng.

The principal features of the relevant myth have already been given in Chapter VI. (p. 202). It will be seen that in this case the facts of the myth are equally acceptable to both sides, but there is disagreement about the formally correct structural rules. The *gumsa* claim that the children of a 'collected widow' are *ipso facto* of lower ranking status than their half siblings, so that the descendants of the former can be treated as commoners by the descendants of the latter. The *gumlao* on the other hand repudiate this notion of rank and claim that siblings or half siblings and all their patrilineal descendants should rank equally as clan brothers. The very essence of the *gumsa-gumlao* opposition is that while the latter repudiate hereditary class distinctions, the former glory in them. Since *gumsa* validate class difference by reference to such features as levirate marriage and the inferior status of secondary wives, it is appropriate that the *gumlao* should validate their own principles by reference to a myth which challenges the *gumsa* on this very point.

The following example is similar. Here again the *gumlao* do

[8] Kawlu Ma Nawng (1942), pp. 2, 7. The names Maju Kinji and Hpyi mean 'unlucky priest's wand' and 'witch' respectively.

not dispute the facts of the myth but challenge the ethical deductions made from it by the *gumsa*, and thereby again deny the principle of hereditary class inferiority.

Pyen Tingsa Marip: Most versions say that the descendants of the fifth son of Wahkyet Wa are either Marip or Pyen Tingsa. The *gumsa* version is that the oldest son of Wahkyet Wa, Marip Wa Gumja, was married to Woigawng Sumpyi. Marip Wa Gumja went on a long journey leaving his wife at home. While he was away Woigawng Sumpyi had four children by Pyen Tingsa Tang, fifth son of Wahkyet Wa and younger brother of Marip Wa Gumja. As punishment for this offence the descendants of Woigawng Sumpyi and Pyen Tingsa Tang, though classed as Marip, are for ever commoners and hereditary serfs of the descendants of Woigawng Sumpyi and Marip Wa Gumja the true aristocratic Marip.

The *gumlao* accept most of the above story but say that it was Marip Wa Gumja's own fault if his wife was unfaithful, he should not have left her alone so long. In any case many Kachins hold that if a husband is away for a long time, it is quite proper for the wife to sleep with the husband's brother. The ancestors of the Pyen Tingsa sub-clan therefore rightly refused to accept a status of inferiority and joined the *gumlao* movement.[9]

This particular story appears to serve as a banner for several different kinds of faction. It is commonly held that the modern representatives of the Pyen Tingsa sub-clan are the N'Ding major lineage of which there are a large number of branches. Some of these are *gumlao*, others include chiefs of great influence. The story cited above can therefore be used not only to point out the opposition between *gumsa* and *gumlao* Marips but also to justify factions between rival *gumsa* sections of the Marip clan—the N'Ding on the one hand and the Um, Ningrang, Rureng on the other.[10]

It will be agreed, I think, that all the examples of tradition which I have cited in this chapter are unquestionably myth in an orthodox classical sense. Yet in every case the structural implications of the myth are wholly ambiguous and vary according to the vested interests of the individual who is citing the story.

In Chapter IV, when describing the feuds and factions of

⁹ Kawlu Ma Nawng (1942), pp. 4, 5, 13.
¹⁰ cf. Kawlu Ma Nawng (1942), pp. 6, 8.

Hpalang, I showed how traditions about the fairly recent past are used to make argumentative assertions about the relative status of living individuals. I referred to these Hpalang stories as 'myth', though I pointed out that they do not fall into the ordinary definition of myth, since the events purport to be recent and the characters ordinary humans. The tales I have now given are myths in a classical sense; they concern gods and demi-gods and ancestors of semi-divine status and most of them are very widely shared among all Jinghpaw-speaking peoples. I don't think that it is going too far to say that any Jinghpaw saga-teller (*jaiwa*) in the Kachin Hills, if suitably questioned, would give a version of the creation and of the beginning of mankind which could readily be seen to be the 'same story' as that given in Figs. 6 and 7 (pp. 269, 272). But it would be the same story only in general framework, the minor details would vary in such a way as to enhance (by implication) the personal status of the story-teller. In other words, what the evidence of this chapter has shown is that myth of the orthodox kind varies in the same way and for the same reasons as myth of the unorthodox kind which I cited for Hpalang.

My conclusion is that the ordinary anthropological definition of myth is an inappropriate category as far as the Kachins are concerned. Sacred tales—that is to say tales about divine beings which are widely known—have no special character-istics which make them any different from tales about local happenings 20 years ago. Both kinds of tale have the same function—the telling of them is a ritual act (in my sense of the term) which justifies the particular attitude adopted by the teller at the moment of the telling.

I am led therefore to the conclusion that the existence of an agreed framework is in no sense an index of social solidarity or equilibrium. This view conflicts with what most anthropo-logists have held—at any rate until very recently. Since Malinowski's day it has been a commonplace that myth serves to sanction social behaviour and to validate the rights of particular individuals and groups within a particular social system. Since any social system, however stable and balanced it may be, contains opposing factions, there are bound to be different myths to validate the particular rights of different groups of people. Malinowski himself saw this and the point has been forcefully made by others—notably Fortes[11] and Firth.[12] But the argument of these writers, if I understand them correctly, is that whatever may be the local tensions and oppositions within a social system, the overall structure is somehow in equilibrium, the claims of one group balancing out against the claims of another. In Fortes' analysis, for example, the very fact that the rival Namoos and Talis in Tallensi society use a common language of ritual expression seems to be taken as evidence for the overall stability of the total system.[13]

What I am suggesting is exactly the opposite to this. Myth and ritual is a language of signs in terms of which claims to rights and status are expressed, but it is a language of argument, not a chorus of harmony. If ritual is sometimes a mechanism of integration, one could as well argue that it is often a mechanism of disintegration. A proper assimilation of this point of view requires, I would maintain, a fundamental change in the current anthropological concept of social structure.

[11] Fortes (1945).   [12] Firth (1932).   [13] Fortes (1945), especially pp. 24 ff.

CHAPTER X

CONCLUSION

In my first chapter I set out my problem as being a study of how particular structures can assume a variety of cultural interpretations and how different structures can be represented by the same set of cultural symbols.

What we have found is roughly this. The population of the Kachin Hills Area is not culturally uniform; one would not expect it to be so for the ecology varies. But if we neglect that very large part of culture which is concerned with practical economic action—that is the whole of what Malinowski might have considered to be the apparatus for the satisfaction of basic human needs—we are still left with something, that something which in this book I have dealt with under the heading of ritual action. And as concerns these ritual aspects of culture the population of the Kachin Hills Area is relatively uniform. The people may speak different languages, wear different kinds of clothes, live in different kinds of houses, but they understand one another's ritual. Ritual acts are ways of 'saying things' about social status, and the 'language' in which these things are said is common to the whole Kachin Hills Area.

The Burmese who administered the area before the British came understood this very well. We have an account dating from 1835 of a ritual act which illustrates my point perfectly. I give the story in precis.[1]

In 1836 the Hukawng Valley was administered by the Burmese Governor of Mogaung. So far as the Kachins were concerned, he had assumed the ritual functions of the former Shan *saohpa* of Mogaung. At this time there were kept in the Buddhist monasteries of Mogaung three portable shrines (? images) which were said to house the nats of the founder ancestors of the Mogaung *saohpa* lineage—in other words they were the *möng* nats of Mogaung. Their names were Chow Pya Ho Seng; Chow Sue Kap Ha; Chow Sam Loung Hue Mong. In life they had been three brothers. The names are orthodox Shan royal titles. On all occasions of

[1] Hannay (1837) and Hannay (1847) contain accounts which are substantially identical but certain details in each are missing from the other.

279

state cermony or whenever the Governor of Mogaung went on tour the three nats were brought out and 'placed in three small temples made of bamboo carried on men's shoulders'.

In 1836 the Burmese Governor visited Maingkwan and received the submission of local Shan and Kachin celebrities.   The procedure was as follows.   'The ceremony commenced by killing a buffalo which was effected with several strokes of a mallet and the flesh of the animal was cut up to be cooked for the occasion, each Tsobua[2] then presented his sword and spear to the spirits of the three brothers. . . .   Offerings of rice, meat, etc., were made to these nats and on this being done each person concerned in taking the oath received a small portion of rice in his hand and in a kneeling posture with his hands clasped above his head heard the oaths read in both the Shan and Burmese languages.   After this the paper on which the oaths were written was burned to ashes and mixed with water when a cupful of the mixture was given to each of the Tsobuas to drink, who, before doing so, repeated the assurance that they would keep the oath.   The ceremony was concluded by the chiefs all sitting down together and eating out of the same dish.   The chieftains to whom this oath of forbearance was administered were the headman of Maingkwan, a Shan, the Daipha Gam,[3] a Tsasen Jinghpaw, the Panwa Tsobua, a Lahpai Jinghpaw, Wing Kong Moung (? N'Wanghkang Nawng) and the 'Situngyen' Chief, Marip Jinghpaws, Tarepoung Moung, a Tsasen Jinghpaw, and 'Ngeemen Gyaung', a Shan, all of whom by this act virtually acknowledged the supremacy of the Burmese authorities and their own subjugation to the Kingdom of Ava.

This surely is an almost perfect example of ritual in a Durkheimian sense.   Every detail, from the slaying of the buffalo to the final drinking of the oath and the eating from the same dish, seems to denote an act of social solidarity. Even the mystic sense of 'euphoria' seems to have been there, for Hannay, a shrewd and critical observer, was clearly greatly impressed.   Yet are the contributors to this performance to be thought of as members of 'one society'?   By the standards of normal ethnography certainly not; by the standards of this book perhaps yes.   But does a ritual of this kind really denote social 'integration', 'solidarity' or 'equilibrium'?

In this particular case we happen to know that the Daihpa

---

[2] Hannay applies Tsobua (saohpa) to Kachins and Shans alike.
[3] The Burmese Governor later died and the following year the Daihpa Gam married his widow (see p. 220).

Gam and Tarepoung Moung (Tari Bum Nawng) had been at feud the year before, that for a year or two after Daihpa Gam had the status of a kind of sub-Governor for the whole Hukawng area, and that within five years the N'Ding *gumsa* (Marip chiefs) had joined forces with the *gumlao* and driven the Daihpa Gam out of his home village altogether. This does not seem to indicate any marked degree of continuing social solidarity. If then we accept the Durkheimian view that religious rituals are representations of the solidarity of the participating group, we need clearly to understand that the solidarity need exist only at the moment at which the ritual takes place; we cannot infer a continuing latent solidarity after the ritual celebrations are over.

All my example really shows is that the Burmese, the Shans and the Kachins of the Hukawng Valley in 1837 shared a common language of ritual expression; they all knew how to make themselves understood in this common 'language'. It doesn't mean that what was said in this 'language' was 'true' in political reality. The statements of the ritual in question were made in terms of the supposition that there existed an ideal stable Shan state with the *saohpa* of Mogaung at the head of it and with all the Kachin and Shan chiefs of the Hukawng Valley his loyal liege servants. We have no real evidence that any real *saohpa* of Mogaung ever wielded such authority, and we know for a fact that when this particular ritual took place there had been no genuine *saohpa* of Mogaung at all for nearly 80 years. At the back of the ritual there stood not the political structure of a real state, but the 'as if' structure of an ideal state. This 'as if' system needs to be distinguished from the categories of political fact which, at first sight, appear to be manifest in overt cultural differences.

A part of my objective in writing this book has been to demonstrate that in contexts such as we find in North Burma the ordinary ethnographic conventions as to what constitutes *a* culture or *a* tribe are hopelessly inappropriate. I am not suggesting that this is a wholly new idea but I consider it to be a matter of general theoretical importance that calls for emphasis.

A great deal of modern anthropological field work has been carried out in areas where there is a palpable lack of coincidence between the boundaries of cultural and structural phenomena. My thesis is simply that the conventional use of the concept of unit cultures serves to obscure the significance of such facts. Let me cite an example remote from the Kachin field. The Tswana of Bechuanaland are distinguished politically into ten tribes; rather more than half the total population belong to the Ngwato and Tawana tribes. Of these we are told:

'About four-fifths of the Ngwato tribe . . . consists of what were originally foreign peoples, and among the Tawana the proportion is even greater. The members of a tribe moreover sometimes differ in customs and language. Among the Ngwato, for instance, there are Sarwa, who by language and custom are Bushmen and not Bantu; Kalaka, Koba, Herero, Rotse and others, who although Bantu do not belong to the Sotho group (of which the Tswana are a division), but speak their own languages and have many customs different from those of their rulers; and Kwena, Kaa, Kgatla, Khurutshe and many others, who are of Tswana stock but differ in various details of law and custom from the Ngwato proper.'[4]

Despite this empirical situation we find that, for comparative purposes, Murdock has treated the Tswana both as *a* society and *a* culture.[5] I find it difficult to understand what this notion of cultural unity really signifies in such a case.

As regards my own area I have sought to do much more than merely break down existing conventions regarding the separateness of Shans and Kachins, I have tried also to say something about the mechanisms of one type of social process which overrides these cultural distinctions.

This has led me into great difficulties in the matter of presentation. The generation of British anthropologists of which I am one has proudly proclaimed its belief in the irrelevance of history for the understanding of social organisation. What is really meant by these arguments is not that history is irrelevant but that it is too difficult to put on paper. We functionalist anthropologists are not really 'antihistorical' by principle; it is simply that we do not know how to fit historical materials into our framework of concepts. Thus Professor Evans-Pritchard, who is one of the most staunch upholders of equilibrium theory in British social anthropology, is also an advocate of the use

[4] Schapera (1952), p. v.   [5] Murdock (1949), pp. x; 353, 374.

of history in anthropological analysis,[6] but he has not yet explained how the inconsistencies between the two positions can be resolved. The beautiful lucidity of Evans-Pritchard's own writing is only possible because he limits himself to the description of certain unreal types of situation—namely the structure of equilibrium systems. What I have tried to do in this book is to describe the structure of a system that is not in equilibrium and my method of demonstration has involved trying to display two or three different 'ideal systems' at one and the same time. I do not claim that the result is either simple or lucid, but it does seem to me to contain some propositions that have not been stated in quite this form before.

Let me try to elaborate this doctrine of ideal or model systems a bit further.

The sociologist as opposed to the ethnographer *always* deals with ideal rather than empirical societies. It has been so since the very beginning. Spencer, for example, originally proposed that the second part of his *Principles of Sociology* should contain

'General facts, structural and functional, as gathered from a survey of societies and their changes; in other words the empirical generalisations that are arrived at by comparing different societies and successive phases of the same society.'[7]

The 'general facts' are conceived of as being fitted to the ideal model of human society at a particular stage of development and are obtained from observation of societies assumed by definition to be at a particular phase—i.e. in an unreal static condition. The evolutionists never discussed in detail—still less observed—what actually happened when a society in Stage A changed into a society at Stage B; it was merely argued that all Stage B societies must somehow have evolved out of Stage A societies. It was consistent with this approach that when the evolutionists used empirical ethnographic material to illustrate their arguments they purposely chose 'societies' which were not interdependent. If the societies were contemporary they were spatially remote—preferably separated by large areas of sea; if they were adjacent they were not contemporary; one might pronounce upon the technical superiority

[6] Evans-Pritchard (1951), *passim.*   [7] Spencer (1858), cited in Rumney (1934).

of the Greeks over the Ancient Egyptians, but the problem of the contemporary interrelationship of political structure in Athens and Sparta was outside the field of anthropology.

The model systems of all the earlier anthropologists, whether expressed in cultural or structural terms—the Kava People, the Megalithic Culture, the Matriarchal Phase and so on— are vast and vague. Indeed learned men still write great volumes about the matriarchal peoples of the past without providing any detailed explanation of how a matriarchal society could possibly work.[8] But these model systems have a common element in that they are conceived of as stable fixed systems, they are ideal types.

Modern social anthropologists usually operate on a much more modest scale in much greater detail, but their 'societies' are still, I maintain, largely model systems, the stability of which is an hypothesis not an established fact. But because anthropologists, right from the beginning, have always treated the figment 'a society' as an isolate, they still have no language in which they can describe social systems which are both contemporary and adjacent—that is in actual interrelation.

As late as 1938 Malinowski was still describing such situations as the 'contact' or 'impact' between discrete cultures. The Wilsons, who in 1945 published a work entitled *The Analysis of Social Change*, still clearly regarded the products of such interaction as being somehow fundamentally immoral and 'destructive of law, logic and convention'.[9]

American anthropologists long ago coined the expression *acculturation*, but they do not seem to have developed any framework of concepts which could make possible a sociological theory of the contemporary process involved. In most cases an acculturation study turns out to be the analysis of the swapping of particular traits between particular isolate cultures over a particular historical period of time.[10]

My own view is that equilibrium theory in social anthro-

---

[8] e.g. Thomson (1949). This author supposes that the Khasis of Assam provide a concrete example of matriarchy. The Khasis are not now matriarchal. Whether they ever were so in the past is a matter for speculation.

[9] Wilson (1945), p. 133. cf. the same authors' categorical assertion 'all objective analysis of social relations rests on the assumption that they form coherent systems, that within any one field they support and determine one another inexorably', op. cit., p. 23.

[10] See Herskovits (1948), Part 6; Tax (1952).

pology was once justified but that it now needs drastic modification. We can no longer be satisfied with attempting to set up a typology of fixed systems. We must recognise that few if any of the societies which a modern field worker can study show any marked tendency towards stability. On the other hand I hold that it should be possible for anthropologists to develop methods for the analysis of changing social systems which avoid metaphysical generalisations of the type which Professor Popper has rightly condemned as 'historicism'.[11]

Candid recognition that social systems are not necessarily naturally stable need not compel the structurally minded social anthropologist to abandon all his traditional techniques of analysis, for he will still be justified in continuing his use of scientific fictions.[12] In practical field work situations the anthropologist must always treat the material of observation *as if* it were part of an overall equilibrium, otherwise description becomes almost impossible. All I am asking is that the fictional nature of this equilibrium should be frankly recognised.

In this book my descriptions of *gumsa, gumlao* and Shan patterns of organisation are largely *as if* descriptions—they relate to ideal models rather than real societies, and what I have been trying to do is to present a convincing model of what happens when such *as if* systems interact. A sociological description of process in social change, if it is to have any generality at all, must relate to a model of this type rather than to any one particular instance. It is not possible, I maintain, to describe such a process of change directly from the observation of first-hand ethnographic data. What one must do is first analyse out the ethnographic facts by reference to abstract whole systems conceived of as existing in unstable equilibrium, and then postulate that the confusion of reality arises from the interpenetration of these unstable ideal systems.

Thus described my method sounds like a scholastic device of the purest pedantry. But my claim is that Kachins and Shans actually think of their own society in this sort of way. Kachins *themselves* tend to think of the difference between *gumsa* and *gumlao* and the difference between *gumsa* and Shan as being differences of the same general kind. Further they recognise that these differences are not absolute—individuals

[11] Popper (1945).   [12] Vaihinger (1924).

may change from one category into another. Kachins speak of people 'becoming *gumlao*' or 'becoming Shan' (*gumlao tai; sam tai*). This implies that the Kachins themselves think of the difference between Shan and *gumsa* Kachin as being a difference of ideal, and not, as the ethnologists would have us believe, a difference of ethnic, cultural or racial type.

It also implies that Kachins of the *gumsa* persuasion can conceptualise fairly clearly other ways of living. The *gumsa* ritual organisation provides, for a *gumsa* Kachin, a model society to which he imagines his own real society conforms. But he is also aware of other possible stereotype models, *gumlao* and Shan, against which his own society can be compared.

The stereotype or model version of each of these three societies is fairly precise, but the application of these categories to actual communities is decidedly flexible. Although the ideal types are quite distinct, the practical types overlap.

From the abstract verbal descriptions which Kachins themselves provide one would not suppose that there could be much confusion between the three types of organisation. Yet in practice one frequently finds communities which are regarded as *gumsa* from some points of view, and *gumlao* from others; there are other communities which are simultaneously Kachin *gumsa* and Shan. In other words the question whether a particular community is *gumlao*, or *gumsa*, or Shan is not necessarily ascertainable in the realm of empirical facts; it is a question, in part at any rate, of the attitudes and ideas of particular individuals at a particular time. There are, as we have seen, a large number of 'ritual acts' which can be said to have the same meaning whether the actor is a Shan, a *gumsa* Kachin or a *gumlao* Kachin, but the inferences that are to be drawn from such acts will be entirely different in each case.

That such ambiguity does not lead to intolerable misunderstandings is due to the essential vagueness of all ritual statements. Ritual and mythology 'represents' an ideal version of the social structure. It is a model of how people suppose their society to be organised, but it is *not* necessarily the goal towards which they strive. It is a simplified description of what is, not a fantasy of what might be. But the statements made in ritual acts are vague statements; they have not the quality of scientific descriptions and because of this the same ritual act can have significance in a Shan and also in a Kachin context.

From the point of view of the external observer, a Kachin political domain (*mung*) which is favourably situated from an economic point of view, may merge into and become part of a Shan *möng*. Again from the external observer's point of view the process may result in some of the Kachins 'becoming Shans', but to the actor this change may be hardly noticeable. In becoming sophisticated, the individual merely begins to attach Shan values to ritual acts which previously had only a Kachin significance.

I began this book with the evidence of a Kachin who had become a Shan. Here is another statement from the same source:

'We were virtually absorbed, gradually becoming Shans by race because the result of intermarriage looks more like a Shan than a Kachin. The transition to Buddhism was an easy one because our Buddhism includes nat worship. The only thing they (his Shan brothers) took from us were a couple of outstanding blood feuds'.[13]

It is only the external observer who tends to suppose that shifts in the culture and structural organisation of a group must be of shattering significance. It is a prejudice of the ethnocentric anthropologist to suppose that change is 'destructive of law, logic and convention'.

Apart from this tendentious problem of the intervariability of culture and structure in a single area, the most important theme in this book is, it seems to me, my documentation of the relationship between the Kachin *mayu-dama* marriage system and the class structure of Kachin society. The hypothesis that there might be such a relationship originates with Lévi-Strauss and I have devoted a previous publication to showing that, at the formal idea level, this principle is fundamental to an understanding of Kachin *gumsa* society.[14] Lévi-Strauss made the further suggestion that the existence of a *mayu-dama* type marriage system, while leading to a class stratified society, would for that very reason result in the breakdown of Kachin society. The material I have assembled here partly supports

[13] Harvey and Barton (1930), p. 81n.   [14] Lévi-Strauss (1949); Leach (1952).

Lévi-Strauss' argument though the instability in Kachin *gumsa* organisation is not, I think, of quite the kind that Lévi-Strauss supposed. From the point of view of general anthropological theory this case is of great interest.

In some ways the Kachin pattern is that of a classical segmentary type primitive society—the 'gentile' organisation which Morgan found exemplified in the social organisation of the Iroquois and of Ancient Greece. Some of the best work of modern British anthropologists has been done in African societies of this type and what may be called the typical principles of lineage organisation are now well understood. Numerous generalisations that could be made for the Nuer and the Tallensi and the Tiv have equal application to the Kachins. Where Kachins are atypical is that they have a class system associated with a lineage system. But as we have seen, the Kachin polity is, as it were, only half a step removed from that of the Shans which resembles very closely what we understand in Europe by the term feudalism. The transition from Kachin-type organisation to Shan-type organisation involves the substitution of a straight landlord-tenant relationship for a relationship based either on common lineage or affinal dependence. On the evidence of this book it is a difficult transition to make and one would like to know whether other peoples at other times have dealt with similar political choices in the same way.

And now to turn to another matter. I have stressed throughout that my problem is not only to try to understand why Kachins should be different from Shans; I need also to understand why Kachins should differ from one another—why we have Gauri and Atsi living cheek by jowl and sharing the same kinship system yet speaking fundamentally different languages. Here again we are dealing with a problem of social dynamics rather than of social statics; the differentials that distinguish one sub-category from another are not fixed, Atsi can become Jinghpaw, Gauri can become Atsi. Why does this happen in some cases and not in others?

In Chapter III I discussed this problem in terms of the single criterion *language*. I argued that we need some sociological explanation for the fact that some Kachin groups change their language affiliation very readily while others are linguistically conservative to the point of absurdity. Why should my type community in Hpalang have had six dialect groups within a community of 130 households when in other parts of the Kachin area we have phenomena of ultra rapid linguistic assimilation such as those recorded in Appendix I?

In Chapter III I suggested that in situations where there is an open choice as to whether an individual, or a group of individuals should use one language rather than another, language must be regarded as a status symbol. If that be so, I argued that in stable *gumsa* systems or stable feudal hierarchies we should expect to find linguistic uniformity, the favoured language being that of the ruling group; similarly in stable *gumlao* systems we should expect each self-contained community to be dialectically different from the next. I showed that this theory does not fit the actual distribution of *gumsa* and *gumlao* communities as we now find them.

I have now shown, however, that few existing *gumlao* and *gumsa* communities can be regarded as in any sense stable. How does this affect the argument?

If the reader refers again to Map 3, p. 31, he will see that the regions in which Kachin languages are all mixed up and small groups are obstinately conservative about language are my ecological zones B and C (Map 2, p. 23). In Zone A, on the other hand, the Kachins are almost uniformly Jinghpaw speaking.

The analysis of the latter part of the book has shown the existence of political stability in two types of situation.

a. A feudal type structure has persisted in all the Shan rice plains. The language is more or less consistently Tai except for a recent switch over to Burmese near Burmese urban areas.

b. A *gumlao*-type organisation seems to have persisted throughout most of the northern part of Zones B and C (Map 2, Htawgaw and Nam Tamai areas). Here dialects (Maru and Nung) change every few miles, almost from village to village.

So far the facts are in accord with the theory advanced in Chapter III.

But throughout the rest of the Kachin Hills Area we have, I maintain, endemic political instability. What then? I argued earlier that in most of Zone B and in the southern part of Zone C (Map 2, Sinpraw area), because of relative dryness and relative high population density the economy of the hill communities is essentially unbalanced. Temporary stability can only be achieved by political and military expedients. In these zones, both in *gumsa* and in *gumlao* areas, the only continuing unit of political structure is the village; all larger scale political federations are constantly changing. In such circumstances peculiarity of language serves to uphold the continuing unity of the village community in the face of rapid shifts of power in the external political world.

It is in these situations that we find small village units obstinately retaining their linguistic uniqueness, even within the framework of a *gumsa* political organisation.

In Zone A, on the other hand, there is much less pressure on resources, the economy is more soundly based, it is less essential for the village group to retain its territorial identity in face of political change. But here, precisely because economic conditions are potentially easier, it is less risky to resort to political experiment. Factionalism now takes a different form. Instead of one territorially based village competing against the next, we have the rivalry between *gumsa* and *gumlao* and between *uma du* (youngest son chief) and *ma gam* (eldest son aristocrat). In these conditions language ceases to be useful as a banner of solidarity, for the grouping of persons is now in terms of kinship rather than of locality. All this is consistent with the fact that throughout Zone A there is only one major form of Kachin speech, namely Jinghpaw, and alien groups in this area are very quickly assimilated into the Jinghpaw system.

This perhaps is not the whole of the matter but it provides I think at least a partial explanation of my original problem.

Finally let me make the plea that the general type of analysis which I have attempted in this book may have value in other contexts besides that of the Kachin Hills Area. The cultural situation in the Kachin Hills, as I have described it, is both confused and confusing but it is not exceptional. On the contrary I would claim that it is largely an academic fiction to suppose that in a 'normal' ethnographic situation one ordinarily finds distinct 'tribes' distributed about the map in orderly fashion with clear-cut boundaries between them. I agree of course that ethnographic monographs frequently suggest that this is the case, but are the facts proved? My own view is that the ethnographer has often only managed to discern the existence of 'a tribe' because he took it as axiomatic that this kind of cultural entity must exist. Many such tribes are, in a sense, ethnographic fictions.

A case in point is provided by the literature of the Naga and Chin Hills Areas which lie to the west of the Kachin Hills Area (see Map 1). The ethnography of this region has been very thoroughly recorded in a large number of highly competent monographs by various authors, the work of Hutton, Mills and Parry being outstanding. In all these books it is taken as axiomatic that the group which speaks a distinct language or dialect is, by definition, a separate tribe or tribal section. Each such section is then treated as a distinct cultural and ethnographic entity with a distinct history and a separate continuity in time. Some tribes, the Sema Nagas for example,[15] have an organisation which differs hardly at all from that described in this book under the title *gumsa*. Other tribes such as the Angami Nagas[16] come closer to my *gumlao* pattern. But the assumption is made that such tribal categories are independent. The Sema and the Angami are geographically adjacent, but they are not represented as interacting in any institutional sense. This whole approach seems to me to rest on false premises.

I do not deny of course that within the Chin-Naga area there is great diversity of culture, but that it should be a stable diversity seems to me inconceivable. It surely must be the case that over a period there is a shifting of economic and political power from one geographical centre to another, along with corresponding readjustments in the total network of intergroup relations, at every level of scale, throughout the whole area?

In such a situation, I suggest, it is futile to attempt to record all the stereotyped ethnographic variations for they are almost numberless. The assiduous ethnographer can find just as many different 'tribes' as he cares to look for.

Mills's account of the Ao Nagas provides an example of this. The tribal category Ao is here represented as comprising three sub-tribal categories or sections—Chongli, Mongsen and Changki. These sections, according to Mills, 'undoubtedly

---

[15] Hutton (1921*b*).   [16] Hutton (1921*a*).

represent different waves of immigrants speaking different dialects'.[17]   Local communities usually contain several distinct wards (*khel*) which correspond to the villages (*kahtawng*) of my Kachin analysis.   The wards of an Ao local community are usually all of one tribal section (Chongli, Mongsen or Changki), but this is not always the case.   Some communities are composite.   In some of the composite communities the members of the different wards all speak the same dialect; in other cases, however, the members of adjacent wards in a single community maintain differences of dialect and social custom.   In short, it appears that the difference between the categories Chongli, Mongsen and Changki is analogous to that between Jinghpaw, Atsi and Maru in parts of the Kachin Hills.

Mills admits the difficulty of using dialect difference as a crucial criterion of cultural distinction, yet he assumes that it is sensible to write of Chongli, Mongsen and Changki as separate ethnographic entities.   There is no suggestion in his book that the social organisation of the Mongsen may be interdependent with that of Chongli and Changki and vice versa.

I cannot believe that any analysis along these lines can correspond at all closely to the facts.   It seems to me axiomatic that where neighbouring communities have demonstrable economic, political and military relations with each other then the field of any useful sociological analysis must override cultural boundaries.

In my own study I have avoided any attempt to represent the variations of Kachin culture as characteristics of 'tribal' entities of any scale.   I have also tried to avoid the common ethnographic device of representing cultural variation as aberrant deviation from an orthodox central norm.   I am not concerned with *average* Kachin behaviour; I am concerned with the relationship between actual Kachin behaviour and ideal Kachin behaviour.   And with this in mind I have tried to represent Kachin cultural variations as differing forms of compromise between two conflicting systems of ethics.

I believe that this type of analysis is capable of considerable further development and that it might usefully be applied to many parts of the ethnographic map.   The Chin and Naga Hills region to which I have referred is only one of these.

[17] Mills (1926), p. 2.

SOME DOCUMENTED CASES OF LINGUISTIC CHANGE

1. *Jinghpaw become Shan*

The first European to visit Hkamti Long (Putao) was Wilcox in 1828. He recorded of the Shan area that 'the mass of the labouring population is of the Kha-phok tribe whose dialect is closely allied to the Singpho'. Other non-Shan dependents of the Shans were the Kha-lang with villages on the Nam Lang 'whose language more nearly resembles that of the Singpho than that of the Nogmung tribe who are on the Nam Tisang'.

The prefix 'Kha-' in Hkamti Shan denotes a serf: 'phok' (*hpaw*) is a term applied by Maru and Hkamti Shans to Jinghpaw. Kha-phok therefore means 'serf Jinghpaw'.

In 1925 Barnard described Hkamti Long as he knew it. He noted that the Shan population included a substantial serf class (*lok hka*) divided into various 'tribes' which he supposes to have been of Tibetan origin, but he remarks: 'I have not been able to obtain even a small vocabulary of their language as they have been absorbed into the Shans whose language and dress they have completely adopted.' It would appear that Barnard's *lok hka* must include the descendants of Wilcox's Kha-phok and Kha-lang. The inhabitants of 'the villages on the Nam Lang' now speak Shan; but the Jinghpaw-speaking population on the other side of the Mali Hka—who call themselves Duleng—claim to be related to these 'Shans' of the Nam Lang.

Of the Nogmung, Barnard recorded: '(They) are gradually being absorbed by the Shans . . . they have adopted the Shan dress and nearly all speak Shan in their houses.' Some Nogmung, however, still spoke a variety of Jinghpaw in 1925. They called themselves *Sam-hpyen*, which is Jinghpaw for 'Shan soldier' and presumably they at one time had the status of mercenaries to their Shan overlords.

Feudal obligations of this kind were broken down during the British occupation and in 1940 a Jinghpaw school was started at Nogmung. The tendency for the local inhabitants to become Shan may therefore have gone into reverse. The Nogmung are probably becoming Jinghpaw again.

References

Wilcox (1832). Barnard (1925); (1934).

2. *Assamese become Jinghpaw*

During the period 1824–1837, in which the British first made contact with the Jinghpaw of Assam and the Hukawng Valley, there are repeated references to the fact that the Jinghpaw enslaved Assamese in large numbers and traded them back into Burma through the Hukawng. Some of these slaves were traded onwards to Shans and Burmese, but some were retained in the Hukawng. It is quite clear that in 1835 when Bayfield and Hannay visited the Hukawng these Assamese slaves were still palpably Assamese.

Throughout the 19th century the descendants of these Assamese slaves continued to play a vital part in the economy of the Hukawng. They remained 'slaves' but became Jinghpaw in speech and custom. In 1925 the slaves were compulsorily released. There were found to be 3,466 slaves out of an estimated total population of 7,903. Of the slaves released, all of whom spoke Jinghpaw, 2,051 claimed to be of Assamese origin.

References

Selection of Papers (1873), especially Bayfield and Hannay. Barnard (1930).

3. *Nagas become Jinghpaw*

The following is a quotation from Dewar (1931):

'The Pangaw and Pyengoo Nagas, who reside in the hills lying north and east of the confluence of the Namhpuk and Tanai rivers, were the first to leave their ancestral homes at the headwaters of the Namhpuk. They migrated about ten generations ago, occupying their present sites with the permission of the Kachins to whom, according to the Kachin tribal custom, they gave presents. The Pangaw Nagas have intermarried freely with Kachins and, but for a few households who in appearance, dress, habits and customs are practically the same as Kachins, may at the present day be considered an extinct clan. The Pyengoo Nagas, chiefly the men, have almost entirely adopted the Kachin dress, but they still observe many of the habits and customs of their ancestors. The validity of their long residence in their present hills is amply proved by their appearance, the familiarity with which they speak the Kachin dialect, and the statements of their neighbours in the Dalu Valley, the Shans and Kachins.'

Of the Pyengoo Nagas mentioned here, their overlord, the Kachin chief of the Lajawn tract, says: 'We have been their overlords for the past four or five generations. I do not know how we became their overlords. It was during the time of the Mogaung Wa (i.e. the Shan *saohpa* of Mogaung) when the Hawseng (Shans) ruled all the country.'

The other ethnographic details recorded by Dewar concerning the 'Pyengoo Nagas' are consistent with the view that these people are now culturally indistinguishable from other Kachins.

References
Dewar (1931), pp. 268, 277, 278–9.

4. *Shans become Jinghpaw. Assamese become Jinghpaw and then becoming Shan*

When the British took Assam in 1824 there were a number of distinct Shan groups living in the general area of Sadiya and Ledo. Among these were a group referred to by contemporary writers as *Phakeal*. It was then reported that when Mogaung was sacked by the Burmese King Alompra (Alaungpaya), in the mid-18th century, a Mogaung prince, one Chow Ta Khuen Meng, had founded a Shan colony on the Tarung river at the west of the Hukawng Valley. It is probable that this was close to the modern Ningbyen. While there, these 'Phakeal' Shans appear to have formed an alliance with Jinghpaw of the Tsasen clan. Later a sub-colony was established in Assam. The Phakeal in Assam lived at Moongkong Tat (i.e. Möng Kawng Tat), their Jinghpaw allies close by at Ningroo (Ningru). Both groups there acquired large numbers of Assamese serfs.

The British policy in Assam from 1824 onwards was to

release slaves held by Shan and Jinghpaw chiefs. To escape this 'persecution' most of the 'Phakeal' Shans and their Jinghpaw allies returned to their former sites on the Tarung river in the Hukawng Valley. This time the Shans put themselves in alliance with the Jinghpaw chief of Ningbyen. Some remained at Ningbyen while others went south down the Chindwin and either founded or usurped control of the Shan state now known as Sinkaling Hkamti. They appear to have taken some of their Assamese serfs with them. Some of the descendants of these Assamese serfs, intermarried perhaps with their Kachin and Shan masters, fetched up, eventually, at the village of Maukkalauk (Chindwin river, lat. 25° 35'). They have lately been described as follows: 'The people of this village now talk Kachin, wear Kachin dress and are called Kachins. They have learnt Shan, however, and if the present processes continue will no doubt in time 'become' Shans and eventually Burmans. When this has happened someone may perhaps discover that they are of Shan origin. Yet they are not even Kachins. Their headmen says they came from the neighbour-hood of Ningbyen . . . where they had settled for a time and adopted the Kachin language and customs, but they had arrived there when his father was a little boy from Assam where they wore white clothes and spoke some language they have entirely forgotten.' (Grant Brown).

Here we seem to have a case of Assamese slaves becoming Jinghpaw and then becoming Shan.

At Ningbyen there is still a population described as Shan. They are subordinate to the Ningbyen Jinghpaw chief. Pre-sumably they regard themselves as being the descendants of the 'Phakeal' Shans. They speak Jinghpaw.

References

Hannay (1847), ii. Kawlu Ma Nawng (1942), pp. 31, 32, 42. Grant Brown (1925), Chapter 2. Various items in the early literature, such as that given in *Selections of Papers* (1873) and Butler (1846), add details to this story.

5. *Miscellaneous 'Kachins' become Jinghpaw*

In 1825 the Assam 'Singpho' comprised two main groups. One of these, consisting of Tsasen-Jinghpaw, was subordinate to an Assamese district ruler known as the Muttuck Gohain;

the other was a more miscellaneous group subordinate to the Hkamti Shan ruler of Sadiya. Many of these 'Singpho' had apparently arrived in Assam along with their Shan overlords direct from the Putao area to the east (Map 4). We have contemporary evidence that the language they spoke was not comprehensible to the other Singpho. Name lists of Singpho village headmen from this Sadiya-Tenga Pani area suggest that the group included Lisu, Northern Nung and Duleng families.

As a result of the British occupation of Assam and the later development of the Assam tea industry the Hkamti Shans of Assam lost both their political status and their lands. The survivors live mixed up with the surviving Singhpo. The principal language of the joint community appears to be Tsasen-Jinghpaw. All Assam 'Singpho' now speak the same language.

References

The evidence is very scattered but see especially: Neufville (1828), Wilcox (1832), Butler (1846), *Selection of Papers* (1873), Michell (1883), Mackenzie (1884), Needham (1889), Kawlu Ma Nawng (1942).

THE HPALANG FEUD AS OFFICIALLY REPORTED

The following is an extract from the *Report on the North Eastern Frontier for the year 1899/1900* (Rangoon 1900):

'On the 6th December Mr. Rae left Bhamo for Sinlum. At Latan he was met by the Sima *taungok* who reported that the Atsis of Hkona, Hpakum, Sadon and Panlum and the Kauries [Gauri] of Auragatoung [Aura *kahtawng*] and South Hoton intended re-establishing the Atsi Duwa of Hpalang who had been turned out many years before by his villagers and the Marans by force. Orders were at once issued to the Duwas and the elders of villages named to keep the peace. On the 8th Mr. Rae was joined by Mr. Faunce, who took command of his escort which consisted of fifty men, and by the Deputy Commissioner and they proceeded to Hpalang to settle the feud between the Atsis and the Marans. . . . On the 17th January assisted by Mr. Rae, the Deputy Commissioner held a thorough enquiry into the feud between the Marans of Hpalang and the Atsi *duwa* of Hpalang, which resulted in permission being granted to the *duwa* to re-establish himself as Summutgatoung [Sumnut *kahtawng*], a purely Atsi village of the Hpalang group. At the same time a division was made of the paddy lands at the foot of the ridge which owing to this feud had remained uncultivated for years. The Marans appear to be a bit dissatisfied just now over this division, but in a few years time will forget all about it. It is a great thing to have got this famous feud finally settled as it has been smouldering for at least 20 years, preventing both Atsis and Marans from cultivating freely and keeping them in an unsettled state, and it is noteworthy how readily both sides assented to the decision though most of them were new subjects of ours and neither party was very well satisfied.'

The naïve and optimistic tone is delightful. It is to be noted that important factors in the judgement were that the Atsi and Gauri relatives of the Atsi chief had got the ear of the Government first, and the fact that the people of Sumnut village were 'purely Atsi' (i.e. Atsi-speaking), the assumption being that Atsis and Marans were of different 'tribes'.

THE NATURE OF KACHIN 'SLAVERY'

The following is an extract from J. H. Green, *The Tribes of Upper Burma North of 24° Latitude and their Classification* (Dissertation for Diploma in Anthropology 1934; typescript available in the Haddon Library, Cambridge). [The footnotes have been added by me.—E. R. L.]

Pp. 86 f. '. . . . It is a pity that the word "slave" was ever used as a translation of the Chinghpaw (Jinghpaw) word *"mayam"*, for the Hkahku[1] slavery system is in no way comparable with all that is usually associated with that word. It is, however, in many respects similar to the serf system in England and the *"boi"* system amongst the Chins.

In the Triangle the *mayam* were found to be fairly contented with their lot, and on the whole living on good terms with their masters.

There are two distinct types of *mayam*: the *ngong mayam*[2] and the *tinung mayam*,[2] but several grades of *Tinung mayam* can be identified and a few of these may be rightly called slaves.

The *ngong mayam* is the outside *mayam*. He is in many respects similar to the serf. He owns his own house and property and, when living in a *mayam* village, shares in the ownership of communal land. The dues they pay their master are heavy and include amongst other things every alternate calf born, the first bunch of plantains of each tree, half the marriage price of a bride, and so much labour, etc., etc. In relation to their owner they have no rights, but few owners are oppressive, as *mayam* are valuable subjects whose prosperity is always advantageous. Some of them even become slaves voluntarily and pay their dues in return for land and protection.

The *tinung mayam* are the household *mayam*. In relation to their master they have no rights and no rights of ownership. In a similar way it is of interest to note that unmarried children have no rights in relation to their fathers. In practice,

---

[1] Roughly speaking Green uses Hkahku to denote Jinghpaw-speaking Kachins north of Myitkyina plus those of the Htingnai. cf. Map. 2. p. 23.

[2] The significance of the terms *ngong* (? *n-gawng*; ? *ngawn*) and *tinung* (? *ti-nang*) is not clear to me.

however, they are well cared for and hardly distinguishable from a child of the house.   They are generally contented to receive their food, clothing, drink and opium.   They are given wives and sacrifices are made on their behalf when they are sick. In practice there is very little difference between the life of a *mayam* and of a *ma gam* (i.e. an ordinary member of the chief's household).   The *mayam* is, however, a socially inferior being and now, after generations of being *mayam*, are actually inferior beings, are listless, and suffer from an inferiority complex.

There are many grades of household *mayam*; one may be a half-witted menial who is bullied by all, while another may become the owner's right-hand man and most trusted and confidential adviser.   I have actually seen a case of a Hkahku chief slave owner hand the money he had received for the release of his slaves to one of his slaves to take care of.

Mayam are occasionally bought and sold.   The price for the best type—a young able-bodied girl—is the equivalent of Rs. 200/–.   In Administered Territory where slaves were liable to appeal to a British court where slavery was not recognised, the price was naturally slightly less.   It was about three buffaloes, a cooking tripod, a gong, a gun, a blanket and *kauya* (sundry small things).

The grades of *tinung mayam* vary according to the way in which they were obtained.   Some are bought, a few captured, others obtained as handmaids to brides and others purchased as wives.   The big majority, however, are inherited or born as *mayam*.

Nearly every unmarried slave woman is burdened with one or two bastards, sometimes by different fathers some of whom are of the ruling class.   Children of the latter are not, however, classed as *mayam* and are known as *surawng*.   It is not unusual for a free-born woman to have bastards by a *mayam* man although it brings much shame upon the woman who is generally given in marriage elsewhere leaving her child behind. Strictly speaking free-born women who go with *mayam* become *mayam* but this rule is not always followed; her children how-ever are *mayam*.[3]

It is customary where a woman of *Du* (chiefly) family is

[3] I think Green has misunderstood the rule.   The slave father of a free woman's bastard is liable to the ordinary penalty of *sumrai hka*.   If the slave's master chooses to pay the *sumrai hka* he will acquire the child as his slave, but not otherwise.

married for her parents to give a slave as handmaiden. The handmaiden is also, as it were, a reserve woman for the man in case the wife dies suddenly or is sterile.

Some *mayam* have become so voluntarily, either in payment of debts or in order to get wives and food, forfeiting their liberty by taking on a *mayam* woman and thereby themselves becoming the property of her owner.[4] These types of *mayam* are comparable with the *sho* and *chengcha* of the Thado Kukis[5] and with the Lushai *boi*.[6] It is interesting to note that since the slaves of the Triangle have been released all have decided to continue to live in the hill tracts and that very few have left their old owners.[7]

Ordinarily a *mayam* takes the Clan name of his master and to the ordinary Hkahku name given in order of birth is added *Sha* or *Mai*;[8] e.g. a *gam* (firstborn male) may be a *Kum Mai* or *Kum Sha*, a *kaw* (firstborn female) *Kaw Sha*, etc. They are often given nicknames generally approbious and, in the case of a girl, the name sometimes has an indelicate reference to something in the girl's anatomy or habits. The ceremony of making a *mayam* includes the shaving of the head which is anointed with ashes from the owner's hearth.

An analysis of the following figures regarding slaves released in the Triangle and adjacent areas will give a good idea of the *mayam* system among the Hkahkus

Estimated free-born population	80,011[9]
Total slaves: Male, 1,798; Female, 2,191	3,989[10]
Born in bondage	2,367
Obtained as part of dowry	480
Purchased, including those purchased as wives	916
Became slaves voluntarily	55
Seized by force	5
Obtained in payment of debt	16
Inheritance	12[11]
Ownerless	126

[4] The husband becomes in effect *dama* to the wife's owner.
[5] Shaw (1929), p. 63.   [6] Shakespear (1912), pp. 46–50.
[7] The Hukawng Valley slaves, who were released a year earlier than those in the Triangle, were, I believe, prohibited from remaining with their former masters.
[8] *Sha* = child; *mai* = orphan.
[9] It is not clear how Green computed this figure or what geographical area it refers to; cf. Appendix V.
[10] According to the official report to the League of Nations (1928), 3,445 slaves were released in the Hukawng Valley in 1925–6; 3,989 were released in the Triangle in 1926–27; 1,028 were released in the Triangle and 370 from neighbouring areas in 1927–28; the grand total of released slaves is given as 8,852. cf. Barnard (1930), p. 185.
[11] It is not clear how this group differ from those 'born in bondage'.

The ownerless are often *Ngong mayam* who have been power-ful enough to declare their independence upon the death of their owner.   Although free they are socially graded as *mayam*.

Absolute freedom can be obtained by the *mayam* being ceremoniously received into the clan of which he is a real blood member.

Part of the ceremony consists in the *mayam* making offerings to the clan nats; but such seldom happens except in the first generation.'

This account makes it quite clear that the status of the male *mayam* was that of a 'semi-permanent debtor' rather than a chattel.   It also makes it clear that the relationship between the master and his *mayam* resembled closely that between a chief and an adopted or illegitimate son, or that be-tween a rich man and a poor son-in-law.   The analogy with the Chin *tefa* system described by Stevenson[12] seems very close.

The status of female *mayam* was rather different.   They were classed by Kachins as *hpaga* (see pp. 146 f.), and thus rated as a kind of chattel.   They were goods of value which could be put to use as servants or concubines or converted into other forms of wealth through marriage exchanges at the master's whim.   Green's statistics unfortunately are inadequate to make a full analysis on this point.   The various 'released slaves' must in fact have fallen into the following categories

A. *Ngong mayam*

i. Independent male householders in debtor status.
Their wives.
Their male and female children.

It would appear that the master had few rights over the females in this group other than the right to take a share of the bride-price of the daughters.

B. *Tinung mayam*

i. Male dependents resident in the house of their master.
Their wives.
Their male and female children.

It is the unmarried females of this group who approximate most closely to chattels.

[12] Stevenson (1943), pp. 176 f.

ii. Concubines received as dowry or by purchase. Such women will not ordinarily go through the ceremony of *num shalai* and therefore they are not properly speaking 'wives'. Their children have such status as they can manage to assert. The term *surawng* which applied to children of this category would seem to mean 'proud spirited ones'.

Green stresses that female slaves formed part of the *dowry* of a chief's daughter, but they also often formed part of the *bride-price* of a chief's daughter. In terms of my general analysis one would assume that where a slave is an item of dowry the status of the bride's father is much higher than that of the bridegroom, whereas when a slave is an item of bride-price the exchange of women denotes the status equality of bridegroom and father-in-law. I have no conclusive evidence to prove this point.

An aspect of the Kachin *mayam* system which is not covered by Green's account is that some *mayam* were simply pledges for *hpaga* which the parents of the *mayam* had borrowed from the master for the purposes of settling a 'debt'. The following quotation from Pritchard (1914) gives clear evidence of this:

'On this march a lad accompanied Captain Pritchard who described himself as a Peshe Lagu and not a Naingvaw. He was sixteen years old and had been a slave in Kachin country for two years. His people had sold him originally for a coat and cooking pots. He had nothing but good to say of his Kachin owners, and was found to be most useful, probably because the two years away from his own people had enlarged his mental horizon. Pritchard asked him why he did not run away from his Kachin masters, and he replied that, in the first place, he had no wish to do so, as he was very well treated; and in the second his own people who had sold him had told him that sooner or later they would buy him back.'

JINGHPAW KINSHIP TERMINOLOGY

A detailed analysis of the logic of Jinghpaw kinship terminology has appeared in a previous publication (Leach, 1945). For reference purposes I here reprint the two tabulations that appeared in that earlier paper.

TABLE I.   RECIPROCAL TERMS

The terms in the two right-hand columns are the reciprocals of those in the two left-hand columns and vice versa.

Senior		Junior	
Male	Female	Male	Female
Wa	*Nu*	*Sha*	*Sha*
Ji	*Woi*	*Shu*	*Shu*
Hpu	*Na*	*Nau*	*Nau*
Tsa	*Ni*	*Hkri*	*Hkri*
	Rat	*Rat*	
Gu	*Moi*	*Nam*	*Nam*
	Ning		*Ning*
Hkau		*Hkau*	

Note.   In the *ni-hkri* relationship, the *hkri* is always male.   In the *tsa-hkri* relationship, the *hkri* is male or female, and if female, unmarriageable.

The explanation of Table II (facing) is as follows :

In each of the columns headed AA, A, B, C, CC the terms on the left designate females, the terms on the right males. Each horizontal band within a vertical column designates a group of siblings. Thus in column B, NA, HPU and NAU are EGO's siblings; NA and HPU being older than EGO and NAU younger than EGO. Similarly, MOI and WA are the 'fathers' and 'father's sisters' of EGO while MOI and JI are the 'father's fathers' and 'father's father's sisters' of EGO. In each column the males have married, or will marry, the females in the column immediately to their right; they are the brothers (*hpu-nau*) of the females in the column immediately to their left; they are the sons (*sha*) of the males in the generation level immediately above them; and they are the fathers (*wa*) of both the males and the females in the generation level immediately below, in the same column. The central B group male is shown as 'EGO', his sister as 'ego'. In respect of each individual represented in the diagram, the term of address used by 'EGO' is shown in capital letters, and the corresponding term used by 'ego' is shown in lower case letters immediately below, thus: $\frac{RAT}{ning}$. The terms DAMA, HPU-NAU, MAYU, shown at

TABLE II. THE TERM SYSTEM IN RELATION TO EGO

AA (SHU)		A DAMA		B HPU-NAU (own group)		C MAYU		CC (JI)	
Female	Male	Female	Male	Female	Male	Female	Male	Female	Male
			GU gu	MOI moi	JI ji	WOI woi	JI ji	WOI woi	JI ji
	SHU hkri	HKRI ning	GU gu	MOI moi	WA wa	NU nu	TSA tsa	NI ning	JI ji
SHU ning	SHU hkri	HKRI ning	HKAU gu	NA na	HPU hpu	RAT ning	HKAU tsa	NI ning	JI ji
			(madu wa)	ego	EGO	(MADU JAN)			
SHU ning	SHU hkri	HKRI ning	HKAU rat	NAU nau	NAU nau	NAM ning	HKAU tsa	NI ning	JI ji
SHU ning	SHU hkri	HKRI sha	HKRI sha	SHA nam	SHA nam	NAM ning	NAM tsa	NI ning	JI ji
SHU shu	SHU shu	SHU shu	SHU shu	SHU nam	SHU nam	NAM ning	NAM tsa		

the head of columns A, B and C, are the Jinghpaw terms for these lineage groupings, as used by both 'EGO' and 'ego'. *Madu wa* and *Madu jan* signify 'husband' and 'wife', respectively.

In practice, the terms denoting affinal relationship are used in the same sense, whether or not all the marriages envisaged by the ideal system have actually taken place. Thus EGO's wife's father may not stand in any blood relationship to EGO's mother, but EGO's wife's father is nevertheless called *tsa*, EGO's wife's father's sister *nu*, EGO's wife's father's sister's husband *wa*, and so on.   It is this type of adoptive relationship which makes the system appear unduly complicated when first encountered in the field.

In reading the diagram it should be understood that siblings of the same sex are always denoted by the same term, and that the children of siblings of the same sex are treated as siblings; thus the mother's sister is called *nu*, the mother's sister's husband *wa*, and the mother's sister's son (older than the speaker) *hpu*.

In Table II, the horizontal bands can be regarded either as age-groups or generations.   The distinction is arbitrary except in the speaker's own patrilocal group, where the stratification is definitely by biological generation.   Outside the local group, this may not be so.   Old men may marry young girls as their second wives; a husband may then be as old as his wife's father, or older.   The distinction between *hkau* and *tsa* here becomes somewhat indefinite.

In practice, a distinction is made between real and classificatory parents.   Usages vary locally.   Gilhodes (1922, pp. 199 f.) gives a long list of distinguishing particles recorded in the Gauri area.   In general usage are the terms below:

> *Wa di* for *wa* older than the real father
> *Wa doi* for *wa* younger than the real father
> *Nu tung* for *nu* older than the real mother
> *Nu doi* for *nu* younger than the real mother

By abbreviation, the particularising particle may sometimes be used alone.   Thus some observers have recorded *tung* as the term for the mother's elder sister, and *n'doi* as the term for the mother's younger sister.   Similar particles, for use with *ji* and *woi*, are listed by Hanson (1906).   The following variants fall into a rather different category.

(a) *In parts of Myitkyina District*

jum	..	..	.. father's father
ji ..	..	..	.. father's father's father

(b) *In the Bhamo and Northern Shan States Areas*

ji hkai	..	..	.. father's father
ji ke	..	..	.. father's father's father
ji dwi	..	..	.. mother's father

ji ke dwi ..	..	..	mother's father's father
woi hkai ..	..	..	father's mother
woi ke ..	..	..	father's father's mother
woi dwi	..	..	mother's mother
woi ke dwi (dwi ke)		..	mother's father's mother

But in contrast to the above are the terms Gilhodes (1922) gives for the Gauri:

hkai ji ..	..	..	mother's father
hkai woi ..	..	..	mother's mother
ji ..	..	..	father's father
woi	..	..	father's mother

The essential kinship category in all these phrases is *ji* (male), *woi* (female); the other particles merely provide sub-categories of these classes and should not be regarded as kinship terms in themselves, even if, by abbreviation, they may occasionally be used alone. In the Tsasen dialect the phrase *mayu-shayi* is used where I have used *mayu-dama*. Doubtless there are numerous other dialect variations.

To distinguish between two relatives of the same class the personal name is added, as in *Hpu Gam, Hpu Naw*. In the normal form of address to equals or seniors, the relationship term is used and not the personal name: thus, '*Hpu E!*' (not '*Gam E!*'). On the other hand, parents speaking to their own children address them by their personal name, or nickname, rather than indiscriminately as *sha*. Husbands and wives usually address one another by their personal names. *Madu wa* may sometimes be used by a wife, but is formal; the reciprocal *madu jan* is a term of reference only. *Hpu ba, na ba* ('big brother,' 'big sister') are common ways of distinguishing the eldest real brother and the eldest real sister, respectively.

Complete strangers are addressed by kinship terms of low affective content. The following are common verbal usages:

EGO (male) speaking: to old man, *wa di*; to male of own age, *hkau*; to child, *sha*; to old woman, *woi*; to adult woman of own age, or younger, *hkri*.

ego (female) speaking: to male of own age, *tsa*; to male much younger, *shu*; to child, *shu*; to any other female, *ning*.

As has been explained in Chapters IV and V there is an implied order of seniority such that in relation to any ego of group B (Table II), group A is junior to group B, and group AA junior to group A, while likewise group C is senior to group B and group CC senior to group C. The fact that AA are (for a male Ego) collectively *shu*—'grandchildren', while CC are collectively *ji*—'grandfathers' is consistent with this.

It should be noted that, for a man, the following degrees of female relationship are theoretically incestuous:

nu—mother; *woi*—grandmother; *moi*—father's sister; *ni*—mother's brother's wife; *na*—elder sister; *rat*—elder brother's wife; *hkri*—father's sister's daughter; *nau*—younger sister; *sha*—daughter; *shu*—granddaughter.

On the other hand the proper marriage is with a female standing in the relationship of

nam—mother's brother's daughter.

In practice little notice will be taken of the theoretical exogamy rules unless the relationship is close. Marriage of a man to a *close* female relative in any of the prohibited degree would upset the structure of *mayu-dama* links between localised kingroups and would therefore be opposed. But if the relationship is remote (*lawu lahta*)[1] 'incest' becomes irrelevant. A man is quite likely in practice to marry a woman who, strictly speaking, might be rated as a *nau*, a *ni*, a *hkri* or a *shu*.

So far as I am aware the term system of Atsi can be translated word for word into Jinghpaw with identical ranges of meaning. This does not seem to be true of the other Maru languages or of Lisu. Nung has the crucial *mayu-dama* distinction of the Jinghpaw system but is not otherwise structurally identical with Jinghpaw (see Barnard (1934), p. 47).

[1] cf. p. 74.

APPENDIX V

ESTIMATE OF 'SHAN' AND 'KACHIN' POPULATION IN KACHIN HILLS AREA

Data derived from *Census* (1931); *Command Paper* (1947); *Linguistic Survey* (1917); unpublished Census data supplied by J. L. Leyden, Esq.

Region Map 2	Census Area	Valley People Shans, Burmese, Chinese	Jinghpaw	Hill People (Kachins)				Lisu	Kachin Total
				Atsi	Maru	Lashi	Nung		
ASSAM	Assam	2,000* Hkamti Shan	1,500 (Singpho)	—	—	—	—	—	1,500
PUTAO	Putao	6,500 Hkamti Shan	3,000 (Duleng)	—	—	—	9,000	3,500	15,500
NAM TAMAI		—							
HUKAWNG	Hukawng	1,000? Hkamti Shan	7,500 (partly Tsasen)	—	—	—	—	—	7,500
HKAHKU	Sumprabum Triangle	300? Shan	54,500	—	2,500	—	—	—	66,000
	Myitkyina Hill Tracts	—	—	—	—	—	—	—	
HTAWGAW	Htawgaw	—	9,000	—	11,500	11,500	—	5,000	28,000
JADE MINES HTINGNAI	Kamaing and Mogaung Townships	36,000 Burmese	17,500 (Kamaing Hill Tracts)	—	—	—	—	—	33,500
		36,000 Shan	16,000 (Mogaung Hill Tracts)	—	—	—	—	—	
	Myitkyina Township	38,000 mostly Shan	8,000 (Sadon)	3,000	6,000	3,000	—	—	20,000
SINPRAW	Bhamo	75,000 50% Shan	50,500 (including Gauri)	2,000	500	500	—	500	54,000
	Northern Shan States (Burma)	300,000 Shan	39,000 [110,000 Palaung]	8,000	12,000	6,000	—	6,000	71,000†
	Chinese Shan States	100,000? Shan	20,000?	10,000?			—	?	30,000?†

Estimated Total Valley Population in Kachin Hills Area: 594,800

* Excludes Assamese.

Estimated Total Kachins: 327,000*†

* Excludes all Palaung.
† Excludes all Lisu groups resident in China.

APPENDIX VI

RAINFALL: ANNUAL PRECIPITATION IN INCHES

Data based in part on published weather reports and in part on figures supplied by J. L. Leyden Esq.

Hill Districts	Average.	Highest Recorded.
Putao	155	172
Sumprabum	149	175
Hukawng	150 approx.	—
Sadon	122	132
Htawgaw	97	—
Sinlum	(110?)	—
Mogok	105	—
Northern Shan States (Lashio)	55	—
Valley Areas		
Myitkyina-Mogaung	85	96
Kamaing	105	116
Mohnyin	72	92
Bhamo	72	—

In general, valleys receive less rain than the western face of mountain ranges. Rainfall decreases as one proceeds either North to South or West to East.

Vegetation cover and human ecology is dependent upon geological factors as well as rainfall. For details, see Stamp (1924).

A NOTE ON THE QUALIFICATIONS OF THE AUTHOR

The form and subject matter of this book have naturally been greatly influenced by the special experiences of the author. It may be useful to state what these are.

In 1939 I was engaged in study for a higher degree in anthropology under the supervision of the late Professor Malinowski. I proceeded to Burma intending to do a year's field-work and present my results as a functionalist study of a single community. I chose Hpalang on the advice of Mr. H. N. C. Stevenson who had recently been Assistant Superintendent, Sinlum, and who had also worked under Professor Malinowski. The timing of my expedition was unfortunate. I arrived in Burma four days before the declaration of war. Of the next twelve months I spent seven in Hpalang itself. I dispensed with the services of an interpreter very early. Though this had its disadvantages, it meant that I learnt to understand the Jinghpaw language very quickly.

From the autumn of 1940 until the summer of 1945 I served as an officer in the Burma Army. During much of this time I was in the company of Kachins but I never had the opportunity to carry out detailed anthropological study. My military duties did, however, have the advantage that I travelled very widely in the Kachin Hills Area. I visited the Northern Shan States, the Sima and Sadon Hills, the Htawgaw Area, Kamaing and the region north of Myitkyina in the course of recruiting duty. In 1942 I saw military service in the Northern Shan States and later made an undignified withdrawal from Burma on my feet. This took me through many Kachin byways little known to Europeans and enabled me to see something of the Chinese Shan states. By the end of August 1942 I had re-entered Burma from Assam and was engaged in raising a force of Kachin irregulars. My centre of operations this time was the Putao, Sumprabum, North Triangle area. In 1943 I visited the Nung country in the Nam Tamai on a political mission.   In all, the only main sections of the Kachin Hills Area of which I have no direct experience at all are the Hukawng Valley and Jade Mines areas.   There are comparatively few Europeans who· have had similar opportunities for assessing the totality of Kachin culture.

My Hpalang field notes and photographs were all lost as the result of enemy action.   During 1941, however, I had found time to write up much of my Hpalang material in the form of a functionalist economic study of the Hpalang community.   This manuscript is also lost but the effort was not entirely wasted.   The fact that I had worked out this draft fixed many details in my mind which would otherwise have been confused.   In 1942 when I reached India I sketched out notes of Hpalang as I then recollected it and I think the details were probably fairly accurate though some names and figures may have got confused.   I took such notes as I could during my military tours of 1942–43 and these are preserved.   In 1944–45 I was away from the Kachin Hills Area though I saw something of the Naga Hills further to the west.

In 1946 I was released from the Army and was permitted by the University of London to prepare a thesis based largely on historical materials relating to the Kachin Hills Area. While preparing this thesis I made a very thorough study of government records and other publications relating to the area, mainly from sources preserved in the India Office library. There are one or two documents which I have never managed to trace, but in general, excluding ephemeral publications issued by the missions, I think I have at one time or another probably read nearly everything that has been published in English, French or German about the Kachin Hills Area during the past 130 years.

Since 1947 I have held a teaching post at the London School of Economics and it is during the course of this latter work that the sociological ideas contained in this book have been worked out.

BIBLIOGRAPHY

The best bibliographical sources for the Kachin Hills Area are cited below as Embree and Dotson (1950) and Wehrli (1904). Leach (1946) contains a number of references missing in both of these.

The Bibliography which follows only contains items cited in the text of this book.

ANDERSON, J. 1871. *A Report on the Expedition to Western Yunnan via Bhamo* (Calcutta).

—— 1876. *Mandalay to Momien* (London).

BARNARD, J. T. O. 1925. 'The History of Putao', *J. Bur. Res. Soc.*, XV.

—— 1930. 'The Frontier of Burma', *J. Roy. Cen. As. Soc.*, XVII.

—— 1934. *A Handbook of the Rawang Dialect of the Nung Language* (Rangoon).

BATESON, G. 1936. *Naven* (Cambridge).

BAYFIELD, G. T. 1873. 'Narrative of a Journey from Ava to the Frontiers of Assam and back, performed between December 1836 and May 1837 under the orders of Col. Burney....' (see *Selection of Papers* (1873)).

BENNISON, J. J. 1933. See *Census*, 1931, XI, Report.

BURNEY, H. 1837. 'Some account of the Wars between Burma and China together with Journals and Route of the different Embassies sent to Pekin by the King of Ava; taken from Burmese Documents', *J. As. Soc. Bengal*, VI.

—— 1842. 'On the Population of the Burman Empire', *J. Stat. Soc.* (London), IV (cf. *J. Bur. Res. Soc.* XXXI (1941)).

BUTLER, J. 1846. *A Sketch of Assam* . . . by an *Officer in the Hon. East India Company's Bengal Native Infantry* (London).

CAMERON, A. A. 1911. 'A Note on the Palaungs of the Kodaung Hill Tracts of the Momeik State', *Census*, 1911, IX Report, App.

CARRAPIETT, W. J. S. 1929. *The Kachin Tribes of Burma* (Rangoon).

Census. Burma Census data relating to the years 1891, 1901, 1911, 1921, 1931 were published as part of the Census of India. In most cases the Burma volume is in two parts. Part 1, Report. Part 2, Tables. For 1941, only incomplete data were published; see *Command Paper* (1947).

Command Paper. 1947. 'Burma Frontier Areas: Committee of Enquiry', *Parliamentary Command Paper* No. 7138, June 1947.

CLERK, F. V. 1911. *A Manual of the Lawngwaw or Maru Language* (Rangoon).

DALTON, E. T. 1872. *Descriptive Ethnology of Bengal* (Calcutta).

DAVIES, H. R. 1909. *Yunnan* (Cambridge).

DEWAR, T. P. 1931. 'Naga Tribes and their Customs. A general Description of the Naga Tribes inhabiting the Burma Side of the Patkoi Range', *Census*, 1931, XI, Report, App.

DOOLITTLE, J. 1876. *Social Life of the Chinese*, 2 vols. in one (New York).

DURKHEIM, E. 1925. *Les Formes élémentaires de la vie religieuse* (2nd Edn.) (Paris).

—— 1947. *The Division of Labour in Society* (trans. G. Simpson), (Glencoe, Illinois).

DURKHEIM, E. 1951. *Suicide* (trans. J. A. Spaulding and G. Simpson), (Glencoe, Illinois).

EICKSTEDT, E. FR. VON. 1944. *Rassendynamik von Ostasian* (Berlin).

ELIAS, NEY. 1876. *Introductory Sketch of the History of the Shans of Upper Burma and West Yunnan* (Calcutta).

EMBREE, J. F., and DOTSON, L. O. 1950. *Bibliography of the Peoples and Cultures of Mainland South East Asia.* (New Haven).

ENRIQUEZ, C. M. 1923. *A Burmese Arcady* (London).

—— 1933. *The Races of Burma* (Handbooks for the Indian Army) (Calcutta).

EVANS-PRITCHARD, E. E. 1939. 'Nuer Time Reckoning', *Africa*, IX.

—— 1940. *The Nuer* (London).

—— 1951. *Social Anthropology* (London).

FIRTH, R. 1936. *We, the Tikopia* (London).

—— 1932. 'Totemism in Polynesia', *Oceania*, 1.

—— 1939. *Primitive Polynesia Economy* (London).

—— 1951. *Elements of Social Organisation* (London).

FORTES, M. 1945. *The Dynamics of Clanship among the Tallensi* (London).

—— 1949. 'Time and Social Structure: an Ashanti Case Study', in *Social Structure: Studies presented to A. R. Radcliffe-Brown* (Fortes, M., Editor), (Oxford).

FORTES, M., and EVANS-PRITCHARD, E. E. (Eds.). 1940. *African Political Systems* (London).

FRASER, J. O. 1922. *Handbook of the Lisu (Yawyin) Language* (Rangoon).

FRAZER, J. G. 1918. *Folklore in the Old Testament*, 3 vols. (London).

GAIT, E. A. 1906. *A History of Assam* (Calcutta).

GEIS, G. J. 1911. Cited in *Census*, 1911, IX, Report, p. 152.

GEORGE, E. C. T. 1891. 'Memorandum on the Enumeration of the Tribes inhabiting the Kachin Hills'; 'Memorandum on the Kachins of our Frontier', *Census*, 1891, IX, App.

GILHODES, C. 1922. *The Kachins; Religion and Customs* (Calcutta).

GRANET, M. 1939. 'Catégories matrimoniales et relations de proximité dans la Chine ancienne', *Ann. Soc.*, Ser. B., Fasc. 1–3.

GRANT BROWN, R. 1925. *Burma as I saw it* (London).

GRAY, ERROL. 1894. 'Diary of a Journey to the Borkhamti and the Sources of the Irrawaddy, 1893', *Govt of India Foreign Affairs Proceedings*, May 1894, Nos. 7–15 (published in abstract in *Geo. J.*, III (1894), pp. 221–8).

GREEN, J. H. 1933. 'A Note on the Indigenous Races of Burma', *Census*, 1931, XI, Report, App.

—— 1934. *The Tribes of Upper Burma North of 24° Latitude and their Classification* (Typescript dissertation, Haddon Library, Cambridge).

HAMILTON, A. 1912. *In Abor Jungles* (London).

HANNAY, S. F. (otherwise Hannah, S. F.). 1837. 'Abstract of the Journal of a Route travelled by Captain S. F. Hannay in 1835–36 from the Capital of Ava to the Amber Mines of the Hukawng Valley on the South Eastern Frontier of Assam' by Captain R. Boileau Pemberton. *Trans. As. Soc. Bengal*, VI, April 1837 (also in *Selection of Papers* (1873)).

—— 1847. (*a*) *Sketch of the Singphos or Kakhyens of Burma . . .* (Calcutta).

—— 1847. (*b*) *The Shan or Tai Nation* (Calcutta), (follows previous item without change of pagination).

—— 1848. *Continuation of Notes on the Shans*, Part II, Shans of Assam (Calcutta), (forms supplement to previous item).

HANSON, O. 1906. *A Dictionary of the Kachin Language* (Rangoon).
—— 1913. *The Kachins: their Customs and Traditions* (Rangoon).
HARVEY, G. E. 1925. *History of Burma* (London).
HARVEY, G. E., and BARTON, G. E. 1930. *Mengmao Succession* (Burma Secretariat file; Imprint No. 99 H.P.D. 29.10.30), (Rangoon).
[My citations from this most important scarce source are made by permission of Mr. G. E. Harvey. A popular account of some of the events to which it refers will be found in Metford (1935).]
HERTZ, H. F. 1943. *A Practical Handbook of the Kachin or Chingpaw Language* . . . (Calcutta), (identical with the 1902 Edition published Rangoon).
HERTZ, W. A. 1912. *Burma Gazetteer*, Myitkyina District, Vol. A. (Rangoon).
HERSKOVITS, M. J. 1948. *Man and His Works* (New York).
HODSON, T. C. 1925. 'The Marriage of Cousins in India' *Man in India*, V.
HOGBIN, H. I. 1934. *Law and Order in Polynesia* (Introduction by Malinowski B.), (London).
HOMANS, G. C. 1951. *The Human Group* (London).
HOWORTH, H. H. 1876. *History of the Mongols*, Part I (London).
HUTTON, J. H. 1921. (*a*) *The Angami Nagas* (London).
—— 1921. (*b*) *The Sema Nagas* (London).
—— 1929. 'Diaries of two tours in the unadministered area east of the Naga Hills.' *Mem. As. Soc. Bengal*, XI, No. 1, pp. 1–71.
IMBAULT-HUART, M. C. 1878. *Histoire de la conquête de la Birmanie par les Chinois sous le règne de Tç'ienn Long (Khien Long)* (trans. from the Chinese), (reprinted from Journal Asiatique).
Kachin Hill-tribe Regulation. 1895 (Rangoon). Amended 1898, 1902, 1910, 1921, 1922, 1938. Cf. also *The Hill Tracts Regulation, 1942* (Govt. of Burma, Simla).
KAWLU MA NAWNG. 1942. *The History of the Kachins of the Hukawng Valley* (translation and notes by J. L. Leyden) (Bombay) (privately printed). [There exists also a later edition of this work with different pagination.]
KROEBER, A. L. 1952. *The Nature of Culture* (Chicago).
KROEBER, A. L., and KLUCKHOHN, CLYDE. 1952. *Culture* (Peabody Museum Papers, Vol. XLVII, No. 1).
LAHIRI, S. C. 1951. *Principles of Modern Burmese Buddhist Law* (Calcutta).
LASKER, B. 1950. *Human Bondage in Southeast Asia* (Chapel Hill).
LEACH, E. R. 1945. 'Jinghpaw Kinship Terminology', *J.R.A.I.*, LXXV.
—— 1946. *Cultural Change with Special Reference to the Hill Tribes of Burma and Assam* (Ph.D. Dissertation, London University; typescript.)
—— 1949. 'Some Aspects of Dry Rice Cultivation in North Burma and British Borneo', *The Advancement of Science*, VI, No. 21, pp. 26–28.
—— 1952. 'The Structural Implications of Matrilateral Cross-Cousin Marriage', *J.R.A.I.*, LXXXI.
League of Nations. 1928. Slavery Convention. 'Memorandum on Measures for the Abolition of Slavery in Burma', *Publications of the League of Nations*, VI B, Slavery, 1928, VI, B.2.
LEVI-STRAUSS, C. 1949. *Les Structures élémentaires de la parenté* (Paris).
LEWIS, C. S. 1936. *The Allegory of Love* (London).
LIANG CHI CHAO. 1930. *History of Chinese Political Thought during the early Tsin Period* (London).

Linguistic Survey. 1917. *Linguistic Survey of Burma: Preparatory Stage of Linguistic Census* (Rangoon).

Lowis, C. C. 1903. In *Census, 1901*, XII, Report.

—— 1906. *A Note on the Palaungs of Hsipaw and Tawngpeng* (Ethnographical Survey of India: Burma, No. 1), (Rangoon).

—— 1919. *The Tribes of Burma* (Ethnographical Survey of India: Burma, No. 4), (Rangoon).

Luce, G. H. 1940. 'Economic Life of the Early Burman', *J. Bur. Res. Soc.*, XXX.

Luce, G. H., and Pe Maung Tin. 1939. 'Burma down to the Fall of Pagan', *J. Bur. Res. Soc.*, XXIX.

Mackenzie, A. 1884. *History of the Relations of the Government with the Hills Tribes of the North Eastern Frontier of Bengal* (Calcutta).

MacGregor, C. R. 1887. 'Journal of the Expedition under Colonel Woodthorpe, R. E., from Upper Assam to the Irrawadi, etc.', *Proc. R.G.S.*, IX.

—— 1894. 'Rough Notes on the Traditions, Customs, etc., of the Singphos and Khamptis', Babylonian and Oriental Record, VII, pp. 172–6.

Malcom, H. 1839. *Travels in South Eastern Asia . . .*, 2 vols. (Boston).

Malinowski, B. 1926. *Myth in Primitive Psychology* (London).

—— 1944. *A Scientific Theory of Culture and Other Essays* (University of North Carolina).

—— 1945. *The Dynamics of Culture Change* (New Haven).

Martin, R. M. 1838. *The History, Antiquities, Topography and Statistics of Eastern India: collated from the Original Documents*, 3 vols. (London).

Mauss, M. 1947. *Manuel d'Ethnographie* (Paris).

Metford, B. 1935. *Where China meets Burma* (London).

Merton, R. K. 1951. *Social Theory and Social Structure* (Glencoe, Illinois).

Michell, St. J. F. 1883. *Report (Topographical, Political, and Military) on the North-East Frontier of India*. Confidential (Calcutta). [This important work has not been mentioned in earlier Kachin bibliographies. Like Mackenzie (1884) and *Selection of Papers* (1873) it is compiled from earlier sources but contains many details not reported elsewhere.]

Mills, J. P. 1922. *The Lhota Nagas* (London).

—— 1926. *The Ao Nagas* (London).

Milne, L. 1924. *The Home of an Eastern Clan* (Oxford).

Milne, L., and Cochrane, W. W. 1910. *Shans at Home* (London).

Morgan, L. H. 1877. *Ancient Society* (London).

Murdock, G. P. 1949. *Social Structure* (New York).

Nadel, S. F. 1951. *The Foundations of Social Anthropology* (London).

Needham, J. F. *Outline Grammar of the Singpho Language as spoken by the Singphos, Dowanniyas, and others residing in the neighbourhood of Sadiya* (Shillong).

Neufville, J. B. 1828. 'On the Geography and Population of Assam', *As. Res.*, XVI.

Parry, N. E. 1932. *The Lakhers* (London).

Parsons, Talcott. 1949. *Essays in Sociological Theory: Pure and Applied* (Cambridge, Mass.).

Parsons, Talcott and Shils, E. A. (Eds.). 1951. *Toward a General Theory of Action* (Cambridge, Mass.).

Pemberton, R. B. 1835. *Report on the Eastern Frontier of India* (Calcutta).

PELLIOT, P. 1904. 'Deux itinéraires de Chine en Inde à la fin du VIIIme. siècle', *Bull. Ec. Franc. Extr. Orient.* (Hanoi).

POPPER, K. R. 1945. *The Open Society and its Enemies* (London).

PRITCHARD, B. E. A. 1914. 'A Journey from Myitkyina to Sadiya via the N'Mai Hka and Hkamti Long', *Geo. J.*, XLVIII.

RADCLIFFE-BROWN, A. R. 1940. 'On Social Structure', *J.R.A.I.*, LXX.

RADCLIFFE-BROWN, A. R., and FORDE, D. (Eds.). 1950. *African Systems of Kinship and Marriage* (London).

RICHARDSON, D. 1837. 'Copy of papers relating to the route of Captain W. C. McCleod from Moulmein to the Frontiers of China and to the route of Dr. Richardson on his fourth mission to the Shan Provinces of Burma (1837), or extracts from the same',—*Parliamentary Papers 1868–9*, XLVI. See also *J. As. Soc. Bengal*, VI (1837).

—— 1912. *The Damathat or the Laws of Menoo* (trans. from the Burmese), (Rangoon). (1st Edition dates from 1847.)

R.N.E.F. *Report on the North-East Frontier.* Annually from 1892–1923. (*Report on the Administration of the Shan States* (same dates) contains related material.)

RUMNEY, J. 1934. *Herbert Spencer's Sociology* (London).

RUSSELL, B. 1948. *Human Knowledge* (London).

SANDEMAN, J. E. 1882. 'The River Irrawadi and its Sources', *Proc. R.G.S.*, IV, p. 257.

SANGERMANO, V. 1893. *The Burmese Empire a Hundred Years Ago as described by Father Sangermano.* Introduction and Notes by John Jardine (London).

SCHAPERA, I. 1952. *The Ethnic Composition of Tswana Tribes* (London).

SCOTT, J. G. n.d. [1925]. *Burma: a Handbook of Practical Information* (London).

SCOTT, J. G., and HARDIMAN, J. P. 1900–1. *Gazetteer of Upper Burma and the Shan States*, Part 1, 2 vols.; Part 2, 3 vols. (Rangoon).

Selection of Papers. 1873. *Selection of Papers regarding the Hill Tracts between Assam and Burma and on the Upper Brahmaputra* (Calcutta).

SHAKESPEAR, J. 1912. *The Lushei Kuki Clans* (London).

SHAKESPEAR, L. W. 1914. *History of Upper Burma, Upper Assam and North Eastern Frontier* (London).

SHAN STATES and KARENNI. 1943. *Shan States and Karenni: List of Chiefs and Leading Families* (corrected up to 1939). (Confidential) (Simla).

SHAW, W. 1929. *Notes on the Thadou Kukis* (Calcutta). (Reprinted from *J. As. Soc. Bengal*).

SIGURET, J. 1937. *Territoires et Population des Confins du Yunnan* (Peiping) (trans. from various Chinese sources).

SLADEN, E. B. 1868. 'Official Narrative of the Expedition to explore the Trade Route to China via Bhamo', *Parliamentary Papers*, 1867–8, L1.

SMITH, W. C. 1925. *The Ao Naga Tribe of Assam* (London).

SPATE, O. H. K. 1945. 'The Burmese Village', *Geo. Rev.*, XXXV.

SPENCER, H. 1858. 'Prospectus of a System of Philosophy' (in Rumney (1934)).

STAMP, L. D. 1924. (a) 'Notes on the Vegetation of Burma' *Geo. J.*, LXIV.

—— 1924. (b) *The Vegetation of Burma from an Ecological Standpoint* (Rangoon).

STEVENSON, H. N. C. n.d. [1943]. *The Economics of the Central Chin Tribes* (Bombay).

STEVENSON, H. N. C.   1944.   *The Hill Peoples of Burma* (Burma Pamphlets, No. 6), (Calcutta).
STRETTEL, G. W.   1876.   *The Ficus Elastica in Burma Proper, or a Narrative of my Journey in Search of it . . .* (Rangoon).
STUART, J.   1910.   *Burma through the Centuries* (London).
TAX, SOL and others.   1952.   *Heritage of Conquest* (Glencoe, Illinois).
TAYLOR, L. F.   1923.   'Indigenous Languages and Races (of Burma)', *Census*, 1921, X, Report, App.
T'IEN JU-K'ANG.   1949.   'Pai Cults and Social Age in the Tai Tribes of the Yunnan Burma Frontier' *Am. Anth.* LI.
THOMAS, W. L.   1950.   *Ethnic Groups of Northern South East Asia* (New Haven).
THOMSON, G.   1949.   *Studies in Ancient Greek Society. The Prehistoric Aegean* (London).
VAIHINGER, H.   1924.   *The Philosophy of 'As If'* (London).
VAN GENNEP, A.   1909.   *Les Rites de Passages* (Paris).
WALKER, J. J.   1892.   'Expeditions among the Kachin Tribes of the North East Frontier of Upper Burma compiled by General J. J. Walker from the reports of Lieut. Elliot, Assistant Commissioner', *Proc. R.G.S.*, XIV.
WARD, F. KINGDON.   1921.   *In Farthest Burma* (London).
WEHRLI, H. J.   1904.   *Beitrag zur Ethnologie der Chingpaw (Kachin) von Ober Burma.*   Supplement to *Int. Archiv. f. Ethnog.*, XVI.
WILCOX, R.   1832.   'Memoir of a Survey of Assam and the Neighbouring Countries executed in 1825-28', *As. Res.* XVII (also in *Selection of Papers* (1873)).
WILSON, G. and M.   1945.   *The Analysis of Social Change* (Cambridge).
WILLIAMS, C.   1863.   *Through Burma to Western China* (London).
WITTGENSTEIN, L.   1922.   *Tractatus Logico-Philosophicus* (London).

INDEX